CHRIS SCOTT updated this new edition of the book. As well as doing the Coast to Coast Path and the Pennine Way he's walked in many of the wilder parts of Britain, the USA, France and Australia.

Among other books he's written, for Trailblazer he's the author of the *Adventure Motorcycling Handbook*, *Morocco Overland, Sahara Overland* and the forthcoming *Overlanders' Handbook*.

Born in Chatham, Kent, HENRY STEDMAN has been writing guidebooks for over fifteen years and is the author or co-author of half a dozen titles, including Trailblazer's *Kilimanjaro – The Trekking Guide to Africa's Highest Mountain, Dolomites Trekking* and *Hadrian's Wall Path,* as well as *The Bradt Guide to Palestine* and the *Rough Guides* to *Indonesia* and *Southeast Asia*.

When not travelling or writing, Henry lives in England editing other people's guidebooks, maintaining his Kilimanjaro website and arranging climbs on the mountain through his company, Climb Mount Kilimanjaro.

Coast to Coast Path
First edition: 2004; this fourth edition: 2010

Publisher
Trailblazer Publications
The Old Manse, Tower Rd, Hindhead, Surrey, GU26 6SU, UK
Fax (+44) 01428-607571, info@trailblazer-guides.com
www.trailblazer-guides.com

British Library Cataloguing in Publication Data
A catalogue record for this book is available from the British Library

ISBN 978-1-905864-30-0

Editor: Anna Jacomb-Hood
Proof-reading: Nicky Slade
Layout: Anna Jacomb-Hood
Illustrations: © Nick Hill (pp62-3); Rev CA Johns (p65-6)
Photographs (flora): C1 Row 3 left and centre, C2 Row 2 centre,
C3 Row 1 centre and right, © Charlie Loram; all others © Bryn Thomas
All other photographs: © as indicated: CS = Chris Scott, HS = Henry Stedman,
JM = Jim Manthorpe, SG = Stuart Greig
Cartography: Nick Hill
Index: Lucy Ridout and Anna Jacomb-Hood

Warning: hill walking can be dangerous
Please read the notes on when to go (pp29-31) and outdoor safety (pp71-5).
Every effort has been made by the author and publisher to ensure that the information
contained herein is as accurate and up to date as possible. However, they are unable
to accept responsibility for any inconvenience, loss or injury sustained by anyone
as a result of the advice and information given in this guide.

Printed on chlorine-free paper by
D2Print (☎ +65-6295 5598), Singapore

Coast to Coast
PATH

ST BEES TO ROBIN HOOD'S BAY
planning, places to stay, places to eat,
includes 109 large-scale walking maps

HENRY STEDMAN

FOURTH EDITION RESEARCHED AND UPDATED BY

CHRIS SCOTT

with contributions by
Stuart Greig, David and Maria Bull,
Noelle Cox and Chris Foster

TRAILBLAZER PUBLICATIONS

Acknowledgements

From Chris Scott: Thanks to contributors and updates sent by letter and email from: Stuart Greig, David and Maria Bull, Noelle Cox, Chris Foster, Gillian Beggs, Martin Bentham, Peter and Mary Burton, John Cooper, Peter Coulson, Tim Day, Tom Driscoll, Jack Filmore, Holland Gidney, Nichola Hele, Jane Johnson, Colin Lindsay, Colin McHugo, Julie Odell, Graham Pepper, Christine Perkin, Adrian Pickup, Veronica Piekosz, Lee Richardson, Vincent Rockey, Gary Taylor, K Vaughan and Keith Wren.

Thanks also to Anna Jacomb-Hood for forensic editing and last-minute fact checking and to Nick Hill for the new maps.

A request

The author and publisher have tried to ensure that this guide is as accurate and up to date as possible. Nevertheless, things change. If you notice any changes or omissions that should be included in the next edition of this book, please write to Trailblazer (address on p2) or email us at ⌨ info.trailblazer-guides.com. A free copy of the next edition will be sent to persons making a significant contribution.

Updated information will be available on:
⌨ **www.trailblazer-guides.com**

Front cover: Deepdale Hause above Grisedale Tarn (Stage 4) © Chris Scott

CONTENTS

INTRODUCTION

In devising a walk that would span the north of England from the Cumbrian coast to the North Sea, the legendary fell walker, guidebook writer and illustrator, Alfred Wainwright, created an enduring concept that 40 years later continues to inspire hikers in ever-growing numbers.

Despite not being an official National Trail with all the support that entails, the Coast to Coast path has almost certainly become the most popular long-distance footpath in England. At around 200 miles (see box p13) it's not the longest in the country and certainly doesn't, as some mistakenly think, cross the country at its widest point. It makes no claim to being especially tough (though we can safely predict that those who attempt it in one go will find it sufficiently challenging). Nor does it, unlike the long-distance paths that run alongside Hadrian's Wall or Offa's Dyke, follow any ancient construction or border.

In truth, the Coast to Coast is but one of an infinite number of routes that could be devised by joining the various footpaths and byways to form a trail across northern England and in doing so providing those who follow it with a snapshot of the country.

But what a magnificent snapshot that is! Around two-thirds of the walk is spent in the national parks of the Lake District, the Yorkshire Dales and the North York Moors. These parks encompass the most dramatic upland scenery in England, from its highest fells to its largest lakes, some of its most beautiful woods and parts of its bleakest, barest moors. The walk also passes through areas alive with some of Britain's rarest wildlife, including red squirrels and otters, and even skirts around the eyrie of England's last surviving golden eagle.

Furthermore, where man has settled on the trail he has, on the whole, worked in harmony with nature to produce some of England's finest villages, from idyllically situated Grasmere to unspoilt Egton Bridge. The trail itself is a further example of this harmony; these paths and bridleways have existed for centuries and though man-made, do not feel or look like an imposition on the landscape but are very much part of it.

While these paths and villages continue to thrive under the steady stream of Coast to Coasters, in other places nature has reclaimed the poignant ruins of mills and mines, ancient Iron Age sites and mysterious stone circles which between them bear witness to thousands of years of human endeavour. They punctuate the path and provide absorbing highlights along the way.

But the walker on the Coast to Coast path experiences additional, unquantifiable rewards. There is the pleasure of acquiring a developing level of fitness, the satisfaction of unravelling a route-finding conundrum and the relief when a hard-won day finally ends at the doorstep of a cosy B&B or in a centuries-old hostelry. Most memorably, it's the cheery camaraderie shared by your fellow pilgrims bound for Robin Hood's Bay and the window into the lives of the people who live and work in this fabulous landscape that stay with you as you transit the country from coast to coast.

About this book

This guidebook contains all the information you need. The hard work has been done for you so you can plan your trip from home without the usual pile of books, maps and guides. It includes:

● All standards of accommodation from campsites to B&Bs and luxurious hotels
● Walking companies if you want an organised tour and baggage-carrying services if you just want your luggage carried
● Itineraries for all levels of walkers
● Answers to all your questions: when to go, degree of difficulty, what to pack, and how much the whole walking holiday will cost.

When you're all packed and ready to go, the comprehensive public transport information will get you to and from the trail and 109 detailed maps and town plans to help you find your way along it. The route guide section includes:

● Walking times and GPS waypoints
● Reviews of campsites, bunkhouses, hostels, B&Bs, guesthouses and hotels
● Cafés, pubs, tearooms, takeaways, restaurants and shops for buying supplies
● Rail, bus and taxi information for all the villages and towns along the path
● Street plans of the main towns: St Bees, Grasmere, Shap, Orton, Kirkby Stephen, Reeth, Richmond, Grosmont and Robin Hood's Bay
● Historical, cultural and geographical background information

Minimum impact for maximum insight

Man has suffered in his separation from the soil and from other living creatures ... and as yet he must still, for security, look long at some portion of the earth as it was before he tampered with it. **Gavin Maxwell**, *Ring of Bright Water*, **1960**

Why is walking in wild and solitary places so satisfying? Partly it is the sheer physical pleasure: sometimes pitting one's strength against the elements and the lie of the land. The beauty and wonder of the natural world and the fresh air restore our sense of proportion and the stresses and strains of everyday life slip away. Whatever the character of the countryside, walking in it benefits us mentally and physically, inducing a sense of well-being, an enrichment of life and an enhanced awareness of what lies around us.

All this the countryside gives us and the least we can do is to safeguard it by supporting rural economies, local businesses, and low-impact methods of farming and land-management, and by using environmentally sensitive forms of transport – walking being pre-eminent.

In this book there is a detailed and illustrated chapter on the wildlife and conservation of the region and a chapter on minimum-impact walking, with ideas on how to tread lightly in this fragile environment; by following its principles we can help to preserve our natural heritage for future generations.

PART 1: PLANNING

About the Coast to Coast path

HISTORY

The Coast to Coast path owes its existence to one man: Alfred Wainwright (see box pp10-11). It was in 1972 that Wainwright, already renowned for his exquisitely illustrated guides to walking in the Lake District, finally completed a trek across the width of England along a path of his own devising. It was an idea that he had been kicking around for a time: to cross his native land on a route that, as far as he was aware, would 'commit no offence against privacy nor trample on the sensitive corns of landowners and tenants'. The result of his walk, a guidebook, was originally printed by his long-time publishers, *The Westmoreland Gazette*, the following year. It proved hugely successful. Indeed, a full twenty years after the book was first published, a television series of the trail was also made in which Wainwright himself starred, allowing a wider public to witness firsthand his wry, abrupt, earthy charm.

Wainwright reminds people in his book that his is just **one of many such trails** across England that could be devised, and since Wainwright's book other Coast to Coast walks have indeed been established. Yet it is still *his* trail that is by far and away the most popular, and in order to distinguish it from the others, it is now commonly known as Wainwright's Coast to Coast path.

The route has been amended slightly since 1973 mostly because, though careful to try to use only public rights of way, in a few places Wainwright's original trail actually intruded upon private land. Indeed, even today the trail does in places cross private territory and it's only due to the largesse of the landowners that the path has remained near-enough unchanged throughout its 200 miles.

Though the trail passes through three national parks, crosses the Pennine Way and at times joins with both the Lyke Wake Walk and the Cleveland Way, it's not itself one of the 15 national trails in the UK, nor is it likely to become one anytime soon. What is certain is that despite this lack of official support, the Coast to Coast has become one of the most popular of Britain's long-distance paths, with estimates of up to 10,000 people attempting it annually.

HOW DIFFICULT IS THE COAST TO COAST PATH?

Undertaken **in one go** the Coast to Coast path is a long, tough walk. Despite the presence of some fairly steep gradients, every mile is 'walkable' and no mountaineering or climbing skills are necessary. All you need is some suitable clothing, a bit of money, a backpack full of determination and a half-decent pair of calf muscles. In the 200-odd miles from sea shore to sea shore you'll have ascended and of course descended the equivalent height of Mount Everest.

That said, the most common complaint we've received about this book, particularly from North American readers, is that it doesn't emphasise how tough it can be. So let us be clear: **the Coast to Coast is a tough trek**, **particularly if undertaken in one go**. Ramblers (formerly the Ramblers' Association of Great Britain; see box p48) describe it as 'challenging' and they're not wrong. When walkers begin to appreciate just how tough the walk can be, what they're really discovering is the reality of covering a daily average of just over 14 miles or 23km, *day after day*, for two weeks, in fair weather or foul and while nursing a

❑ Mr Coast to Coast – Alfred Wainwright

The popular perception of the man who devised the Coast to Coast path is that of a gruff, anti-social curmudgeon with little time for his fellow men, though one who admittedly knew what he was doing when it came to producing guidebooks. It's an unflattering portrait, but one that the man himself did little to destroy. Indeed, many say that he deliberately cultivated such a reputation in order to make himself unapproachable, thus allowing him to continue enjoying his beloved solitary walks without interruptions from the cagoule-clad masses who trudged the fells in his wake.

Yet this unflattering and rather dull two-dimensional description disguises a very complex man: artist, father, divorcé, pipe smoker, accountant, part-time curator at Kendal Museum, TV personality, romantic and cat-lover.

Alfred Wainwright was born in Blackburn on 17 January 1907, to a hardworking, impoverished mother and an alcoholic father. Bright and conscientious, his early years gave little clue to the talents that would later make him famous, though his neat handwriting – a feature of his guidebooks – was frequently praised by his teachers. Leaving school to work in accounts at the Borough Engineer's Office in Blackburn Town Hall, he regularly drew cartoons to entertain his colleagues. When, in December 1931, he married Ruth Holden, it seemed that Wainwright's life was set upon a course of happy – if humdrum – conformity.

Wainwright, however, never saw it like that. In particular, he quickly realised that his marriage had been a mistake and felt stifled and bored with his home life; feelings that not even the arrival of a son, Peter, could erase. His wife, though loyal, good and obedient, left Wainwright unfulfilled and any trace of romantic love that had been in the marriage at the beginning quickly drained away.

To escape the misery at home, Wainwright threw himself into his new-found hobby, fellwalking. He first visited the Lakes in 1930 and soon after was making detailed notes and drawings on the walks he made. Initially, these visits were few and far between, but a move to Kendal ten years later to take up a position as an accounting assistant allowed Wainwright to visit the Lakes virtually every weekend. Yet it wasn't until the early 1950s that Wainwright struck upon the idea of shaping his copious notes and drawings into a series of walking guides.

The idea wasn't a new one: guides to the Lakes had existed since at least the late 18th century and previous authors had included such literary luminaries as William Wordsworth. Where Wainwright's guides differed, however, was in their detail and the unique charm of their production.

For Wainwright was a publisher's dream: his writing was concise and laced with a wry humour, his ink sketches were delightful, and every page was designed and laid varying array of aches and pains. After all, how often do any of us walk 14 miles in a day, let alone continuously for *two weeks*?

The Lake District, in particular, contains many steep sections that will test you to the limit; however, there are also plenty of genteel tearooms and accommodation options in this section should you prefer to break your days into easier sections.

The topography of the eastern section is less extreme, though the number of places with accommodation drops too, and for a couple of days you may find yourself walking 15 miles or more in order to reach a town or village on the trail that has somewhere to stay.

down by the author himself, with the text justified on both sides (and without hyphens!) around the drawings. As a result, all the publisher really needed to do was crank up the printing press, load in the paper, and hey presto! They had another bestseller on their hands.

His first seven books, a series of guides to the Lakeland fells, took fourteen years to produce and by the end he had built up quite a following amongst both walkers and those who simply loved the books' beauty. Further titles followed, including one on the Pennine Way (a walk that he seemed to have enjoyed rather less than the others, possibly because at one point he had needed to be rescued by a warden after falling into a bog). As an incentive to walkers, however, he offered to buy a pint for every reader who completed the entire walk, telling them to put it on his bill at the Border Hotel at the end of the Pennine Way. The Coast to Coast was the follow-up to the Pennine Way, with the research starting in 1971 and the book published in 1973. It was a project that Wainwright seemed to have derived much greater enjoyment from (though, unfortunately, there was no offer of a free drink this time!).

While all this was going on, however, Wainwright's private life was in turmoil. Though his homelife with Ruth remained as cold as ever, Wainwright had found the love of his life in Betty McNally, who had visited him in his office on official matters sometime in 1957. For Wainwright, it was love at first sight, and he began courting Betty soon after. They married eventually in 1970, and by all accounts this union provided Wainwright with the contentment and happiness he had so signally failed to find in his first marriage. She also accompanied Wainwright on his forays into television, where his gruff, no-nonsense charm proved a big hit.

At the time of their marriage Wainwright, already 63, promised Betty ten happy years. In the event, he was able to provide her with 21, passing away on Sunday, January 20, 1991. His last wish, fulfilled two months later by Betty and his long-time friend Percy Duff, was to have his ashes scattered on Hay Stacks. At the end of his autobiography, *Ex-Fellwanderer*, he sums his life up thus:

I have had a long and wonderful innings and enjoyed a remarkable immunity from unpleasant and unwelcome incidents. ... I never had to go to be a soldier, which I would have hated. I never had to wear a uniform, which I also would have hated. ... I was never called upon to make speeches in public nor forced into the limelight; my role was that of a backroom boy, which suited me fine. I never went bald, which would have driven me into hiding. ... So, all told, I have enjoyed a charmed life, I have been well favoured. The gods smiled on me since the cradle. I have had more blessings than I could ever count.

Regarding safety, there are few places on the regular trail where it would be possible to fall from a great height, save perhaps for the cliff walks that book-end the walk. On some of the high-level Lakeland alternatives (see pp112-13 and pp120-1), however, there is a chance of being blown off a ridge. In 2009 a walker suffered this fate and broke his ankle, as did the rescuer who came in a helicopter, though sustaining such a serious injury by being blown over is highly unusual.

The greatest danger to trekkers is, perhaps, the likelihood of **losing the way**, particularly in the Lake District with its greater chance of poor visibility, bad weather and a distinct **lack of signposting**. A compass and knowing how to use it is vital, as is appropriate clothing for inclement weather and most importantly of all, a pair of boots (more on pp41-2) which you ease on each morning with a smile not a grimace.

Not pushing yourself too hard is important too (more on pp74-5), as this leads to fatigue with all its inherent dangers, not least poor decision making. In case all this deters you from the walk bear in mind that in 2009 a 71-year-old finished the walk for the fifth time, and a 7-year-old girl once completed the walk with her father – and they all managed it in 13 days! At the same time young men with all the right kit and a previous crossing under their belt were finished after storming across to Shap in three days.

Route finding

(See the box on pp81-2 for more details.) The presence of signposts and way-marking varies along the path. Once over the Pennines and into Yorkshire the trail becomes fairly well signposted and finding the way shouldn't be a problem. In the Lakes, on the other hand, there are no Coast to Coast signposts and you'll have to rely on the descriptions in this book to find the way. For much of the time the path is well-trodden and obvious, though of course there are situations where there are a number of paths to choose from, and other occasions where the ground is so boggy no clear path is visible at all. Misty conditions are another problem, particularly in the Lake District. In these instances a compass or GPS will help you move in the right direction or follow the correct path.

In the Lakes in particular there are a number of high-level alternatives to the main route, and on a clear day fit trekkers should consider taking them. Though obviously more tiring, the rewards in terms of the views and sense of achievement are all worthwhile.

GPS

I never carried a compass, preferring to rely on a good sense of direction... I never bothered to understand how a compass works or what it is supposed to do... To me a compass is a gadget, and I don't get on well with gadgets of any sort.   **Alfred Wainwright**

While Wainwright's acolytes may scoff, other walkers will accept GPS technology as an inexpensive, well-established if non-essential, navigational aid. To cut a long story short, within a minute of being turned on and with a clear view of the sky, GPS receivers will establish your position as well as elevation in a variety of formats including the British OS grid system, anywhere on earth to an accuracy of within a few metres.

❑ **Just how long is Wainwright's Coast to Coast path?**
The figure of **191$^{1}/_{2}$ miles** has been bandied around for years as this is close to the 190 miles which Wainwright's original edition quoted back in 1972. Disregarding the fact that these days this route is no longer followed, for this edition each stage was logged using a GPS odometer. While one or two stages were actually shorter than previously quoted, most were longer, so the final tally showed the actual distance walked to be around 198$^{1}/_{2}$ miles (319.5km) or at least 200$^{1}/_{2}$ miles (323km) if combining all the longest alternative routes.

This, of course, does not account for walking to the pub or B&Bs off the track, going the wrong way and even, as some Pythagorians like to consider, the fact that walking up and down hills technically covers more ground than if the ground was flat.

The fact is Wainwright's Coast to Coast (and doubtless many other long-distance paths) is a little longer than the distance commonly given; not of great import in the big picture as you'll walk the walk however long it is, but it's something worth knowing when psyching yourself up for a long day. Other guides and maps usually show shorter distances, often constrained to fit the immutable figure estimated by Alfred Wainwright; this edition is probably the first Coast to Coast path guidebook to use technology to work out the actual distance walked.

One thing must be understood however: **treating GPS as a replacement for maps, a compass and common sense is a big mistake**. Although current units are robust, it only takes the batteries to go flat or some electronic malfunction to leave you in the dark. GPS is primarily a navigational aid or backup to conventional route finding and, in almost all cases, is best used in conjunction with a paper map. At its most basic level a GPS stops you exacerbating navigational errors and saves you time in correcting them. Unlike the satellite navigation systems now common in cars, handheld 'hiking' GPS units do not come with an inbuilt map that is of much use for driving let alone walking across the moors. Though such units are now entering the market and while it's possible to buy **digital mapping** (see box p46) to import into a regular GPS unit with sufficient storage capacity, it might be considered as practical as having internet on a mobile phone – you still end up scrolling and zooming across a tiny screen.

Using GPS with this book
This book identifies key waypoints on the route maps. It's anticipated you won't tramp along day after day, ticking off the book's waypoints, transfixed by the GPS screen; the route description and maps are more than adequate most of the time. Only when you're **unsure of your position** or which way to go might you feel the need to even turn on the unit for a quick affirmation.

The book's waypoints correlate to the list on pp244-8 which gives the OS grid reference and a description. You'll find more waypoints across bleak mountain and moorland sections where the walk can degenerate into a prolonged stumble through thick mist. Typically cairns and other significant landmarks and junctions are marked. In towns and villages waypoints are less common, but in places can still be useful to pin down an unsigned turn off up a lane, for example.

You can either simply read off the nearest presumed waypoint from the list on pp244-8 as and when the need arises and work out where you are in relation to it or, less confusingly, key it in as a new point and press 'go to'. As there will probably be only a handful of times you need to do this, for most that will suffice but, with less margin for keystroke error, you can download the complete list as a GPS-readable .gpx file of grid references (but with no descriptions) from Trailblazer website's 'Coast to Coast' page.

Another way of using a GPS unit is to download a **track log** of the route from the internet. Where waypoints are single points like cairns, a track log is a continuous line like a path that appears on your GPS screen; all you have to do is keep on that line. If you lose it on the screen you can zoom out until it reappears and walk towards it. While it's impressive to see the trail unfold as a track log on a calibrated map or Google Earth, many of these 'user-generated' track logs available online are imperfect because it takes an extremely trail-savvy and committed Coast to Coaster to record a perfect, 200-mile-long track log without any gaps or confusing diversions; we certainly didn't manage it. The fact is thousands have managed the walk without this feature and you certainly don't need a track log to walk from one end of Kirkby Stephen High St to the other. On the Coast to Coast, waypoints will be adequate.

Using GPS with this book, be it someone's tracklog or just the key waypoints listed on pp244-8, is *an option*. Without them you could find yourself staggering around a mist-clad moor, or ambling confidently down the wrong path. With GPS, when the need arises, you can reliably establish your position in relation to the path, or quickly find out how far and in what direction it is to a known point on the trail.

It's worth repeating that 98% of people who've ever walked the Coast to Coast did so without GPS so there's no need to rush out and buy one. Your spending priorities ought to be on good waterproofs and above all, footwear. However, correctly using this book's GPS data could get you back on track and dozing in front of the pub fireplace or tucked up in bed all the sooner.

HOW LONG DO YOU NEED?

We've heard about an athlete who completed the entire Coast to Coast path in just 37 hours and a walker who managed it in eight days. We also know somebody who did it in ten and another guy who did four four-day stages over four years. Continuously or over several visits, for most people, the Coast to Coast trail takes a minimum of **14 walking days**, in other words an average distance of just over 14 miles (23km) a day.

Indeed, even with a fortnight in which to complete the trail, many people still find it tough going, and it doesn't really allow you time to look around places such as Grasmere or Richmond which can deserve a day in themselves. So, if you can afford to build a couple of rest days into your itinerary or even break it up into shorter stages over several weeks, you'll be very glad you did.

Of course, if you're fit there's no reason why you can't go a little faster if that's what you want to do, though you'll end up having a different sort of trek to most of the other people on the route. For where theirs is a fairly relaxing holiday, yours will be more of a sport as you try to reach the finishing line on schedule. There's nothing wrong with this approach, though you obviously won't see as much as those who take their time; *chacun à son goût*, as the French probably say. However, what you mustn't do is try to push yourself beyond your body's ability; such punishing challenges often end prematurely in exhaustion, injury or, at the absolute least, an unpleasant time.

When deciding how long to allow for their trek, those intending to camp and carry their own luggage shouldn't underestimate just how much a heavy pack can wear you down. On pp36-7 there are some suggested itineraries covering different walking speeds. If you've only got a few days, don't try to walk it all; concentrate, instead, on one area such as the Lakes or North York Moors. You can always come back and attempt the rest of the walk another time.

Practical information for the walker

ACCOMMODATION

From one coast to the other, businesses and families alike today owe a lot to Wainwright's inspired concept. Smaller towns and villages as well as isolated farms far from the reliable Lakeland honeypots have come to rely on accommodating and feeding the seasonal flow of coastbound walkers.

The route guide (Part 4) lists a fairly comprehensive selection of places to stay along the trail. The three main options are: camping, staying in hostels/ bunkhouses, or using B&Bs/pubs/hotels. Few people stick to just one of these the whole way, preferring, for example, to camp most of the time but spend every third night in a hostel, or perhaps take a hostel where possible but splash out on a B&B or hotel every once in a while.

The table on pp34-5 provides a snapshot of what type of accommodation and services are available in each of the towns and villages, while the tables on pp36-7 provide some suggested itineraries. The following is a brief introduction as to what to expect from each type of accommodation.

Camping

It's possible to camp all along the Coast to Coast path, though few people do so every night. You're almost bound to get at least one night where the rain falls relentlessly, sapping morale; it's then that most campers opt to spend the next night drying out in a hostel or B&B somewhere. There are, however, many advantages with camping. It's more economical, for a start, with most campsites charging somewhere between £4 and £8; one or two charge nothing at all. Best of all there's **rarely any need to book**, except possibly in the very high season, and even then you'd be highly unlucky not to find somewhere, even if it means camping discreetly in the woods.

The campsites vary and you get what you pay for: some are just pub gardens or a farmer's spare field with basic toilet/shower facilities; others are full-blown caravan sites with a few spaces put aside for tents, security access codes and sparkling ablutions blocks with wi-fi. Showers are usually available, occasionally for a fee, though more often than not for free. Note that the youth hostels on the Coast to Coast path no longer accept campers. Note, too, that some of the bigger towns such as Richmond and Grasmere do not have recognised campsites, with the nearest being at least three miles away.

Wild camping (ie camping not in a regular campsite; see p69) is also possible along the route but please don't do so in a field without first gaining permission from the landowner. Some good wild camping locations include the level areas surrounding mountain lakes such as Innominate Tarn (on the high route to Borrowdale), Grisedale Tarn (out of Grasmere) and Angle Tarn (two miles from Patterdale). Further east old mine ruins, such as those on the high route to Reeth, provide good shelter and 'cover' as well as patches of level grass and nearby running water. Beyond there, wild camping might be misconstrued as 'vagrancy' so woodland or plantations will be your best bet.

Remember that camping wild or 'tame' is not an easy option, especially for a solo walker. Walked continuously, the route is wearying enough without carrying the means to sleep and cook with you. Should you decide to camp at campsites, consider employing one of the baggage-carrying companies mentioned on pp24-7, though this does mean the loss of spontaneity which is the whole point of camping, and of course they can't deliver to Angle Tarn!

Bunkhouses and camping barns

A bunkhouse and a camping barn are different things. In most cases a **camping barn** is pretty much what it sounds like: an old barn in the corner of a farmer's field with a couple of wooden benches to sleep on; sleeping bags and usually sleeping mats are thus necessary, though bedding is provided in many of the YHA-franchised camping barns. A camping barn is probably the nearest non-campers will get to sleeping outside, while at the same time providing shelter from the elements. Note also that camping barns are sometimes booked for sole occupancy and thus it is essential to call in advance to check availability.

Bunkhouses can be much more agreeable places, with fluffed-up bedding, bathrooms you'd be happy to show to your parents and even kitchen and lounge areas. The description 'bunkhouse' is often used in place of 'small hostel' or 'independent hostel' to distinguish a private enterprise from lodgings under the YHA banner (see opposite) which can often be huge properties with scores of beds, hyperactive school groups and, depending on your age, unhappy memories of a long-gone institutional past.

Hostels

Youth hostels are plentiful along the Coast to Coast path and if you haven't visited one recently – and thus the words 'youth' and 'hostel' still conjure up images of limited opening hours, crowded dorms, lousy food and staff who really wish you'd move on – we advise you to take a second look. Over the years the venerable YHA (Youth Hostel Association) has acquired some of the best-located and most interesting accommodation along the path, from two pretty country houses at Grasmere to a former shepherd's bothy at Black Sail, some former workers' cottages at Osmotherley and an old corn mill at Robin Hood's Bay.

Each hostel comes equipped with a whole range of facilities, from drying rooms to washing machines, televisions to pool tables and fully equipped kitchens. Many also have a shop selling a selection of groceries, snacks and souvenirs and some even have internet access (though for some reason, the YHA always charges a fortune to use the internet at their hostels, perhaps because you should be outside doing something more wholesome). Many offer breakfast and/or dinner (of varying quality), some offer a packed lunch, and several even have a licence to sell alcohol. They are also great places to meet fellow walkers, swap stories and compare blisters.

Weighed against these advantages is the fact that even though many hostels now have rooms with two to four beds you may have to share your night with a heavy snorer. A couple of the hostels also suffer from uncomfortably small dorms when they're full. Some rooms now have en suite facilities but in others you have to share a shower room and in a couple of cases facilities may be limited. The curfew (usually 11pm) is annoying, too. Nor is it possible to stay in hostels every night on the trail, for there are some areas where hostels don't exist and when they do they're occasionally at least a mile or two off the path.

If you're travelling out of the main season (particularly between November and February) you may find some hostels are shut to walkers during the week, or completely. Even in high season most are not staffed during the day and walkers may have to wait until 5pm before checking in, though in some cases you can access the kitchen and you may be able to leave luggage in a secure room before 5pm. Furthermore, youth hostels save booked beds only until 6pm unless they have been informed of your late arrival – though to be fair, this rule doesn't seem to be rigidly enforced on this route. And finally, the cost of staying in a hostel, once breakfast has been added on, is in most instances not that much cheaper (around £17-21 for members) than staying in a B&B, especially if you're walking with someone.

Booking a hostel Despite the name, anybody of any age can join the YHA. This can be done at any hostel, or by contacting the **Youth Hostels Association of England and Wales** (☎ 01629 592700, 🖳 www.yha.org.uk). The cost of a year's membership is £15.95 for an adult, less for anyone under 18.

Having secured your membership, youth hostels are easy to book, either online or by phone through the contact details above. If you're booking only a few days in advance it may be better to ring each hostel direct; if you haven't actually booked in advance hostel staff will reserve a bed at the next stop on the path for you. Since non members have to pay £3 more per night it is worth joining if you expect to stay in a hostel for more than six nights in a year.

Bed and breakfast

Bed and Breakfasts (B&Bs) are a great British institution and many of those along the Coast to Coast are absolutely charming, with buildings often three or four hundred years old. Older owners often treat you as surrogates for their long-departed offspring and enjoy nothing more than looking after you.

As the name suggests, they provide you with a bed in a private room, and breakfast – a hearty, British-style cooked one (see p19) unless you specify otherwise beforehand – though they range in style enormously. Most B&Bs have en suite rooms and/or rooms with either private or shared facilities. En suite facilities often mean a shower squeezed into a room but with private/shared facilities there may be a bath, which is what most walkers prefer at the end of a long day, and the bathroom is never more than a few feet away. These rooms

---

❏ Should you book your accommodation in advance?

With the trend in recession-beating 'staycations' and the general rise in the popularity of walking holidays, the Coast to Coast path could be entering something of a boom time and some have predicted that accommodation may struggle to cope. In the high season of **June to August**, unless camping it's essential you have your night's accommodation secured. Nothing is more deflating than arriving at the end of a long day only to find that you've then got to walk another few miles or even take a detour off the route, because everywhere is booked up.

How soon you start booking is up to you but doing so the night before is no longer dependable. If you start booking **up to six months** in advance you'll have a good chance of getting precisely the accommodation you want. Booking so early does leave you vulnerable to changing circumstances of course, but with enough notice it's likely your deposit will be returned as they can easily fill your bed; ask on booking.

Outside the high season and away from weekends, as long as you're **flexible** and willing to take what's offered, you should get away with booking just a couple of weeks or even just days in advance. Having said that, some establishments we've spoken to told us that May and September were in fact their busiest months, early September being dubbed 'Saga week' when older hikers return to the hills once the schools have re-absorbed all the kids. As mentioned, at any time the exceptions to this rule are the **weekends**, when everywhere, especially **the Lakes**, is busy – or in places like Keld or Blakey Moor where conveniently close accommodation is limited.

If you've left it too late and can only get accommodation for parts of the walk but are set on a certain period, **consider camping** to fill in the gaps. It's not to everyone's taste and it helps if you already own the gear, but it can save you money which you can lavish on yourself later without guilt and, if using a baggage service, they can cart the gear from door to door at no extra effort to yourself.

If you're planning on staying in hostels the same applies though do be careful when travelling out of high season as many **hostels** close during the week and shut altogether from around November to February. Once again, it's well worth booking in advance. Campers, whatever time of year, should always be able to find somewhere to pitch their tent, though ringing in advance can't hurt and will at least confirm that the campsite is still open.

usually contain either a double bed (known as a double room), or two single beds (known as a twin room). Family rooms are for three or more people. Solo trekkers should take note: single rooms are not so easy to find so you'll often end up occupying a double room, for which you'll have to pay a single occupancy supplement (see below).

Smoking is banned in all enclosed places open to the public in England but places to stay are able to designate rooms for smokers, so do check this if it's important to you; see also box p23.

Some B&Bs provide an evening meal (see pp20-1); if not, there's often a pub or sometimes a restaurant nearby or, if it's far, the owner may give you a lift to and from the nearest place with food. Always **let the owner know** if you have to cancel your booking so they can offer the bed to someone else.

B&B rates B&Bs in this guide start at around £23 per person for the most basic accommodation to over £40 for the most luxurious en suite places in a popular tourist haunt like Grasmere. Most charge around £28-35 per person. A typical **single occupancy supplement** is between £5 and £10. An evening meal (usually around £10-15) is sometimes provided, but you may need to book in advance. Packed lunches are often available too for around £5.

Guesthouses, hotels, pubs and inns
A guesthouse offers bed and breakfast but should have a better class of décor and more facilities such as offering evening meals and a lounge for guests. However, they are unlikely to offer room service, unlike a hotel.

Pubs and inns may also offer bed and breakfast accommodation and tariffs are no more than in a regular B&B. However, you need to be prepared for a noisier environment, especially if your room is above the bar. **Hotels** do usually cost more, however, and some might be a little displeased by a bunch of muddy trekkers turning up. Most places on the Coast to Coast walk, particularly in the quieter towns and villages, are used to seeing trekkers, make a good living from them and welcome them warmly. Prices in hotels and pubs start at around £35 per person. When booking say if you want a room designated for smokers, see box p23.

FOOD AND DRINK

Breakfast
Stay in a B&B/guesthouse/hotel and you'll be filled to the gills each morning with a cooked English breakfast. This can consist of a bowl of cereal followed by a plateful of eggs, bacon, sausages, mushrooms, tomatoes, and possibly baked beans or black pudding, with toast and butter, and all washed down with coffee, tea and/or juice. Enormously satisfying the first time you try it, by the fourth or fifth morning you may start to prefer the lighter continental breakfast or porridge, which most establishments now offer.

Alternatively, and especially if you're planning an early start, you might like to request a packed lunch instead of this filling breakfast and just have a cup of coffee before you leave.

PLANNING YOUR WALK

☐ **Is a full English breakfast healthy?**
You've paid for the bed, it's understandable you want the breakfast too, and enough breakfast to fuel you down the trail all the way to lunch. But is the traditional 'FEB' the way to go? Most probably not which is why you begin to gag at the very idea after a few days. The former national dish never recovered from the muesli revolution of the 1970s and only truck drivers, whose legendary obesity has them blacklisted by the WHO, will tolerate such a dreadful diet on a daily basis.

At the beginning of the day it's complex carbohydrates you want, not a stomach full of fat and salt. Slow-release carbs keep you going till lunchtime, don't put your gall bladder on action stations and contain negligible fat. Ask for a big bowl of **porridge**, ideally cooked with milk and a little salt and if you do go fried, keep off offal-packed sausages, hope the bacon and tomatoes are grilled not fried, and throw fried bread and black pudding back into the kitchen. (A black pudding is a sausage of oat-soaked congealed blood, in case you didn't know, and a constituent of a 'Full *Yorkshire* breakfast').

The youth hostels mentioned in this guide offer breakfast; usually it's a good meal but they charge an additional £4-5.

Lunch
Your B&B host or youth hostel can usually provide a packed lunch at an additional cost, though of course there's nothing to stop you preparing your own. There are some fantastic locally made cheeses and pickles that can be picked up along the way, as well as some wonderful bakers still making bread in the traditional way (the bakeries in Kirkby Stephen, see p152, and Reeth, see p176, spring to mind). Alternatively, stop in a pub (see 'Evening meals' below).

Remember, too, to plan ahead: at least four of the stages in this book are devoid of eateries or shops so read ahead about the next day's walk to make sure you never go hungry.

Cream teas
Never miss a chance to avail yourself of the treats on offer in the tearooms and farmhouses of Cumbria and Yorkshire. Nothing relaxes and revives like a decent pot of tea, and the opportunity to accompany it with a scone served with jam and cream, or a cake or two, is one that should not be passed up.

Evening meals
If your B&B doesn't do an evening meal you may find that in many villages, the pub is the only place to eat out. **Pubs** are as much a feature of this walk as moorland, churches and views, and in some cases the pub is a tourist attraction as much as the finest ruined abbey. Most of them have become highly attuned to the needs of walk-

ers and offer both lunch and evening meals (with often a few regional dishes and usually a couple of vegetarian options), some locally brewed beers, a garden to relax in on hot days and a roaring fire to huddle around on cold ones. The standard of the food varies widely, though portions are usually large, which is often just about all walkers care about at the end of a long day.

That other great British culinary tradition and a favourite of Wainwright's is the **fish 'n' chip shop** which will deep fry your dinner in the bigger towns and then slather it in a layer of mushy peas and brown sauce. Larger towns also have Chinese and Indian **takeaways**; a welcome change from too much pub food and usually the only places still serving food late in the evenings, staying open until at least 11pm.

Catering for yourself

The list of village shops (often combined with a post office) along the route grows sadly shorter with each edition but those that manage to remain in business have a pretty good selection of foods and your diet will depend on what you can find there. A couple of these small stores sell camping gas stove cartridges (which you can also pick up in the bigger towns such as Grasmere, Kirkby Stephen and Richmond). Part 4 goes into greater detail about what can be found where.

Drinking water

There are plenty of ways of perishing on the Coast to Coast trail but thirst won't be one of them. Be careful, though, for on a hot day in some of the remoter parts of the Lake District after a steep climb or two you'll quickly dehydrate, which is at best highly unpleasant. Always carry some water with you and in hot weather aim to drink **three or four litres** per day, supplemented by rehydration tablets such as Nuun.

Out of the hills, don't be tempted by the water in the streams you come across in lowland areas where the chemicals from the pesticides and fertilisers used on the farms may become concentrated. It's a lot safer to fill up from taps or high mountain pools and becks. Remember, what makes you ill can't be seen by the naked eye so filling up from a peat-stained tarn or fellside beck will probably be much less polluted than a dribbling brook in somewhere like the intensively farmed Vale of Mowbray.

MONEY

Banks are very few and far between on the Coast to Coast path. There's one in Shap open a couple of hours a day, a couple in Kirkby Stephen, and Richmond has branches of all the major banks, but apart from in these places there's nothing.

Post offices thus provide a very useful service. You can get cash (by debit card with a PIN number, or by cheque with a debit card) for free at any post office counter if you bank with certain banks/building societies (for a full list see 🖳 www.postoffice.co.uk; click 'Counter Services' and then 'Using your bank account' on the left).

P L A N N I N G   Y O U R   W A L K

   A number of post offices also play host to the village **cashpoint/ATM** (usually a Link machine). These machines are useful for people who can't get cash from the counter but a number of these are privately operated and charge £1.25-1.75 whatever amount is withdrawn.

   Another way of getting cash is to use the **cashback** system: find a store that will accept a debit card and ask them to advance cash against the card. A number of the local village stores as well as some pubs will do this, though you'll usually have to spend a minimum of £5 with them first. It pays to ask.

   As not all local stores, pubs or B&Bs accept credit or debit cards, it's essential to carry plenty of cash (reckon on £200 per person). A chequebook could prove useful as a back-up, so that you don't have to keep on dipping into your cash reserves. **Travellers' cheques** can only be cashed at banks, foreign exchanges and some of the large hotels so their use is limited; cash and cards are best.

❏ Information for foreign visitors

● **Currency** The British pound (£) comes in notes of £100, £50, £20, £10 and £5, and coins of £2 and £1. The pound is divided into 100 pence (usually referred to as 'p', pronounced pee) which come in silver coins of 50p, 20p 10p and 5p and copper coins of 2p and 1p.

● **Rates of exchange** Up-to-date exchange rates can be found at 🖳 www.xe.com/ucc.

● **Business hours** Most **shops** and main **post offices** are open at least from Monday to Friday 9am-5pm and Saturday 9am-12.30pm. Many choose longer hours and some open on Sundays as well. However, some also close early one day a week, often Wednesday or Thursday. **Banks** are usually open 10am-4pm Monday to Friday.

   Pub opening hours have become more flexible – up to 24 hours a day seven days a week – so each pub may have different times. However, most pubs on the Coast to Coast route continue to follow the traditional 11am to 11pm and some still close in the afternoon.

● **National (Bank) holidays** Most businesses are shut on 1 January, Good Friday (March/April), Easter Monday (March/April), the first and last Monday in May, the last Monday in August, 25 December and 26 December.

● **School holidays** School holiday periods in England are generally as follows: a one-week break late October, two weeks around Christmas, a week mid-February, two weeks around Easter, a week in late May and from late July to early September.

● **Travel/medical insurance** The European Health Insurance Card (EHIC) entitles EU nationals (on production of the EHIC card) to necessary medical treatment under the UK's National Health Service while on a temporary visit here. However, this is not a substitute for proper medical cover on your travel insurance for unforeseen bills and for getting you home should that be necessary. Also consider cover for loss or theft of personal belongings, especially if you're camping or staying in hostels, as there will be times when you'll have to leave your luggage unattended.

● **Weights and measures** The European Commission is no longer attempting to ban the pint or the mile: so, in Britain, milk can be sold in pints (1 pint = 568ml), as can beer in pubs, though most other liquid including petrol (gasoline) and diesel is sold in litres. Distances on road and path signs will also continue to be given in miles (1 mile = 1.6km) rather than kilometres, and yards (1yd = 0.9m) rather than metres.

INTERNET ACCESS

If you have the means to get online, places to stay are increasingly offering **wi-fi** free to visitors, or in the case of some pubs and hotels, for a small fee. Some clued-up B&Bs and hotels provide an internet-enabled **computer** in the guest lounge free of charge while, as already mentioned, the bigger youth hostels do so for around £4 an hour. Otherwise, where present and open, the local **library** is the place to find internet access if there's no cyber café.

OTHER SERVICES

Most small villages have a **post office** that doubles as the local store, and nearby you'll usually find a **phone box**, though be warned, to combat vandalism some only accept cards, taking a £1 connection fee which is charged whether you get an answer or not! Otherwise 40p, supposedly in any non-copper combination of coins, is the minimum fee to make a cash call.

The population remains split between those who still use inches (1 inch = 2.5cm), feet (1ft = 0.3m) and yards and those who are happy with millimetres, centimetres and metres; you'll often be told that 'it's only a hundred yards or so' to somewhere, rather than a hundred metres or so.

Most food is sold in metric weights (g and kg) but the imperial weights of pounds (lb: 1lb = 453g) and ounces (oz: 1oz = 28g) are often displayed too. The weather – a frequent topic of conversation – is also an issue: while most forecasts predict temperatures in centigrade (C), many people continue to think in terms of fahrenheit (F; see temperature chart on p30 for conversions).

● **Time** During the winter the whole of Britain is on Greenwich Meantime (GMT). The clocks move one hour forward on the last Sunday in March, remaining on British Summer Time (BST) until the last Sunday in October.

● **Smoking** Smoking in enclosed public places is banned. The ban relates not only to pubs and restaurants, but also to B&Bs, hostels and hotels. These latter have the right to designate one or more bedrooms where the occupants can smoke, but the ban is in force in all enclosed areas open to the public – even in a private home such as a B&B. Should you be foolhardy enough to light up in a no-smoking area, which includes pretty well any indoor public place, you could be fined £50, but it's the owners of the premises who suffer most if they fail to stop you, with a potential fine of £2500.

● **Telephones** The international access code for Britain is +44, followed by the area code minus the first 0, and then the number you require. To call a number with the same area code as the phone you are calling from you can omit the code. It's cheaper to phone at weekends and after 6pm and before 8am on weekdays. **Mobile phone reception** is better than you think. Even in the Lakes you're often actually quite close to a town and on high ground where a weak signal can often be picked up. It's said the Vodaphone network works best across rural northern England followed by O2 or Orange; in our experience Virgin was pretty poor.

● **Internet access** See above.

● **Emergency services** For police, ambulance, fire and mountain rescue dial ☎ 999 (or the EU standard number ☎ 112).

There are **outdoor equipment shops** and **pharmacies** in the larger towns of Grasmere, Kirkby Stephen and Richmond and **tourist information centres** at Kirkby Stephen, Ullswater (near Patterdale), Reeth and Richmond.

WALKING COMPANIES

It's possible to turn up with your boots and backpack at St Bees and just start walking without planning much other than your accommodation (about which, see the box on p18). The following companies, however, are in the business of making your holiday as stress-free and enjoyable as possible.

Baggage carriers

There are several baggage-carrying companies serving the Coast to Coast route, from national organisations, such as Sherpa, to companies that consist of little more than one man and his van. With all these services you can usually book up to around 9pm the previous evening, though it can be cheaper if you book in advance. All stipulate a maximum weight per bag of around 20kg. The cost is around £8 to take your bag to your next destination. Nearly all these services also offer an **accommodation-booking service** (see box p48).

Two of the better known are The Coast to Coast Packhorse and Sherpa Van. **Sherpa Van** (baggage line ☎ 0871 520 0124, 🖥 www.sherpavan.com, also see p26), based at The Old Brewery Guesthouse on the path in Richmond, is a much bigger organisation than the others. It also runs a baggage-delivery service from April to mid-October for many of Britain's other walking and cycling trails including the Coast to Coast. They charge from £7 a bag and will transfer (or effectively, store) your excess baggage left at St Bees and deliver it to Robin Hood's Bay for £25. They also operate a daily **passenger bus service** from Richmond to St Bees and from Robin Hood's Bay to Richmond; contact them for details and to book a seat.

The **Coast to Coast Packhorse** (see p26; early Apr-Sep) based near Kirkby Stephen receives regular recommendations from our readers and also shifts the baggage for many other Coast to Coast operators. Having paid for baggage transfers – from £6.45 per stage – Packhorse customers are welcome to ride on the minibus with their bags, at no extra cost, should the need arise (great if the weather's foul or the feet are causing mayhem). Non-baggage customers are also welcome to hop on and off as the Packhorse passes through, paying only the appropriate fee for the distance so effectively this adds up to **a daily westbound bus service** along the entire route.

One van departs Kirkby Stephen at 8.30am, arriving at St Bees around 10.15am, before travelling via the pick-up points back to Kirkby Stephen. A second bus also leaves Kirkby Stephen at 8.30am, stopping at the drop-off points before reaching Robin Hood's Bay at 3.30pm, departing at 4pm for the direct trip back to Kirkby Stephen, arriving around 6.15pm. In other words, the buses stop at the various drop-off points only when travelling from west to east. The cost of travelling directly from Kirkby Stephen to St Bees or Robin Hood's Bay to Kirkby Stephen is £24 per person. As if that wasn't enough help they also have a secure parking lot in Kirkby Stephen, where you can leave a car for the duration of the walk for £3.10 per day.

This service has two important consequences for trekkers. Firstly, it means that, should you be attempting the walk from west to east and want to skip a stage, you can get the Packhorse van to pick you up and drive you to the next stage. Secondly, you can use Kirkby Stephen as your base, getting a lift on the Packhorse van to St Bees, and another at the end of the walk back from Robin Hood's Bay. Thus you can leave your car in Kirkby Stephen (which is better than the alternative of leaving it in St Bees and travelling all the way back from the east coast to pick it up again). Or you can buy a return train ticket from your home to Kirkby Stephen, which may be cheaper and quicker than having to buy one ticket to St Bees, and another from Robin Hood's Bay.

Other companies offering a similar service include **Brigantes Walking Holidays** (see below). Brigantes' baggage courier service is family operated with 16 vehicles which support trails across the north of England. If you wish, at the end of your walk, they can return you by minibus to an agreed railway/bus terminal, or to their free car park, in Kirkby Malham.

All baggage forwarders will give an estimated latest time by which you can expect your bags to be delivered. The two most popular forwarders used on the Coast to Coast, Packhorse and Sherpa, promise to deliver by around 4.30pm as these are the estimated times each service ends its eastbound luggage run. For Packhorse that run ends at Kirkby Stephen and Robin Hood's Bay, and for Sherpa it's Richmond and Robin Hood's Bay. If you happen to arrive well before the above times at say Shap or Kirby Stephen with Packhorse, or Reeth and Richmond with Sherpa, there's a chance your bag may still be in transit so you should plan accordingly.

Self-guided holidays

Self-guided means that the company will organise accommodation, baggage transfer (some contracting out the work to other companies), transport to and from the walk and various maps and advice, but leave you on your own to actually walk the path and cover lunch and dinner. In addition to these, don't forget the specialist Coast to Coast websites (see box p48) that can also book accommodation and provide details of the walk.

● **Absolute Escapes** (☎ 0131 447 2570, 🖥 www.absoluteescapes.com) This Edinburgh-based company offers the full walk as well as shorter walks covering half the route.

● **AMS Adventures** (☎ 01236 722664, 🖥 www.ams-adventures.com) also offers the Coast to Coast walk in full and in two parts.

● **Brigantes Walking Holidays** (☎ 01729 830463, 🖥 www.brigantesenglish walks.com) Based near Skipton, North Yorkshire, this is primarily a baggage-transfer and accommodation-booking service but they also offer walks west to east, for 14 days. In addition they are introducing budget packages where all the necessary equipment for camping is provided; further details on the website.

● **Coast to Coast Holidays & Baggage Services** (☎ 01642 489173, 🖥 www .coasttocoast-holidays.co.uk) Based in Redcar, near Robin Hood's Bay, they

PLANNING YOUR WALK

organise walks taking from 11 to 17 days and offer a car transport service from St Bees to Robin Hood's Bay.

● **Contours Walking Holidays** (☎ 017684 80451, 🖳 www.contours.co.uk) Based in Greystoke, north of Patterdale in Cumbria, they offer seven itineraries covering the Coast to Coast from the strenuous to the easy over 12 to 18 days. Also offer either western or eastern sections only and can tailor-make walks. Baggage transfer included.

● **Discovery Travel** (☎ 01904 632226, 🖳 www.discoverytravel.co.uk) Operating from York, they offer a standard 15-day Coast to Coast walk, as well as, unusually, the walk from east to west. Can tailor-make walks.

● **Explore Britain** (☎ 01740 650900, 🖳 www.xplorebritain.com) Based in Ferryhill, north of Richmond, County Durham, Explore Britain lays on 14-, 17- and 18-day treks along the entire path, as well as dividing the walk into two, with a seven-day walk from St Bees to Kirkby Stephen, and an eight-day walk from Kirkby Stephen to Robin Hood's Bay. Offer walks in both directions and can tailor-make walks. Offer full package and luggage transfer.

● **HF Holidays** (☎ 020 8732 1250, 🖳 www.hfholidays.co.uk) A reliable and frequently recommended Hertfordshire and Penrith-based company that offers the Coast to Coast in its entirety (17 nights) as well as St Bees to Keld and Keld to Robin Hood's Bay in 9 nights. Walks are west to east.

● **Macs Adventure** (☎ 0141 530 8886, 🖳 www.macsadventure.com) A Glasgow-based company that offers the full trail in 13 days, and also two parts, the western section and the eastern section in 6-7 days each. The walks are west to east and can be tailor-made.

● **Mickledore** (☎ 017687 72335, 🖳 www.mickledore.co.uk) Offers the complete trail in 12-19 days, and both halves in 5-9 days. Walks are west to east and can be tailor-made.

● **Northwest Walks** (☎ 01257 424889, 🖳 www.northwestwalks.co.uk) Though one of the smaller companies serving the route, Wigan-based Northwest has an excellent reputation and organises 7- to 11-day walks along half of the path, or 12-18 days for the complete trail. Walks are west to east and can be tailor-made.

● **Sherpa Expeditions** (☎ 020 8577 2717, 🖳 www.sherpa-walking-holidays.co.uk) Sherpa offers an 8- and 15-day itinerary for half or the full walk respectively, starting on any day you choose (Apr-Oct). They can extend the 15 day itinerary if required.

● **The Coast to Coast Packhorse** (☎ 017683 71777, 🖳 www.c2cpackhorse.co.uk) Coast to Coast specialist Packhorse offers a tailor-made approach to scheduling your trip depending on your own preferences. Any number of nights can be accommodated, ranging from short sections to full trips and at whatever pace suits you.

● **UK Exploratory** (☎ 01942 826270, 🖳 www.ukexploratory.com) A small and flexible Wigan-based company. Offers basic trail (14 days) but can tailor-make walks and do both west to east and east to west.

Group/guided walking tours

If you don't trust your navigational skills or simply prefer the company of other walkers as well as an experienced guide, the following companies will be of interest. Packages nearly always include all meals, accommodation, transport arrangements, minibus back-up and baggage transfer.

Have a close good look at each company's website before booking as each has its own speciality and it's important to choose one that's suitable for you.

● **Footpath Holidays** (☎ 01985 840049, 💻 www.footpath-holidays.com) Runs guided walking tours along the trail in three 4- to 6-day sections from individual bases (one in the Lake District, one in the Yorkshire Dales, and one in North York Moors) so avoiding the hassle of daily packing. Guests can book one section or all three to complete the whole trail. Can tailor-make walks if required.

● **HF Holidays** (see opposite) Offers the Coast to Coast in its entirety (15 days) five times a year as well as both St Bees to Keld and Keld to Robin Hood's Bay (9 nights) once a year.

● **Northwest Walks** (see opposite) Northwest offers a 15-day walk along the entire trail, undertaken around five times a year from west to east in groups of around ten people. Also offers walks along half the trail.

● **Ramblers Countrywide Holidays** (☎ 01707 386800, 💻 www.ramblerscoun trywide.co.uk) No specific Coast to Coast itinerary but this walking specialist does offer packages to Grasmere and the Lakes as well as a Highlights of Wainwright walk.

● **Sherpa Expeditions** (see opposite) Runs two to three 15-day Coast to Coast treks a year.

TAKING DOGS ALONG THE COAST TO COAST PATH

The Coast to Coast is a dog-friendly path, though it's extremely important that dog owners behave in a responsible manner. Dogs should always be kept on leads while on the footpath to avoid disturbing wildlife, livestock and other walkers. Dog excrement should be cleaned up and not left to decorate the boots of others; take a pooper scooper or plastic bag if you're walking with a dog.

It's particularly important to **keep your dog on a lead** when crossing fields with livestock in them, especially around calving or lambing time (see box p71) which can be as early as February or as late as the end of May. Most farmers would prefer it if you did not bring your dog at all at this time.

In addition, in certain areas on the Coast to Coast trail (particularly around Sunbiggin Tarn, east of Shap) there are notices ordering owners to keep their dogs on a lead to protect endangered ground-nesting birds between March and June; dogs can frighten them off and possibly cause them to desert their nests.

Remember when planning and booking your accommodation that you'll need to check if your dog will be welcome. Youth hostels do not permit them unless they're for assistance. Many inns and hotels charge extra for a dog and not all farms will want your mutt frightening the chickens. Note, too, that your dog needs to be extremely fit to complete the Coast to Coast path. You may not

PLANNING YOUR WALK

> ### ❑ Walking with a dog near cattle
> In August 2009, following four fatal tramplings by cows that summer (not on the
> Coast to Coast, it must be said) as well as who knows how many more less serious
> and unreported incidents, Ramblers (see box p48) in conjunction with the National
> Farmers Union issued the following guidelines when passing bovine livestock:
> ● Move quickly and quietly and, if possible, walk around the herd;
> ● Try not to get between cows and their calves;
> ● Be prepared for cattle to react to your presence, especially if you have a dog with you;
> ● Keep your dog close and under effective control on a lead;
> ● Don't put yourself at risk. Find another way round the cattle and rejoin the footpath
> as soon as possible;
> ● Don't hang onto your dog. If you are threatened by cattle let your dog go as the cat-
> tle will chase the dog;
> ● Don't panic or run! Most cattle will stop before they reach you. If they follow just
> walk on quietly.

believe it when you watch it haring around the fields, but they do have a finite
amount of energy (the hyperactive collies of some walkers we met finally went
lame around Osmotherley), so make sure your dog is up to the task of walking
for 10-20 miles a day.

Budgeting

England is not a cheap place to go travelling and, while the north may be one
of the less expensive regions, the towns and villages in the Lakes especially can
get all the business they can handle and charge accordingly. You may think
before you set out that you're going to keep your budget to a minimum by
camping every night and cooking your own food, but it's a rare trekker who
sticks to this. Besides, the B&Bs and pubs on the route are amongst the Coast
to Coast's major attractions and it would be a pity not to sample their hospitality from time to time.

If the only expenses of this walk were accommodation and food, budgeting
would be a piece of cake. Unfortunately, in addition to these there are all the little **extras** that push up the cost of your trip: for example beer, cream teas, internet use, buses or taxis, baggage carriers, laundry, souvenirs. It's surprising how
much these add up!

CAMPING

You can survive on less than £12 per person per day if you use the cheapest
campsites, don't visit a pub, avoid all the museums and tourist attractions in the
towns, forage for or cook all your own food from staple ingredients ... and generally have a pretty miserable time of it. Even then, unforeseen expenses will

probably nudge your daily budget up. Include the occasional pint, and perhaps a pub meal every now and then, and the figure will be nearer £15 per day.

HOSTELS, BUNKHOUSES AND CAMPING BARNS

The charge for staying in a **hostel** is £12-17 per night. Whack on another £5 for breakfast and an evening meal (£9-12), though you can use their self-catering facilities for both, and there's also lunch (packed lunches about £5.50) to consider. This means that, overall, it will cost £25-35 per day, or £40-45 to live in a little more comfort, enjoy the odd beer and go out for the occasional meal.

There are a few basic **camping barns** along the Coast to Coast. They vary in quality and price (expect to pay around £8).

B&BS, GUESTHOUSES AND HOTELS

B&B prices start at around £23 per person per night but can be up to twice this. Add on the cost of food for lunch and dinner and you should reckon on about £40 minimum per day. Staying in a guesthouse or hotel will cost more. Remember that there is often a supplement of £5-10 for single occupancy of a room.

When to go

SEASONS

Britain is a notoriously wet country and the north-west of England is an infamously damp part of it. Rare indeed is the trekker who manages to walk the Coast to Coast path without suffering at least one day of rain; three or four days per trek is more likely, even in summer. That said, it's equally unlikely that you'll spend a fortnight in the area and not see any sun at all, and even the most cynical of walkers will have to admit that, during the walking season at least, there are more sunny days than showery ones. That **walking season**, by the way, starts at Easter and builds to a crescendo in August, before quickly tailing off in September. By the end of that month there are few trekkers on the trail, and in late October many places close down for the winter.

Spring

Find a couple of dry weeks in springtime and you're in for a treat. The wild flowers are beginning to come into bloom, lambs are skipping in the meadows and the grass is green and lush. Of course, finding a dry fortnight in spring (around the end of March to mid-June) is not easy but occasionally there's a mini-heatwave at this time. Another advantage will be few trekkers on the trail so finding accommodation without booking is relatively easy. Easter is the exception, the first major holiday in the year when people flock to the Lake District and other national parks.

Summer

Summer, on the other hand, can be a bit *too* busy and, in somewhere like the Lakes over a weekend in August, at times depressingly congested. Still, the chances of a prolonged period of sunshine are of course higher at this time of year than any other, the days are much longer and the heather is in bloom, too, turning the hills a fragrant purple. If you like the company of other trekkers summer will provide you with the opportunity of meeting scores of them, though do remember that you'll need to book your accommodation well in advance or be prepared to camp occasionally. Despite the higher than average chance of sunshine, take clothes for any eventuality – it's bound to rain at some point.

Autumn

September can be a wonderful time to walk; many of the families have returned home and the path is clear although accommodation gets filled up in early September by a wave of older visitors who've been waiting for the school holidays to clear the way. The weather is usually sunny, too, at least at the beginning of September. By the end of the month the weather will begin to get a little wilder and the nights will start to draw in. For most mortals the walking season is almost at an end.

Winter

A few people trek the Coast to Coast in winter, putting up with the cold, damp conditions and short days for the chance to experience the trail without other tourists and maybe even under snow. Much of the accommodation will be closed too but whilst it may also be a little more dangerous to walk at this time, particularly on the high-level routes through the Lakes, if you find yourself walking on one of those clear, crisp, wintry days it will all seem absolutely worth it.

RAINFALL

At some point on your walk, it will rain; if it doesn't, it's fair to say that you haven't really lived the full Coast to Coast experience properly. At nearly 4.7 metres (185 inches), the hills over Borrowdale on Stage 2 (see p106) record the **highest rainfall in England**; a staggering eight times more than the south-east of England, for example! The question, therefore, is not whether you will be rained on, but how often and how hard. But as long as you dress accordingly and take note of the safety advice given on pp71-5, this shouldn't be a problem.

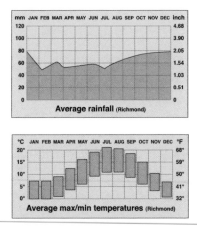

Average rainfall (Richmond)

Average max/min temperatures (Richmond)

Do, however, think twice about tackling some of the high-level alternatives if the weather is bad and visibility poor, and don't do so on your own.

DAYLIGHT HOURS

If walking in autumn, winter or early spring, you must take account of how far you can walk in the available light. It won't be possible to cover as many miles as you would in summer. Remember though, that you'll get a further 30-45 minutes of usable light before and after sunrise and sunset depending on the weather. In June, because the path is in the far north of England, those coming from the south may be surprised that there's enough light for walking until at least 10pm. Conversely, in early spring, late autumn and winter you'll be equally amazed how quickly the nights draw in.

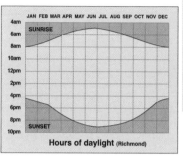

JAN FEB MAR APR MAY JUN JUL AUG SEP OCT NOV DEC

4am · 6am · 8am · 10am · 12pm · 2pm · 4pm · 6pm · 8pm · 10pm

SUNRISE

SUNSET

Hours of daylight (Richmond)

PLANNING YOUR WALK

ANNUAL EVENTS

Thanks largely to its undying appeal with tourists, Grasmere has become something of a mecca for those interested in those peculiarly Lakeland sports such as fell running, and Cumberland and Westmoreland wrestling.

In addition to the events outlined below, all kinds of **agricultural shows** take place annually in towns and villages on the Coast to Coast trail. These shows are an integral and traditional part of life all over rural England and particularly in the Lake District. Too numerous to list here, details of all the shows can be found by looking at the websites of the places concerned, of which you'll find a number in the box on p48. For further information about events in the southern Lake District see 🖳 www.lakelandgateway.info and click on Events.

Being aware of the bigger festivals is also useful when planning your walk as there's a good chance that available accommodation will be all the more in demand should you turn up on a busy weekend. For example early June's Appleby Horse Fair (🖳 www.applebyfair.org) can drain accommodation opportunities in Kirkby Stephen and Orton.

January to March

Grasmere hosts an annual **Art and Book Festival** (🖳 www.wordsworth.org.uk; click on What's on) at one of Wordsworth's old houses, Dove Cottage (or at a hotel very nearby). The festival usually takes place in January, is residential and consists of lectures, surgeries and workshops.

April to June

The villages of Swaledale, which include Keld, Muker, Thwaite, Gunnerside and Reeth, hold an annual music festival (**Swaledale Festival**); this usually takes place at the end of May to early June. The festival has an annual theme (eg stringed instruments), and in addition to the music there are all kinds of other activities from art exhibitions and guided walking trails to craft workshops; information can be found and tickets bought on the dedicated website 🖥 www .swaledale-festival.org.uk. Another event in June is the **Swaledale Marathon** (🖥 www.swaledaleoutdoorclub.org.uk; click on Swaledale Marathon) so accommodation in the area can dry up.

Robin Hood's Bay hosts a **folk music weekend** (🖥 www.robin-hoods-bay .co.uk – click on What's on), usually on the first or second weekend of June.

July to September

Richmond Live (🖥 www.richmondlive.org) is a pop music festival usually held over one weekend in July or August. Some readers have advised that if you want a quiet night's sleep, Richmond can be well worth avoiding at this time.

The annual **Grasmere Lakeland Sports and Show** (🖥 http://grasmere sportsandshow.co.uk), the origins of which date back over 300 years, takes place at the end of August. Other sports featured include tug-of-war, hound-trailing and the more recent addition of mountain biking. If you're in the Lakes at this time, don't miss the opportunity to witness this unique event.

October to December

For something a bit different, if you happen to be in Robin Hood's Bay in winter don't miss the **Victorian weekend** (🖥 www.robin-hoods-bay.co.uk – click on What's on) at the beginning of December, where the town turns out in 19th-century costume. It's all good fun, with quizzes, recitals, concerts and demonstrations, and it's all in aid of charity too.

Itineraries

Most people tackle the Coast to Coast from west to east, mainly because this allows them to walk 'with the weather at their back' (most of the time the winds blow off the Atlantic from the south-west). It's also usual for people to attempt the walk in one go, though there's much to be said for breaking it up and not crawling into Robin Hood's Bay in an Ibuprofen daze.

Part 4 of this book has been written from west to east, but there is of course nothing to stop you from tackling it in the opposite direction (see opposite). To help plan your walk look at the **planning map** (see opposite inside back cover) and the **table of village/town facilities** (on pp34-5), which gives a run-down on the essential information you'll need regarding accommodation possibilities and services at the time of writing. You could follow one of the suggested itineraries (see boxes pp36-7) which are based on preferred type of accommodation and walking speeds. There's also a list of recommended linear day and week-end walks on pp38-9 which cover the best of the Coast to Coast path, all of which are well served by public transport or the Packhorse/Sherpa van. The services table is on pp52-4 and public transport map on p55.

Once you have an idea of your approach turn to Part 4 for detailed information on accommodation, places to eat and other services in each village and town on the route. Also in Part 4 you will find summaries of the route to accompany the detailed trail maps. See also the box below and the boxes on p40 for tips from previous Coast to Coasters on what they'd do next time.

WHICH DIRECTION?

There are a number of advantages in tackling the path in a west to east direction, not least the fact that the prevailing winds will, more often than not, be behind you. If you are walking alone but wouldn't mind some company now and again you'll find that most of the other Coast to Coast walkers are heading in your direction too. However, there is also something to be said for leaving the Lake District – many people's favourite part of the British Isles, let alone the path – until the end of the walk.

❏ Next time ...

Next time we do the coast to coast we will make sure that we have booked into B&Bs that have baths! It's incredible how hard it is to stand up in a shower after a day's walking and also it is good to soak your muscles. We would highly recommend Ennerdale View B & B just outside Ennerdale Bridge as they offer the luxury of a hot tub and a glass of wine on arrival which is just what we needed after our first day's walking.

Parts of the walk are very remote and it is therefore important to make sure you have plenty of cash and/or your cheque book. Very few places accept cash cards and it is easy to get caught out. Likewise we would suggest that you take plenty of Compeed plasters for your possible blisters and pain killers as they are hard to get hold of once you get going on the walk and if you have a similar experience to ours then you'll go through plenty!

Be prepared for all weathers no matter what time of year you are walking. We experienced five days of horrendous weather in the Lakes at the end of July. A pair of gloves and a woolly hat are essential, along with a trusty compass for the top of mountains when you can't see beyond your arm!

Walking poles are a must for all ages – they saved our knees. In our experience they worked for us for a number of reasons from taking some of the weight off our feet, to clearing pathways, supporting our leaps across fast flowing streams and warning off angry looking cattle!

Invest in a camel pack (at least two litres). By having easy access to water it means that you don't get dehydrated.

Take innersoles to cushion feet as they came into their own, especially on the middle section of the walk when it is very flat and your feet take a pounding.

Birkdale Farm B&B in Keld is a find. It is the best accommodation we had the pleasure of staying in en route and if we knew this prior to our walk, we may well have stayed there for more than one night. The accommodation is a converted barn and completely self sufficient with a great open fire and a whole stash of logs!

Noelle Cox and Chris Foster

PLANNING YOUR WALK

Place name (Places in brackets are a short walk off the Coast to Coast path)	Distance from previous place approx miles/km	Cash Machine/ ATM	Post Office	Tourist Information Centre/Point (TIC/TIP)
St Bees		✔	✔	TIP
Sandwith	4.5/7.2			
Moor Row	3.5/5.6			
Cleator	1/1.6			
Ennerdale Bridge	6/9.6 (via Dent)			
Seatoller	14/22.5			National Trust information centre
Borrowdale	2/3.2 (to R'thwaite)			
(Longthwaite, Rosthwaite, Stonethwaite)				
Grasmere	9.5/15.3 (from R'thwaite)	✔	✔	
Patterdale	7.5/12 (not Helvellyn routes)		✔	TIC (at Glenridding)
Shap	16/25.7	✔	✔	
(Orton)	8/12.9		✔	
Kirkby Stephen	20.5/33 (from Shap)	✔	✔	TIC
Keld	14.5/23.3 (not Green route)			
(Thwaite)	2/3.2			
(Muker)	3.5/5.6 (from Keld)			
(Gunnerside)	2.5/4 (from Muker)			
Reeth	4/6.4 (from Gunnerside) 12.5/20.1 (from Keld on high route)	✔	✔	TIC/NPC*
Marrick	3.5/5.6			
Richmond	10.5/16.9	✔	✔	TIC
Colburn	3/4.8			
Catterick Bridge	2/3.2			
(Brompton-on-Swale)	0.5/0.8			
Danby Wiske	7.5/12.1			
Oaktree Hill	2.5/4			
Ingleby Cross/Arncliffe	8/12.9		✔	
(Osmotherley)	3/4.8 (from Ingleby Cross)		✔	
Clay Bank Top#	12/19.3			
Blakey Ridge	8.5/13.7			
Glaisdale	10/16.1		✔	
Egton Bridge	2/3.2			
Grosmont	2/3.2	✔	✔	NPC*
Littlebeck	3.5/5.6			
High Hawsker	7.5/12			
Robin Hood's Bay	4.5/7.2		✔	

TOTAL DISTANCE 198.5 miles (318.9km)

* NPC = National Park Centre

TOWN FACILITIES

Eating Place ✔=one; ✔✔=two; ✔✔✔=three +	Food Store	Campsite	Hostels Y (YHA) H-B (IndHostel or Bunkhouse) B (Barn)	B&B-style accommodation ✔=one; ✔✔=two; ✔✔✔=three+	Place name (Places in brackets are a short walk off the Coast to Coast path)
✔✔	✔	✔		✔✔✔	**St Bees**
			B		**Sandwith**
✔				✔	**Moor Row**
✔	✔			✔✔	**Cleator**
✔✔		✔(1.5 miles)	B(5 miles)/ H-B(1.5 miles)/YHA (5miles)	✔✔	**Ennerdale Bridge**
✔		✔	YHA (1.5 miles/2.5km)	✔✔	**Seatoller**
✔✔✔	✔(essentials)	✔	YHA/B	✔✔✔	**Borrowdale** (Longthwaite, Rosthwaite, Stonethwaite)
✔✔✔	✔	✔	YHA/H-B	✔✔✔	**Grasmere**
✔✔	✔	✔	YHA	✔✔✔	**Patterdale**
✔✔✔	✔	✔	H-B	✔✔✔	**Shap**
✔	✔	✔		✔✔✔	**(Orton)**
✔✔✔	✔	✔	H-B	✔✔✔	**Kirkby Stephen**
✔✔	✔	✔	H-B	✔✔✔	**Keld**
✔				✔	**(Thwaite)**
✔	✔			✔✔✔	**(Muker)**
✔				✔	**(Gunnerside)**
✔✔✔	✔	✔	YHA/H-B	✔✔✔	**Reeth**
		✔		✔	**Marrick**
✔✔✔	✔	✔ (3miles)	H-B (3miles)	✔✔✔	**Richmond**
		✔			**Colburn**
✔		✔		✔	**Catterick Bridge**
		✔	B		**(Brompton-on-Swale)**
✔		✔		✔✔	**Danby Wiske**
			B	✔	**Oaktree Hill**
✔		✔		✔✔✔	**Ingleby Cross/Arncliffe**
✔✔✔	✔	✔	YHA	✔✔✔	**(Osmotherley)**
✔		✔(3.5miles)		✔✔✔	**#Clay Bank Top**
✔		✔		✔✔	**Blakey Ridge**
✔	✔			✔✔✔	**Glaisdale**
✔✔				✔✔✔	**Egton Bridge**
✔	✔	✔		✔✔✔	**Grosmont**
		✔		✔	**Littlebeck**
✔		✔			**High Hawsker**
✔✔✔	✔	✔	YHA	✔✔✔	**Robin Hood's Bay**

§ DISTANCE Distances are between places directly on the Coast to Coast path
# Clay Bank Top This refers to Urra & Great Broughton

PLANNING YOUR WALK

CAMPING

Night	Relaxed pace Place	Approx Distance miles/km	Medium pace Place	Approx Distance miles/km	Fast pace Place	Approx Distance miles/km
0	St Bees		St Bees		St Bees	
1	Cleator*	11/17.5	Ennerdale Br*	14.5/23.5	Ennerdale Br*	14.5/23.5
2	Ennerdale Br*	7/11	Borrowdale§	16.5/26.5	Borrowdale§	16.5/26.5
3	Seatoller	13/21	Grasmere*	9.5/15	Patterdale	17/27.5
4	Grasmere*	11/17.5	Patterdale	7.5/12	Shap	16/25.5
5	Patterdale	7.5/12	Shap	16/25.5	K. Stephen	20.5/33
6	Shap	16/25.5	Kirkby Stephen	20.5/33	Reeth	28/45
7	Orton	8/13	Keld	14.5/23.5	Colburn	17/25
8	Kirkby Stephen	13/21	Reeth	12.5/20	Ingleby Cross	20/32
9	Keld	14.5/23.5	East Applegarth	11/18	Blakey Ridge	20.5/33
10	Reeth	11/17.5	Danby Wiske*	17.5/26.5	Grosmont	14/22.5
11	East Applegarth	8/13	Osmotherley	12/19	R. Hood's Bay	15.5/25
12	Brompton-o-S	8.5/14	Blakey Ridge	20.5/33		
13	Danby Wiske*	8.5/14	Grosmont	14/22.5		
14	Ingleby Cross	9/14.5	R. Hood's Bay	15.5/25		
15	Clay Bank Top§*	11.5/17.5				
16	Blakey Ridge	9/14.5				
17	Grosmont	13.5/21.5				
18	High Hawsker	10/16				
19	R. Hood's Bay	5.5/9				

Note: campsites may be seasonal
* No campsite but alternative accommodation is available
§ See **note** opposite

STAYING IN B&Bs

Night	Relaxed pace Place	Approx Distance miles/km	Medium pace Place	Approx Distance miles/km	Fast pace Place	Approx Distance miles/km
0	St Bees		St Bees		St Bees	
1	Cleator	11/17.5	Ennerdale Br	14.5/23.5	Ennerdale Br	14.5/23.5
2	Ennerdale Br	5/8	Borrowdale§	16.5/26.5	Borrowdale§	16.5/26.5
3	Seatoller§	14/22.5	Grasmere	9.5/15	Patterdale	17/27.5
4	Grasmere	10.5/17	Patterdale	7.5/12	Shap	16/25.5
5	Patterdale	7.5/12	Shap	16/25.5	K. Stephen	20.5/33
6	Shap	16/25.5	K. Stephen	20.5/33	Reeth	28/45
7	Orton	8/13	Keld	14.5/21	Colburn	17/22.5
8	K. Stephen	13/21	Reeth	14/22.5	Ingleby Cross	20/37
9	Keld	14.5/25	Richmond	10.5/17	Blakey Ridge	20.5/33
10	Reeth	12.5/20	Danby Wiske	14/22.5	Littlebeck	17.5/23
11	Richmond	14/22.5	Osmotherley	12/19	R. Hood's Bay	12/19
12	Danby Wiske	14/22.5	Clay Bank Top§	11/17.5		
13	Ingleby Cross	9/14.5	Blakey Ridge	8.5/14		
14	Clay Bank Top§	12/19	Grosmont	14/21.5		
15	Blakey Ridge	8.5/14	R. Hood's Bay	15.5/25		
16	Glaisdale	10/16				
17	Littlebeck	7/11				
18	R. Hood's Bay	12/19				

§ See **note** opposite

SUGGESTED ITINERARIES

The itineraries in the box opposite and below are based on different accommodation types – camping (not including wild camping which opens your options right out), hostels/bunkhouses/camping barns, and B&Bs – with each one divided into three alternatives depending on your walking speed (relaxed, medium and fast). They are only suggestions so feel free to adapt them. **Don't forget** to add your travelling time before and after the walk.

Note: **Borrowdale** refers to Longthwaite, Rosthwaite & Stonethwaite; **Clay Bank Top** actually means nearby Urra & Great Broughton

SIDE TRIPS

The Coast to Coast path is long enough and few walkers will be tempted to make side trips. However, Wainwright's series of guides to Lakeland fells describes other walks around the Lake District in further detail and it may be worth making time for an ascent of some of the hills in the area as they give an entirely different perspective of the Lakeland landscape. Old favourites include Great Gable, Striding Edge on Helvellyn, High Street and England's highest mountain Scafell Pike (3209ft/978m).

	STAYING IN HOSTELS/CAMPING BARNS/BUNKHOUSES					
	Relaxed pace		**Medium pace**		**Fast pace**	
Night	Place	Approx Distance miles/km	Place	Approx Distance miles/km	Place	Approx Distance miles/km
0	St Bees		St Bees		St Bees	
1	Sandwith	3/5	Sandwith	3/5	Ennerdale	20/32
2	Ennerdale Br*	12/19	Ennerdale	15.5/25	Grasmere	20.5/33
3	Black Sail YH	8.5/13.5	Borrowdale§	10.5/17	Shap	23.5/38
4	Borrowdale§	5.5/9	Grasmere	10/16	K. Stephen	20.5/33
5	Grasmere	10/16	Patterdale	10/16	Reeth [Dales]	29/47
6	Patterdale	10/16	Shap	16/25.5	East Applegarth	10/16
7	Shap	16/25.5	K. Stephen	20/32	Osmotherley	28.5/46
8	Orton*	8/13	Keld	13/21	Blakey Ridge*	20.5/33
9	K. Stephen	13/21	Reeth [Grinton]	12.5/20	Grosmont*	13.5/21.5
10	Keld	13/21	East Applegarth	9.5/15	R. Hood's Bay	15.5/25
11	Reeth [Dales]	12.5/20	Danby Wiske*	16.5/26.5		
12	East Applegarth	9.5/15	Osmotherley	12/19		
13	Danby Wiske*	16.5/26.5	Clay Bank Top§*	11/17.5		
14	Osmotherley	12/19	Glaisdale*	19/30.5		
15	Clay Bank Top§*	11/17.5	R. Hood's Bay	19/30.5		
16	Blakey Ridge*	9/14.5				
17	Glaisdale*	10/16	* No camping barns, bunkhouses or hostels but			
18	Littlebeck*	7/11	alternative accommodation is available			
19	R. Hood's Bay	12/19	§ See **note** above			

Note: some of the above are seasonal so check in advance

PLANNING YOUR WALK

❏ DAY AND WEEKEND WALKS

The best day loops and weekend walks on the Coast to Coast
The following suggested trails are for those who don't want to tackle the entire path in one go or just want to get a flavour of the challenge before committing themselves. In our opinion they include the best parts of the Coast to Coast path, and are all described in more detail in Part 4.

Day walks bring you back to your starting point, either along other routes not mapped in this book or in some cases it is possible to use public transport.

There is good public transport (see pp52-4 for details) to the start and end points on the suggested weekend walk but no direct service between Reeth and Kirkby Stephen. However, if there are two of you, you can shuttle with two cars, or a car and bike as many walkers do.

Day walks
● **St Bees to Sandwith** 5 miles/8km (pp83-6) Get a flavour of setting out from St Bees and striking off along the red rock sea cliffs – even if you're back in St Bees that night on the bus or by walking from Sandwith.

● **Around Ennerdale Water** 11 miles/17.5km (pp94-6) The first truly gorgeous stretch of the Coast to Coast passes along the south shore of Ennerdale Water to the River Liza. You can carry on to Black Sail along an easy track, then take a walk back along the northern access track.

● **Borrowdale to Grasmere and back** 15 miles/21km (pp109-18) Grasmere for lunch? In good weather it's a great training walk and you'll be able to pin down the Greenup Edge crossing to boot. Warm yourself up on the long climb to the Edge and we recommend you take the regular valley route down to Grasmere. Rest up, revive yourself in the fleece-wearing capital of the UK, and then take the haul back with the sun to Borrowdale. We don't recommend the high route via Helm Crag unless you're really on form.

● **Grasmere to Grasmere** 8 miles/13km (pp113-110) A very popular day trip for the more active visitor to Grasmere. It's up to you which direction you take; probably reversing the Coast to Coast by tackling the acute climb up to Helm Crag is best. At the junction at the top of Easedale (Wpt 36, p111) you come down the valley. A great day out but tougher than you think.

● **Grasmere to Patterdale and back** $16^{1}/_{2}$ miles/16km (p118-27) A pretty hefty proposition and another great training walk through the heart of the Lakes. The walk takes you up to Helvellyn summit and along Striding Edge, lunch at the pub and then back either up the valley or along St Sunday Crag (same distance but more climbing on the latter) and back down the other side of Tongue Gill. With very little overlapping, it's easily one of the best days out in the Lakes.

● **Patterdale to Kidsty Pike and back** 13 miles/19.5km (pp128-32) Take a $6^{1}/_{2}$ mile walk to the 791-metre (2995ft) summit of Kidsty Pike on the eastern edge of the Lakes and the highest point on the original Coast to Coast route (though Helvellyn and St Sunday are much higher).

Have a sandwich and a look around then walk right back down again to Patterdale for a slap-up meal in the pub. It's a stiff old climb up to Angle Tarn but from there on the gradients just blend in with the surroundings and the views all the way up and down are well worth the effort. Another Lakeland classic that will have you fired up for the real thing.

● **Kirkby Stephen to Nine Standards and back** 12 miles/19.5km (pp153-7) An easy climb to the mysterious stone cones atop Nine Standards Rigg. From the top you might try a southward link towards Rigg Beck and the Green Route back to town, adding a mile or two, but that can involve some messy bog-trotting.

● **Keld to Reeth** 12¹/₂ miles/20km (pp163-77) Whether you take the high route via a string of evocative mine ruins between breezy moors, or the lowland amble past the hamlets of Upper Swaledale, you're sure to find something you like. If you want to return to Keld you can either take a bus or, with a bit of forward planning, can cycle-shuttle back to the car.

● **Lord Stones Café to Clay Bank Top and back** 7¹/₂ miles/12km (pp212-13) On some days a rather too popular run with Teeside dog walkers but the gradients will all be good training for the big day.

● **The Esk Valley**: **Glaisdale to Grosmont** 4 miles/6.5km (see pp225-9) Not so much a trek as an easy pub crawl, this path takes you along the Esk Valley following the course of the river through woodland and along country tracks, via pretty Egton Bridge. Grosmont, at the end of the trail, has steam trains to Pickering or Whitby or buses and regular trains to Scarborough, Whitby, and even the beginning of the trail. There are also buses back to Glaisdale.

● **Little Beck Woods excursion** 4¹/₂ miles/7km (pp231-3) A shady afternoon's round trip to Falling Foss waterfall and the adjacent tea room through the lovely Little Beck Woods.

● **Whitby to Robin Hood's Bay** 7 miles/11km (p237) Not on the Coast to Coast until the last few miles but a stirring cliff-top tramp nonetheless, ending at the hallowed slipway below the Bay Hotel. You won't be the first to pretend you've just finished the entire Coast to Coast, but no one need know. Take the regular bus service back to Whitby, which is a fun place too.

Weekend walk

In addition to the walk described below, any number of the day walks can be combined into a two-day trek, particularly in the Lake District.

● **Kirkby Stephen to Reeth** 28 miles/45km (p153) Anyone who manages to scramble over the Pennines and negotiate the boggy ground down to the old mining village of Keld deserves a reward of some sort, and picturesque Swaledale is just that. As an encore, take Wainwright's high route over the moors to Reeth or the less demanding stroll down the dale, passing through or near the villages of Muker, Gunnerside and Thwaite to end up in Reeth.

❏ Next time I do the C2C...

I'll have to go east to west; with the promise of the Lake District always ahead of me and the mid-day rush of fellow C2C-ers to meet coming from the west. I will happily take the gamble of walking into the weather when I know that ascending to Helvellyn will be so much easier from Patterdale than it is at the end of a long, tiring day from Rosthwaite. The east to west route also means that you meet different people in the pub every evening and you can swap information on the path conditions ahead.

I will also discipline myself to take more time on the trail and to savour the experience of the walking. The metronomic, almost trance-like state that can occur when all you need to do is put one foot in front of the other is rarely achieved when you're focussing on getting to the end. Too often I arrived at my destination by 3pm or even 2pm and although this means more time relaxing in the pub it also means I could have taken more time on the hills, perhaps sitting quietly enjoying a view or taking time to divert from the path to explore the landscape.

I will of course use Brookfield House in Shap again, as I have on my two previous crossings. The welcome you receive from Margaret when you knock on the door here is second to none. I will also make sure I book early because her reputation means the place is always in demand.

Stuart Greig

❏ Next time...

Take our time. It's a holiday. Forget about the keen types who set off before 8am – let them go. Plan most days at 10-14 miles, that gives plenty of time.

Expect to feel tired, especially on days 2-4. It isn't Pennine Way-tough, but it isn't an easy stroll either.

Stay in B&Bs, especially farms. Last time, except for the terrific Langstrath, the pubs and hotels were a bit disappointing while the B&Bs were all good to great.

See the eagle in Riggindale again. We saw it for a few seconds last time, fabulous.

Do the high routes, weather permitting – Helm Crag and St Sunday Crag are fantastic on clear days. Helvellyn next time?

If we've time, have a rest day in Kirkby Stephen as well as in Richmond. It's welcome after the Lakes. (And there's a launderette!).

Take the Swale route from Keld to Reeth. The mines are interesting but bleak; everyone said the river is beautiful ... but then, lots of them wished they'd done the high-level route.

Spend longer in the Swaledale Museum in Reeth, and stay overnight in their lovely quirky cottage. Then stock up in the Reeth Bakery.

Take a lightweight camera, binoculars, a notebook. Make notes at least every evening – it's easy to forget the details, the days merge into one another. Take more notice of the small things: wild flowers, how the dry-stone walls change, curlews. The big things are dramatic, but the small ones are fascinating.

Make sure boots are 100% waterproof. A tiny damp spot on a Sunday stroll in Cheshire is trench foot on Nine Standards Rigg.

Think about going east to west. The Lakes are the highlight but they're hard work at the start. They'd be a great climax starting from the east, when we're more walking-fit. As for the rain-in-your-face argument ... what rain?!

David Bull

What to take

Not ending up schlepping over the fells like an overloaded mule with a migraine takes experience and some measure of discipline. **Taking too much** is a mistake made by first-time travellers of all types, an understandable response to not knowing what to expect and not wanting to be caught short. The village store in Patterdale even has a special counter for Coast to Coasters sending stuff home.

By UK standards the Coast to Coast is a long walk but it's not an expedition into the unknown. Experienced independent hill walkers trim their gear down to the essentials because they've learned that an unnecessarily heavy pack can exacerbate injuries and put excess strain on the already hard-pressed feet. Note that if you need to buy all the gear listed, keep an eye out for the ever-more frequent online **sales** at outdoor gear shops; time it right and you could get it all half price.

TRAVELLING LIGHT

Organised tours apart, baggage-forwarding services tempt walkers to partially miss the point of long-distance walking: the satisfaction of striding away from one coast knowing that you're carrying everything you need to get to the other. But if you've chosen to carry it all you must be ruthless in your packing choices.

HOW TO CARRY IT

Today's rucksacks are hi-tech affairs that make load-carrying as tolerable as can be expected. Don't get hung up on anti-sweat features; unless you use a wheelbarrow your back will always sweat a bit. It's better to ensure there is thick padding and a **good range of adjustment**. In addition to hip belts (allied with some sort of stiff back frame/plate), use an unelasticated **cross-chest strap** to keep the pack snug; it makes a real difference.

If camping you'll need a pack of at least 60-litres' capacity. Staying in hostels 40 litres should be ample, and for those eating out and staying in B&Bs a 20- to 30-litre pack should suffice; you could even get away with a daypack.

Few backpacks these days claim to be waterproof, use a waterproof **liner** or the elasticated backpack cover like a shower cap that comes with some packs. It's also handy to **compartmentalise** the contents into smaller bags so you know what is where. Take a few (degradable) **plastic bags** for wet things, rubbish etc; they're always useful. Finally, pack intelligently with the most frequently used things readily accessible.

FOOTWEAR
Boots
A good pair of boots is vital. Scrimp on other gear if you must – you'll only use waterproofs some days but you'll be walking every mile on every day. Expect

to spend up to £150 on quality, three-season items which are light, breathable and waterproof, and have ankle support as well as flexible but thick **soles** to insulate your own pulverised soles. Don't buy by looks or price and avoid buying online until you've been to a shop and tried on an identical pair (and even this can backfire on you). Go to a big outdoor shop on a quiet weekday and spend an hour trying on everything they have in stock that appeals to you.

With modern fabric boots **breaking in** is a thing of the past (traditional one-piece leather Meindels are not so accommodating, as I found to my cost...), but arriving in St Bees with an untried pair of boots is courting disaster. You must try them out beforehand, first round the house or office, and then on a full day's walk or two.

An old and trusted pair of boots can be resoled and transformed with shock-absorbing after-market **insoles**. Some of these can be thermally moulded to your foot in the shop, but the less expensive examples are also well worth the investment, even if the need for replacement by the end of the walk is likely. Some walkers wisely carry old trusted boots in their luggage in case their new footwear turns on them. Blisters are possible even with a much-loved boot if you walk long and hard enough; refer to p73 for blister-avoidance strategies.

Boots might be considered over the top for the Coast to Coast; much of the walking is on easy paths and some experienced walkers have turned to trail shoes. They won't last as long as boots, be as tough or crucially, have the height to keep your socks dry in the bogs and streams, but the rewards of nimbleness and greater comfort can transform your walk, just as bad footwear can cast a shadow over it.

Socks

As with all outdoor gear, the humble sock has not escaped the technological revolution (with prices to match) so invest in two non-cotton pairs designed for walking. Although cushioning is desirable, avoid anything too thick which will reduce stability. A correctly sized boot with an anatomically shaped insole gives a sure-footed feel. As well as the obvious olfactory benefits, frequent washing will maintain the socks' springiness.

CLOTHES

Tops

The proven system of **layering** is a good principle to follow. A quick-drying synthetic, or a less odiferous merino wool, **base layer** transports sweat away from your skin; the mid-layer, typically a **fleece** or woollen jumper, keeps you warm; and when needed, an outer 'shell' or **jacket** protects you from the wind and rain.

Maintaining a comfortable temperature in all conditions is the key, and this means not **overheating** just as much as the more obvious effects of **wind chill**. Both can prematurely tire you. Trudging out of Patterdale on a warm day will soon have you down to your base layer, but any exposed and prolonged descent, or rest on an unsheltered summit like Kidsty Pike, with a strong wind will soon chill you. Although tedious, the smart hiker is forever fiddling with zips and managing their layers and headwear to maintain an optimal level of comfort.

Avoid cotton; as well as being slow to dry, when soaked it saps away body heat but not the moisture – and you'll often be wet from sweat if not rain. Take a change of **base layers** (including underwear), a **fleece** suited to the season, and the best **breathable waterproof** you can afford. **Soft shells** are an alternative to walking in rustling nylon waterproofs when it's windy but not raining.

It's useful to have a **spare set of clothing** so you're able to get changed should you arrive chilled at your destination, but choose **quick-drying clothes** as washing them reduces your payload. Once indoors your body heat will quickly dry out a synthetic fleece and nylon leggings. However, always make sure you have a **dry base layer** in case you or someone you're with goes down with hypothermia. This is why a quality waterproof is important.

Leg wear

Your legs are doing all the work and don't generally get cold so your trousers can be light which will also mean quick-drying. Although they lack useful pockets, many walkers find leg-hugging cycling polyester **leggings** very comfortable (eg Ron Hill Tracksters). Poly-cotton or microfibre trousers are excellent. Denim jeans are cotton and a disaster when wet.

If the weather's good, **shorts** are very agreeable to walk in, leaving a light pair of trousers clean for the evenings. It also means your lower legs get muddy and not the trousers. On the other hand **waterproof trousers** would only suit people who really feel the cold; most others will find them unnecessary and awkward to put on and wear; quick drying or minimal legwear is better. For Lakeland stream crossings and Pennine peat bogs, **gaiters** are a great idea; they also stop irritating pebbles dropping into your footwear. You don't have to wear them all the time.

Headwear and other clothing

Your head is both exposed to the sun and loses most of your body heat so, for warmth, carry a woolly beany that won't blow away and for UV protection a peaked cap; a bandana makes a good back-up or sweat band too. Between them they'll conserve body heat or reduce the chances of dehydration. **Gloves** are a good idea in wintry conditions (carry a spare pair in winter).

TOILETRIES

Besides **toothpaste** and a brush, **liquid soap** can also be used for shaving and washing clothes, although a ziplock bag of **detergent** is better if you're laundering regularly. Carry **toilet paper** and a lightweight **trowel** to bury the results out on the fells (see pp68-9). Less obvious items include **ear plugs**, **sun screen**. **moisturiser**; **insect repellent** if camping and possibly a means of **water purification** (see p21).

FIRST-AID KIT

Apart from aching limbs your most likely ailments will be blisters so a first-aid kit can be minimal. **Ibuprofen** and **paracetamol** help numb pain although rest of course is the only real cure. '**Compeed**', or '**Second Skin**' all treat blisters. An **elastic knee support** is a good precaution for a weak knee as are walking poles (see box p33). A tube of Nuun tablets can flavour water and restore lost minerals on the march, and a few sachets of Dioralyte or Rehydrat powders will quickly remedy more serious dehydration. Other items worth considering are: **plasters** for minor cuts; a small selection of different-sized **sterile dressings** for wounds; **porous adhesive tape**; **antiseptic wipes**; **antiseptic cream**; **safety pins**; **tweezers**; and **scissors**.

GENERAL ITEMS

Essential
Carry a **compass**, a **whistle** and a **mobile phone** as well as at least a one-litre **water bag** or bottle; an LED **headtorch**; **emergency snacks**, a **penknife** and a **watch**.

Useful
If you're not carrying a proper bivi bag or tent, a compact foil **space blanket** is a good idea in the cooler seasons. Many people take a **camera**, **batteries** and **sunglasses**. A **book** is a good way to pass the evenings, especially mid-summer wild camps. A **vacuum flask**, for hot drinks or soup, is recommended if walking in a cooler season. Studies have shown that nothing improves a hilltop view on a chilly day like a cup of hot tea or soup.

SLEEPING BAG & CAMPING GEAR

If you're camping or planning to stay in camping barns you'll need a sleeping bag. Many bunkhouses now offer bedding, some at a nominal cost. All youth hostels provide bedding and insist you use it.

A **two-season bag** will do for indoor use, but if you can afford it or anticipate outdoor use, go warmer. The choice over a **synthetic** or **down** filling is a debate without end. Year by year less expensive synthetic-filled bags (typically under £100) approach down's enviable qualities of good compressability while expanding or 'lofting' fully once unpacked to create maximum warmth. But get a down bag wet (always a risk in the UK) and it clogs up and loses all its thermal qualities; and drying down bags takes half a day at the laundrette.

If committed to the exposure of wild camping you'll need a **tent** you can rely on; light but able to withstand the rain and wind. In campsites you may just get away with a cheap tent. Otherwise, a good 1-man tent suited to the wilds can cost under £120 and weigh just 1.5kg, with a sub-2kg two-man example costing around £250. An inflatable **sleeping mat** is worth many times its weight.

As for **cooking**, is it really worth the bother on the Coast to Coast? The extra weight and hassle in buying provisions is only viable when shared by a group of three or more; otherwise get down the pub and help support the local economy.

MONEY

Cash machines (ATMs) are infrequent along the Coast to Coast path, with none between Richmond and Grosmont, though their numbers are growing as post offices and shops along the trail install them or turn to the simpler **cashback** system. Banks are even rarer, with only Shap, Kirkby Stephen and Richmond boasting any. Not everybody accepts **debit** or **credit cards** as payment either – though many B&Bs and restaurants now do. As a result, you should always carry plenty of cash with you, just to be on the safe side. Though its days are said to be limited, a **cheque book** from a British bank is useful in those places where credit cards are not accepted. See also p21 and p34. Crime on the trail is thankfully rare but it's always a good idea to carry your money in a **moneybelt**.

MAPS

The much-improved hand-drawn maps in this edition cover the trail at a scale of just under 1:20,000: one mile equals $3^1/8$th of an inch (1km = 5cm). At this generous scale, combined with the notes and tips written on the maps and now waypoints, they should be enough to stop you losing your way as long as you don't stray too far off the route. That said, a supplementary map of the region – ie one with contours, can prove invaluable should you need to abandon the path and find the quickest route off high ground in bad weather. They also help you to identify local features and landmarks and devise possible side trips.

Unfortunately, the two Outdoor Leisure strip maps produced by the **Ordnance Survey** (☎ 08456 050505, 💻 www.ordnancesurvey.co.uk) that covered the entire trail at a scale of 1:27,777 went out of print in 2002 although it may be possible to get second-hand copies; look for sheets OL33 covering the trail from St Bees to Keld and OL34 covering it from Keld to Robin Hood's Bay. If you find a set going cheap – apparently on Ebay they're selling for about £30 – get one though they may be getting tatty by now. The good news is that electronic copies are available online and could of course be printed off. Have a look at 💻 www.walkingplaces.co.uk/c2c/osmaps.htm.

In their place the Ordnance Survey now have The Explorer series of maps at a scale of 1:25,000 but in order to cover the whole trail you will need eight maps. The trouble here, of course, is one of weight and expense and also, **they don't always show the path** and are sometimes out of date with details like plantations (Dent Hill and Ennerdale on the OL4 being good examples in 2009). The details are: 303 (for St Bees); Outdoor Leisure (OL) 4 for the western Lake District; OL5 for the eastern Lake District; OL19 for the upper Eden Valley (Kirkby Stephen); OL30 for Swaledale; Explorer Series 304 for Richmond and the Vale of Mowbray; OL26 for the western North York Moors; and OL27 for the eastern half to Robin Hood's Bay. While it may be extravagant to buy all of these maps, members of Ramblers (see box p48) can borrow up to 10 maps for a period of six weeks at 30p per map from their library.

We say again that with a bit of nous many readers manage with the maps in this book, but if any two of the above OS maps are worth getting they are the

OL4 and OL5 covering the Lake District where the weather can be bad, the waymarking is worse and the consequences of losing the path vexing in the extreme. By a stroke of luck both these double-side sheets can be neatly cut in half while still retaining the full extent of the path from west to east.

The alternatives to OS are the strip maps produced by either **Footprint** (🖳 www.stirlingsurveys.co.uk) or **Harvey Maps** (🖳 www.harveymaps.co.uk), both of which cover the trail over two maps at a scale of around 1:50,000 and 1:40,000 respectively. The problem is that, like our maps, they only cover a narrow strip either side of the trail and consequently give limited opportunities for exploring further afield. Footprint's maps have a useful cumulative mile count and cost around £4.95; Harvey's are £11.95 each but are made of more weatherproof plastic paper.

❏ **Digital mapping**

There are a number of software packages available on the market today that provide Ordnance Survey maps for a PC or handheld computer. The two best known are Memory Map and Anquet, but more suppliers join the list every year. Maps are supplied not in traditional paper format, but electronically on CD or DVD media. They are then loaded into a PC program, normally supplied with the maps, where you can view them, print them and work with them.

Digital maps are normally purchased for an area such as a National Park, but the Coast to Coast walk is available as a distinct product from some vendors. When compared to the eight OS Explorer maps that are needed to cover the walk, they aren't that much more expensive either. Once you own the electronic version of the map you can print any section of the map you like, as many times as you like.

The real value of the digital maps though, is the ability to draw a route onto the map using your computer mouse. The map, or the appropriate sections of it, can then be printed out with the route marked on it, so you no longer need the full versions of the OS maps. Additionally, the route can be uploaded to a GPS device, providing you with the whole C2C route in your hand at all times while walking. If you set your GPS to record the route as you walk, you can then upload this recorded data into the digital mapping software when you return from your walk, providing information on distance walked, time, speed, ascent and so on.

Many websites now have free routes you can download for the more popular digital mapping products. Anything from day walks around the Lakes to complete Long Distance Paths like the Coast to Coast. Taking OS quality maps with you on the hills has never been so easy. There are dozens of different devices on the market now that will display a detailed map on a screen in a small portable format; everything from small handheld computers like the HP iPaq down to mobile phones. Almost any device with built-in GPS functionality now has some mapping software available for it. One of the most popular manufacturers of dedicated GPS devices is Garmin, who have an extensive range of map-on-screen devices. Prices vary from around £100 to £600.

GPS devices should not replace the traditional method of navigation, a map and compass, as any electronic device is susceptible to failure and if nothing else, battery failure. Remember that battery life will be significantly reduced, compared to normal usage, when you are using the built-in GPS and running the screen for long periods.

Stuart Greig

RECOMMENDED READING

Most of the following books can be found in the tourist information centres; the centre at Richmond has a particularly good supply of books about the path and the places en route. As well as stocking many of the titles listed below, the tourist offices also have a number of books about the towns and villages en route, usually printed by small, local publishers.

Guidebooks, travelogues and DVD

We have to mention here Wainwright's original *A Coast to Coast Walk* (*Wainwright Pictorial Guides*, 2003), a veritable work of art and now reprinted by local publisher, Frances Lincoln. For the coffee table *Coast to Coast with Wainwright* (also Frances Lincoln, 2009) marries Wainwright's original text with photos by Derry Brabbs; it makes a great souvenir of the walk. *Ancient Feet* (Matador, 2008) by Alan Nolan, is a humourous tale of five friends in their sixties tackling the path. Returning with the Wainwright theme, Hunter Davies's *Wainwright: The Biography* (Orion Press) is an absorbing account of this complex man. And finally *Rick Stein's Coast to Coast* (2008) has nothing to do with the walk, but does have some lovely seafood recipes.

Getting back to practicalities, towards the end of each year Doreen Whitehead produces the latest edition of her long-running publication *Coast to Coast Bed & Breakfast Accommodation Guide*. For ordering details see 🖥 www .coasttocoastguides.co.uk.

It's possible you saw *Coast to Coast with Julia Bradbury* (DVD; Acorn Media, 2009, 165 mins), the five-part BBC show broadcast twice in 2009 and part of a 'Wainwright Walks' series. Julia Bradbury makes an engaging presenter and approaches the task with gusto, interviewing characters along the way (including writer Alan Nolan, mentioned above). Unfortunately, the production hit terrible weather in the Lakes which dampened the impression of that part of the walk; many of the aerial shots were filmed in much better conditions. Rumours circulated on the web and along the trail about body doubles standing in on long shots while she got choppered to the summits looking fresh as a daisy, and whether she walked the entire route. The reality of television as well as of filming outdoors makes the former likely (though she may well have done the walk on another occasion) and watching the parts in quick succession you can't help thinking that it's more fun to walk than to watch. Nevertheless, to have the Coast to Coast featured on mainstream TV at all is something of a coup for British long-distance paths and has further enshrined the popularity of the trail. The DVD contains no 'special features' of any significance.

If you're a seasoned long-distance walker, or even new to the game and like what you see, check out the other titles in the Trailblazer series; see pp253-6.

Flora and fauna field guides

Collins *Bird Guide* with its beautiful illustrations of British and European birds continues to be the favourite field guide of both ornithologists and laymen alike. For a pocket-sized guide to the flora you'll encounter on the Coast to Coast path, *The Wild Flowers of Britain and Ireland: A New Guide to Our Wild*

❏ SOURCES OF FURTHER INFORMATION

Online trail information

🖳 www.coast2coast.co.uk Run by Sherpa Van, this site is crammed full of information and has an online shop for books and maps as well as a popular accommodation-booking and luggage-transfer service (see p25). Best of all, they have the most active Coast to Coast forum around, where trekkers share their experiences and others post questions, although it does suffer from a level of flippancy by the 'seen-it-all' regulars who dominate the board. Scrutinise at length before enquiring; it's probably been asked before.

🖳 www.coasttocoastguides.co.uk Richmond-based organisation and another excellent website with books and maps for sale and a thorough accommodation guide based on Doreen Whitehead's booklet (see p47).

🖳 www.walkingplaces.co.uk/c2c An extensive and cleanly designed website that's not trying too hard to do everything or sell you something. Run by a Coast to Coast enthusiast, there are some excellent resources here that you won't find anywhere else, as well as a tolerant and supportive forum.

Tourist information organisations

● **Tourist information centres (TICs)** TICs are based in towns throughout Britain and provide all manner of locally specific information and an accommodation-booking service. There are four centres relevant to the Coast to Coast path: **Ullswater/Glenridding** (near Patterdale, p125), **Kirkby Stephen** (p150), **Reeth** (p175) and **Richmond** (pp185-6).

● **Yorkshire Tourist Board** (🖳 www.yorkshire.com) The tourist board oversees all the local tourist information centres in the county. It's a good place to find general information about the county as well as on outdoor activities and local events. They can also help with arranging holidays and accommodation.

● **Cumbria Tourist Board** (🖳 www.cumbria-the-lake-district.co.uk) Performing much the same role as the Yorkshire board above but, of course, for the county encompassing the Lake District.

Organisations for walkers

● **Backpackers' Club** (🖳 www.backpackersclub.co.uk) A club aimed at people who are involved or interested in lightweight camping through walking, cycling, skiing and canoeing. They produce a quarterly magazine, provide members with a comprehensive advisory and information service on all aspects of backpacking, organise weekend trips and also publish a farm-pitch directory. Membership is £12/15/7 per year for an individual/family/anyone under 18 or over 65.

● **The Long Distance Walkers' Association** (🖳 www.ldwa.org.uk) Membership includes a journal (*Strider*) three times per year with details of challenge events and local group walks as well as articles on the subject. Information on over 730 paths is presented in their newly revised *UK Trailwalkers' Handbook*, published by Cicerone. Membership is £13 a year.

● **Ramblers** (formerly Ramblers' Association; 🖳 www.ramblers.org.uk) Looks after the interests of walkers throughout Britain. They publish a quarterly *Walk* magazine (£3.40 to non-members) and *Walk Britain's Great Views* (£14.99), a guide to Britain's top 50 viewpoints. Membership costs £27/36 individual/joint.

(Opposite) Passing Eagle Crag (see p109) on the long climb up from Borrowdale to Greenup Edge. (© CS).

Flowers (Tandem) by Marjorie Blamey and Richard Fitter, with illustrations by Alastair Fitter, is comprehensive but, alas, not for the beginner, with the plants arranged by families. It's also too big to take with you. Another in the Collins Gem series, *Wild Flowers*, is thus more suitable for walkers and only costs £5.

Getting to and from the Coast to Coast path

Both St Bees and Robin Hood's Bay are quite difficult to reach. For this reason, many people opt to use Kirkby Stephen as their base. Not only is this town well connected by public transport (it lies on the Carlisle to Leeds line) but it's also the home of Packhorse who offer van rides to the start at St Bees and other

❏ GETTING TO BRITAIN

● **By air** Manchester Airport (🖳 www.manchesterairport.co.uk) is the nearest major international airport to St Bees but for most foreign visitors one of the London airports is likely to be their entry point to the country. Nevertheless, if you've no business in London do check out flights to Manchester. Trans-Pennine Express (see p50) operates services from the airport to Barrow-in-Furness and Northern Rail (see p50) from there to St Bees.

Leeds Bradford (convenient for Kirkby Stephen) and Teeside (7 miles/11km outside Darlington and useful for Richmond; also the nearest airport to Robin Hood's Bay) are also worth investigating but are served mainly by domestic flights.

A number of **budget airlines** (easyJet 🖳 www.easyjet.com, bmibaby 🖳 www .bmibaby.com and Ryanair 🖳 www.ryanair.com) fly from many of Europe's major cities to Manchester and the London terminals (Stansted, Luton, Gatwick and Heathrow). See pp50-2 for details about Getting to St Bees, Kirkby Stephen or Robin Hood's Bay from London.

● **From Europe by train** Eurostar (🖳 www.eurostar.com) operates a high-speed passenger service via the Channel Tunnel between Paris, Brussels (and some other cities) and London St Pancras International – convenient for both the trains for Carlisle (which leave from nearby Euston) and to the north-east coast (which leave from neighbouring King's Cross). For more information about rail services from Europe contact your national rail operator, or Railteam (🖳 www.railteam.eu).

● **From Europe by coach** Eurolines (🖳 www.eurolines.com) have a huge network of long-distance coach services connecting over 500 cities in 25 European countries to London. Check carefully, however: often, once such expenses as food for the journey are taken into consideration, it often does not work out that much cheaper than taking a flight, particularly when compared to the prices of some of the budget airlines.

● **From Europe by ferry (with or without a car)** Numerous ferry companies operate routes between the major North Sea and Channel ports of mainland Europe and the ports on Britain's eastern and southern coasts as well as from Ireland to ports in both Wales and England. For further information see websites like 🖳 www.directferries.com.

● **From Europe by car** Eurotunnel (🖳 www.eurotunnel.com) operates the shuttle train service for vehicles via the Channel Tunnel between Calais and Folkestone taking one hour between the motorway in France and the motorway in Britain.

(Opposite) Looking down on Ullswater from The Cape, St Sunday Crag route. (© CS).

destinations on the Coast to Coast path, and will also bring customers back to Kirkby Stephen from Robin Hood's Bay. See pp24-5 for details.

If you want to make your own way to **St Bees**, it's best to take a train to Carlisle or Barrow-in-Furness, and then take the train to St Bees. Alternatively take a bus from Carlisle to Whitehaven (Stagecoach No 300, 301 & No 600; see box p53) and then walk, bus or train the 4½ miles south from Whitehaven.

For **Robin Hood's Bay**, Arriva's No 93 Middlesbrough to Scarborough bus service operates daily (see box p54); all these towns are well connected by rail.

NATIONAL TRANSPORT

All train **timetable and fare information** can be found at National Rail Enquiries (☎ 08457 484950, 24hrs; 🖳 www.nationalrail.co.uk). Alternatively, and to book tickets, you can look on the websites of the train companies concerned: **Virgin Trains** (🖳 www.virgintrains.co.uk), **East Coast** (🖳 www.eastcoast.co.uk), **Northern Rail** (🖳 www.northernrail.org) and **Trans-Pennine Express** (🖳 www .tpexpress.co.uk). Timetables and tickets are also available on 🖳 www.thetrain line.com and 🖳 www.qjump.co.uk. You are advised to book in advance. Turning up at Darlington at the end of the walk, a train to London will cost £100; if booked in advance it would cost about £35.

Coach travel is generally cheaper (though with the excellent advance-purchase train fares that is not always true) but takes longer. The principal coach (long-distance bus) operator in Britain is **National Express** (☎ 08717 818181 Mon-Sat 8am-8pm, Sun 10am-8pm, 🖳 www.nationalexpress.com). **Megabus** (🖳 www.megabus.co.uk) has a more limited service though may be cheaper.

Getting to St Bees
● **Train** Carlisle and Barrow-in-Furness are the main access points for St Bees. Virgin's London Euston to Glasgow service calls at Carlisle; trains operate approximately hourly during the day and the journey takes 3¼-4 hours. Virgin's Birmingham New St to Edinburgh/Glasgow service stops in Carlisle hourly.

Trans-Pennine Express operates a service from Manchester Airport/ Manchester Piccadilly to Barrow-in-Furness (Mon-Sat 8-10/day, Sun 3-6/day). They also operate a service from Manchester Airport/Piccadilly to Glasgow/Edinburgh via Carlisle (Mon-Sat 8-9/day, Sun 7/day).

Northern Rail (see above) operates a service from Carlisle to Barrow-in-Furness calling at St Bees (Mon-Sat 7-9/day). On Sunday the service only goes from Carlisle to Whitehaven (3/day). However, Whitehaven is just over four miles up the road from St Bees and AA Travel (see box p53) operates a bus service between the two on Sunday.

● **Coach/bus** Whitehaven is the closest place to St Bees that National Express services operate to; stops on the once daily NX570 London to Whitehaven service include Grasmere, and Kendal for bus services to Kirkby Stephen. See above for details of how to get to St Bees from Whitehaven.

Alternatively, National Express has services to Carlisle from several towns and cities in Britain. Services that stop at least once a day in Carlisle include:

NX590/592 London to Aberdeen; NX920 London to Stranraer; NX538 Coventry to Inverness; NX536 Cardiff to Edinburgh; NX539 Bournemouth to Edinburgh; NX336 Penzance to Edinburgh; and NX533 Wrexham to Glasgow.

From Carlisle take a train (see opposite) to St Bees, or a bus to Whitehaven (Stagecoach No 300, 301 & No 600; see box p53). From there trekkers can either take 3D Travel's No 20 bus to St Bees or, if a Sunday, AA Travel's X6 (see box p53).

● **Car** You can of course drive to St Bees and leave your car (for a fee) at a B&B there. The nearest motorway is the M6 to Carlisle which joins the M1 just outside Coventry. From the south, leave the M1 at junction 36 (the Southern Lakes turn-off), then take the A590 till it meets the A5092; this then meets the A595 (to Whitehaven) and turn off just before Egremont.

Getting to Robin Hood's Bay

● **Train** Robin Hood's Bay is, if anything, even harder to reach than St Bees. The nearest rail station is at Whitby: East Coast's London King's Cross to Newcastle/Edinburgh/Glasgow service calls at Darlington from where you need to take a Northern Rail train to Middlesbrough and change there for a train to Whitby (see box p52). From London to Whitby takes 5-6 hours. From Whitby Arriva's No 93/X93 (see box p54) bus takes 20 minutes to Robin Hood's Bay.

A better way, involving only one change of train, is to get off the East Coast train at York and take one of TransPennine Express's trains to Scarborough and then take Arriva's No 93/X93 (see box p54) bus to the Bay. The bus journey is longer (approximately 40 minutes) but the train journey is only around three hours including changes.

● **Coach/bus** National Express operates one direct service (NX563) a day to Whitby (leaving London Victoria at 1pm, arriving in Whitby at 8.40pm). Arriva's No 93 service (Scarborough to Middlesbrough) calls in at Whitby and Robin Hood's Bay and it should be possible to get a bus to Robin Hood's Bay on the same day but this would mean arriving very late.

● **Car** It's not entirely straightforward to get to Robin Hood's Bay by car either, though compared to public transport it is at least the simplest. From London head up to Doncaster on the M1/A1(M), then the M18/A19 to York. From there you can head north-east to Scarborough on the A64, then follow the A171 heading towards Whitby, turning off on the B1447 for Robin Hood's Bay. Coming from Manchester take the M62 north-east to Leeds, then the A64 all the way to Scarborough, from where you pick up the A171 as outlined above.

Getting to Kirkby Stephen

● **Train** Kirkby Stephen is a stop on the Carlisle to Settle line. Coming from London (Kings Cross) either take an East Coast train from King's Cross to Leeds ($2^{1}/_{2}$ hours) and then catch a Northern Rail train to Kirkby Stephen (Mon-Sat 6-8/day, Sun 3/day; $1^{3}/_{4}$ hours), or take a Virgin train to Carlisle ($3^{1}/_{4}$ hours) from London Euston and then a Northern rail train to Kirkby Stephen (Mon-Sat 6-8/day, Sun 3/day; 50 mins).

● **Coach/bus** National Express coach services run to Kendal and Grasmere (both stops on the NX570 service; see p50). Stagecoach's No 564 operates from Kendal to Kirkby Stephen and their No 555 from Kendal to Grasmere.

● **Car** The A685 runs through the town and the trans-Pennine A66 (which shadows the Coast to Coast path to the north) crosses the A685 just four miles north of the town. The nearest motorway, the M6, is 22 miles west of the A66 interchange. See p24 for information about Packhorse's parking facilities.

LOCAL TRANSPORT

Public transport is limited along the Coast to Coast path. While most places do have some sort of bus service, these services may be irregular and often just two

---

❑ PUBLIC TRANSPORT SERVICES

Notes
● Service details were as accurate as possible at the time of writing but it is essential to check before travel
● Services on Bank Holiday Mondays are usually the same as Sunday services; services that operate Monday to Saturday generally don't operate on Bank Holiday Mondays
● Services generally operate at the same frequency in both directions
● In rural areas where there are no fixed bus stops it is usually possible to 'hail and ride' a passing bus though it is important to stand where visibility is good and also somewhere where it would be safe for the driver to stop
● See pp24-5 for details of Packhorse's and Sherpa Van's services along this route.

Rail services
Northern Rail Ltd (🖳 www.northernrail.org)
See pp50-1 for details of the services to Carlisle for St Bees, to Whitby (for Robin Hood's Bay) and to Kirkby Stephen
● Middlesbrough to Whitby (Esk Valley Railway) via Glaisdale, Egton & Grosmont, Mon-Sat 4/day plus 1/day Fri evening Jul-Sep, Sun 5/day May-Sep

North York Moors Railway (enquiries ☎ 01751 472508, talking timetable ☎ 01751-473535, 🖳 www.nymr.co.uk)
Grosmont to Pickering/Whitby via Goathland, Newtondale Halt & Levisham, daily Mar-Oct plus in holiday periods such as Christmas/New Year and February half-term, weekends only at other times; 4-8/day depending on the time of year.

Bus services
Yorkshire Coastliner (☎ 01653 692556 Mon-Fri 9am-3pm, Sat 9am-noon, 🖳 www.yorkshirecoastliner.co.uk)
840   Leeds to Whitby via York, Mon-Sat 4/day; Sun Leeds to Malton (843) and Malton to Whitby (840) 2/day

Stagecoach North West (🖳 www.stagecoachbus.com)
22   Whitehaven to Egremont via Cleator Moor & Cleator, Mon-Sat 6-7/day
77/77A Keswick to Keswick (Honister Rambler) a circular route via Buttermere,
       Honister slate mine & Seatoller, Apr-Oct 4/day in each direction; no
       service Nov-Mar

or three times per day (although this didn't stop one Coaster we met doing the walk by taking a bus back to his car every night!). Usually the choice of destination is limited too, often the nearest big town.

If you have difficulty getting through to the transport companies in the box on pp52-4, contact **traveline** (☎ 0871 200 2233; 🖳 www.traveline.org.uk), which has public transport information for the whole of the UK. For additional information about transport in Cumbria contact Cumbria County Council (🖳 publictransport@cumbriacc.gov.uk, 🖳 www.cumbria.gov.uk\buses) and ask for a copy of *Cumbria and Lakesrider*, which gives details of buses, trains and ferries in the county. For information about services in the Yorkshire Dales visit 🖳 www.dalesbus.org.

PLANNING YOUR WALK

Bus services *(cont'd)*
Stagecoach North West *(cont'd)*

78   Keswick to Seatoller (Borrowdale Rambler) via Rosthwaite, Easter to Sep
         Mon-Sat 1/hr, end July-Aug Mon-Sat 2/hr, Sun 8/day

106   Penrith to Kendal via Shap & Orton (also operated by Apollo 8 Travel),
         Mon-Sat 7/day

108   Penrith to Patterdale Hotel (Patterdale Bus) via Glenridding,
         Mon-Sat 4-5/day; Apr-late Aug Sun 4/day

300/301 Whitehaven to Carlisle, Mon-Sat hourly

301   Whitehaven to Carlisle, Sun 5/day

517   Bowness to Glenridding (Kirkstone Rambler) via Windermere & Patterdale
         Hotel, Easter to mid-Jul & Sep-Oct, Sat, Sun & Public Hols 3/day; mid-Jul
         to end Aug daily 3/day; no service Nov to Mar

555   Keswick to Lancaster via Grasmere, Ambleside, Windermere & Kendal,
         Mon-Sat 8/day plus Keswick to Kendal school summer holidays Mon-Fri
         7/day, Sun Easter-Oct 10/day, Nov-Easter 5/day

599   Grasmere to Bowness (Open-top Lakeland Experience) via Ambleside &
         Windermere, Easter-Aug daily 3/hr; Sep-Oct daily 2/hr, Nov-Easter Mon-
         Sat 1/hr

600   Carlisle to Whitehaven via Cockermouth, Mon-Fri 3/day, Sat 5/day

3D Travel (☎ **01946 812828**)

6   Whitehaven to Muncaster via Moor Row, Egremont & Seascale, Mon-Sat
         2/day plus 1-2/day Whitehaven to Seascale

20   Whitehaven to St Bees via Sandwith, Mon-Sat 4-6/day

AA Travel (☎ **01900-606707**)

X6   Millom to Whitehaven via Muncaster, Egremont & St Bees, Sun 4/day

Rosie's Travel (☎ **01900-810393**)

217   Cockermouth to Frizington via Kirkland, Rowrah, and Ennerdale Bridge,
         Mon-Sat 1-3/day

Grand Prix Coaches (☎ **017683 41328**)

563   Penrith to Kirkby Stephen, Mon-Sat 5-6/day

(cont'd on p54)

PUBLIC TRANSPORT SERVICES *(cont'd from p53)*

Bus services

Ken Routledge (daily 7am-10pm ☎ 01900 822795)
949   Cockermouth to Buttermere via Lorton and Loweswater (dial-a-ride Mon-Sat 3/day)

NBM Hire (☎ 01768 892727)
111   Penrith to Burnbanks Village (Haweswater Rambler), Tue 2/day, Sat 3/day

Little Red Bus (☎ 01423 526655, 💻 www.littleredbus.co.uk)
30   Keld to Richmond via Thwaite, Muker, Gunnerside Bridge & Reeth, Mon-Sat 2-3/day; and Reeth to Richmond Mon-Sat 3-4/day

Kirkby Lonsdale Coach Hire (☎ 01524-733831, 💻 www.kirkbylonsdalecoach hire.co.uk/bus_services.html or 💻 www.dalesbus.org)
564   Kirkby Stephen to Kendal, Mon-Sat 4-5/day
831   (Northern Dalesman) Hawes to Leyburn via Thwaite, Keld, Muker, Gunnerside & Reeth, May-Oct Sun 1/day

Arriva North East (💻 www.arrivabus.co.uk)
X26   Catterick Village/Colburn to Darlington via Richmond, Mon-Sat 2/hr, Sun 1/hr
27   Catterick Garrison to Darlington via Richmond, daily 1/hr evening only until 11pm
X27   Catterick Garrison to Darlington via Richmond, Mon-Sat 2/hr, Sun 1/hr
29   Darlington to Richmond, Mon-Sat 6/day
X34   Richmond to Darlington via Catterick, Mon-Sat 2-3/day plus 1/day Catterick via Colburn to Darlington
93/X93   Scarborough to Middlesbrough via Robin Hood's Bay (not all services stop at Robin Hood's Bay), Hawsker Village & Whitby, Apr-Oct Mon-Sat 11/day, Sun 6/day plus Scarborough to Whitby Mon-Sat 12/day, Sun 12/day; Nov-Mar 8/day plus Scarborough to Whitby Mon-Sat 4/day, Sun 3/day plus Scarborough to Whitby 11/day
5/5A   Whitby to Middlesbrough Mon-Sat 1/hr. Sun 1/hr

Dales & District (☎ 01677 425203, 💻 www.procterscoaches.co.uk)
54   Richmond to Northallerton via Catterick Bridge, Mon-Sat 3/day
55   Richmond to Northallerton via Bolton on Swale, Mon-Sat 4-5/day

Moorsbus Network (☎ 01845 597000, 💻 www.moors.uk.net/moorsbus)
Note: The details for the M2/M9 services were not available at the time of writing but it is expected that services will operate daily in the summer and up to 4/day
M2   Helmsley to Guisborough via Clay Bank Top and Stokesley, Easter-Oct Sun & Bank Hols 1/day
M9   Osmotherley to Helmsley, Easter-Oct Sun & Bank Hols 1/day

G Abbott & Sons (☎ 01677 422858)
80   Stokesley to Northallerton via Ingleby Cross & Osmotherley, Mon-Sat 5/day
89   Stokesley to Northallerton via Gt Broughton, Ingleby Cross & Osmotherley, Mon-Sat 5/day

M&D Minicoaches (☎ 01947 895418)
99   Whitby to Lealholm via Grosmont, Egton Bridge & Glaisdale, Mon-Sat 4-5/day. This is a hail-and-ride service.

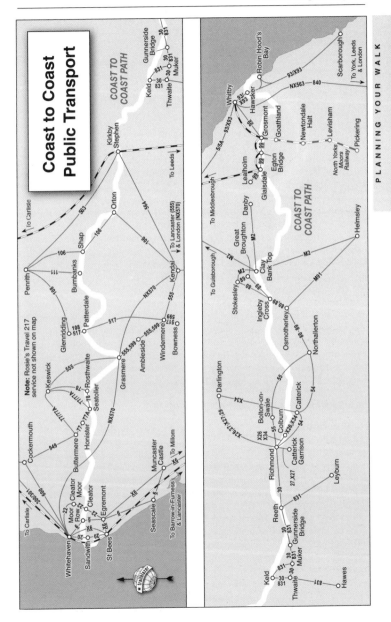

Coast to Coast Public Transport

COAST TO COAST PATH

To Carlisle

To Leeds

Gunnerside Bridge — 30/831 — Keld — 30/831 — Thwaite — 30/831 — Muker

Kirkby Stephen

Orton — 563
Shap — 106
Burnbanks
Penrith — 106 — Shap
108
104
Patterdale — 108/517
Glenridding
Keswick — 555
Rosthwaite — 78/77A
Seatoller
Honister — 77/77A
Buttermere — 949
Cockermouth
Grasmere — 555/599
Ambleside — 555/599
Windermere — 599
Bowness
Kendal — 555 — NX570
To Lancaster (555) & London (NX570)

Note: Rosie's Travel 217 service not shown on map

To Carlisle
600/X600
22
Whitehaven — 20
Moor Row — Cleator Moor — Cleator — Egremont
Sandwith
St Bees — 20
Seascale — 6 — X6
Muncaster Castle — X6
To Millom
To Barrow-in-Furness & Lancaster

COAST TO COAST PATH

Robin Hood's Bay
Whitby — 93/X93
Hawsker — 93/X93
Scarborough
NX563 — 840
To York, Leeds & London

Grosmont — 5/6A — 93/X93
Lealholm — 99
Egton Bridge — 99
Glaisdale — 99
Danby
Goathland
Newtondale Halt
Levisham
North Yorks Moors Railway
Pickering

To Middlesbrough
To Guisborough

Great Broughton — M2
Stokesley — M2
Clay Bank Top — M2
Ingleby Cross — 80/89
Helmsley — M2 — M91
Osmotherley — 80/89
Northallerton — 80/89

Darlington — X34
Bolton-on-Swale
Colburn — X26/X27/X34
Catterick — 54
Catterick Garrison — 54
Richmond — 27/X27
Reeth — 30
Leyburn — 831
55 — 54

Keld — 831 — 30/831
Thwaite — 30/831
Muker — 30/831
Gunnerside Bridge — 30/831
Hawes — 831

Trailblazer

PART 2: ENVIRONMENT AND NATURE

Conserving the Coast to Coast path

With a population of over 61 million Britain is an overcrowded island, and England is the most densely populated part of it. As such, the English countryside has suffered a great deal of pressure from both over-population and the activities of an ever more industrialised world. Thankfully, there is some enlightened legislation to protect the surviving pockets of forest and heathland.

Apart from these, it is interesting to note just how much man has altered the land that he lives on. Whilst the aesthetic costs of such intrusions are open to debate, what is certain is the loss of biodiversity that has resulted. The last wild boar was shot near the Coast to Coast trail a few centuries ago; add to that the extinction of bear and wolf as well as, far more recently, a number of other species lost or severely depleted over the decades and you get an idea of just how much of an influence man has over the land, and how that influence is all too often used negatively.

There is good news, however. In these enlightened times when environmental issues are quite rightly given more precedence, many endangered species, such as the otter, have increased in number thanks to the active work of voluntary conservation bodies. There are other reasons to be optimistic. The environment is no longer the least important issue in party politics and this reflects the opinions of everyday people who are concerned about issues such as conservation on both a global and local scale.

GOVERNMENT AGENCIES AND SCHEMES

Natural England

Natural England is responsible for enhancing biodiversity, landscape and wildlife in rural, urban, coastal and marine areas; promoting access, recreation and public well-being; and contributing to the way natural resources are managed. One of its roles is to identify, establish and manage: national trails, national parks, areas of outstanding natural beauty (AONBs), national nature reserves (NNRs), sites of special scientific interest (SSSIs), and special areas of conservation (SACs) and to enforce regulations relating to these sites.

The highest level of landscape protection is the designation of land as a **national park** which recognises the national importance of an area in terms of landscape, biodiversity and as a recreational resource. At the time of writing there were nine national parks in England (plus the Norfolk and Suffolk Broads which enjoy comparable status and protection). Three of these are bisected by the Coast to Coast path (Lake District, Yorkshire Dales and North York Moors national parks). This designation does not signify national ownership and these are not uninhabited wildernesses, making conservation a knife-edged balance between protecting the environment and the rights and livelihoods of those living in the parks.

The second level of protection is **area of outstanding natural beauty** (AONB). The only AONB passed on the Coast to Coast trail covers the very southern extremity of the North Pennines as you pass Nine Standards Rigg and before you enter the Yorkshire Dales. The primary objective for an AONB is conservation of the natural beauty of a landscape. As there is no statutory administrative framework for their management, this is the responsibility of the local authority within whose boundaries they fall. Some AONBs, including the North Pennines, have also been designated **geoparks** (🖳 www.european geoparks.org), a European Union initiative originally set up as a socio-economic project to help the development and management of deprived areas which nevertheless benefited from a rich geological heritage, defined as both unique and important. The concept has since moved on, with today's geoparks designed to raise awareness of an area and to educate the general public.

National nature reserves (NNRs) are places where the priority is protection of the wildlife habitats and geological formations. There are over 200 (including Smardale in Cumbria) in England and they are either owned or managed by Natural England or by approved organisations such as wildlife trusts.

Local nature reserves (LNRs) are places with wildlife or geological features that are of special interest to local inhabitants; there are nine in Cumbria and 18 in North Yorkshire.

Sites of Special Scientific Interest (SSSIs) range in size from little pockets protecting wild flower meadows, important nesting sites or special geological

---

❏ Government agencies and other bodies
● **Department for Environment, Food and Rural Affairs** (🖳 www.defra.gov.uk) Government ministry responsible for sustainable development in the countryside.
● **Natural England** (🖳 www.naturalengland.org.uk) See opposite.
● **English Heritage** (🖳 www.english-heritage.org.uk) Organisation whose central aim is to make sure that the historic environment of England is properly maintained. It is officially known as the Historic Buildings and Monuments Commission for England.
● **Forestry Commission** (🖳 www.forestry.gov.uk) Government department for establishing and managing forests for a variety of uses.
● **National Association of Areas of Outstanding Natural Beauty** (🖳 www.aonb .org.uk); for further information on the North Pennines AONB visit 🖳 www.north pennines.org.uk.
● **Lake District National Park Authority** (🖳 www.lake-district.gov.uk); **Yorkshire Dales National Park Authority** (🖳 www.yorkshiredales.org.uk); **North York Moors National Park Authority** (🖳 www.northyorkmoors.org.uk). The government authorities charged with managing the respective areas. None of these has much in the way of specific Coast to Coast trail information on their websites, though they might be worth contacting to find out the latest developments to the path.

THE ENVIRONMENT AND NATURE

features, to vast swathes of upland, moorland and wetland. SSSIs, of which there are over 4000 in England, are a particularly important designation as they have some legal standing. They are managed in partnership with the owners and occupiers of the land who must give written notice before initiating any operations likely to damage the site and who cannot proceed without consent from Natural England. Many SSSIs are also either a NNR or a LNR.

Special Area of Conservation (SAC) is an international designation which came into being as a result of the 1992 Earth Summit in Rio de Janeiro, Brazil. This European-wide network of sites is designed to promote the conservation of habitats, wild animals and plants, both on land and at sea. Every land SAC is also an SSSI.

CAMPAIGNING AND CONSERVATION ORGANISATIONS

These voluntary organisations started the conservation movement in the mid-19th century and are still at the forefront of developments. Independent of government but reliant on public support, they can concentrate their resources either on acquiring land which can then be managed purely for conservation purposes, or on influencing political decision-makers by lobbying and campaigning.

Managers and owners of land include well-known bodies such as the RSPB, the NT and the CPRE. The **Royal Society for the Protection of Birds** (RSPB), has over 150 nature reserves and more than a million members. There are two reserves on the Coast to Coast path, both of great significance. St Bees Head, at the very start of the trail, is the largest seabird colony in north-west England, home in spring and summer to guillemots, kittiwakes, fulmars and razorbills; while Haweswater, at the eastern end of the Lake District, is England's only golden eagle territory.

The **National Trust** (NT) is a charity with over three million members which aims to protect, through ownership, threatened coastline, countryside, historic houses, castles and gardens, and archaeological remains for everybody to enjoy. On the Coast to Coast trail, the NT's properties are concentrated in the Lakes where they look after such beauty spots as Ennerdale, supposedly England's wildest valley; parts of Ullswater; and 4925 hectares (12,170 acres) of Grasmere and Great Langdale including, curiously, the bed of Grasmere Lake, Johnny Wood (see p106) and Bay Ness (see Map 93, p237).

❏ **Campaigning and conservation organisations**
- **Royal Society for the Protection of Birds** (RSPB; 🖳 www.rspb.org.uk) See above.
- **National Trust** (NT; 🖳 www.nationaltrust.org.uk) See above.
- **Campaign to Protect Rural England** (CPRE; 🖳 www.cpre.org.uk) See p59.
- The umbrella organisation for the 47 wildlife trusts in the UK is **The Wildlife Trusts** (🖳 www.wildlifetrusts.org). Two relevant to the Coast to Coast path are **Cumbria Wildlife Trust** (🖳 www.cumbriawildlifetrust.org.uk) and **Yorkshire Wildlife Trust** (🖳 www.ywt.org.uk)
- **Woodland Trust** (🖳 www.woodland-trust.org.uk) Restores woodland throughout Britain for its amenity, wildlife and landscape value.

The **Campaign to Protect Rural England** (CPRE) exists to promote the beauty and diversity of rural England by encouraging the sustainable use of land and other natural resources in both town and country.

A huge increase in public interest and support of these and many other conservation/campaigning groups since the 1980s indicates that people are more conscious of environmental issues and believe that it cannot be left to our political representatives to take care of them for us without our voice. We are becoming the most powerful lobbying group of all, an informed electorate.

BEYOND CONSERVATION

Pressures on the countryside grow year on year. Western society, whether directly or indirectly, makes constant demands for more oil, more roads, more houses, more cars. At the same time awareness of environmental issues increases, as does the knowledge that our unsustainable approach to life cannot continue. Some governments appear more willing to adopt sustainable ideals, others less so.

Yet even the most environmentally progressive of governments are some way off perfect. It's all very positive to classify parts of the countryside as national parks and Areas of Outstanding Natural Beauty but it will be of little use if we continue to pollute the wider environment, the seas and skies. For a brighter future we need to adopt that sustainable approach to life. It would not be difficult and the rewards would be great.

The individual can play his or her part. Walkers in particular appreciate the value of wild areas and should take this attitude back home with them. This is not just about recycling the odd green bottle or two and walking to the corner shop rather than driving, but about lobbying for more environmentally sensitive policies in local and national government.

The first step to a sustainable way of living is in appreciating and respecting this beautiful, complex world we live in and realising that every one of us plays an important role within the great web. The natural world is not a separate entity. We are all part of it and should strive to safeguard it rather than work against it. So many of us live in a way that seems far removed from the real world, cocooned in centrally heated houses and upholstered cars. Rediscovering our place within the natural world is both uplifting on a personal level and important regarding our outlook and approach to life.

Flora and fauna

The beauty of walking from one side of England to the other is that on the way you pass through just about every kind of habitat this country has to offer. From woodland and grassland to heathland, bog and beach, the variety of habitats is surpassed only by the number of species of flower, tree and animal that each supports.

The following is not in any way a comprehensive guide – if it were, you would not have room for anything else in your rucksack – but merely a brief guide to the more commonly seen flora and fauna of the trail, together with some of the rarer and more spectacular species.

MAMMALS

The Coast to Coast path is alive with all manner of native species and the wide variety of habitats encountered on the way means that the wildlife is varied too. Unfortunately, most of these creatures are shy and many are nocturnal, and walkers can consider themselves extremely lucky if during their trek they see more than three or four species.

One creature that you will see everywhere along the walk, from the cliffs at St Bees to the fields outside Robin Hood's Bay, is the **rabbit** (*Oryctolagus cuniculus*). Timid by nature, most of the time you'll have to make do with nothing more than a brief and distant glimpse of their white tails as they stampede for the nearest warren at the first sound of your footfall. Because they are so numerous, however, the laws of probability dictate that you will at some stage get close enough to observe them without being spotted; trying to take a decent photo of one of them, however, is a different matter.

If you're lucky you may also come across **hares**, often mistaken for rabbits but much larger, more elongated and with longer back legs and ears.

Rabbits used to form one of the main elements in the diet of the **fox** (*Vulpes vulpes*), one of the more adaptable of Britain's native species. Famous as the scourge of chicken coops, their reputation as indiscriminate killers is actually unjustified: though they will if left undisturbed kill all the chickens in a coop in what appears to be a mindless and frenzied attack, foxes will actually eat all their victims, carrying off and storing the carcasses in underground burrows for them and their families to eat at a later date. These days, however, you are far more likely to see foxes in towns, where they survive mostly on the scraps and leftovers of the human population, rather than in the country. While generally considered nocturnal, it's not unusual to encounter a fox during the day too, often lounging in the sun near its den.

One creature that is strictly nocturnal, however, is the **bat**, of which there are 14 species in Britain, all protected by law. Your best chance of spotting one is just after dusk while there's still enough light in the sky to make out their flitting forms as they fly along hedgerows, over rivers and streams and around street lamps in their quest for moths and insects. The most common species in Britain is the pipistrelle (*Pipistrellus pipistrellus*).

The Lakes offer one of the few chances in England to see the rare **red squirrel** (*Sciurus vulgaris*). While elsewhere in the country these small, tufty-eared natives have been usurped by their larger

CAUTION
Red squirrels
crossing

cousins from North America, the **grey squirrel** (*Sciurus carolinensis*), in the Lakes the red squirrel maintains a precarious foothold.

Patterdale offers walkers on the Coast to Coast their best chance of seeing the **badger** (*Meles meles*). Relatively common throughout the British Isles, these nocturnal mammals with their distinctive black-and-white-striped muzzle are sociable animals that live in large underground burrows called setts, appearing after sunset to root for worms and slugs.

One creature which you almost certainly won't encounter, though they are said to exist in the Lakes, is the **pine marten** (*martes martes*). Extremely rare in England since being virtually wiped out during the 19th century for their pelts and their reputation as vermin, there are said to be a few in the valley of Ennerdale.

In addition to the above, keep a look out for other fairly common but little-seen species such as the carnivorous **stoat** (*Mustela erminea*), its smaller cousin the **weasel** (*Mustela nivalis*), the **hedgehog** (*Erinaceus europaeus*) – these days, alas, most commonly seen as roadkill – and a number of species of **voles**, **mice** and **shrews**.

One of Britain's rarest creatures, the **otter** (*Lutra lutra*), is enjoying something of a renaissance thanks to concerted conservation efforts. Though more common in the south-west, otters are still present in the north of England. At home both in salt and freshwater, they are a good indicator of a healthy unpolluted environment. Don't come to the north expecting otter sightings every day. If you see one at all you should consider yourself *extremely* fortunate, for they remain rare and very elusive. There are said to be some in Swaledale.

A surprisingly large number of trekkers encounter deer on their walk. Mostly this will be the **roe deer** (*Capreolus capreolus*), a small native species that likes to inhabit woodland, though some can also be seen grazing in fields. As with most creatures, your best chance of seeing one is very early in the morning, with sightings particularly common in Ennerdale, the upper end of Swaledale and the Vale of Mowbray.

Britain's largest native land mammal, the **red deer** (*Cervus elaphus*), is rarely seen on the walk though it does exist in small pockets around the Lakes.

REPTILES

The **adder** is the only common snake in the north of England, and the only poisonous one of the three species in Britain. They pose very little risk to walkers – indeed, you should consider yourself extremely fortunate to see one, providing you're a safe distance away. They only bite when provoked, preferring to hide instead. The venom is designed to kill small mammals such as mice, voles and shrews, so deaths in humans are very rare, but a bite can be extremely unpleasant and occasionally dangerous to children or the elderly. You are most likely to encounter them in spring when they come out of hibernation and during the summer when pregnant females warm themselves in the sun. They are easily identified by the striking zigzag pattern on their back. Should you be lucky enough to encounter one, enjoy it but leave it undisturbed.

THE ENVIRONMENT AND NATURE

BIRDS

The Coast to Coast is without doubt an ornithologist's dream. The seaside cliffs, woods, moorland and hedgerows encountered on the path provide homes for a wealth of different species including the golden eagle, Britain's rarest and most majestic bird, and a flock of parrots.

The red sandstone cliffs above St Bees (see p83) have been owned by the RSPB since 1973 and dotted along the trail are viewpoints where you can gaze down at the nesting seabirds. This is in fact the only colony of cliff-nesting seabirds in north-west England to which birds return year after year to lay their eggs and hatch chicks.

The most common of the seabirds is the **guillemot** (*Uria aalge*), with an estimated minimum of 5000 crowding onto the cliff's open ledges, including the rare **black guillemot** (*Cepphus grylle)*; indeed, the cliffs are believed to be the only place where this rare sub-species nests in England.

GUILLEMOT
L: 450MM/18"

Razorbills (*Alca torda*), a close relative of the guillemot, are also present, as are **puffins** (*Fratercula arctica*), though their numbers seldom rise above two dozen or so.

Kittiwakes (*Rissa tridactyla*), **fulmars** (*Fulmarus glacialis*) and **gulls** (family *Larus*) are also present, while a little further inland **ravens** (*Corvus corax*) and **peregrine falcons** (*Falco peregrinus*) nest.

Away from the coast, the rarest species in England is the **golden eagle** *(Aquila chrysaetos)*, a pair of which had set up an eyrie near the Coast to Coast trail, on the way down to Haweswater Reservoir from Kidsty Pike (see p132). Enthusiastic twitchers could be seen peering up the valley most hours of the day, and there was also a 24hr guard

BLACK GUILLEMOT
L: 350MM/13.5"

GOLDEN EAGLE
L: 910MM/36"

keeping watch to protect it from the predations of the egg collectors. This was the only pair of breeding golden eagles in England. However, since the female has disappeared it is hoped another one can be attracted down from Scotland for the lone male.

The first wild **ospreys** (*Pandion haliaetus*) to breed in England for centuries are also present in the Lakes, though not near the trail.

Other birds of prey include **kestrel** (*Falco tinnunculus*), **buzzard** (*Buteo buteo*), **barn owl** (*Tyto alba*) and **short-eared owl** (*Asio flammeus*).

One of the most common birds seen on the path, particularly in the latter half of the walk, is the **pheasant** (*Phasianus colchicus*). Ubiquitous on the moors, the male is distinctive thanks to his beautiful long, barred tail feathers, brown body and glossy green-black head with red head-sides, while the female is a dull brown. Another way to distinguish them is by the distinctive strangulated hacking sound they make together with the loud flapping of wings as they fly off.

Another reasonably common sight on the moors of Yorkshire is the **lapwing** (*Vanellus vanellus*), also known as the peewit. Black and white with iridescent green upper parts and approximately the size of a pigeon or tern, the lapwing's most distinctive characteristic is the male's tumbling, diving swooping flight pattern when disturbed, believed to be either a display to attract a female or an attempt to distract predators from its nest, which is built on the ground.

LAPWING/PEEWIT
L: 320MM/12.5"

Less common but still seen by most walkers is the **curlew** (*Numenius arquata*), another bird that, like the lapwing, is associated with coastal and open fields, moors and bogs. With feathers uniformly streaked grey and brown, the easiest way to identify this bird is by its thin elongated, downward curling beak.

CURLEW
L: 600MM/24"

Both the lapwing and the curlew are actually wading birds that nest on the moors in the spring, but which winter by the coast.

Other birds that make their nest on open moorland and in fields include the **redshank** (*Tringa totanus*), **golden plover** (*Pluvialis apricaria*), **snipe** (*Gallinago gallinago*), **dunlin** (*Calidris alpina*) and **ring ouzel** (*Turdus torquatus*).

Somewhat ironically, these birds have benefited from the careful management of the moors which is mainly done to protect the populations of game birds such as **black grouse** (*Tetrao tetrix*).

In the deciduous woodland areas on the trail, look out for **treecreepers** (*Certhia familiaris*), **tits** (family *Paridae*, including blue, coal and great), **nuthatches** (*Sitta europaea*), **pied flycatchers** (*Ficedula hypoleuca*) and **redstarts** (*Phoenicurus phoenicurus*), while in the conifers watch out for **crossbills** (*Loxia curvirostra*) and **siskins** (*Carduelis spinus*).

Finally, for something completely different, in Kirkby Stephen there are ten or so '**homing parrots**': macaws let out by their owner to fly around the town during the day, before returning home each night.

THE ENVIRONMENT AND NATURE

FLOWERS

Spring is the time to come and see the spectacular displays of colour on the Coast to Coast path. Alternatively, arrive in August and you'll see the heathers carpeting the moors in a blaze of purple flowers.

The coastal meadows

The coastline is a harsh environment subjected to strong, salt-laced winds. One plant that does survive in such conditions, and which will probably be the first you'll encounter on the path, is **gorse** (*Ulex europeous*) with its sharp-thorned bright yellow, heavily perfumed flowers. Accompanying it are such cliff-top specialists as the pink-flowering **thrift** (*Armeria maritima*) and white **sea campion** (*Silene maritima*) and **fennel** (*Foeniculum vulgare*), a member of the carrot family which grows to over a metre high.

Woodland and hedgerows

From March to May **bluebells** (*Hyacinthoides non-scripta*) proliferate in the woods along the Coast to Coast, providing a wonderful spectacle. Littlebeck (see p232) and Clain (see p210) woods are particularly notable for these displays. The white **wood anemone** (*Anemone nemorosa*) and the yellow **primrose** (*Primula vulgaris*) also flower early in spring. **Red campion** (*Silene dioica*), which flowers from late April, can be found in hedgebanks along with **rosebay willowherb** (*Epilobium augustifolium*) which also has the name fireweed due to its habit of colonising burnt areas.

In scrubland and on woodland edges you'll find **bramble** (*Rubus fruticosus*), a common vigorous shrub, responsible for many a ripped jacket thanks to its sharp thorns and prickles. **Blackberry** fruits ripen from late summer into autumn. Fairly common in scrubland and on woodland edges is the **dog rose** (*Rosa canina*) which has a large pink flower, the fruits of which are used to make rose-hip syrup.

Other flowering plants common in wooded areas and in hedgerows include the tall **foxglove** (*Digitalis purpurea*) with its trumpet-like flowers, **forget-me-not** (*Myosotis arvensis*) with tiny, delicate blue flowers and **cow parsley** (*Anthriscus sylvestris*), a tall member of the carrot family with a large globe of white flowers which often covers roadside verges and hedgebanks.

Heathland and scrubland

There are three species of heather. The most dominant one is **ling** (*Calluna vulgaris*), with tiny flowers on delicate upright stems. The other two species are **bell heather** (*Erica cinera*), with deep purple bell-shaped flowers, and **cross-leaved heath** (*Erica tetralix*) with similarly shaped flowers of a lighter pink, almost white colour. Cross-leaved heath prefers wet and boggy ground. As a result, it usually grows away from bell heather which prefers well-drained soils.

Heather is an incredibly versatile plant which is put to many uses. It provides fodder for livestock, fuel for fires, an orange dye and material for bedding, thatching, basketwork and brooms. It is still sometimes used in place of hops to flavour beer, and the flower heads can be brewed to make good tea. It is also

Spear Thistle
Cirsium vulgare

Common Knapweed
Centaurea nigra

Sea Campion
Silene maritima

Bell Heather
Erica cinerea

Heather (Ling)
Calluna vulgaris

Violet
Viola riviniana

Devil's-bit Scabious
Succisa pratensis

Harebell
Campanula rotundifolia

Bluebell
Endymion non-scriptus

Marsh Marigold (Kingcup)
Caltha palustris

Meadow Buttercup
Ranunculis acris

Cowslip
Primula veris

Tormentil
Potentilla erecta

Birdsfoot-trefoil
Lotus corniculatus

Ox-eye Daisy
Leucanthemum vulgare

Common Ragwort
Senecio jacobaea

Primrose
Primula vulgaris

Dandelion
Taraxacum officinale

Gorse
Ulex europaeus

Rowan tree
Sorbus aucuparia

Rosebay Willowherb
Epilobium angustifolium

Lousewort
Pedicularis sylvatica

Herb-Robert
Geranium robertianum

Scarlet Pimpernel
Anagallis arvensis

Hemp-nettle
Galeopsis speciosa

Ransoms (Wild Garlic)
Allium ursinum

Yarrow
Achillea millefolium

Foxglove
Digitalis purpurea

Meadow Cranesbill
Geranium pratense

Water Avens
Geum rivale

Common Vetch
Vicia sativa

Heartsease (Wild Pansy)
Viola tricolor

Germander Speedwell
Veronica chamaedrys

Early Purple Orchid
Orchis mascula

Thrift (Sea Pink)
Armeria maritima

Red Campion
Silene dioica

incredibly hardy and thrives on the denuded hills, preventing other species from flourishing. Indeed, at times, highland cattle are brought to certain areas of the moors to graze on the heather, allowing other species a chance to grow.

Not a flower but worthy of mention is the less attractive species, **bracken** (*Pteridium aquilinum*), a vigorous non-native fern that has invaded many heathland areas to the detriment of native species.

Grassland

There is much overlap between the hedge/woodland-edge habitat and that of pastures and meadows. You will come across **common birdsfoot-trefoil** (*Lotus corniculatus*), **Germander speedwell** (*Veronica chamaedrys*), **tufted** and **bush vetch** (*Vicia cracca* and *V. sepium*) and **meadow vetchling** (*Lathyrus pratensis*) in both.

Often the only species you will see in heavily grazed pastures are the most resilient. Of the thistles, the three most common species are **creeping thistle**, **spear thistle** and **marsh thistle** (*Cirsium arvense, C. vulgare* and *C. palustre*). Among them you may find **common ragwort** (*Senecio jacobaea*), **yarrow** (*Achillea millefolium*), **sheep's** and **common sorrel** (*Rumex acetosella* and *R. acetosa*), and **white** and **red clover** (*Trifolium repens* and *T. pratense*).

Other widespread grassland species include **harebell** (*Campanula rotundifolia*), delicate yellow **tormentil** (*Potentilla erecta*) which will often spread up onto the lower slopes of mountains along with **devil's-bit scabious** (*Succisa pratensis*). Also keep an eye out for orchids such as the **fragrant orchid** (*Gymnaadenia conopsea*) and **early purple orchid** (*Orchis mascula*).

TREES

It seems incredible that, before man and his axe got to work, most of the bleak, empty moors and windswept Lakeland fells were actually covered by trees. These days, the biggest and most ubiquitous areas of tree cover are the ghastly pine plantations of Ennerdale and other places in the Lakes. But the overgrazing of land by sheep and, to a lesser extent, deer, which eat the young shoots of trees, has ensured that the ancient forests have never returned. Yet there are still small patches of indigenous woodland on the Coast to Coast path. Perhaps the most interesting are the Atlantic Oakwoods at Borrowdale, including Johnny Wood (see p106, map p107) on the way to Longthwaite. The woods are owned and cared for by the National Trust and are actually correctly known as temperate rainforest, the moist Atlantic climate creating a landscape of boulders covered by liverworts and ferns, under **oaks** (*Quercus petraea*) dripping in moss and lichen.

There are other areas of woodland in the Lakes, including Easedale Woods on the way into Grasmere and Glenamara Park, just before Patterdale, which has some truly spectacular mature trees. One

OAK LEAVES SHOWING GALLS

THE ENVIRONMENT AND NATURE

HAZEL (WITH FLOWERS)

interesting thing about oak trees is that they support more kinds of insects than any other tree in Britain and some of these insects affect the oak in interesting ways. The eggs of the gall-fly, for example, cause growths on the leaves, known, appropriately enough, as galls. Each of these contains a single insect. Other kinds of gall-flies lay eggs in stalks or flowers, leading to flower galls – growths the size of currants.

Oak woodland is a diverse habitat and not exclusively made up of oak. Other trees that flourish in oak woodland include **downy birch** (*Betula pubescens*), its relative the **silver birch** (*Betula pendula*), **holly** (*Ilex aquifolium*), and **hazel** (*Corylus avellana*) which has traditionally been used for coppicing (where small trees are grown for periodic cutting). Further east there are some examples of limestone woodland. **Ash** (*Fraxinus excelsior*) and oak dominate, along with **wych elm** (*Ulmus glabra*), **sycamore** (*Acer*) and **yew** (*Taxus*).

The **hawthorn** (*Crataegus monogyna*) also grows on the path, usually in isolated pockets on pasture. These species are known as pioneer species and play a vital role in the ecosystem by improving

ASH (WITH SEEDS)

the soil. It is these pioneers, particularly the **rowan** (*Sorbus aucuparia*) and hawthorn, that you will see growing all alone on inaccessible crags and ravines. Without interference from man, these pioneers would eventually be succeeded by longer-living species such as the oak. In wet, marshy areas and along rivers and streams you are more likely to find **alder** (*Alnus glutinosa*).

ALDER (WITH FLOWERS)

THE ENVIRONMENT AND NATURE

PART 3: MINIMUM IMPACT AND OUTDOOR SAFETY

Minimum impact walking

In this world in which people live their lives at an increasingly frenetic pace, many of us living in overcrowded cities and working in jobs that offer little free time, the great outdoors is becoming seen as an essential means of escape.

Walking in the countryside is a wonderful means of relaxation and gives people the time to think. However, as the popularity of the countryside increases so do the problems that this pressure brings. It is important for visitors to remember that the countryside is the home and workplace of many others.

By following a few simple guidelines while walking the Coast to Coast path you can have a positive impact, not just on your own well-being but also on local communities and the environment, thereby becoming part of the solution.

ENVIRONMENTAL IMPACT

A walking holiday in itself is an environmentally friendly approach to tourism. The following are some ideas on how you can go a few steps further in helping to minimise your impact on the environment while walking the Coast to Coast path.

Use public transport whenever possible
Public transport along the Coast to Coast trail is not bad (though it can be a little infrequent at times), with just about everywhere served by at least one bus or train a day. Public transport is always preferable to using private cars as it benefits everyone: visitors, locals and the environment.

Buy local
Look and ask for local produce to buy and eat. Not only does this cut down on the amount of pollution and congestion that the transportation of food creates, so-called 'food miles', it also ensures that you are supporting local farmers and producers.

Support local businesses

Never leave litter
'Pack it in, pack it out'. Leaving litter is ugly so carry a degradable plastic bag for all your rubbish, organic or otherwise and even other people's too, and pop

it in a bin in the next village. Or better still, reduce the amount of litter you take with you by getting rid of packaging in advance.

● **Is it OK if it's biodegradable?** Not really. Apple cores, banana skins, orange peel and the like are unsightly, encourage flies, ants and wasps, and ruin a picnic spot for others; they can also take months to decompose. In high-use areas such as the Coast to Coast path either bury them or take them away with you.

Erosion

● **Stay on the main trail** The effect of your footsteps may seem minuscule but when they're multiplied by several thousand walkers each year they become rather more significant. Avoid taking shortcuts, widening the trail or taking more than one path, especially across hay meadows and ploughed fields. This

The mire below Nine Standards Rigg (see p158)

is particularly true on parts of the Coast to Coast with the boggy Pennine stage now divided into three trails to be used for four months a year (see p154), so reducing erosion on any one trail.

● **Consider walking out of season** Maximum disturbance by walkers coincides with the time of year when nature wants to do most of its growth and repair. In high-use areas, like that along much of the Coast to Coast path, the trail is often prevented from recovering.

Walking at less busy times eases this pressure while also generating year-round income for the local economy. Not only that, but it may make the walk a more relaxing experience with fewer people on the path and less competition for accommodation.

Respect all flora and fauna

Care for all wildlife you come across along the path; it has as much right to be there as you. Tempting as it may be to pick wild flowers leave them so the next people who pass can enjoy them too. Don't break branches off or damage trees in any way.

If you come across wildlife keep your distance and don't watch for too long. Your presence can cause considerable stress, particularly if the adults are with young, or in winter when the weather is harsh and food is scarce. Young animals are rarely abandoned. If you come across young birds keep away so that their mother can return.

The code of the outdoor loo

'Going' in the outdoors is a lost art worth reclaiming, for your sake and everyone else's. As more and more people discover the joys of the outdoors this is becoming an important issue. In some parts of the world where visitor pressure is higher than in Britain, walkers and climbers are required to pack out their excrement. This might one day be necessary here. Human excrement is not only offensive to our senses but, more importantly, can infect water sources.

● **Where to go** Wherever possible **use a toilet**. Public toilets are marked on the trail maps in this guide and you'll also find facilities in pubs, cafés and campsites along the path. If you do have to go outdoors, avoid ruins which can otherwise be welcome shelter for other walkers, as well as sites of historic or archaeological interest, and choose a place that is at least **30 metres away from running water**. Use a stick or trowel to **dig a small hole** about 15cm (6") deep to bury your excrement. It decomposes quicker when in contact with the top layer of soil or leaf mould. Stiring loose soil into your deposit speeds up decomposition. Do not squash it under rocks as this slows down the composting process. If you have to use rocks to cover it make sure they are not in contact with your faeces.

● **Toilet paper and tampons** Toilet paper takes a long time to decompose whether buried or not. It is easily dug up by animals and may then blow into water sources or onto the path.

The best method for dealing with it is to **pack it out**. Put the used paper inside a paper bag which you then place inside a plastic bag. Then simply empty the contents of the paper bag at the next toilet you come across and throw the bag away. If this is too much bother, light your used toilet paper and watch it burn until the flames are out, you don't want to start a wild fire. Pack out **tampons** and **sanitary towels**; they take years to decompose and may also be dug up and scattered about by animals.

Wild camping

Wild camping is not encouraged within the national parks which make up the majority of the walk. This is a shame since wild camping is much more fulfilling than camping on a designated site. Living in the outdoors without any facilities provides a valuable lesson in simple, sustainable living where the results of all your actions, from going to the loo to washing your plates, can be seen.

If you do wild camp always ask the landowner for permission. In most cases this is, of course, completely impractical so don't camp on farmland at all, but out on the uncultivated moors or in forests, and follow these suggestions:

● **Be discreet** Camp alone or in small groups, spend only one night in each place, pitch your tent late and leave early.

● **Never light a fire** Accidental fire is a great fear for farmers and foresters. Never make a camp fire and take matches and cigarette butts out with you to dispose of safely. Aside from that, the deep burn caused by camp fires, no matter how small, damages turf which can take years to recover. Cook on a camp stove instead.

● **Don't use soap or detergent** There is no need to use soap; even biodegradable soaps and detergents pollute streams. You won't be away from a shower for more than a couple of days. Wash up without detergent; use a plastic or metal scourer, or failing that, a handful of fine pebbles or some bracken or grass.

● **Leave no trace** Endeavour to leave no sign of having been there: no moved boulders, ripped up vegetation or dug drainage ditches. Make a final check of your campsite before departing; pick up any litter leaving the place in the same state you found it in, or better.

ACCESS

Britain is a crowded island with few places where you can wander as you please. Most of the land is a patchwork of fields and agricultural land and the terrain through which the Coast to Coast path marches is no different. However, there are countless public rights of way, in addition to the Coast to Coast path, that criss-cross the land.

This is fine, but what happens if you feel a little more adventurous and want to explore the moorland, woodland and hills that can also be found near the walk?

Right to roam

The Countryside & Rights of Way Act 2000 (CRoW), or 'Right to Roam' as dubbed by walkers, came into effect in 2005 after a long campaign to allow greater public access to areas of countryside in England and Wales deemed to be uncultivated open country; this essentially means moorland, heathland, downland and upland areas.

Some land is covered by restrictions (ie high-impact activities such as driving a vehicle, cycling, horse-riding are not permitted) and some land is excluded (such as gardens, parks and cultivated land). Full details are given on 🖳 www .countrysideaccess.gov.uk.

With more freedom in the countryside comes a need for more responsibility from the walker. Remember that wild open country is still the workplace of farmers and home to all sorts of wildlife. Have respect for both and avoid disturbing domestic and wild animals.

The Countryside Code

The Countryside Code seems like common sense but sadly some people still appear to have no understanding of how to treat the countryside they walk in.

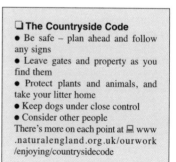

❏ **The Countryside Code**
● Be safe – plan ahead and follow any signs
● Leave gates and property as you find them
● Protect plants and animals, and take your litter home
● Keep dogs under close control
● Consider other people
There's more on each point at 🖳 www .naturalengland.org.uk/ourwork /enjoying/countrysidecode

The Countryside Code has now been revised, in part because of the changes brought about by the CRoW Act (see above). The following is an expanded version of the new Countryside Code, launched under the logo 'Respect, Protect and Enjoy':

● **Be safe** The Coast to Coast path is pretty much hazard free but you're responsible for your own safety so follow the simple guidelines outlined on pp71-5.

● **Leave all gates as you found them** Normally a farmer leaves gates closed to keep livestock in but may sometimes leave them open to allow livestock access to food or water. Leave them as you find them and if there is a sign, follow the instructions.

● **Leave livestock, crops and machinery alone** Help farmers by not interfering with their means of livelihood.

● **Take your litter home** See pp67-8.

● **Keep your dog under control** See pp27-8. During lambing time they should not be taken with you at all.

● **Enjoy the countryside and respect its life and work** Access to the countryside depends on being sensitive to the needs and wishes of those who live and work there.

Being courteous and friendly to those you meet will ensure a healthy future for all based on partnership and co-operation.

❏ **Lambing**

Lambing takes place from mid-March to mid-May when dogs should not be taken along the path. Even a dog secured on a lead can disturb a pregnant ewe.

If you see a lamb or ewe that appears to be in distress contact the nearest farmer.

Also, be aware of cows with calves (see box p28).

● **Keep to paths across farmland** Stick to the official path across arable or pasture land. Minimise erosion by not cutting corners or widening the path.

● **Use gates and stiles to cross fences, hedges and walls** The Coast to Coast path is well supplied with stiles where it crosses field boundaries. On some of the side trips you may find the paths less accommodating. If you have to climb over a gate because you can't open it always do so at the hinged end.

● **Guard against all risk of fire** See p69.

● **Help keep all water clean** Leaving litter and going to the toilet near a water source can pollute people's water supplies. See p21 for more guidelines.

● **Take special care on country roads** Drivers often drive dangerously fast on narrow winding lanes. To be safe, walk on the right facing the oncoming traffic and carry a torch or wear highly visible clothing when it's getting dark.

● **Protect wildlife, plants and trees** Care for and respect all wildlife you come across along the Coast to Coast path. Don't pick plants, break trees or scare wild animals. If you come across young birds that appear to have been abandoned leave them alone.

● **Make no unnecessary noise** Enjoy the peace and solitude of the outdoors by staying in small groups and acting unobtrusively.

Outdoor safety

AVOIDANCE OF HAZARDS

With good planning and preparation most hazards can be avoided. This information is just as important for those out on a day walk as for those walking the entire Coast to Coast path. Always make sure you have suitable **clothing** (see pp42-3) to keep warm and dry, whatever the conditions, and a change of inner clothes. Carrying plenty of food and water is vital too.

The **emergency signal** is six blasts on the whistle or six flashes with a torch, best done when you think someone might see or hear them.

MINIMUM IMPACT & OUTDOOR SAFETY

Safety on the Coast to Coast path

Sadly every year people are injured while walking the Coast to Coast path. The most dangerous section is the Lake District, where the visitor numbers, eleva-

tion, lack of signage and the sometimes extreme weather all combine to imperil walkers. Locally based mountain-rescue teams are staffed by volunteers who are ready 24 hours a day 365 days of the year.

In an emergency phone ☎ 999 and the police will activate the service. Rescue teams rely on donations (the Patterdale's running costs are estimated to be £30,000 a year), and are called on average about 60 times a year. There is another rescue team based at Kirkby Stephen.

All rescue teams should be treated as very much the last resort, however, and it's vital you take every precaution to ensure your own safety:

● Avoid walking on your own if possible, particularly on the Lakeland fells.
● Make sure that somebody knows your plans for every day that you're on the trail. This could be a friend or relative whom you have promised to call every night, or the place you plan to stay in at the end of each day's walk. That way, if you fail to turn up or call that evening, they can raise the alarm.
● If the weather closes in suddenly and mist descends while you're on the trail, particularly on the moors or fells, and you become uncertain of the correct trail, do not be tempted to continue. Just wait where you are and you'll find that mist often clears, at least for long enough to allow you to get your bearings. If you're still uncertain, and the weather does not look like improving, return the way you came to the nearest point of civilisation.
● Fill up with water at every opportunity and carry some high-energy snacks.
● Always carry a torch, compass, map, whistle, mobile phone and wet-weather gear with you.
● Wear sturdy boots or shoes, not trainers.
● Be extra vigilant if walking with children.

Dealing with an accident

● Use basic first aid to treat the injury to the best of your ability.
● Work out exactly where you are. If possible leave someone with the casualty while others go to get help. If there are only two people, you have a dilemma. If you decide to get help leave all spare clothing and food with the casualty.
● In an emergency dial ☎ 999 (or the EU standard number ☎ 112). Don't assume your mobile won't work up on the fells. In 2009 a rescue was called in in this way on Greenup Edge, out of Borrowdale.

WEATHER FORECASTS

The Coast to Coast suffers from enormously unpredictable weather so it's wise to try to find out what the weather is going to be like before you set off for the day, especially if heading for high routes in the Lakes. Many hostels and tourist information centres will have pinned up somewhere a summary of the weather forecast. Otherwise you can get a telephone forecast (**Weather Call** ☎ 09068 500419 for Cumbria/Lake District and 500417 for Yorkshire, ☎ 0901 471 0310 for the next six hours in your local town; 🖥 www.weathercall.co.uk); these are frequently updated and generally reliable but calls are charged at the premium-rate (60p/min); if you have internet access you can look at the website. Pay close attention to the forecast and consider altering your plans accordingly. That said, even if a fine sunny day is forecast, always assume the worst and pack some wet-weather gear.

BLISTERS

It's essential to try out new boots before embarking on your long trek. Make sure they're comfortable and once on the move try to avoid getting them wet on the inside and remove small stones or twigs that get in the boot. Air and massage your feet at lunchtime, keep them clean, and change your socks regularly.

As soon as you start to feel any hot spots developing, stop and apply a few strips of low-friction zinc oxide tape. Leave it on until the foot is pain free or the tape starts to come off. As you're walking continuously the chances are it won't get better, but it won't get worse so quickly. If you know you have problems apply the tape pre-emptively. If you've left it too late and a blister has developed you should apply a plaster such as Compeed (or the slightly cheaper clone now made by Boots). Many walkers have

Footsore in Marrick

Compeed to thank for enabling them to complete their walk; they can last for up to two days even when wet and work with a combination of good adhesive, a gel pad and a slippery outer surface. Popping a blister reduces the pressure but can lead to infection. If the skin is broken keep the area clean with antiseptic and cover with a non-adhesive dressing material held in place with tape.

Blister-avoiding strategies include rubbing the prone area with vaseline or wearing a thin and a thick sock as well as adjusting the tension of your laces. All are ways of reducing rubbing and foot movement against the inside of the boot.

HYPOTHERMIA

Also known as exposure, hypothermia occurs when the body can't generate enough heat to maintain its normal temperature, usually as a result of being wet, cold, unprotected from the wind, tired and hungry. It's usually more of a problem in upland areas such as in the Lakes and on the moors.

Hypothermia is easily avoided by wearing suitable clothing, carrying and consuming enough food and drink, being aware of the weather conditions and checking the morale of your companions. Early signs to watch for are feeling cold and tired with involuntary shivering. Find some shelter as soon as possible and warm the victim up with a hot drink and some chocolate or other high-energy food. If possible give them another warm layer of clothing and allow them to rest until feeling better.

If allowed to worsen, erratic behaviour, slurring of speech and poor co-ordination will become apparent and the victim can quickly progress into unconsciousness, followed by coma and death. Quickly get the victim out of wind and rain, improvising a shelter if necessary.

Rapid restoration of bodily warmth is essential and best achieved by bare-skin contact: someone should get into the same sleeping bag as the patient, both having stripped to the bare essentials, placing any spare clothing under or over them to build up heat. Send or call urgently for help.

HYPERTHERMIA

Not an ailment that you would normally associate with the north of England, hyperthermia (heat exhaustion and heatstroke) is a serious problem nonetheless.

Symptoms of **heat exhaustion** include thirst, fatigue, giddiness, a rapid pulse, raised body temperature, low urine output and, if not treated, delirium and finally a coma. The best cure is to drink plenty of water.

Heatstroke is another matter altogether, and even more serious. A high body temperature and an absence of sweating are early indications, followed by symptoms similar to hypothermia (see p73) such as a lack of co-ordination, convulsions and coma.

Death will follow if treatment is not given instantly. Sponge the victim down, wrap them in wet towels, fan them, and get help immediately.

SUNBURN

It can happen, even in northern England and even on overcast days. The only surefire way to avoid it is to stay wrapped up or smother yourself in sunscreen (with a minimum factor of 15) and apply it regularly throughout the day. Don't forget your lips, nose and the back of your neck.

COLLAPSE OF MORALE

This is not something that can be quickly treated with medication, but is probably the biggest cause of abandoned attempts on the Coast to Coast walk. Weather and injury which add up to exhaustion might be presumed to be the most common culprit, but as we know plenty manage the walk in monsoonal conditions and hobble into Robin Hood's Bay with a great experience behind them. Others though, can suddenly think: 'what's the point, I'm not enjoying this'.

One morning we met a teenager tramping along the road to Kirkby. He had all the right gear but we could tell he'd had enough that day if not altogether. A morning's rain in the patchy bogs west of Ravenseat had weakened his resolve to tackle the notorious Nine Standards (he was heading Lakeward). He'd done a long-distance path before, but in company, and at that age he'd had much more fun. He was merely lonely, but for others it's the wrong company that leads to resentment and thus a no less miserable experience.

What it all boils down to is this: knowing your limitations and addressing your motivation; matching expectations with your companions; avoiding putting yourself under stress and being flexible rather than insisting on hammering out every last mile without repetition, hesitation or deviation. You can add having good equipment to that list too.

Above all, settle on a **realistic schedule** with at least one, if not two, rest day(s) over the full trek. Even then, it's amazing how sore muscles and feet can recover overnight, especially if you can at least start the day in sunshine. Don't assume a rest day has to be in a town like Kirkby or Richmond. A big room in a lone moorland farmhouse or even two nights in a holiday cottage with a telly or a fat book may suit those who find the bigger towns an intrusion on the spirit of the walk.

A paradox of the Coast to Coast's popularity is the need to book accommodation or baggage-carrying services, so erasing all spontaneity in the adventure. How nice it would be to be able to walk as far as you feel on any given day; on most stages there's certainly enough accommodation to do so, but unfortunately, to paraphrase Jack Nicholson, 22 million people live within 100 miles of the trail and usually some have got there before you. And so every day for the next fortnight is rigidly mapped out, but how can you predict at what point your knee or festering blisters will make walking intolerable? The only alternative is to put up with camping or plan an unbooked accommodated schedule out of the high season and which furthermore avoids weekends in busy spots. Or swallow your pride and skip a stage if you can't face it, catching a lift with the Packhorse van (see p24) or public transport to keep on schedule with your B&Bs or hostels.

It's not fashionable to admit it, but not every day on the Coast to Coast will necessarily be a winner. It's one reason why many people go on to do the walk again and again; the first time is often looked back on as an eye-opening reconnaissance (see box p33 and the boxes on p40).

Perhaps the best way to avoid the risk of getting fed up is not to tackle the full 200 miles in one go. Wainwright certainly didn't (but then he was in his sixties). Thirteen days non-stop on the trail, come rain or shine, really is a bit much for most people (a schedule which at first glance the thirteen stages of this book may seem to encourage). Some days end up as nothing more than forced marches or gritty lessons in pain management because, for many, our prized vacation time is treated as an extension of our busy work life where we must make the most of every minute, 24/7. Here at Trailblazer we propose: turn on, tune in and slow down.

Using the guide

The route is described from west to east and divided into 13 stages. Though each of these roughly corresponds to a day's walk between centres of accommodation, it's not necessarily the best way to structure *your* trek. There are enough places to stay – barring a couple of stretches – for you to pretty much divide the walk up however you want. This is even more true if you're prepared to camp, in which case you can pitch your tent virtually anywhere, as long as you follow the guidelines on p69.

On pp36-7 are tables to help you plan an itinerary. To provide further help, practical information is presented on the trail maps, including waypoints (WPT) and walking times, places to stay, camp and eat, as well as shops from which to buy provisions. Further service details are given in the text under the entry for each settlement. See box pp81-2 for navigation trouble spots.

TRAIL MAPS   [for map key see p243]
Scale and walking times
The trail maps are to a scale of 1:20,000 (1cm = 200m; $3^1/_8$ inches = one mile). Walking times are given along the side of each map; the arrow shows the direction to which the time refers. Black triangles indicate the points between which the times have been taken. These times are merely a tool to help you plan and are not there to judge your walking ability.

Hopefully, after a couple of days you'll know how fast you walk compared with the time bars and can plan your days more accurately as a result. **See note on walking times in the box below**.

Up or down?
The trail is shown as a dashed line. An arrow across the trail indicates the gradient; two arrows show that it's steep. Note that the *arrow points uphill*, the opposite of what OS maps use on steep roads.

A good way to remember our style is: '**front-pointing** on crampons **up** a steep slope' and 'open arms – Julie Andrews-style – **spreading out** to unfold the view **down** below'.

❑ **Important note – walking times**
Unless otherwise specified, **all times in this book refer only to the time spent walking**. You will need to add 20-30% to allow for rests, photography, checking the map, drinking water etc. When planning the day's hike count on 5-7 hours' actual walking.

Accommodation

Accommodation marked on the map is either on or within easy reach of the path. Many B&B proprietors based a mile or two off the trail will offer to collect walkers from the nearest point on the trail and return them next morning.

Details of each place are given in the accompanying text. The number of rooms of each type is given at the beginning of each entry, ie: S=Single, T=Twin room, D=Double room, F=Family room (sleeps at least three people). The rates are also given; some establishments quote rates *per person* (pp) per night (with a supplement for single occupancy) and others *per room* based on two people sharing (in this case there may be a discount for single occupancy). Unless otherwise specified, the rates are for the summer high season. DB&B means dinner, bed and breakfast.

The majority of accommodation options on the Coast to Coast Path have shower facilities; 'bath available' signifies that at least one room has a bath, or access to a bath, for those who prefer a relaxed soak at the end of the day.

Other features

Features are marked on the map when they are pertinent to navigation. In order to avoid cluttering the maps and making them unusable, not all features have been marked each time they occur.

The route guide

ST BEES   see map p79

The settlements along the Cumbrian coast are not all jewels, but situated close to the county's westernmost point, the ancient village of St Bees makes a fine starting point to your walk, with just enough facilities and services to set you on your way.

The village is agricultural in origin; many of the buildings along the main street were once farms dating back to the 17th century and, on Outrigg, there's even an ancient **pinfold** – a circular, stone-walled enclosure once used to house stray livestock recovered from the surrounding hills. The livestock would remain in the pinfold until the farmer could afford to pay a fine to retrieve them.

The town's main sight is its distinctive red sandstone **Priory Church**, once part of a thriving 12th-century Benedictine priory dedicated to the saints Bega (see box p78) and Mary. Original Norman features include the impressively elaborate Great West Door

and, standing opposite, the curious carved Dragon Stone, a door lintel also from the 12th century. The church is believed to stand on a site that had been holy to Christians for centuries prior to the monastery's foundation and has seen over eight hundred years of unbroken worship since then. Not even the dissolution of the monasteries ordered by Henry VIII in 1538, which led to the closure of this and every other priory you'll come across on the Coast to Coast path, could stop the site from being used by the villagers as their main centre of worship, even though Henry's commissioners had removed the lead from the roof, and the whole building, for much of the 16th century, was left open to the elements. Restoration began in the early 17th century, with a major overhaul of the building taking place in the 19th. Thankfully, however, the architects kept intact much of the church's sturdy Norman character.

As with quite a few of the larger churches on the route, there's a table just inside the door with various pamphlets (each costing about 20p) on the history of both the church and the village. Don't miss the glass case in the southern aisle displaying a shroud and a lock of woman's hair unearthed in the excavation of a 14th-century grave; and the graveyard to the north of the church, where you'll find the shaft of a stone cross from the 10th century (in other words, older than every other part of the church), with its Celtic decorations still visible.

Incidentally, the **grammar school** across the road from the church is one of the most venerable in Cumbria, having been founded by **Edmund Grindal** on his deathbed in 1583. Grindal rose to become Archbishop of Canterbury during the reign of Elizabeth I and his birthplace, on the junction of Finkle St and Cross St, is the oldest surviving house in St Bees.

There's a statue of **St Bega** (see box below) just to the west of the railway station on Station Rd.

Services

There's a well-stocked **post office** and **shop** (☎ 01946 822343, 🖳 www.stbees-post office.co.uk; post office Mon-Fri 9am-5.30pm, Sat & Sun 9am-12.30pm, shop Mon-Fri 6am-8pm, Sat 7.30am-8pm, Sun 7.30am-6pm) with a decent selection of groceries, including delicious hot pies, as well as a few Coast to Coast maps, T-shirts and souvenirs. It's also the home of the local Link **cash machine** (£1.50 fee); the last on the trail before Grasmere.

There's a **tourist information point** by the train station but it has limited information; a better bet is St Bees' website (🖳 www.stbees.org .uk). There's also a **public phone**.

One thing the town lacks is an outdoor shop and a pharmacy, but a 10-minute train ride north to Whitehaven will deliver you alongside a huge Tesco as well as both a Millets and a Boots on King St, ten minutes' walk into town. Alternatively you have to wait until you reach Grasmere.

Where to stay

On the front behind the RNLI lifeboat station and owned by the adjacent hotel (see p80) are the serried cabins of *Seacote Caravan Park* (Map 1, p84; ☎ 01946 822777, 🖳 www.seacote.com) where you can **camp** for £10 for a 1-person tent and £18 for a 2- to 5-person tent.

Camping (£4pp) is also available in the back garden of the central *Stonehouse Farm* (☎ 01946 822224, 🖳 www.stone housefarm.net; 1S/2D/1T/4F; most en suite with showers, bath available), where you can fall asleep to the hooting of the barn owl. A long-established and reliable **B&B**, Stonehouse is situated just 30 metres from the station and is one of only two working farms within St Bees (the other is Town Head at the top of the hill beyond Fairladies). Stonehouse's en suite rooms

---

❏ **Who was St Bees?**
St Bees is actually a corruption of St Bega, an Irish princess who fled her native country sometime between the 6th and 9th centuries to avoid an arranged marriage with a Norwegian prince.

Landing on England's north-west coast, so the story goes, St Bega lived as a hermit and became renowned for the good deeds she carried out for the locals. And that's about it really, or at least it would be, if it wasn't for the legends that have grown up over the centuries. In the most famous of these, St Bega approached the local landlord, Lord Egremont, for some land for a convent she wished to found.

Egremont promised St Bega all the land covered by snow the next day; which, seeing as it was to be midsummer's day, was not as generous an offer as it first appeared. Miraculously, however, snow did fall that day and St Bega was able to build her convent, around which the village was founded.

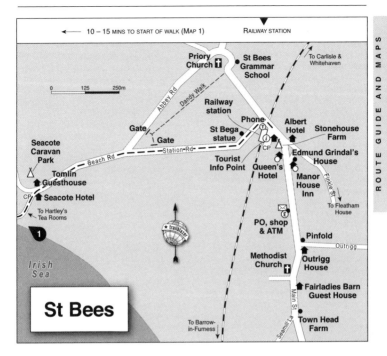

St Bees

with TV are located in its Georgian farm-house, while the dairy next door has been converted into a spacious family cottage. On the other side of the farmhouse is an even older cottage (dating back to 1660) where the character of the building more than compensates for the lack of en suite facilities. Finally, long-term parking (£2.50 per night) is also available. B&B rates are £35-40pp. They accept most credit cards. Packed lunches are about £5 and breakfast is available for campers (around £7).

Further up Main St the 17th-century *Queen's Hotel* (☎ 01946 822287; 🖳 www .marstonspubs.co.uk/queenshotelcumbria; 4S/6D/3T/1F, all en suite, two twin with bath) charges £38-45 for a single and £52-65 for two sharing a room.

Manor House Inn (☎ 01946 820587, 🖳 www.manorhousestbees.com; 1S/3D/ 3T/1F, all en suite some with bath) is anoth-er impressive-looking hotel in St Bees with

rates from £55 per room, £35 for the single/ single occupancy. *Outrigg House* (☎ 01946 822348, Main St; 1S/1T/1D or F; shared bathroom), open Easter to Sep, is a lovely place charging £25pp; £4 for a packed lunch (request in advance).

Albert Hotel (☎ 01946 822345, 🖳 www.alberthotel-stbees.co.uk; 1 Finkle St; 2S/1D/3T/1F, some en suite, others share shower facilities) has B&B from £30 per person; evening meals are available as are packed lunches (£3.50). Up at the top of Main St, *Fairladies Barn Guest House* (☎ 01946 822718, 🖳 www.fairladiesbarn.co .uk; 5D/4T/2F, all en suite with shower) is a cut above the rest; a large, restored 17th-century sandstone barn with varied and charming rooms. The most popular is the unusually shaped studio room under the roof at the end of the barn. They also have a small **bar** (daily in the evenings). Rates are £40-60 per room; single occupancy is £40.

Beyond Finkle St, *Fleatham House* (☎ 01946 822341, 🖥 www.fleathamhouse .com, High House Rd; 3S/3D, all en suite, some with bath) is another impressive B&B, a red sandstone Victorian villa situated up a steep driveway at the top of the village and charging £45pp for two sharing (£64.50-74.50 for a single/single occupancy).

Tomlin Guest House (☎ 01946 822284, 🖥 id.whitehead@which.net; 1D/2D or T/1F, some en suite, bath available) is on Beach Rd, a short walk from Mile Zero (see Map 1, p84) and is a friendly little place charging £23-30pp. Off-street parking is £1 per night, or you can hire a lock-up garage for the duration of your walk for £2.50 per night; since there is only one garage this should be booked in advance. Packed lunches cost £5.

Under new management and fully refurbished, *Seacote Hotel* (Map 1, p84; ☎ 01946 822300, 🖥 www.seacotehotel.com; 7S/28D/24T/16F, all en suite with bath) is the massive complex by the beach car park. Rooms cost £60-75 for two sharing, £50 for a single/single occupancy and £85-105 for a family room; breakfast costs £8.50 per person. Two of the family rooms sleep four, the others sleep three.

Where to eat and drink

Of our selection, *Queen's Hotel* (see Where to stay; food served Easter to Oct daily noon-3pm & 5-9pm, Nov to Easter daily noon-2pm & 5-9pm except Sunday evening) is among the most popular places in town, with a great menu and the bar known for its real ales (such as the Jennings Bitter) and malt whiskies.

Providing healthy competition, *Manor House Inn* (see Where to stay; food served daily noon-2pm & 6.30-9pm) also has a huge menu with a Sunday lunch for £8.50. They also have the *Coast to Coast* bar (daily noon to around 11pm) so how can you resist a swift half here?

For sea views and cream teas, call in at *Hartley's Tea Rooms* (Map 1, p84; ☎ 01946 820175; daily summer 9am-6pm, winter to 5pm) on the foreshore, just a short walk from Mile Zero, and don't forget the pies in the **village shop**; they're out of this world.

Transport (see also pp52-5)

Trains (Mon-Sat) from St Bees go north to Carlisle and south to Barrow-in-Furness; see p50. 3D Travel's **bus** No 20 runs to Sandwith and Whitehaven (Mon-Sat); on Sunday AA Travel's X6 service goes to Whitehaven.

(Opposite) Top: Approaching Fleswick Bay (see p85) on the first day. (© CS). **Bottom**: Parts of the church at St Bees (see p77), including the Great West Door, date back to Norman times. (© HS).

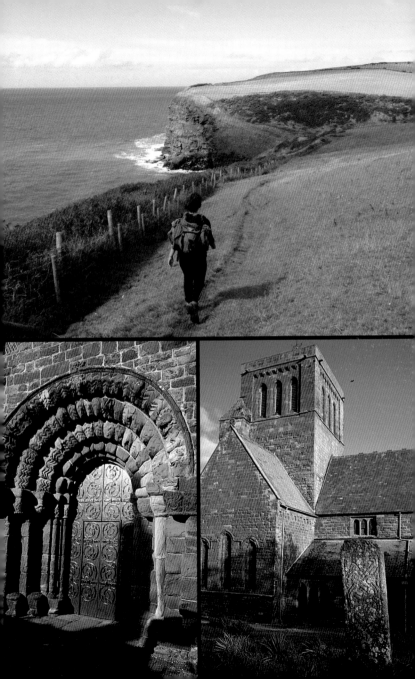

❏ HOW NOT TO LOSE YOUR WAY

Although it's improving year by year, the Coast to Coast path is widely considered to be the least well-signposted of Britain's long-distance trails. Principally it's because it's not been officially designated a 'National Trail' with all the funding benefits that come with it like consistent signage or slabs over bogs that long-distance paths, such as the Pennine Way, get. The trail also passes through the Lake District where the national park authorities have elected not to sully the upland trails with signposts and this, combined with occasions of low visibility, may indeed cause you problems with navigation (see p12). The minute you step out of the Lake District National Park signage by local authorities, local landowners or well-wishers, improves greatly all the way across the Pennines into Yorkshire where, among other signs, the North Yorkshire County Council's yellow waymark discs show the way towards the North Yorkshire Moors and the North Sea. Elsewhere on the trail wooden 'Coast to Coast' signposts clearly point the way.

A few tips
This edition was researched by a first-time Coast to Coaster relying solely on the maps from the previous edition. Secondary maps were only studied when utterly flumoxed, so hopefully leading to improvements or corrections in this guide's mapping and clarifications to the instructions. Nevertheless, many times we went wrong simply because we'd either not read the instructions on the maps fully or followed them correctly. Having made the same mistakes you will, our advice is to **study the book's maps closely** and ideally, read through the entire day's stage before you start it, making a note of possible tricky spots. Once on the move it's easy to be distracted, to blindly follow others who may be on some other walk, or simply to follow an obvious trail while engrossed in a stimulating natter and so miss a crucial turn off.

Secondly, we advise you **keep this book accessible** come rain or shine; at times you'll be referring to it several times an hour. A transparent plastic map holder on a neck string does this best, but the flapping can get on your nerves. Something similar but smaller and hung off a pack's hip belt might be better, or in dry weather, a flat thigh pocket on a pair of shorts or trousers or, of course, a jacket or fleece.

We only used Explorer **OS maps** (see pp45-6) OL4, OL5 and OL19 covering the Lake District and the Pennines, as well as the Footprint 'East' map in North Yorkshire. This could be considered the minimum investment in supplementary mapping to do the walk, although for this edition an effort has been made to make this book's maps good enough to follow without secondary sources. Even then, at its most basic level a **compass** is essential on the occasions when you're not sure the path you're following is heading in the same direction (north-west, south-south-east, and so on) as the one you think you're on according to the book.

Setting aside the GPS data listed in full on pp244-8, on the maps we've also highlighted the places where people frequently get lost – see the list on p81 – with a warning triangle to emphasise the need for vigilance. Look at this carefully. That's not to say that you won't get lost elsewhere, but we think in most places you'll recognise your error within a mile.

See overleaf for **common navigation trouble spots**.

(Opposite) Top: The most remote accommodation on the route: the Black Sail Youth Hostel (p102) at the head of Ennerdale. (© HS). Bottom: Approaching Seatoller, said to be the rainiest place in Britain (but luckily not when we were there). (© CS).

❏ HOW NOT TO LOSE YOUR WAY

Common navigation trouble spots *(cont'd from p81)*

These are the well-known trouble spots on the Coast to Coast path. The list may well be rendered obsolete by improvements in waymarking and signage, and in some cases, drainage – or by simply making use of the book's GPS waypoints.

● **Stanley Pond** (Maps 3 & 4) Just after the rail tunnel the route past the pond is often waterlogged, causing walkers to detour to the south, get disoriented and so take the wrong route through the woods. A helpful map on a gateway off track shows you're not the first. At WPT 003 don't enter the woods and veer off south-east and uphill.

● **Dent Hill** (Maps 5 & 6) Recently cleared forestry only evident in aerial photos (and not on OS maps) as well as a key sign that used to point the other way can all add up to a possibly fractious first day. In bad visibility a compass helped us get from the point where the wall ends on Dent Hill to the stile (WPT 011) but at the key junction (WPT 012), a sign now points clearly east-north-east to the tall stile and Raven Crag hill. If the weather/visibility are terrible on your Dent Hill day, consider taking the quiet road from Black How Farm to Ennerdale Bridge.

● **Top of Loft beck** (WPT 023) (Map 12) Clear as a bell in good conditions, in poor visibility presumably some turn right off the steps too soon or carry on to the fence. The current OS OL4 map is not much help here but if you overshoot and arrive at the fence in the bogs, just follow it east and south to the stile (WPT 024), then carry on towards Grey Knotts (Map 13).

● **Greenup Edge** (Map 16) The 'edge' is actually a broad col preceded by more bogs and an indistinct path marked by hard-to-see cairns piled on low outcrops. Even in perfect visibility hitting the right fence post and twin cairns (WPT 034) takes some luck as other more prominent fenceposts along the col's rim can distract you. Aim for the southern side of the col at a point where a track ascends to Low White Stones. Having located the twin cairns the route down to the next key junction at the top of Easedale is clearer.

● **Boredale Hause** (Map 25) Several converging paths make this grassy junction confusing, but the most used one heading south-east then south is the way to Angle Tarn.

● **High Street** (Map 27) Short of a white-out, it's hard to think what the problem is here other than simply missing the flattened trackside cairn before the col which marks another clear track running north-east to Kidsty Pike.

● **South of Oddendale** (Map 36) Possibly because our map was a bit vague and the OS OL19 map was no help, some experience a brief route-finding wobble here even though there are poles. Just cut past the southern corner of the strip plantation, watch your orientation and use the 'two trees' landmark.

● **Sunbiggin Tarn** (Maps 39 & 40) The route now crosses the moor south of Sunbiggin Tarn but at the time of writing Coast to Coast path waymarks had not quite caught up. Just head east and at the south side of an enclosure aim for the reservoir head on a hilltop. Just before you reach it you cross another back road.

● **Nine Standards routes** (Maps 45, 46 & 47) In very thick mist seeing the mysterious cairns (WPT 092) before they see you can be tricky, as can continuing from there south past the trig point to the key red and blue route junction (WPT 095, half a mile away) while avoiding bogs on the way. If you get to this junction, the Blue route has posts leading to Whitsundalebeck valley, the Red route has less frequent landmarks. The path of the Green route has been optimised and is now easier to follow. The 1:25,000 OS OL19 map shows no paths up here although the 1:50,000 sheet does.

● **Graystone Hills** (Maps 91 & 92) The path across this short stretch of moorland is alas one of many and although you can hear the rush of the nearby A171, even in clear weather one marker pole on the path did not quite seem to lead to the next and others distract you. Watch your orientation or use GPS.

STAGE 1: ST BEES TO ENNERDALE BRIDGE   MAPS 1-7

Introduction

There is a lot of variety in this **14¹/₂-mile (23.5km, 6hr)** stage, beginning with a cliff-top walk along the Irish Sea and ending (weather permitting) with a high-level view from Dent Hill across to the brooding western fells of the Lake District.

Most will find this first day a bit of a struggle, particularly the haul up and over Dent Hill into Ennerdale Bridge (where there are few places to stay). If you think this may include you, pace yourself while you have a choice and consider stopping near Cleator or Egremont, both a mile or two off the path, before continuing on the second day to the youth hostels at High Gillerthwaite or even Black Sail. In a couple of days you may be glad you did.

The route

As far as we and most other walkers are concerned, '**Mile Zero'** (Wᴘᴛ 001) on the path is at the Coast to Coast sign by the RNLI hut facing the Irish Sea. To get there follow Beach Rd to the shore, baptise your boots in the surf and take a photo by the sign. Some walkers even collect a small pebble as a keepsake to drop into the North Sea at the end of the walk. Suitably initiated, turn north-west, steel yourself for the adventure about to unfold, and climb up the steep path to the clifftop. You're now on the Coast to Coast path, with a fence on one side and a 300ft (90m) drop on the other.

'Mile Zero'

The cliffs themselves are made of red St Bees sandstone, used in the construction of many of the buildings in the vicinity since medieval times and part of a broad sedimentary bed which you'll encounter again in the Vale of Eden on the far side of the Lakes.

The first notable landmark is the cleft of **Fleswick Bay** (Map 2) composed of a secluded pebble beach surrounded by red sandstone cliffs with some unusually weathered boulders on the shore, if you can be bothered to make the short detour.

This bay marks the dividing line between the constituent parts of St Bees Head: **South Head**, which you've been on up to now, and **North Head** (Map 2), which you now climb up to from the bay. Two features distinguish this latter part of St Bees Head: the three **RSPB observation points**, to the left of the path, which allow you to safely peer over the cliffs and observe the seabirds nesting there (including puffins, terns and England's only colony of black guillemots); and **St Bees Lighthouse**, a little way inland from the path but clearly visible since South Head.

If you're already puffed out, ***Tarn Flatt Hall*** (☎ 01946 692162, 🖳 www .lakelandcampingbarns.co.uk), a basic **camping barn**, is best reached by turning off the path here towards the lighthouse and continuing east for ¹/₄ mile/400m. It sleeps 12 and costs £7-8 per person.   *(cont'd on p86)*

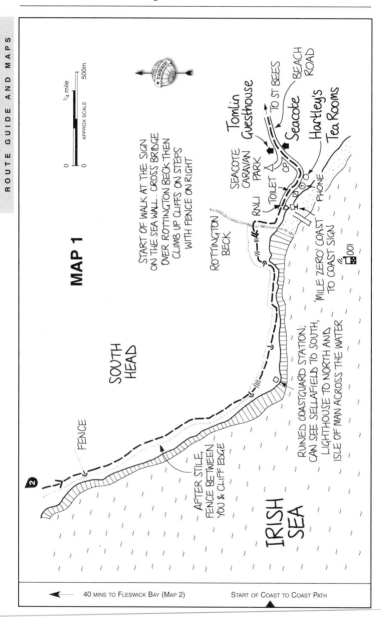

MAP 1

START OF WALK AT THE SIGN ON THE SEA WALL. CROSS BRIDGE OVER ROTTINGTON BECK THEN CLIMBS UP CLIFFS ON STEPS WITH FENCE ON RIGHT

¼ mile
0
APPROX SCALE
0
500m

SOUTH HEAD

FENCE

ROTTINGTON BECK

SEACOTE CARAVAN PARK

TOILET

RNLI

Tomlin Guesthouse

TO ST BEES

Seacote

BEACH ROAD

Hartley's Tea Rooms

CP

PHONE

'MILE ZERO' COAST TO COAST SIGN

001

AFTER STILE, FENCE BETWEEN YOU & CLIFF EDGE

RUINED COASTGUARD STATION; CAN SEE SELLAFIELD TO SOUTH, LIGHTHOUSE TO NORTH AND ISLE OF MAN ACROSS THE WATER

IRISH SEA

2

40 MINS TO FLESWICK BAY (MAP 2)

START OF COAST TO COAST PATH

ROUTE GUIDE AND MAPS

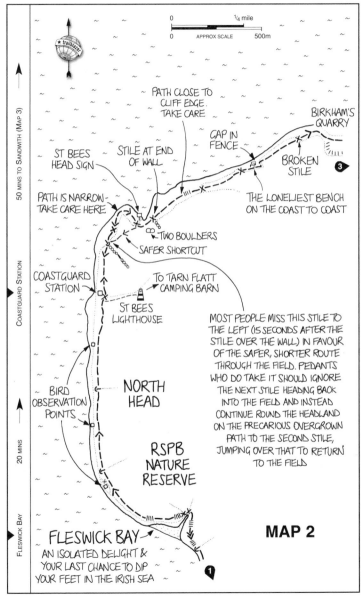

¼ mile

APPROX SCALE   500m

PATH CLOSE TO
CLIFF EDGE.
TAKE CARE

BIRKHAM'S
QUARRY

GAP IN
FENCE

ST BEES
HEAD SIGN

STILE AT END
OF WALL

BROKEN
STILE

3

PATH IS NARROW—
TAKE CARE HERE

THE LONELIEST BENCH
ON THE COAST TO COAST

50 MINS TO SANDWITH (MAP 3)

TWO BOULDERS

SAFER SHORTCUT

COASTGUARD
STATION

TO TARN FLATT
CAMPING BARN

ST BEES
LIGHTHOUSE

MOST PEOPLE MISS THIS STILE TO
THE LEFT (15 SECONDS AFTER THE
STILE OVER THE WALL) IN FAVOUR
OF THE SAFER, SHORTER ROUTE
THROUGH THE FIELD. PEDANTS
WHO DO TAKE IT SHOULD IGNORE
THE NEXT STILE HEADING BACK
INTO THE FIELD AND INSTEAD
CONTINUE ROUND THE HEADLAND
ON THE PRECARIOUS OVERGROWN
PATH TO THE SECOND STILE,
JUMPING OVER THAT TO RETURN
TO THE FIELD

COASTGUARD STATION

BIRD
OBSERVATION
POINTS

NORTH
HEAD

RSPB
NATURE
RESERVE

20 MINS

MAP 2

FLESWICK BAY

FLESWICK BAY
AN ISOLATED DELIGHT &
YOUR LAST CHANCE TO DIP
YOUR FEET IN THE IRISH SEA

1

(cont'd from p83) The barn comes with electric lighting (no power sockets), a slab to put your camping stove on and a wood-burning fire, with wood available from the farm. Showers cost 50p. Booking (online or by phone) is recommended, especially for the peak season.

After the lighthouse the path continues up to the tip of **North Head** before curving east along the coast and eventually turning inland just after **Birkham's Quarry**. Fifteen minutes later you arrive in the village of Sandwith.

SANDWITH   MAP 3

Sandwith (pronounced *Sanith*) is the first settlement of note on the trail; it's almost five miles/8km along the path from St Bees (though only two miles/3km as the crow flies!). Other than the bus stop, phone box, and the ***Dog and Partridge*** pub (☎ 01946 692671; summer daily noon-4pm & 6-11pm, winter Tue-Sun 7-11pm; no food), there's little to warrant much of a stay, particularly as you'll probably be wanting to crack on to the Lakes.

The nearest **accommodation** is *Tarn Flatt Hall* (see p83).

3D Travel's **bus** No 20 (Mon-Sat) passes through en route between St Bees and Whitehaven; see pp52-5 for further details. Some readers have found going back to St Bees for a second night and catching the bus back to Sandwith next morning is a gentle way to break themselves into the trek.

Taking the road past the pub (Dog & Partridge), the path crosses Byerstead Rd and, just over half a mile (0.8km) later, the B5345 linking Whitehaven to St Bees. From the tunnel beneath the railway line (Map 3) at the foot of the hill, the trail crosses waterlogged fields around **Stanley Pond** (with possible navigation issues; see box p82) and a small stream (**Scalegill Beck**; Map 4), before passing underneath the course of a disused railway. If you were to continue straight on and look behind you, you'd see St Bees nestling in the valley of Pow Beck. We, however, advise you to take the steps on your right up the side of the tunnel onto the disused railway track; take a left here and follow the 'track' to Moor Row.

MOOR ROW   MAP 4, p88

Moor Row lacks the village-green charm of Sandwith but does have a **phone** and the *Walkers Pop In Café* (Easter to Nov, daily 10am-6pm, closed Wed), a good spot for a sit down and a cuppa.

Around the corner, *Jasmine House* (☎ 01946 815795, 🖳 www.jasminehouse bandb.com; 1S/2D/2F, all en suite, one with bath) was for sale at the time of writing but the new owners expect to do B&B. The rate is £25-30pp.

3D Travel's No 6 **bus** (Mon-Sat) passes through on its route between Whitehaven and Seascale/Muncaster Castle; see pp52-5 for further details.

Local sculptor Colin Telfer's 'Coast to Coast' figure stands at the seven-mile mark.

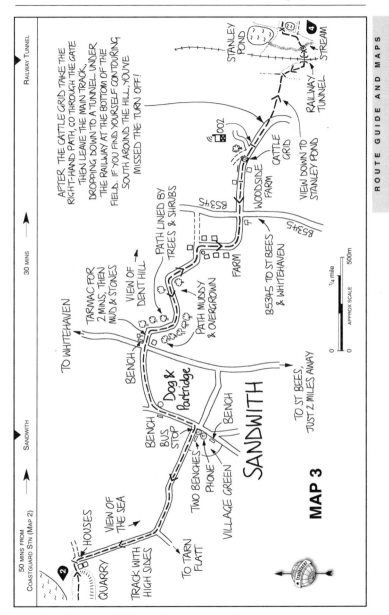

50 MINS FROM COASTGUARD STN (MAP 2)

SANDWITH

30 MINS

RAILWAY TUNNEL

AFTER THE CATTLE GRID TAKE THE RIGHT-HAND PATH, GO THROUGH THE GATE THEN LEAVE THE MAIN TRACK, DROPPING DOWN TO A TUNNEL UNDER THE RAILWAY AT THE BOTTOM OF THE FIELD. IF YOU FIND YOURSELF CONTOURING SOUTH AROUND THE HILL, YOU'VE MISSED THE TURN OFF!

STANLEY POND

STREAM

RAILWAY TUNNEL

VIEW DOWN TO STANLEY POND

CATTLE GRID

WOODSIDE FARM

B5345

PATH LINED BY TREES & SHRUBS

FARM

B5345 TO ST BEES & WHITEHAVEN

TARMAC FOR 2 MINS, THEN MUD & STONES

VIEW OF DENT HILL

PATH MUDDY & OVERGROWN

TO WHITEHAVEN

BENCH

Dog & Partridge

BENCH

BUS STOP

TWO BENCHES

PHONE

BENCH

VILLAGE GREEN

TO ST BEES, JUST 2 MILES AWAY

SANDWITH

¼ mile

APPROX SCALE

500m

HOUSES

VIEW OF THE SEA

QUARRY

TRACK WITH HIGH SIDES

TO TARN FLATT

MAP 3

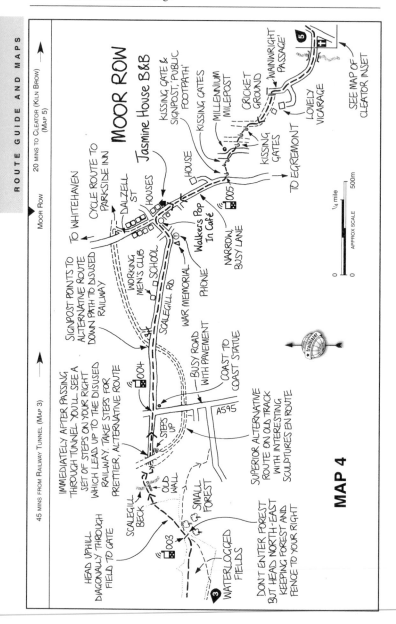

45 MINS FROM RAILWAY TUNNEL (MAP 3)

MOOR ROW

20 MINS TO CLEATOR (KILN BROW) (MAP 5)

MAP 4

MOOR ROW

Jasmine House B&B

KISSING GATE & SIGNPOST 'PUBLIC FOOTPATH'

MILLENNIUM MILEPOST

KISSING GATES

CRICKET GROUND

'WAINWRIGHT PASSAGE'

LONELY VICARAGE

SEE MAP OF CLEATOR INSET

KISSING GATES

HOUSE

TO EGREMONT

DALZELL ST

HOUSES

CYCLE ROUTE TO PARKSIDE INN

TO WHITEHAVEN

Walkers Pop In Café

NARROW, BUSY LANE

SIGNPOST POINTS TO ALTERNATIVE ROUTE DOWN PATH TO DISUSED RAILWAY

WORKING MEN'S CLUB

SCHOOL

SCALEGILL RD

WAR MEMORIAL

PHONE

BUSY ROAD WITH PAVEMENT

COAST TO COAST STATUE

A595

SUPERIOR ALTERNATIVE ROUTE ON OLD TRACK WITH INTERESTING SCULPTURES EN ROUTE

STEPS UP

IMMEDIATELY AFTER PASSING THROUGH TUNNEL YOU'LL SEE A SET OF STEPS ON YOUR RIGHT WHICH LEAD UP TO THE DISUSED RAILWAY. TAKE STEPS FOR PRETTIER, ALTERNATIVE ROUTE

SCALEGILL BECK

OLD WALL

SMALL FOREST

HEAD UPHILL DIAGONALLY THROUGH FIELD TO GATE

WATERLOGGED FIELDS

DON'T ENTER FOREST BUT HEAD NORTH-EAST KEEPING FOREST AND FENCE TO YOUR RIGHT

¼ mile

APPROX SCALE

0   500m

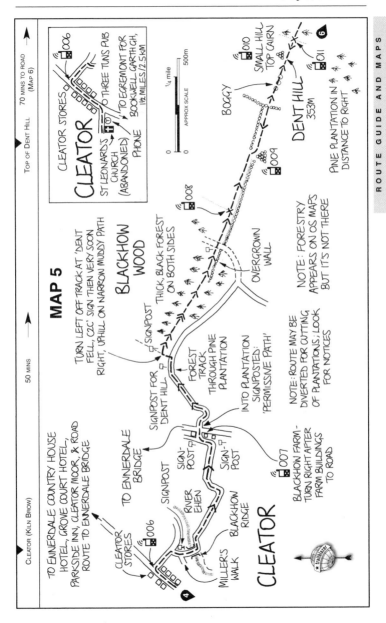

CLEATOR (KILN BROW)   50 MINS   TOP OF DENT HILL   70 MINS TO ROAD (MAP 6)

MAP 5

TO ENNERDALE COUNTRY HOUSE HOTEL, GROVE COURT HOTEL, PARKSIDE INN, CLEATOR MOOR, & ROAD ROUTE TO ENNERDALE BRIDGE

CLEATOR STORES

TO ENNERDALE BRIDGE

SIGNPOST

SIGN-POST

SIGN-POST

RIVER EHEN

MILLER'S WALK

BLACKHOW RIDGE

CLEATOR

BLACKHOW FARM - TURN RIGHT AFTER FARM BUILDINGS TO ROAD

INTO PLANTATION SIGNPOSTED: 'PERMISSIVE PATH'

FOREST TRACK THROUGH PINE PLANTATION

SIGNPOST FOR DENT HILL

TURN LEFT OFF TRACK AT 'DENT FELL, CCC' SIGN THEN VERY SOON RIGHT, UPHILL ON NARROW MUDDY PATH

SIGNPOST

THICK, BLACK FOREST ON BOTH SIDES

BLACKHOW WOOD

NOTE: ROUTE MAY BE DIVERTED FOR CUTTING OF PLANTATIONS: LOOK FOR NOTICES

OVERGROWN WALL

NOTE: FORESTRY APPEARS ON OS MAPS BUT IT'S NOT THERE

CLEATOR

ST LEONARD'S CHURCH (ABANDONED)   PHONE   TO THREE TUNS PUB

TO EGREMONT FOR BOOKWELL GARTH GH, 1½ MILES / 2.5KM

CLEATOR STORES

0 .... 500m
0 .... ¼ mile
APPROX SCALE

BOGGY

PINE PLANTATION IN DISTANCE TO RIGHT

DENT HILL 353M

SMALL HILL TOP CAIRN

Following the uncomfortably narrow and busy road south out of Moor Row (signposted to Egremont), you're pleased to soon get off it and head into a field. A whole series of kissing gates follows as you cross the dismantled railway once more on your way down into Cleator, arriving alongside St Leonard's Church.

CLEATOR   MAP 5, p89

As with Moor Row before it, it's clear that Wordsworth's lyrical ballads never reached out to immortalise the grim, pebbledashed, terraces of Cleator. Remnants of 12th-century masonry in the **church** (St Leonard's) attest to the village's venerability, but the abiding impression dates from a 19th-century iron-ore mining boom at which time Irish migrants flooded into the area (as the many Celtic house names suggest). The mining collapsed in the latter half of the 19th century and the nearby settlements followed suit; a familiar story repeated across west Cumbria, ameliorated today by the ongoing decommissioning of the ageing Sellafield nuclear plant, offering work to the 10,000 who want it. As we passed through, even the old Kangol factory's production of retro-chic headware had just given up the ghost.

Note that **Cleator Stores** (☎ 01946 810038; summer Mon-Fri 6am-7pm, Sat 8am-4pm, Sun 8.30am-3pm; winter Mon-Fri 6am-6pm, Sat 8am-3pm, Sun 8.30am-1pm) is now the **last decent store** until Grasmere although you may be able to get basics in Borrowdale (see p108). Otherwise, **Cleator Moor**, the regional hub with many grand 19th-century edifices, some once painted by Lowry, is a mile to the north, with an external ATM at the NatWest bank, corner shops and several junk-food outlets.

Stagecoach's **Bus** No 22 calls in at Cleator and Cleator Moor on its way between Whitehaven and Egremont; see pp52-5 for details.

Where to stay and eat

Nine miles along the Coast to Coast path from St Bees we still think Cleator can make a better first day of a long, long walk. Set in the former council offices, *Ennerdale Country House Hotel* (☎ 01946 813907, 🖳 www.oxfordhotelsandinns.com/OurHotels/Ennerdale; 1S/19D/8T/3F, all en suite with bath) is pitched at visiting nuclear executives, weddings and conferences, but with online offers from just £60 at the weekend for two sharing (£89 during the week), it could be worth a look as it's closest to the path. Food is served daily 7-9.30pm.

Less than half a mile further up the road, *Grove Court Hotel* (☎ 01946 810503, 🖳 www.grovecourthotel.co.uk; 7D/1T/2F/ two suites, all en suite with bath and shower) is a slightly classier version of the same, with rooms from £80 (£65 for single occupancy). Packed lunches are £3.95 and evening meals are available; booking in advance is recommended.

Two miles north of Cleator along the A5086 is the lonesome *Parkside Inn* (☎ 01946 811001 🖳 www.parksidehotelcumbria.co.uk; 2T/4D or F, most en suite, bath available). The en suite rooms upstairs may have seen better days but then so has the neighbourhood so they're priced appropriately (£25-27.50pp, single occupancy £29.50). Meals won't cost the earth, packed lunches are £2.50-4.50 and the bar is open daily: We're told John, the proprietor, makes a G&T like a pro. It's a dreary roadside schlep up from Cleator to the *Parkside* so it's better to get a bus or follow the quieter cycleway directly from Moor Row (Map 4) north-east for two miles via Cleator Moor to the Inn. Alternatively, if he is not busy John will pick you up/drop you off the next morning.

The Three Tuns (☎ 01946 811996) serves **food** (Easter to Sep daily 11.30am-11pm).

As an alternative to Cleator, **Egremont** is only 1½ miles/2.5km to the south and has *Bookwell Garth Guest House* (☎ 01946 820271, 16 Bookwell; 5S/6T/1F, shared shower facilities); rates start from £25pp. Packed lunches are available if requested in advance. They also have a car park. Stagecoach's No 22, 3D Travel's No 6 (Mon-Sat) and AA Travel's X6 (Sun) **bus** services stop in Egremont; see pp52-5 for details.

From Cleator it's possible to take the road route north and east to Ennerdale Bridge, so avoiding Dent Hill, either off the A5086 or at Black How Farm just before you enter the Dent-side plantation. Either way is said to be not too bad for traffic, though unless the weather is positively treacherous, or you're intent on saving energy, take the high route. It would be a shame to miss the summit of **Dent Hill** (Map 5) and the trickling tranquillity of Nannycatch Beck that lies hidden away at its foot. The long and sweaty climb up Dent Hill takes about an hour from Cleator. At the top there could be views to the Lakeland fells ahead and the sea behind, with the gigantic plant of Sellafield to the south-west,

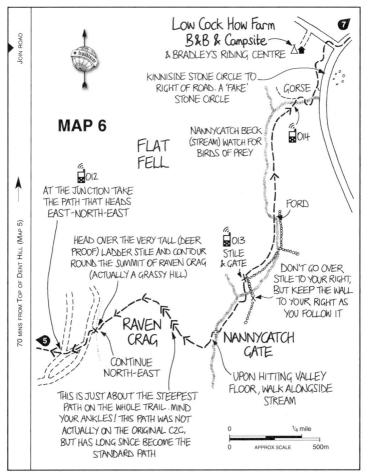

JOIN ROAD

MAP 6

Low Cock How Farm
B&B & Campsite
& BRADLEY'S RIDING CENTRE

KINNISIDE STONE CIRCLE TO RIGHT OF ROAD. A 'FAKE' STONE CIRCLE

GORSE

NANNYCATCH BECK (STREAM) WATCH FOR BIRDS OF PREY

014

FLAT FELL

012

AT THE JUNCTION TAKE THE PATH THAT HEADS EAST-NORTH-EAST

FORD

HEAD OVER THE VERY TALL (DEER PROOF) LADDER STILE AND CONTOUR ROUND THE SUMMIT OF RAVEN CRAG (ACTUALLY A GRASSY HILL)

013
STILE & GATE

DON'T GO OVER STILE TO YOUR RIGHT, BUT KEEP THE WALL TO YOUR RIGHT AS YOU FOLLOW IT

RAVEN CRAG

70 MINS FROM TOP OF DENT HILL (MAP 5)

5

CONTINUE NORTH-EAST

NANNYCATCH GATE

UPON HITTING VALLEY FLOOR, WALK ALONGSIDE STREAM

THIS IS JUST ABOUT THE STEEPEST PATH ON THE WHOLE TRAIL. MIND YOUR ANKLES! THIS PATH WAS NOT ACTUALLY ON THE ORIGINAL C2C, BUT HAS LONG SINCE BECOME THE STANDARD PATH

0   1/4 mile
0   APPROX SCALE   500m

Egremont before it and, on a good day, the silhouette of the Isle of Man and Galloway (Scotland) across the Solway Firth.

After the hilltop the Coast to Coast path signpost points left to the tall stile from where you contour and then descend Raven Crag hill (Map 6). Although very steep, it's become the *de facto* path now, contrary to Wainwright's original instructions. Maybe he had a point as when we say steep we mean it; poles may help and irate readers still write in and complain about the gradient down Raven Crag hill but trust us, it's a lot quicker, good training and more scenic.

From Nannycatch, head due north along the pretty beck, following the course of the water to the road leading into Ennerdale Bridge. Here you'll find **Low Cock How Farm** (Bradley's Riding Centre; Map 6, p91; ☎ 01946 861354, 🖳 www.walk-rest-ride.co.uk; 3D or T/1F, shared shower facilities), a riding centre with B&B from £28pp, a well-equipped 10-berth **bunkhouse** for £16pp as well as **camping** for £8pp. Evening meals cost from £14 but need to be booked in advance and breakfast (for bunkhouse and campers) costs £5.

Joining the road, before continuing north to Ennerdale Bridge, you may like to take a few steps south to check out the 'false' **stone circle of Kinniside Circle**, built in the 20th century by a local academic. From the circle, the trail hugs first one then the other side of the road north and then east into Ennerdale Bridge so walkers do not have to share the tarmac with the traffic.

ENNERDALE BRIDGE   MAP 7

Ennerdale Bridge is the first of the self-consciously pretty Lakeland villages, occupying a wonderful location spanning the River Ehen in one of Britain's least-developed valleys. Unfortunately for east-bound trekkers ending their first day here, there aren't many good lodgings and neither of the two great-looking but pricey pubs receive great plaudits from our readers. In our experience they're not quite tuned in to Coast to Coasters who you'd think make up their most regular clientele.

Rosie's Travel's No 217 **bus** service runs between Cockermouth and Frizington and stops here (Mon-Sat 1-2/day) as well as in Kirkland and Rowrah (both 2-4/day); however, since the services are limited (and only reach Ennerdale Bridge if the weather is good) you shouldn't rely on it and may need to ask for a lift if you stay in either Kirkland or Rowrah (see Where to stay).

Where to stay and eat
In the centre of the village *Shepherd's Arms Hotel* (☎ 01946 861249, 🖳 www .shepherdsarmshotel.co.uk; 2T/4D/2T or D; all private facilities, one with bath) charges

£80 per room, £50 single occupancy. Dogs cost £5 and there is a £2 charge for **wi-fi**. Managed by the same people, the smaller *Fox and Hounds* (☎ 01946 861181, 🖳 www foxandhoundsinn.org.uk; 1T/2D, all en suite with bath) charges the same. Single occupancy and one-night stays are said not to be a problem (as you'll soon learn, many Lakeland lodgings don't offer a discount for single occupancy and require a two-night minimum stay at weekends).

The facilities at *Cloggers* (☎ 01946 862487; 1D/1T, shared bathroom) are fine and the rate (£26pp/single occupancy £35) for B&B is certainly better value than the pubs.

Otherwise it's more walking or asking for a lift. A mile north in **Kirkland**, *Ennerdale View B&B* (☎ 01946 862311, 🖳 www.ennerdale-view.co.uk; 1S/2D/1T; some en suite, bath available) had great views, new owners as of 2009, and seems to be making an effort for walkers with free internet access and they will pick walkers up and drop them back in the morning; rates are £25-35pp. *The Stork* (☎ 01946 861213, 🖳 www.storkhotel.co.uk; 2S/1D/

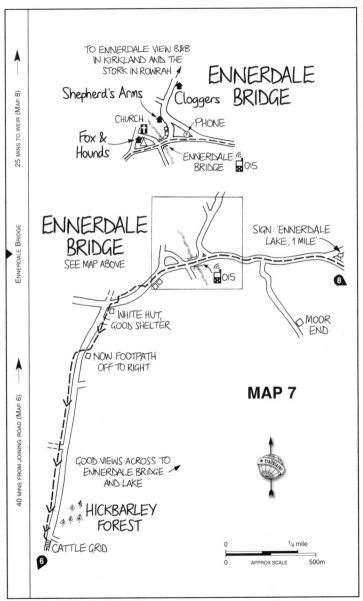

1T/2F, all en suite with shower), a pub, is another mile away in **Rowrah** but offers free lifts for Coast to Coasters who book or call in advance. Rates start at £35 in a single, £60 for two sharing and they do pub **food** (daily 6.30-9pm, Fri & Sun noon-2pm) too.

Food-wise, the only options in Ennerdale Bridge are the *Shepherd's Arms* and the *Fox and Hounds*; both serve food daily (noon-2 & 6-9pm) with a good selection of local ales and main dishes from around £8. They will do packed lunches too (£3.95-5.50).

STAGE 2: ENNERDALE BRIDGE TO BORROWDALE   MAPS 7-14

Introduction

As with any day in the Lakes, the enjoyment of this **16¹/₂-mile (26.5km, 6³/₄hr** via low route) stage depends largely on the weather. And be warned you are heading towards the spot which records the highest rainfall in England; the wryly named **Sprinkling Tarn** just south of Seathwaite receives an average of 185 inches (a phenomenal 4.7m) of rain a year. In the Lakeland wash-out that was 2009, it was probably over 200 inches, helped by no less than 12.4 inches (315mm) falling at Seathwaite Farm in one 24-hour period in late November, a new record for the British Isles since records began nearly 300 years ago. Indeed if it's raining horizontally with waterfalls running off the crags (as it was for us) the chances are the path along the **southern edge of Ennerdale Water** will be one long stream with occasional fords rising halfway up your shin. Unless you like splashing about in such weather the access track along the north shore may be preferable.

Beyond the lake's end, in clear conditions even the high route via Red Pike can get busy, but be warned it's a fair old climb and you can still enjoy great views down to Buttermere from the top of Loft Beck or Grey Knotts on the standard route. If the weather looks like closing in, it would be foolhardy to attempt the fell-top alternative. It's a long walk from Ennerdale Bridge, your first real stage in the Lakes, although you can rearrange this day at any of the four hostels spaced out along the route.

The route

The stage's first half involves a walk along the southern side of **Ennerdale Water** and though it's not quite the dreamy lakeside stroll you may have imagined, navigation couldn't be simpler. At one point the path rises to clamber over the outcrop of **Robin Hood's Chair** (take the easier right route at the top of the crag) to enter mossy light woodland as you near the eastern extremity of the lake. Here it's been reported that the path along the southern banks of the **River Liza**, as shown on Maps 9-11, has been washed away in places; stick to the original route which scenically is no different.

Low Gillerthwaite Field Centre (Map 10; ☎ 01946 861229, 🖳 www.lgfc .org.uk) has **camping** for £4 per person; **bunkhouse** accommodation (40 beds) is available for £13pp. There is a kitchen and a lounge with open wood fire as well as shower and toilet facilities. Note, however, that if they have a school group in residence (which is not unusual) you may not be allowed to stay so call ahead or take your chances.

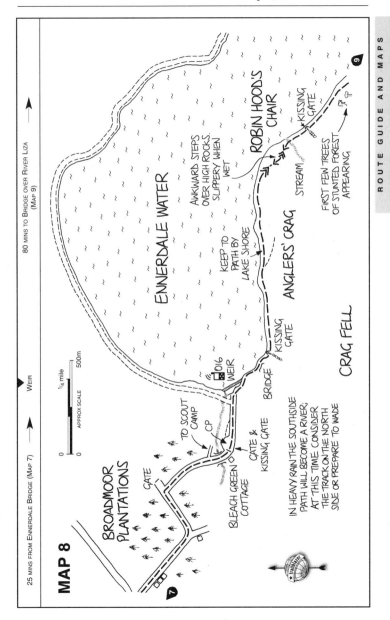

MAP 8

25 MINS FROM ENNERDALE BRIDGE (MAP 7) ⟶

WEIR

80 MINS TO BRIDGE OVER RIVER LIZA (MAP 9)

BROADMOOR PLANTATIONS

GATE

0   ¼ mile

0   APPROX SCALE   500m

TO SCOUT CAMP

CP

WEIR

ENNERDALE WATER

KEEP TO PATH BY LAKE SHORE

AWKWARD STEPS OVER HIGH ROCKS. SLIPPERY WHEN WET

ROBIN HOOD'S CHAIR

KISSING GATE

STREAM

FIRST FEW TREES OF STUNTED FOREST APPEARING.

ANGLERS' CRAG

CRAG FELL

KISSING GATE

BRIDGE

BLEACH GREEN COTTAGE

GATE & KISSING GATE

IN HEAVY RAIN THE SOUTHSIDE PATH WILL BECOME A RIVER; AT THIS TIME CONSIDER THE TRACK ON THE NORTH SIDE OR PREPARE TO WADE

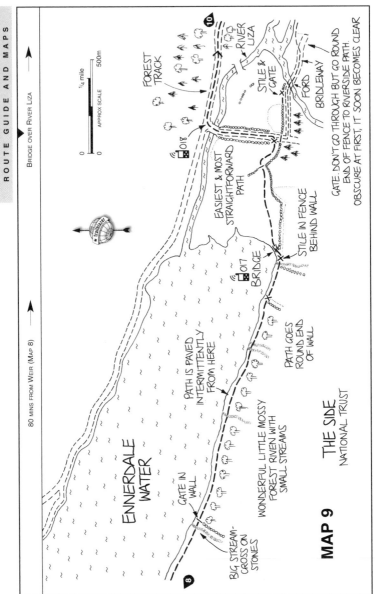

BRIDGE OVER RIVER LIZA

80 MINS FROM WEIR (MAP 8)

APPROX SCALE

0

0

¼ mile

500m

RIVER LIZA

FOREST TRACK

STILE & GATE

FORD

BRIDLEWAY

GATE. DON'T GO THROUGH BUT GO ROUND END OF FENCE TO RIVERSIDE PATH OBSCURE AT FIRST, IT SOON BECOMES CLEAR

EASIEST & MOST STRAIGHTFORWARD PATH

STILE IN FENCE BEHIND WALL

PATH GOES ROUND END OF WALL

BRIDGE

ENNERDALE WATER

PATH IS PAVED INTERMITTENTLY FROM HERE

WONDERFUL LITTLE MOSSY FOREST RIVEN WITH SMALL STREAMS

GATE IN WALL

BIG STREAM- CROSS ON STONES

MAP 9

THE SIDE
NATIONAL TRUST

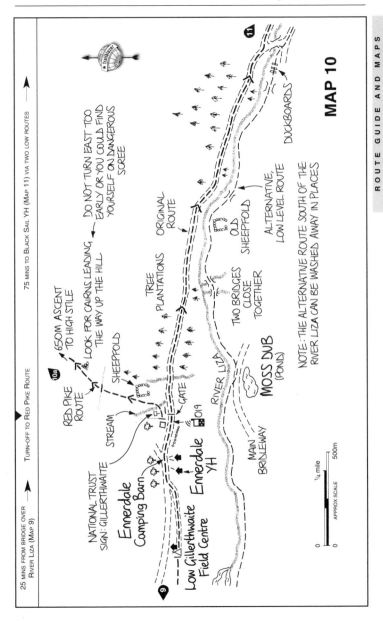

25 MINS FROM BRIDGE OVER RIVER LIZA (MAP 9) → → TURN-OFF TO RED PIKE ROUTE 75 MINS TO BLACK SAIL YH (MAP 11) VIA TWO LOW ROUTES

MAP 10

11

DUCKBOARDS

DO NOT TURN EAST TOO EARLY OR YOU COULD FIND YOURSELF ON DANGEROUS SCREE

650M ASCENT TO HIGH STILE

LOOK FOR CAIRNS LEADING THE WAY UP THE HILL

TREE PLANTATIONS

ORIGINAL ROUTE

OLD SHEEPFOLD

ALTERNATIVE, LOW LEVEL ROUTE

RED PIKE ROUTE

10a

SHEEPFOLD

STREAM

GATE

RIVER LIZA

TWO BRIDGES CLOSE TOGETHER

NOTE: THE ALTERNATIVE ROUTE SOUTH OF THE RIVER LIZA CAN BE WASHED AWAY IN PLACES

NATIONAL TRUST SIGN: GILLERTHWAITE

Ennerdale Camping Barn

10019

MOSS DUB (PONDS)

Ennerdale YH

MAIN BRIDLEWAY

Low Gillerthwaite Field Centre

9

¼ mile

500m

APPROX SCALE

0

0

Up the track a bit ***Ennerdale Youth Hostel*** (Map 10; ☎ 0845 371 9116, 📧 ennerdale@yha.org.uk; 24 beds; from £13.95), at **High Gillerthwaite** is a small hostel that's open from the week before Easter to the end of October. Meals are available (though these should be booked in advance). The hostel is licensed and has a slick self-catering kitchen and cosy lounge, though sharing the tiny, six-bed dorms with five others could require good organisation. The hostel generates its own hydro-powered electricity which seems to impact on the drying room's efficacy, though this may be improved. The hostel reception opens at 5pm but you can get inside and settle in before then.

Next door, ***Ennerdale Camping Barn*** (☎ 01629 592700, 📧 campingbarns @yha.org.uk; 14 beds) is managed by the YHA. Beds here are £8.50pp; there's electric lighting but no plug sockets, and a cooking area though no cooking facilities so you'll either need a stove or have to pop next door for a meal.

Just beyond the camping barn is the start of the alternative trail up to Red Pike, High Stile and Hay Stacks (see below and Maps 10a, and 10b p100).

The Red Pike, High Stile & Hay Stacks route
Maps 10, 10a, 10b & 12

'All I ask for, at the end, is a last, long resting place by the side of Innominate Tarn, on Haystacks where the water gently laps the gravelly shore and the heather blooms and Pillar and Gable keep unfailing watch. A quiet place, a lonely place. I shall go to it, for the last time, and be carried: someone who knew me in life will take me there and empty me out of a little box and leave me there alone. And if you, dear reader, should get a bit of grit in your boot as you are crossing Haystacks in the years to come, please treat it with respect. It might be me.   **Alfred Wainwright** *Memoirs of an Ex-Fellwanderer*

In his *Coast to Coast* guide Wainwright describes this route as suitable only for 'very strong and experienced fellwalkers' in clear weather. While we don't think the group of people who can do this walk is quite as exclusive as Wainwright suggests, we certainly agree that the weather needs to be clear, if only because the views possible at the top – in particular across Buttermere to the north and to Great Gable and Pillar in the south – benefit from it. (If the weather takes a significant turn for the worse up there, you can drop down from Scarth Gap on steps to the Black Sail hostel; see Map 10b, p100.) There are no technically difficult parts, though there are some steep ascents and particularly descents which will hammer the knees, and route finding on the way up to Red Pike can be tricky. This alternative route should add about **1¹/₂ miles (2.5km, 1³/₄hrs)** to this stage, all in all making it a pretty tough day so early in the walk.

The high-level route takes in a number of summits, including Red Pike (755m), High Stile (807m), High Crag (744m) and Hay Stacks (597m), the lowest but the most interesting. The place where some err from the path is on the initial climb up to Red Pike where it's tempting to branch off eastwards too early: make sure that, having crossed the stream, you continue north-east (following cairns) until you're firmly on the grassy upper reaches of Red Pike (Map 10a). There are *just* enough cairns to show the way, though if in doubt, your motto should be: head up the slope rather than along it.

(cont'd on p102)

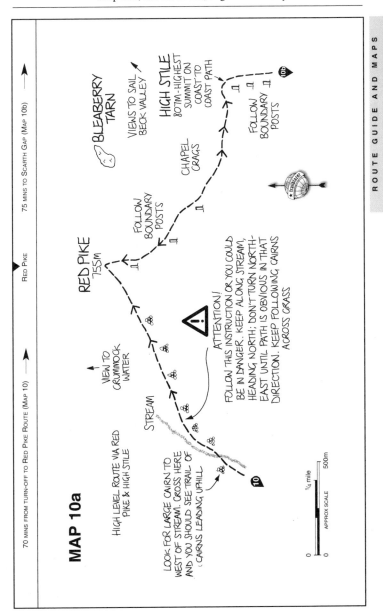

MAP 10a

70 MINS FROM TURN-OFF TO RED PIKE ROUTE (MAP 10) →

RED PIKE

75 MINS TO SCARTH GAP (MAP 10b) →

HIGH LEVEL ROUTE VIA RED PIKE & HIGH STILE

LOOK FOR LARGE CAIRNS TO WEST OF STREAM. CROSS HERE AND YOU SHOULD SEE TRAIL OF CAIRNS LEADING UPHILL

STREAM

VIEW TO CRUMMOCK WATER

RED PIKE 755M

FOLLOW BOUNDARY POSTS

BLEABERRY TARN

VIEWS TO SAIL BECK VALLEY

HIGH STILE 80TM - HIGHEST SUMMIT ON COAST TO COAST PATH

CHAPEL CRAGS

FOLLOW BOUNDARY POSTS

ATTENTION!
FOLLOW THIS INSTRUCTION OR YOU COULD BE IN DANGER. KEEP ALONG STREAM, HEADING NORTH; DON'T TURN NORTH-EAST UNTIL PATH IS OBVIOUS IN THAT DIRECTION. KEEP FOLLOWING CAIRNS ACROSS GRASS

¼ mile

500m

APPROX SCALE

0

0

10

10b

ROUTE GUIDE AND MAPS

ROUTE GUIDE AND MAPS

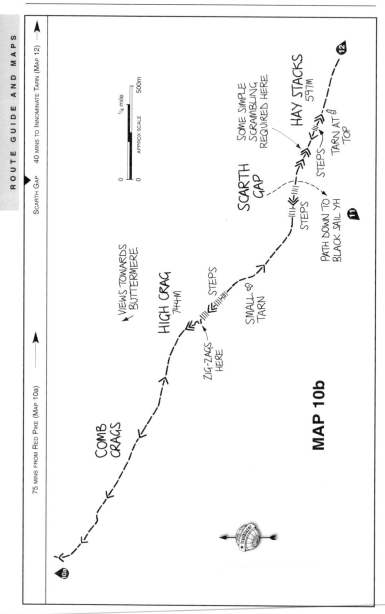

75 MINS FROM RED PIKE (MAP 10a)

SCARTH GAP

40 MINS TO INNOMINATE TARN (MAP 12)

COMB CRAGS

HIGH CRAG
744M

VIEWS TOWARDS BUTTERMERE

ZIG-ZAGS HERE

STEPS

SMALL TARN

STEPS

SCARTH GAP

SOME SIMPLE SCRAMBLING REQUIRED HERE

HAY STACKS
597M

STEPS

TARN AT TOP

PATH DOWN TO BLACK SAIL YH

¼ mile

500m

0

0

APPROX SCALE

MAP 10b

10a

11

12

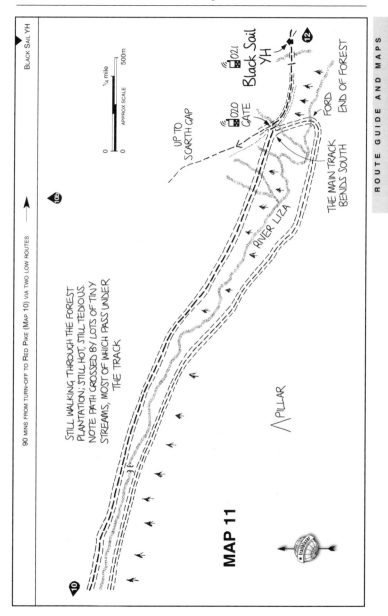

BLACK SAIL YH

MAP 11

STILL WALKING THROUGH THE FOREST
PLANTATION; STILL HOT, STILL TEDIOUS.
NOTE PATH CROSSED BY LOTS OF TINY
STREAMS, MOST OF WHICH PASS UNDER
THE TRACK

90 MINS FROM TURN-OFF TO RED PIKE (MAP 10) VIA TWO LOW ROUTES

∧ PILLAR

RIVER LIZA

THE MAIN TRACK
BENDS SOUTH

UP TO
SCARTH GAP

GATE 020

021

Black Sail
YH

FORD
END OF FOREST

12

APPROX SCALE

¼ mile

500m

(cont'd from p98) Having gained the ridge the path becomes clear and you'll find yourself ticking off one peak after another as you make your way to **Innominate Tarn** (Map 12). From there, Wainwright recommends ignoring the obvious path that continues in an easterly direction to the north of **Blackbeck Tarn**, instead continuing in a south-easterly direction to an unmarked reunion with the low route near the top of **Loft Beck**. Though you'll struggle to follow any clear path in the ground, this trail is marked on Map 12. However, it's said that few trekkers actually manage to successfully rejoin the low route and instead forge their own path to **Honister Quarries**. If you wish to try, the best tactic from Innominate Tarn is to aim for the **Brandreth Fence** to the south and continue along it until you come to a reunion with the regular route at the stile in the fence (WPT 024). Otherwise, the easiest solution is to continue on the clear trail to **Blackbeck**, from where you can follow the wide track down to Honister (see p104). Just make sure you don't start to descend to Buttermere.

Continuing on the low route up the valley, just over 90 minutes after joining the forest track you emerge at the head of Ennerdale and the isolated bothy that is now *Black Sail Youth Hostel* (Maps 11/12; ☎ 0845 371 9680; 16 beds, from £13.95). Even with the rudimentary facilities, who could not wish to wake up here one sunny morning? Breakfast and evening meals are served (these need to be booked in advance) and the hostel is licensed; credit cards aren't accepted. Having a torch is recommended. The hostel is left open during the day, providing welcome shelter from rain and the chance to make a cup of tea in the kitchen. Note that Black Sail is beyond the reach of the baggage carriers and the hostel is only open to individuals from the week before Easter to October. Incidentally, if the weather clears, just before the hostel are some steps leading up to Scarth Gap (Map 10a) on the high route (see p98).

From the hostel things can get a little tricky. You need to follow the correct path east to pick up the stiff climb up the side of **Loft Beck** and from there the path to Grey Knotts from where the long descent to Honister Hause and Borrowdale begins. Armed with this advice, in fine weather the way is crystal clear, but unfortunately such conditions are infrequent in these parts, particularly in the afternoon when most attempt the climb. It's at the top of Loft Beck, when trying to locate the correct path to Honister Hause, that problems can occur in poor visibility: follow Map 12 carefully to negotiate this section and have a compass or GPS at hand. At worst, at the top of the Beck blunder north over the boggy saddle to the Brandreth Fence and follow it east to the stile at WPT 024.

From the stile at **Brandreth Fence**, an initially indistinct path rises to contour around the western face of Brandreth and **Grey Knotts** (Map 13), with occasional cairns along the way. The working Hopper Quarry can be seen in the distance to the north.

The path soon joins the larger track (WPT 026) coming down from Brandreth and Great Gable and drops gently to the **Drum House**, now little more than a massive pile of stones and slate. The path's arrow-straight course betrays its previous incarnation as a quarry tramway, now dismantled, and the

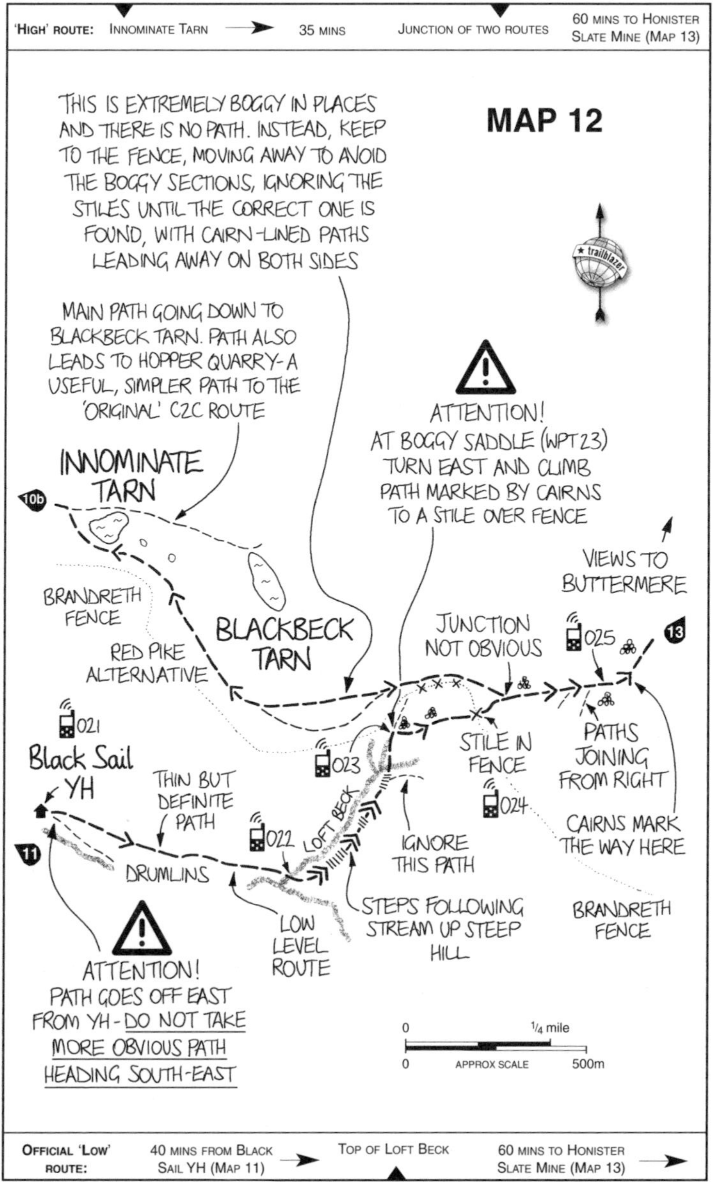

ROUTE GUIDE AND MAPS

THIS IS EXTREMELY BOGGY IN PLACES AND THERE IS NO PATH. INSTEAD, KEEP TO THE FENCE, MOVING AWAY TO AVOID THE BOGGY SECTIONS, IGNORING THE STILES UNTIL THE CORRECT ONE IS FOUND, WITH CAIRN-LINED PATHS LEADING AWAY ON BOTH SIDES

MAP 12

MAIN PATH GOING DOWN TO BLACKBECK TARN. PATH ALSO LEADS TO HOPPER QUARRY - A USEFUL, SIMPLER PATH TO THE 'ORIGINAL' C2C ROUTE

INNOMINATE TARN

10b

⚠️ ATTENTION! AT BOGGY SADDLE (WPT 23) TURN EAST AND CLIMB PATH MARKED BY CAIRNS TO A STILE OVER FENCE

VIEWS TO BUTTERMERE

BRANDRETH FENCE

RED PIKE ALTERNATIVE

BLACKBECK TARN

JUNCTION NOT OBVIOUS

📷 025

13

📷 021

Black Sail YH

THIN BUT DEFINITE PATH

📷 022

📷 023

STILE IN FENCE

📷 024

PATHS JOINING FROM RIGHT

CAIRNS MARK THE WAY HERE

11

DRUMLINS

LOW LEVEL ROUTE

LOFT BECK

IGNORE THIS PATH

STEPS FOLLOWING STREAM UP STEEP HILL

BRANDRETH FENCE

⚠️ ATTENTION! PATH GOES OFF EAST FROM YH - DO NOT TAKE MORE OBVIOUS PATH HEADING SOUTH-EAST

0 ¼ mile

0 APPROX SCALE 500m

ROUTE GUIDE AND MAPS

❑ Honister Slate Mine

The story of mining at Honister began 400 million years ago when volcanic ash, combined with water and subsequent compression, formed the fine-grained rock now called slate. When the glaciers of the last Ice Age retreated up Gatesgarthdale they exposed three parallel veins of slate along the steep sides of the valley and sporadic mining may have taken place before the Roman era. Certainly by the early 1700s slate was being quarried here on an industrial scale and, as well as the disused tramway you walk down, there were roads and aerial ropeways to take the slate to the road. The workers who split and finished the slate lived in barracks in Honister during the week; the adjacent youth hostel is a former quarry workers' building. After closing in the 1980s, the mine (along with the nearby quarry) re-opened in 1997 and has since developed into a slick, tourist-oriented facility backed by small-scale mining operations.

The **Visitors' Centre** (☎ 01768 777230, 🖳 www.honister-slate-mine.co.uk; daily 9am-5pm) is well worth visiting. There are guided tours into the mine daily at 10.30am, 12.30pm and 3.30pm for £9.75. For those with energy to spare they've also set up a *via ferrata*. Common in the Dolomites of northern Italy, a via ferrata, or 'iron way', is essentially a series of fixed iron ropes, ladders and other climbing aids to help non-climbers reach places that would otherwise be inaccessible. The one at Honister, for which a guide is compulsory, takes climbers through the quarry up to Fleetwith Pike on what they claim is the old miners' route to work. The cost is from £25, including equipment hire, with climbs conducted at daily 9am, noon and 3pm. Book via the website. The **shop** is full of slate-based souvenirs, from great slabs of the stuff that have been fashioned into coffee tables, to smaller chippings sold by the bagful. Some of the stuff is lovely but think twice before leaving with a full-size slate coffee table on your back; it's still a long way to Robin Hood's Bay. Something small such as a Coast to Coast coaster may be more appropriate.

Drum House's original purpose was to house the cable that operated the tramway that ran to the cutting sheds. At the bottom of the tramway is **Honister Hause**, and probably a hullabaloo around **Honister Slate Mine Visitor Centre** (see box above) at the crest of the notoriously steep Honister Pass which many a caravanner has regretted tackling. The recently refurbished *Honister Hause Youth Hostel* (☎ 0845 371 9522, 🖳 honister@yha.org.uk; 26 beds; from £13.95) is next door, serves meals and is licensed. Credit cards are accepted. Stagecoach's No 77 **bus** runs from here to Seatoller (eight minutes) and to Keswick (40 minutes) and the 77A goes via Buttermere to Keswick (60 mins); see pp52-5 for details.

From Honister the Coast to Coast path parallels the B5289 down Little Gatesgarthdale. Down in the valley the path loops back on itself to join the road at **Seatoller**, although for a nifty short cut avoiding this village and saving you half a mile, see Map 14.

SEATOLLER   MAP 14, p107

The National Trust village of Seatoller has a tearoom, restaurant and an **information centre** (☎ 01768 777714; Mar-Oct daily 10am-5pm, Nov-Feb weekends only) packed full of souvenirs and books as well as useful advice and a few simple bits of trekking equipment in the shop. The centre was closed for refurbishment in the winter

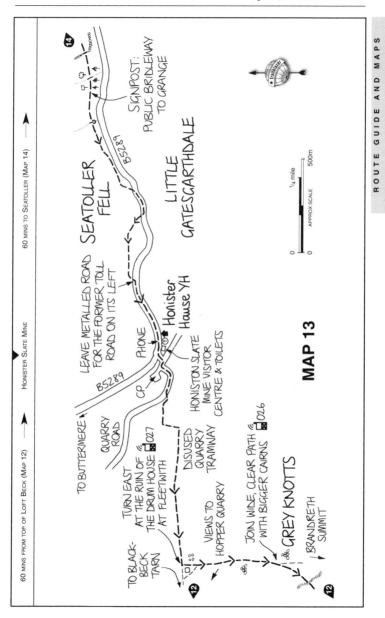

SEATOLLER FELL

LITTLE GATESGARTHDALE

SIGNPOST:
PUBLIC BRIDLEWAY
TO GRANGE

LEAVE METALLED ROAD
FOR THE FORMER TOLL
ROAD ON ITS LEFT

B5289

Honister House YH

PHONE

TO BUTTERMERE

QUARRY
ROAD

B5289

CP

HONISTON SLATE MINE VISITOR
CENTRE & TOILETS

TURN EAST
AT THE RUIN OF
THE DRUM HOUSE 📷 027
AT FLEETWITH

DISUSED
QUARRY TRAMWAY

MAP 13

VIEWS TO
HOPPER QUARRY

TO BLACK-
BECK TARN

JOIN WIDE, CLEAR PATH 📷 026
WITH BIGGER CAIRNS

GREY KNOTTS

BRANDRETH SUMMIT

¼ mile
0   500m
0
APPROX SCALE

ROUTE GUIDE AND MAPS

of 2009 but should be open by spring 2010. Seatoller also has a public phone, toilet, post box and a couple of B&Bs – not bad for a hamlet that can't contain more than 20 houses.

Stagecoach's 77/77A and 78 **bus** services call here between Easter & Sep/Oct; see pp52-5 for details.

Where to stay and eat

As for B&Bs, you're now well and truly among the valleybound Lakeland honeypots with prices which can suddenly make hostelling not seem such a bad idea after all. In the village centre *Seatoller House* (☎ 01768 777218, 🖳 www.seatollerhouse.co .uk; 1D/3T/6F, all with en suite or private bath; Mar-Nov) is a 300-year-old building that's been a guesthouse for over a century.

The rate is £49 per person for B&B, or £61 with a four-course dinner (fixed menu) served at 7pm (light supper on Tuesdays). Single occupancy is subject to a £5 supplement.

Right opposite, *Seatoller Farm* (☎ 01768 777232, 🖳 www.seatollerfarm.co .uk; 2D/1T, all en suite, bath available) is a working National Trust hill farm that charges £35 per person for two sharing; they close mid-Dec to mid-Jan. Their farmhouse breakfasts are said to be the perfect start to the day. Note that dogs are excluded, though **camping** is allowed (£6pp including use of a shower).

The *Yew Tree* (☎ 01768 777634; Apr-Oct daily 10am-6pm) is a traditional English **tearoom** set in a 400-year-old building.

From Seatoller the trail wends its way through **Johnny Wood** (see p65), joining the short cut mentioned above and passing the hostel into Borrowdale (Map 14).

BORROWDALE   MAP 14

Borrowdale is actually made up of three separate settlements: Longthwaite, Rosthwaite and Stonethwaite. Small, picturesque and composed largely of slate-roofed, whitewashed-stone farm cottages, they are the iconic Lake District hamlets tourists from round the world flock to see in their droves.

Stagecoach's No 78 (Easter/Apr-Oct) **bus**, known as the Borrowdale Rambler, runs between Seatoller and Keswick (from where buses run to other destinations in Cumbria) via Rosthwaite; see pp52-5 for details.

Longthwaite

The first building you come to in Borrowdale is *Borrowdale Youth Hostel* (☎ 0845 371 9624, 🖳 borrowdale@yha.org .uk; £15.95-21.95; 86 beds), a spacious and well-run lodge with an alcohol licence and spirited catering well worth crossing the fells for. **Internet access** costs £1 for 15 minutes. Credit cards are accepted.

Longthwaite also plays host to *Gillercombe B&B* (☎ 01768 777602;

1S/4D or T; shared facilities, bath available; Easter-Oct), a fine B&B and the best **campsite** (£6 per person; 50p per shower) in the valley. The owner of both, Rachel Dunckley, is a mine of useful local information and gossip, and her B&B remains a comfortable and convenient place to stay right in the heart of Borrowdale. Rates are £30pp. However, it is essential to book well in advance if you want B&B accommodation here.

Rosthwaite

The biggest settlement of the three is Rosthwaite to the north. Stagecoach's No 78 bus (see column opposite) calls here.

On the way into town there are two National Trust farms offering rooms: *Nook Farm* (☎ 01768 777677, 🖳 nookfarm1 @aol.com; 1D en suite shower/1F private bathroom; Feb-Nov) is a 16th-century farmhouse with lovely open fires – the perfect treat after a rainy day's walk. Rates are £28-32pp. Dogs are not allowed.

Round the corner *Yew Tree Farm* (☎ 01768 777675, 🖳 www.borrowdaleherd wick.co.uk; 2D/1T, all en suite with bath;

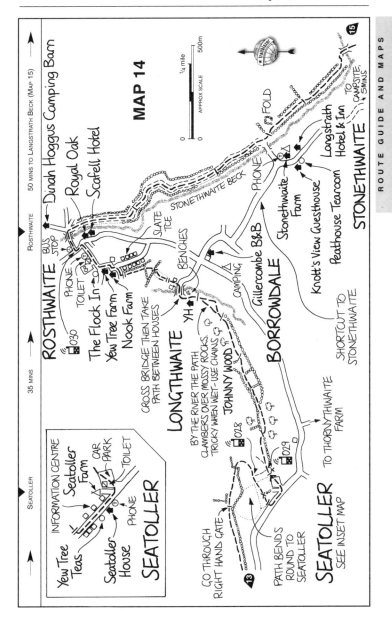

closed Dec & Jan) charges £75 per room, £50 single occupancy. They have taken on the duties of the defunct village **shop** and now sell essentials in their tearoom *The Flock In* (Feb-Dec daily except Wed, 10am-5pm), opposite, where everything, from the tea to the soup, is served in pints or half pints. Many of their dishes are made with produce from the farm, such as 'Herdie-burgers', and the terrace behind is covered by a roof, allowing trekkers to enjoy the outside space even when it's pouring with rain.

Village centre pubs include *The Royal Oak Hotel* (☎ 01768 777214, 🖥 www.royaloakhotel.co.uk; 2S/2T/5D/5D, T or F, most en suite, bath available), a fine-looking place which once hosted the poet William Wordsworth (see p117). Rates start at £55 per person with an extra £4 at weekends, but include an evening meal as well as breakfast.

Next door is *Scafell Hotel and Riverside Bar* (☎ 01768 777208, 🖥 www.scafell.co.uk; 23 rooms, all en suite some with bath), a large place which has served as a coaching inn since 1850. Some of the rooms have been decorated with antique furniture; rates are £62-66pp April to October and from £38pp in the winter. The menu is extensive and the **food** (daily noon-2pm & 6-9pm, school summer holidays noon-9pm), while not of the quality of the nearby Langstrath (see Stonethwaite), is still fine.

On the Coast to Coast path leading over the river out of the village, *Dinah Hoggus Camping Barn* (☎ 01946 758198, 🖥 www.lakelandcampingbarns.co.uk) is a very simple but attractively rustic place sleeping 12 people. They charge £7-8 per person (bring your own sleeping bag and camping stove; mattresses provided); booking in advance is essential.

Stonethwaite

Just under a mile (about 1.6km) to the south and away from the relative clamour of Rosthwaite, Stonethwaite nestles in its own little world at the end of a road running parallel to the beck that shares its name. Although frequently rained on, it is among the prettiest of the Lakeland hamlets.

As for lodgings, as you enter the village *Stonethwaite Farm* (☎ 01768 777234; 1S/2D/1T, some en suite, bath available) comes highly recommended and also offers **camping** (Mar-Oct; £5pp; toilets and cold water) in a field half a mile up the valley (see Map 15). B&B rates are £25-30pp.

Knotts View (☎ 01768 777604; 2D/1T/1T or D, bath available; Apr-Oct) charges £30pp (£35 for single occupancy) for B&B. According to the owner the building is said to be 450 years old and, with its low ceilings, it feels like it. They also own the *Peathouse Tearoom* (flexible opening hours) next door. If you're not familiar with the nature of peat, by the time you get to Greenup Edge tomorrow you'll be an expert.

Best of all is *The Langstrath* (☎ 01768 777239, 🖥 www.thelangstrath.com; 3D/4D or T/1F, all en suite, some with bath; closed Mon, Mon & Tue in Nov, and completely Dec to early Feb) whose reputation for fine **food** (Tue-Sun noon-2pm & 6-8.45pm, to 8pm on Sun; winter hours may vary; bar daily noon-10pm) extends well beyond Borrowdale and includes such locally sourced dishes as slow-roasted Rosthwaite Herdwick lamb. Mains on average cost £9-15 and the rooms are just as worthy of praise. The hotel also has wi-fi. Rates are £42.50-45.50pp; single occupancy supplement £20. All in all, you want to run down from Honister to make the most of this place.

❏ **Important note – walking times**
Unless otherwise specified, **all times in this book refer only to the time spent walking**. You will need to add 20-30% to allow for rests, photography, checking the map, drinking water etc. When planning the day's hike count on 5-7 hours' actual walking.

STAGE 3: BORROWDALE TO GRASMERE   MAPS 14-18

Introduction
In good weather this **8½-mile (13.5km, 4-5½hr high route)** stage is a Lakeland classic, a straightforward climb up past Lining Crag to Greenup Edge, followed by the high-level ridge walk we recommend (see pp112-13) or a less adventurous and slightly shorter plod down the valley to the edge of Grasmere.

Wainwright combines this stage with the next one to Patterdale, adding up to at least a 17-mile (27.5km) hike, and a few walkers do just that. Sticking to the valley routes as Wainwright did, it would not be too demanding. But we strongly recommend you divert along the high-level options on both stages; this is the Lake District after all so you want to get high while you can. However, taking on the high routes in one long day may leave you a little drained for the 16-miler from Patterdale to Shap which follows and along which there are no easy gradients.

The route
The stage begins with a level amble through the fields alongside **Stonethwaite Beck** (Maps 14 and 15), with **Eagle Crag** a permanent, looming presence

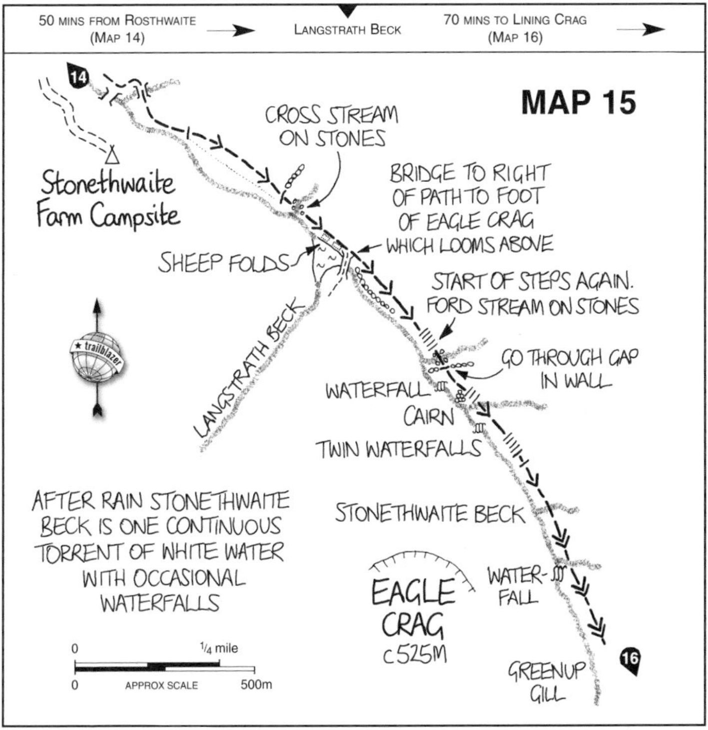

50 MINS FROM ROSTHWAITE (MAP 14) → LANGSTRATH BECK | 70 MINS TO LINING CRAG (MAP 16) →

MAP 15

Stonethwaite Farm Campsite

CROSS STREAM ON STONES

BRIDGE TO RIGHT OF PATH TO FOOT OF EAGLE CRAG WHICH LOOMS ABOVE

SHEEP FOLDS

START OF STEPS AGAIN. FORD STREAM ON STONES

GO THROUGH GAP IN WALL

LANGSTRATH BECK

WATERFALL CAIRN

TWIN WATERFALLS

AFTER RAIN STONETHWAITE BECK IS ONE CONTINUOUS TORRENT OF WHITE WATER WITH OCCASIONAL WATERFALLS

STONETHWAITE BECK

EAGLE CRAG c 525M

WATER-FALL

0   ¼ mile
0   APPROX SCALE   500m

GREENUP GILL

across the water. It looks massive but by the time you get to Greenup Edge you'll be looking *down* on Eagle Crag.

At Stonethwaite you join **Greenup Gill** (Map 15), one long torrent of white water and waterfalls when we came through and with views back down to Borrowdale growing more impressive with every upward step. The path's gradient picks up a notch past Eagle Crag, drops into a basin of drumlins (glacial formations) and a step climb up onto the top of **Lining Crag** (Map 16) from where, weather permitting, views reach over towards Scafell Pike, England's highest summit at 3210ft (978m).

Look to the south and you'll also make out the beginning of the path to the broad col of **Greenup Edge**. This next section is where some lose their way, the boggy ground and indistinct cairns obscuring the correct direction even in ideal conditions. As you near the col look out for the old fence posts which once stretched up and over to Low White Stones, the hill south of the col; see box p82. If you see one on an outcrop (possibly with a broken boot still spiked onto it), aim to the south of it to a less conspicuous fence post at ground level and, a

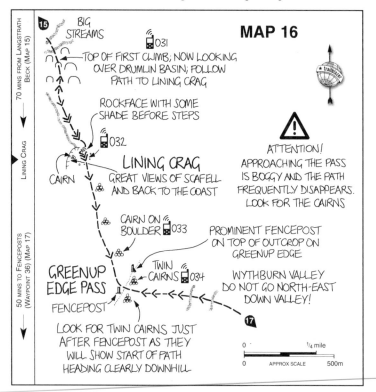

MAP 16

15 BIG STREAMS

📱031

TOP OF FIRST CLIMB; NOW LOOKING OVER DRUMLIN BASIN; FOLLOW PATH TO LINING CRAG

ROCKFACE WITH SOME SHADE BEFORE STEPS

📱032

LINING CRAG

CAIRN

GREAT VIEWS OF SCAFELL AND BACK TO THE COAST

CAIRN ON BOULDER 📱033

GREENUP EDGE PASS

FENCEPOST

TWIN CAIRNS 📱034

LOOK FOR TWIN CAIRNS JUST AFTER FENCEPOST AS THEY WILL SHOW START OF PATH HEADING CLEARLY DOWNHILL

⚠ ATTENTION! APPROACHING THE PASS IS BOGGY AND THE PATH FREQUENTLY DISAPPEARS. LOOK FOR THE CAIRNS

PROMINENT FENCEPOST ON TOP OF OUTCROP ON GREENUP EDGE

WYTHBURN VALLEY DO NOT GO NORTH-EAST DOWN VALLEY!

17

0 ¼ mile
0 APPROX SCALE 500m

70 MINS FROM LANGSTRATH BECK (MAP 15)

LINING CRAG

50 MINS TO FENCEPOSTS (WAYPOINT 36) (MAP 17)

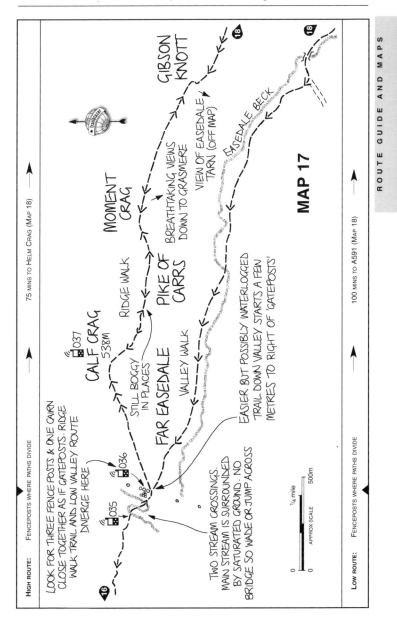

HIGH ROUTE: FENCEPOSTS WHERE PATHS DIVIDE

75 MINS TO HELM CRAG (MAP 18)

LOOK FOR THREE FENCE POSTS & ONE CAIRN CLOSE TOGETHER AS IF GATEPOSTS. RIDGE WALK TRAIL AND LOW VALLEY ROUTE DIVERGE HERE

035

036

037

CALF CRAG 538M

RIDGE WALK

STILL BOGGY IN PLACES

FAR EASEDALE

VALLEY WALK

PIKE OF CARRS

MOMENT CRAG

BREATHTAKING VIEWS DOWN TO GRASMERE

VIEW OF EASEDALE TARN (OFF MAP)

GIBSON KNOTT

18

18

EASEDALE BECK

MAP 17

EASIER BUT POSSIBLY WATERLOGGED TRAIL DOWN VALLEY STARTS A FEW METRES TO RIGHT OF 'GATEPOSTS'

TWO STREAM CROSSINGS. MAIN STREAM IS SURROUNDED BY SATURATED GROUND. NO BRIDGE SO WADE OR JUMP ACROSS

16

¼ mile

0   500m

APPROX SCALE

LOW ROUTE: FENCEPOSTS WHERE PATHS DIVIDE

100 MINS TO A591 (MAP 18)

ROUTE GUIDE AND MAPS

few metres further on, the key twin **cairns** (WPT 034) from where the descent from the Edge commences across the head of **Wythburn Valley**. You cross the upper basin of **Wythburn** on clearer tracks to more gateposts on Map 17 marking its neighbour, **Far Easedale**. From here you choose the valley route or the significantly more demanding high route which most hikers take these days, along with day trippers out of Grasmere who commonly combine both into a loop.

The ridge-walk alternative to Grasmere via Helm Crag
Map 17 p111 & Map 18

The high-level route takes in **Calf Crag**, **Gibson Knott** and **Helm Crag** amongst others. The ground is often saturated but the climbs up to the various

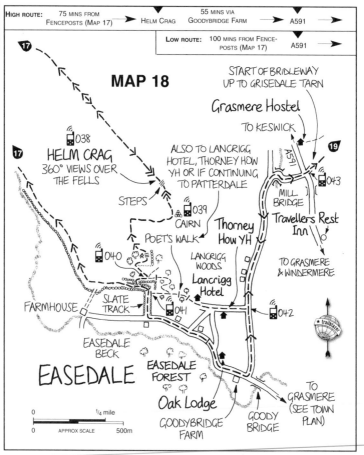

summits take only a few minutes and give some great viewpoints down to Easedale Gill and Easedale Tarn glistening below. It's a long walk with rocky steps and bogs and it can drag on for longer than you might expect. That is the price of surveying Castle, Lang and Silver Hows behind you to the south-west, and Helvellyn and Great Rigg beyond.

By the time you've reached Helm Crag overlooking the following stage, the steep descent to the north-western outskirts of Grasmere may well finish you off but once at the foot of the climb, it's worth a diversion through **Lancrigg Woods** along the **Poet's Walk** (Map 18), a tranquil delight that may soothe sore feet. It comes as no surprise to find that the Lakeland poets enjoyed it; indeed, they planted many of the trees that grow in the woods. Along the way is an inscription, in Latin, describing how Wordsworth's sister Dorothy would sit at this spot while her brother walked up and down composing verses. The path passes across the croquet lawn of Lancrigg Hotel and a minute later, the youth hostel. Here at the road the trail continues over to Patterdale, to the south a 20-minute walk leads to Grasmere, the Lake District's busiest tourist village.

GRASMERE   see map p115

Wordsworth called this valley 'the fairest place on earth' and his association with Grasmere has done so much to popularise the place that on some days you might wish you'd not paused here in your wandering o'er the hills and vales. Fleece-clad hordes stream in all summer to mill about or grab a lunch, but looking out to the glorious hills surrounding the village, you can see why. And with facilities and services that include discount hiking outlets, a cash machine, internet access and more than one shop, it can all add up to a worthwhile stopover.

All together now: '*I wandered lonely as a cloud...*' Though Wordsworth lived in Grasmere for only nine years, the period was a productive one and he wrote many of his best-known works here. His cottage is the main sight in the village and his grave is in the grounds of St Oswald's Church (see p117), one of the more peaceful spots in Grasmere's often overcrowded centre.

More spacious than the preceding valley settlements, to the west the large farmhouses and grand homes share the undulating land with forests of mature deciduous trees and flocks of dozy sheep and through the busy jumble of buildings in the centre flows the River Rothay, a tranquil haven for ducks and other waterfowl; to the south lies brooding Grasmere Lake, flanked by steep, forested hills.

Services

The **post office** (Mon-Wed & Fri 9am-5pm, Thur & Sat 9am-12.30pm) is small but central and plays host to Grasmere's only **cash machine** (£1.75, or free to Alliance & Leicester customers). Alternatively, if you have an account with certain banks and building societies (see p21) you can withdraw cash from the counter at no charge.

If the post office is closed, the **Co-op** (Mon-Sat 8.30am-8pm; Sun 10am-6pm) provides a cashback service and is the best place to stock up on provisions. Next to the Co-op is a **pharmacy** (Mon-Fri 9am-5.30pm, Sat 9am-1pm) if your Compeed supply is in peril.

There are three or four **outdoors (trekking) shops** dotted around the town centre, including Cotswold Rock Bottom near The Harwood Hotel. If you can't find what you need in one of these, take a bus (see Transport) to Ambleside, where there are plenty more.

Internet access is provided by Butharlyp Howe Youth Hostel for the usual rates, at Miller Howe Café (Easter-Oct daily 9am-6/7pm, Nov to Easter daily 9am-5pm; £1 for 15 mins, wi-fi also), opposite The Green, and at the café (Mon-Sat 9.30am-6pm, Sun 11am-5pm; customers only) inside Grasmere Garden Centre.

Where to stay

This is our selection of places to stay in Grasmere; you'll find plenty more on somewhere like ⌨ www.grasmere.com. Being Grasmere, with all the tourist business it can handle, B&Bs will be very reluctant to accept a one-night-only booking on summer weekends. Either stay for two nights or try to avoid the high-season weekends. Single occupancy incurs particularly high surcharges.

Hostels There are two YHA hostels (☎ 0845 371 9319, ⌨ grasmere@yha.org.uk) in Grasmere: *Thorney How* (Map 18, p112; 49 beds; from £13.95) and *Butharlyp Howe* (80 beds; from £17.95). The former is right on the route, though a 15-minute walk from central Grasmere, however the latter is the pick of the two as it is both larger and in a more central location and has internet access, a licence, a smarter self-catering kitchen and more attractive grounds. The food is superior here too. Be warned, however, that because it's the larger it tends to attract school groups, making Thorney How by far the more preferable on these days. Note that in the winter (Nov to mid-Feb) Thorney How is closed to individuals and Butharlyp is open at weekends only. Credit cards are accepted in both hostels.

There's also the great, independent *Grasmere Hostel* (Map 18, p112; ☎ 015394 35055, ⌨ www.grasmerehostel.co.uk; 24 beds) on the main A road north of the village near where the path crosses it. This is a plush joint with features including fully equipped kitchen, a drying room, a really pleasant residents' lounge and even a Nordic sauna. Dorms are either en suite or have a private bathroom and they contain no more than six beds; £19.50pp. However, it is important to note that the hostel focuses on group rather than individual bookings and for that reason individuals cannot book more than six weeks in advance and cannot stay here at weekends. Also, camping is not available.

B&Bs *Oak Lodge* (Map 18, p112; ☎ 015394 35527, ⌨ www.oaklodge-grasmere.co.uk; 2D/1T, all en suite, one room

with bath) is the first place you see as you enter Grasmere on Easedale Rd. It's a very smart little establishment in a wonderful location next to tranquil Easedale Forest and charges from £32 per person.

Silver Lea (☎ 015394 35657, ⌨ www.silverlea.com; 2T or D/2D, all en suite, most with bath), on Easedale Rd, is a charming ivy-clad slate cottage, surprisingly bright inside, where each room has a digital TV as well as, like most places, tea-/coffee-making facilities. Rates are from £44pp for a twin or double, or £48pp for a room with a lounge.

On a few metres towards the centre, the large *Glenthorne* (☎ 015394 35389, ⌨ www.glenthorne.org; Feb-Dec; 7S/12T/4D, most en suite, bath available) is a Victorian, Quaker country house (though folk of any creed can stay) next to another of Wordsworth's old houses, Allan Bank. Though the place feels like a hostel when you first walk in – thanks in part to the wonderfully informal atmosphere to the place – the rooms are fine. Overriding everything, however, is this place's hospitality, with trays of cakes and tea laid out for guests at 4.30pm. Evening meals are offered for £14.50; all they ask is a minute's silence before eating. Packed lunches are also available. There is a voluntary 15-minute (30 mins on Sundays) prayer meeting in the mornings. Rates are £36-42 per person and yes, they do offer porridge for breakfast though it may be necessary to request it in the summer months.

Beck Allans (☎ 015394 35563, ⌨ www.beckallans.com; 5D, all en suite with bath) is a guesthouse overlooking the Rothay. It lies in the heart of the village next to the Wordsworth Hotel (see Hotels), whose pool and gym facilities residents at Beck Allans are allowed to use, though there is a charge. All rooms (£37-43pp) come with TV, tea- and coffee-making facilities, hair dryer – and room No 2 has a four-poster bed. Note that they generally don't take one-night bookings, dogs are not allowed, and there's a single occupancy surcharge of 50 per cent. They also have some self-catering apartments but these are mostly available as weekly lets only. *Lake View Country*

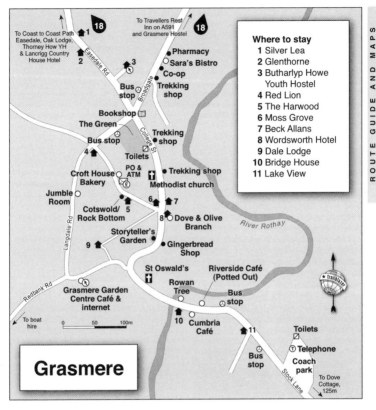

To Travellers Rest
Inn on A591
and Grasmere Hostel

To Coast to Coast Path
Easedale, Oak Lodge,
Thorney How YH
& Lancrigg Country
House Hotel

Where to stay
1 Silver Lea
2 Glenthorne
3 Butharlyp Howe
   Youth Hostel
4 Red Lion
5 The Harwood
6 Moss Grove
7 Beck Allans
8 Wordsworth Hotel
9 Dale Lodge
10 Bridge House
11 Lake View

Pharmacy
Sara's Bistro
Co-op
Trekking
shop

Easedale Rd
Broadgale

Bus
stop

Bookshop
The Green
Bus stop

College St

Trekking
shop

Toilets

PO &
ATM

Croft House
Bakery

Trekking shop
Methodist church

Jumble
Room

Cotswold/
Rock Bottom

Langdale Rd

Storyteller's
Garden

Dove & Olive
Branch

River Rothay

Gingerbread
Shop

St Oswald's

Riverside Café
(Potted Out)

Rowan
Tree

Bus
stop

Redbank Rd

Grasmere Garden
Centre Café &
internet

To boat
hire

0   50   100m

Cumbria
Café

trailblazer

Toilets

Telephone

Coach
park

Bus
stop

Stock Lane

To Dove
Cottage,
125m

Grasmere

House (☎ 015394 35384, 🖥 www.lake
view-grasmere.co.uk; 3D/1T, all en suite,
bath available) is, as its name suggests, one
of the few places to stay from where you
can actually see the lake (from the first
floor). It's a lovely place near the centre of
Grasmere but quietly tucked away at the
end of a lane. Rates are £45.50-52.50pp; no
discount for single occupancy. Stays of two
nights are required except in the winter
months. Dogs are welcome.

Hotels *Moss Grove Organic Hotel* (☎
015394 35251, 🖥 www.mossgrove.com;
10D/1D or T, all en suite with bath and
shower) is a smashing place whose strict

green ethos extends beyond the kitchen to
their accommodation, with beds made from
reclaimed timber sitting atop oak floors
from sustainable forests. All this, and yet
the building still retains its original
Victorian charm. The prices, however, do
reflect the quality, with rooms costing from
£125 (Sun-Thur in the cheaper executive
rooms) up to £250 on a Friday or Saturday.
There is a £15 single occupancy discount.
Breakfast is organic; they do not have a bar
or restaurant.

Red Lion Hotel (☎ 015394 35456, 🖥
www.bestwestern.co.uk; 6T/41D, all en
suite, most with bath and shower) *is* the
centre of town; it's a pleasant-enough place

though one that lacks a little of the charm of some of the other places around here. Rates start at around £70pp (single occupancy £70-105) and do not include breakfast (£9.50) but special rates are sometimes available. Dogs cost £20, regardless of length of stay.

A few metres on down the road, tucked away on a corner across from Cotswold Rock Bottom trekking shop, *The Harwood Hotel* (☎ 015394 35248, 🖳 www.harwood hotel.co.uk; 6D, all en suite most with bath) has been extensively made over into something more fitting of Grasmere, with rooms from £135 per room (less out of season).

Nearby *Dale Lodge Hotel* (☎ 015394 35300, 🖳 www.dalelodgehotel.co.uk; 1T/ 15D, all en suite, some with bath) is a huge, rambling place. An old-fashioned-looking pile on the outside, inside it is all polished floorboards and original tilework and really rather chic. The three acres of sprawling gardens are another attraction, as is its location in the heart of town. Each bedroom is individually decorated and has TV and tea-making facilities. Dogs are allowed for £25 regardless of length of stay. The attached bar, Tweedies (daily noon-11pm or midnight; food served noon-3pm & 6-9pm), is also recommended. Rates start at £100 for a room with breakfast. Single occupancy costs about the same.

The Wordsworth Hotel (☎ 015394 35592, 🖳 www.thewordsworthhotel.co.uk; 3S/11D/22D or T – two with four-poster beds – and two suites; all en suite with bath) was formerly the smartest address in the centre of town, a large but attractive hotel with facilities including gym, pool, sauna, Jacuzzi and cocktail bar. Rooms come with a satellite flat-screen TV, radio, wi-fi and phone. Rates for B&B are £75pp for two sharing, £70 for a single.

Bridge House Hotel (☎ 015394 35425, 🖳 www.bridgehousegrasmere.co .uk; 9D/9D or T, all en suite, most with bath) is another large place near the river; all rooms have the usual facilities. Rates for DB&B are £62-70pp in summer. There is a single occupancy supplement of 1.8% of the per person rate. Unfortunately, they accept one-night bookings only if it's quiet

which, in summer, is unlikely. They also don't allow dogs (apart from guide dogs) which makes the two acres of gorgeous grounds all the more enjoyable.

If you stick to the path via Poet's Walk you'll walk right past *Lancrigg Vegetarian Country House Hotel* (Map 18, p112; ☎ 015394 35317, 🖳 www.lancrigg.co.uk; 10D/2T and a double room in the annexe; all en suite with bath), a large country house with parts dating back to the 17th century. The ambience is rather more conventional 'genteel' than 'vegetarian' in any alternative sense, but in Grasmere £100pp for DB&B is actually not so bad. Like so many fancy Grasmere hotels it's not really a walkers' place but we have no reservations about the food: dinner or breakfast, if what you eat here doesn't get your palate dancing the cancan across the croquet lawn well, at least you tried. The 'organic' restaurant (daily 1-3pm & 6.30-8.30pm, to 7.30pm in winter) is open to non residents.

Where to eat and drink
As you'd expect for a major tourist centre like Grasmere, cafés and restaurants are plentiful throughout the village. Best of all is *The Jumble Room* (☎ 015394 35188, 🖳 www.thejumbleroom.co.uk; summer Wed-Mon 5pm 'till food runs out'; winter Wed-Sun 5pm 'till the food runs out', though check in advance particularly in Dec-Jan; booking advisable), on Langdale Rd. Aptly named, this is a refreshingly quirky little place that resembles an art gallery. Don't be put off, however, for the food is some of the most imaginative in town. The menu changes frequently and includes dishes from all four corners of the globe with a few extra corners you never knew about, including the locally inspired haddock in beer batter for £12.95.

For sandwiches you can't really beat *Croft House Bakery* (Mon-Sat 9am-4pm, Sun 9.30am-4pm), next to the post office; it also does a nice line in pasties, baguettes and butties.

Another place that's open during the day is the *Rowan Tree* (☎ 015394 35528; daily 10am-4.30pm, Wed-Sun Dec & Jan hours depend on demand), overlooking the river. However, our advice is to save a visit until the evening (Feb-Nov 5.30-8.30pm, closed Sun), when they do a fine selection of pizzas from £7.50 and other Italian or English dishes.

A number of other cafés vie for position near the bridge including the contemporary *Riverside Café*, aka *Potted Out* (daily 10am-5.30pm), an offshoot of the Garden Centre café (see p113), and *Cumbria Café* (daily 9am-5pm, Tue-Sun 6pm to late) which does an excellent-value Yorkshire pudding for £3.95.

The *Dove and Olive Branch* (noon-2pm & 6-9pm), part of Wordsworth Hotel (see Where to stay), is a typically upmarket place with an interesting menu, including roasted pork belly for £13.95.

On Broadgate, *Sara's Bistro* (☎ 015394 35266; May-Nov Tue-Sun 10.30am-4pm & 6-9pm; days/hours vary at other times) has also been recommended for its exquisite food.

Finally, at least a 20-minute walk north from town, the *Traveller's Rest Inn* (Map 18, p112; ☎ 0500 600725, 🖳 www.lake districtinns.co.uk/travellers_welcome.cfm; food served Feb-Oct daily all day in the main season, other times noon-2pm & 5-9.30pm) serves hearty portions of mainly local dishes.

What to see

Dove Cottage William Wordsworth lived for less than ten years in beautiful Dove Cottage (☎ 015394 35544, 🖳 www.words worth.org.uk; Mar-Oct daily 9.30am-5pm, Nov-Feb 9.30am-4pm, closed 24-26 Dec and Jan; £7.50, children £4.50; student/ YHA member discounts available; about 500m walk south-east from The Green, just off the A591, yet its importance in both his development as a poet and his life is enormous. Many of his best-loved and most-powerful works were penned here and this is where he first lived with his wife Mary Hutchinson and where his first three children were born.

Today all but the first room is furnished entirely with items owned by the poet, though some have come from other Wordsworth properties. Guides show visitors around the cottage, pointing out such items as Wordsworth's famous **suitcase** (where he's carefully sewn his name inside but didn't leave enough room for the final 'h' tucked up in the corner); a letter of introduction – a precursor to the modern-day passport – penned by the French authorities, and which has been stamped on the back by the border guards of a host of European countries; and the **Royal Warrant** of 1843 in which he was bestowed with the honour of being Queen Victoria's poet laureate. It was an honour he accepted grudgingly, having already turned down the position twice, and one that he never truly fulfilled; indeed, from his acceptance of the post to his death in 1850, Wordsworth wrote precisely no official poems as poet laureate, the first (and so far only) poet laureate to do so.

The cottage is, by the standards of the Lake District, relatively large, containing eight rooms rather than the more typical three or four, thus betraying its origins as a 17th-century pub. One of Wordsworth's frequent visitors at the cottage was that other well-known literary figure (and opium fiend) Thomas de Quincey. De Quincey declared the house to be a fortuitous one for writers and when the Wordsworths vacated it in 1808 the de Quinceys moved in, thus continuing the literary connections of the place.

The **museum** next door contains original manuscripts by both Wordsworth and de Quincey and stages frequent special exhibitions.

Other sights Before you leave Grasmere, you may like to pay a visit to **Wordsworth's family grave** around the back of **St Oswald's**, a 13th-century church named after the 7th-century king of Northumbria who preached on this site. Wordsworth's prayer-book is on display in the church.

Standing by the side entrance to the church grounds is the 150-year-old **Gingerbread Shop** (☎ 015394 35428, 🖳 www.grasmeregingerbread.co.uk; Apr-Oct Mon-Sat 9.15am-5.30pm, Sun 12.30-

5.30pm; Nov-Mar to 5pm), a tiny 'factory' that, incredibly, used to be the local school. It is said that Wordsworth taught here occasionally.

Opposite is the **Storyteller's Garden** (🖥 www.taffythomas.co.uk) which hosts several events throughout the year – ask at the tourist office for a schedule.

Around the village centre are a number of **galleries** displaying works by local artists.

Make sure, too, that you check out Lancrigg Woods and the Poet's Walk (Map 18, p112), the start of which you walked past on your way into Grasmere.

Transport (see also pp52-5)
From Easter to October Stagecoach's open-top No 599 **bus** service travels regularly via Ambleside (15 mins) and the train station and Bowness Pier at Windermere (25 mins), from where in the evening a few buses go on to Kendal. Their No 555 goes from Keswick to Lancaster via Ambleside, Windermere and Kendal (Grasmere to Lancaster takes 1hr 50mins). Buses leave from The Green.

For other destinations, Grasmere **Taxis** can be reached on ☎ 015394 35506.

STAGE 4: GRASMERE TO PATTERDALE   MAPS 18-25

Introduction

Ignoring the alternative routes for the moment, this is the shortest of our stages. Short, but no less sweet for it's another classic hike along which walkers can enjoy some great views back to Grasmere and, once over the pass, down across Grisedale to Patterdale, another gorgeous valley with the lake of Ullswater twinkling away to the north.

The most direct routes avoiding Striding Edge are a mere **7½ miles (12km, 3-4hrs)** and add up to a simple walk up to **Grisedale Pass** and either down the valley or more satisfyingly, up along the ridge of St Sunday Crag. The longer route ascends the 969-metre bulk of Helvellyn, returning to the valley via the stirringly named Striding Edge ridge walk; an additional distance of around **two miles** and a considerable amount of climbing and at times, exposure. Both the high routes are described on pp120-3. You can delay your choice on which path to take until Grisedale Tarn, where the three paths go their separate ways.

The route

First of all you need to reach Grisedale Tarn, which either involves a protracted climb up a bridleway running off the A591 (Map 18, p112) reached by walking up the A591 to the bridleway from Grasmere or, as we've mapped it, picking up the original Coast to Coast path near Thorney How Youth Hostel.

Once off the road the bridleway soon divides at the foot of **Great Tongue** (Map 19) into a steeper route alongside **Little Tongue Gill** with views back down to Grasmere. The less steep path to the east of Great Tongue along Tongue Gill is slabbed for part of its length but anyway, you're still climbing to the same elevation where the two paths rejoin.

At the top of the climb you arrive at the pretty mountain lake of **Grisedale Tarn** (Map 20) with the trail zigzagging up **Dollywaggon Pike** towards Helvellyn. Keeping to the easier path down Grisedale valley, the descent is as uncomplicated as the ascent, with the **Brothers' Parting Stone** just below the

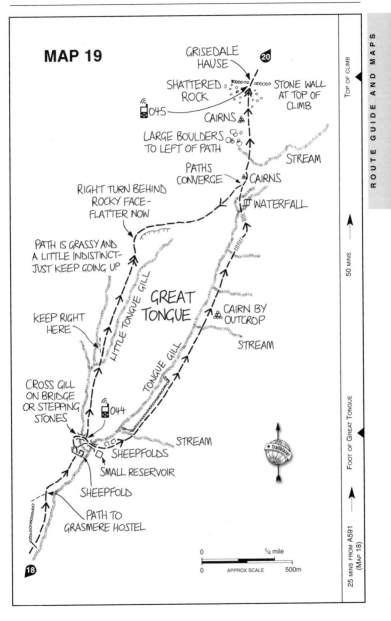

MAP 19

GRISEDALE HAUSE

20

SHATTERED ROCK

STONE WALL AT TOP OF CLIMB

045

CAIRNS

LARGE BOULDERS TO LEFT OF PATH

STREAM

PATHS CONVERGE

CAIRNS

RIGHT TURN BEHIND ROCKY FACE – FLATTER NOW

WATERFALL

PATH IS GRASSY AND A LITTLE INDISTINCT – JUST KEEP GOING UP

LITTLE TONGUE GILL

GREAT TONGUE

KEEP RIGHT HERE

CAIRN BY OUTCROP

TONGUE GILL

STREAM

CROSS GILL ON BRIDGE OR STEPPING STONES

044

STREAM

SHEEPFOLDS

SMALL RESERVOIR

SHEEPFOLD

PATH TO GRASMERE HOSTEL

18

0   ¼ mile

0   500m

APPROX SCALE

TOP OF CLIMB

50 MINS

FOOT OF GREAT TONGUE

25 MINS FROM A591 (MAP 18)

tarn (so-called because it's said that here in 1800 Wordsworth last met with his brother John, who died at sea a few years later). Just under a mile further on by Ruthwaite Beck, **Ruthwaite Lodge** is a usually locked-up climbers' hut.

The path continues down the valley and briefly joins a tarmac road (Map 24) where the Helvellyn route comes in, before leaving it to the right to enter the National Trust's **Glenamara Park** (and where the St Sunday route converges), with some wonderful views over Patterdale and beyond to Ullswater (Norse for 'Water with a Bend'). All being well, you'll drop onto the road just below the post office and pub just over two hours' walking after leaving Grisedale Tarn.

The high-level options: Helvellyn & Striding Edge; St Sunday Crag
If weather conditions allow, one of these two high-level routes should be seriously considered. After all, it would be a shame on this, the penultimate stage in the Lake District, if you didn't try to climb as many peaks as possible.

Helvellyn & Striding Edge   Map 20, Maps 22-24 pp123-4
Of the two high-level options, **Helvellyn**, at 950m (3113ft) the third highest peak in England after Scafell Pike and Scafell, is understandably the more popular. The climb is arduous and, having reached the top, you then face a nerve-tingling drop on a crumbing slope above Red Tarn, followed by a knife-edge walk along Striding Edge ridge to reach the trail dropping to Patterdale; the memorial plaque to Robert Dixon who was killed here in 1858 whilst following his fox hounds during a hunt does little to calm the nerves but with a steady head and light winds the sense of achievement is ample reward for your efforts.

Wainwright himself waxes lyrical about this side trip, describing the notorious Striding Edge as the 'best quarter mile between St Bees and Robin Hood's Bay'. He visited Helvellyn on his first trip to the Lakes in 1930, and it was this trip that inspired his passion for the Lakes. He approached the peak from the opposite direction to that given here and he edged along it 'in agonies of apprehension'.

This route takes about 3hrs 15 mins from Grisedale Tarn to Patterdale, though that assumes you take the lower route just below the knife-edge crest of Striding Edge which can be traversed in as little as 20 minutes. However, with the inevitable waiting that needs to be done to let people coming the other way go by (at least at weekends), expect it to take nearer an hour. You won't regret the extra time – it is truly exhilarating.

St Sunday Crag   Map 20, Map 21 p122, Map 23 p123, Map 24 p124
It's said that better views, if fewer thrills, lie in wait on the south side of the valley along St Sunday Crag. Indeed, for many people these are the best views on the entire route. What's more, the effort required to climb up to St Sunday is, by the standards of the lakes, fairly negligible, a steady plod away from the Tarn followed by a reasonably steady descent, at least until the sudden drop into Glenamara Park.

Soon after leaving Grisedale Tarn, you'll see a trail rising away from the lake, presently joined by the usual path from the tarn's mouth (WPT 046). You join the ridge at Deepdale Hause and soon arrive at the high point known as

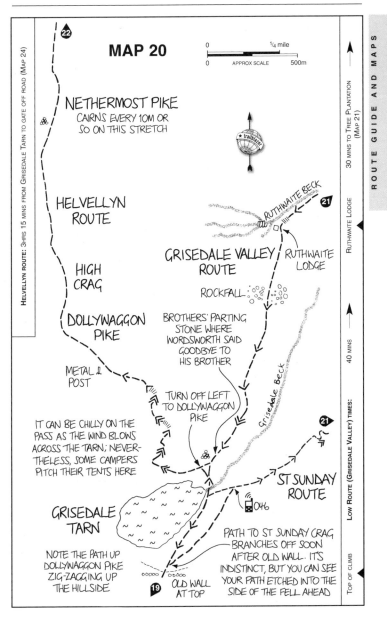

MAP 20

0   ¼ mile

0   APPROX SCALE   500m

22

NETHERMOST PIKE
CAIRNS EVERY 10M OR
SO ON THIS STRETCH

HELVELLYN ROUTE: 3HRS 15 MINS FROM GRISEDALE TARN TO GATE OFF ROAD (MAP 24)

HELVELLYN
ROUTE

HIGH
CRAG

DOLLYWAGGON
PIKE

METAL
POST

IT CAN BE CHILLY ON THE
PASS AS THE WIND BLOWS
ACROSS THE TARN; NEVER-
THELESS, SOME CAMPERS
PITCH THEIR TENTS HERE

GRISEDALE
TARN

NOTE THE PATH UP
DOLLYWAGGON PIKE
ZIG-ZAGGING UP
THE HILLSIDE

RUTHWAITE BECK

21

GRISEDALE VALLEY
ROUTE

ROCKFALL

RUTHWAITE
LODGE

BROTHERS' PARTING
STONE WHERE
WORDSWORTH SAID
GOODBYE TO
HIS BROTHER

TURN OFF LEFT
TO DOLLYWAGGON
PIKE

Grisedale Beck

21

ST SUNDAY
ROUTE

046

19

OLD WALL
AT TOP

PATH TO ST SUNDAY CRAG
BRANCHES OFF SOON
AFTER OLD WALL. IT'S
INDISTINCT, BUT YOU CAN SEE
YOUR PATH ETCHED INTO THE
SIDE OF THE FELL AHEAD

30 MINS TO TREE PLANTATION
(MAP 21)

RUTHWAITE LODGE

40 MINS

Low ROUTE (GRISEDALE VALLEY) TIMES:

TOP OF CLIMB

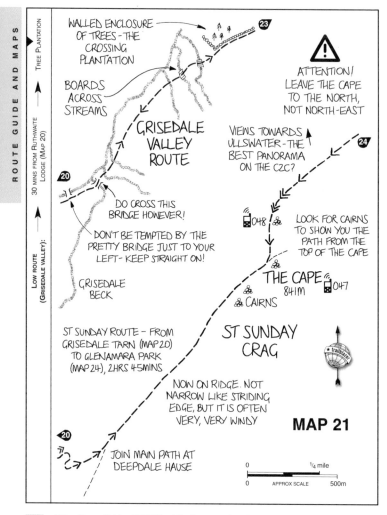

ROUTE GUIDE AND MAPS

TREE PLANTATION

30 MINS FROM RUTHWAITE LODGE (MAP 20)

LOW ROUTE (GRISEDALE VALLEY):

WALLED ENCLOSURE OF TREES - THE CROSSING PLANTATION

23

BOARDS ACROSS STREAMS

ATTENTION! LEAVE THE CAPE TO THE NORTH, NOT NORTH-EAST

GRISEDALE VALLEY ROUTE

VIEWS TOWARDS ULLSWATER - THE BEST PANORAMA ON THE C2C?

24

20

DO CROSS THIS BRIDGE HOWEVER!

DON'T BE TEMPTED BY THE PRETTY BRIDGE JUST TO YOUR LEFT - KEEP STRAIGHT ON!

048

LOOK FOR CAIRNS TO SHOW YOU THE PATH FROM THE TOP OF THE CAPE

THE CAPE 047
841M

GRISEDALE BECK

CAIRNS

ST SUNDAY ROUTE - FROM GRISEDALE TARN (MAP 20) TO GLENAMARA PARK (MAP 24), 2HRS 45MINS

ST SUNDAY CRAG

trailblazer

NOW ON RIDGE. NOT NARROW LIKE STRIDING EDGE, BUT IT IS OFTEN VERY, VERY WINDY

MAP 21

20

JOIN MAIN PATH AT DEEPDALE HAUSE

0 .... 1/4 mile
0 .... 500m
APPROX SCALE

The Cape (841m/2759ft). All along you've fine views of the next stage; a ramp rising steadily past briefly glimpsed Angle Tarn to Kidsty Pike and the unseen depths of Haweswater beyond.

From The Cape make sure you walk briefly north and not east for Gavel Pike. Then at a cairn the path continues north-east before dropping off the ridge and tumbling down to Glenamara Park, where you meet up with the low-level route and enter Patterdale.

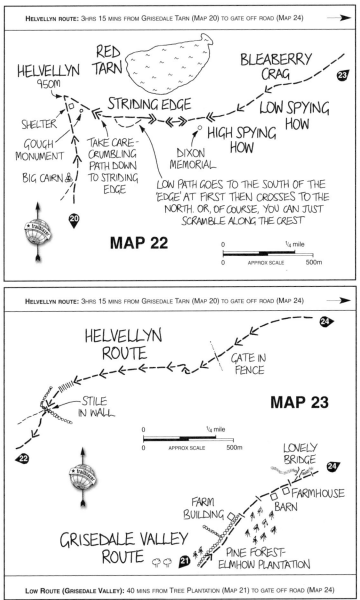

HELVELLYN ROUTE: 3HRS 15 MINS FROM GRISEDALE TARN (MAP 20) TO GATE OFF ROAD (MAP 24) →

RED TARN

HELVELLYN
950M

BLEABERRY CRAG

23

STRIDING EDGE

LOW SPYING HOW

SHELTER

HIGH SPYING HOW

GOUGH MONUMENT

TAKE CARE - CRUMBLING PATH DOWN TO STRIDING EDGE

DIXON MEMORIAL

BIG CAIRN

20

LOW PATH GOES TO THE SOUTH OF THE 'EDGE' AT FIRST THEN CROSSES TO THE NORTH. OR, OF COURSE, YOU CAN JUST SCRAMBLE ALONG THE CREST

MAP 22

0 ¼ mile
0 APPROX SCALE 500m

HELVELLYN ROUTE: 3HRS 15 MINS FROM GRISEDALE TARN (MAP 20) TO GATE OFF ROAD (MAP 24) →

HELVELLYN ROUTE

24

GATE IN FENCE

STILE IN WALL

MAP 23

0 ¼ mile
0 APPROX SCALE 500m

22

LOVELY BRIDGE

24

FARM BUILDING

FARMHOUSE

BARN

GRISEDALE VALLEY ROUTE

21

PINE FOREST - ELMHOW PLANTATION

LOW ROUTE (GRISEDALE VALLEY): 40 MINS FROM TREE PLANTATION (MAP 21) TO GATE OFF ROAD (MAP 24)

ROUTE GUIDE AND MAPS

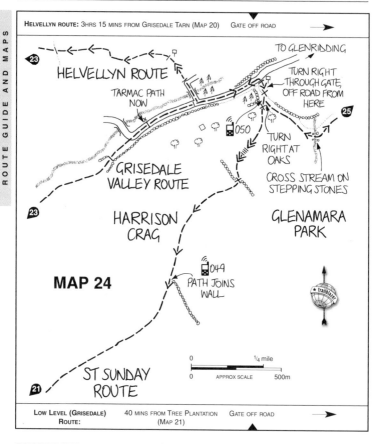

HELVELLYN ROUTE: 3HRS 15 MINS FROM GRISEDALE TARN (MAP 20) GATE OFF ROAD ➡️

23

HELVELLYN ROUTE

TARMAC PATH NOW

TO GLENRIDDING

TURN RIGHT THROUGH GATE, OFF ROAD FROM HERE

📱050

25

GRISEDALE VALLEY ROUTE

TURN RIGHT AT OAKS

CROSS STREAM ON STEPPING STONES

23

HARRISON CRAG

GLENAMARA PARK

MAP 24

📱049
PATH JOINS WALL

trailblazer

0   ¼ mile
0   APPROX SCALE   500m

ST SUNDAY ROUTE

21

LOW LEVEL (GRISEDALE) ROUTE: 40 MINS FROM TREE PLANTATION (MAP 21)   GATE OFF ROAD ➡️

PATTERDALE   MAP 25, p127

Patterdale is little more than a meandering collection of houses strung along the A592. Normally valleys this beautiful would be full of souvenir shops and tearooms. But Patterdale, while not exactly undiscovered, is mercifully free of the crowds which congregate around Grasmere.

The **fountain of St Patrick** (Patterdale is a corruption of St Patrick's Dale) is an ornate Victorian construction set in a bank by the side of the road just outside Glenridding, and is said to mark the spot where the saint baptised the locals.

The valley is also something of a **wildlife** haven, including a population of red squirrels – some of the last remaining in England – and badgers (see p61).

And finally there's **Crookabeck** (ring first for an appointment on ☎ 017684 82742, 🖥 www.crookabeck.co.uk), a farm selling products made from the wool sheared from their flocks of sheep and goats, as well as knitkits.

The only official tourist office (see box opposite) is in Glenridding, but besides Patterdale's community website

(🖳 www.patterdale.org) all your other needs will be met at **Patterdale Village Store** (summer daily 8.30am-6pm, winter to 5.30pm, to noon on Wed & Sun; 🖳 www .patterdalevillagestore.co.uk). Gillian and Tom run one of the best-provisioned village stores along the route and one which, unlike so many others, doesn't look as if it'll be closing down anytime soon.

The shop includes a **post office** (Mon & Tue 8.30am-5.30pm, Wed & Thurs 8.30am to noon), a large variety of hot and cold sandwiches including bacon rolls fit to choke a hog, as well as a lavish array of groceries for those camping, staying in the hostel or just unable to resist temptation. There are also maps and Coast to Coast path souvenirs and maybe even copies of this book.

Both the shop and the post office have **cashback** facilities and outside is a walkers' **message board** plus reams of information on local lodgings, bus times, phone numbers and so on.

Where to stay and eat

There's a range of **accommodation** in Patterdale, though this being the Lakes, booking ahead is vital if you don't want to end up lying in a ditch with a red squirrel for a duvet. Remember, the next stage to Shap is commonly agreed to be the toughest on the Coast to Coast walk, so you'll want to be on form. If you run out of luck in Patterdale, there's more accommodation in Glenridding (see box below); it's listed on the **community website** mentioned opposite, or outside the shop.

For **campers**, across Goldrill Beck is *Side Farm* (☎ 017684 82337; £6 per person; Easter to Oct). The campsite actually lies a little way beyond the farm on the edge of the lake. They insist you check-in at the farm first; also they do not take advance bookings and over bank holiday weekends require a minimum stay of three nights. However, considering they have a **tearoom** (Easter to Oct, school holidays daily 10.30am-5pm; hours vary at other times), it's a great place to recuperate before pitching your tent. And

---

❏ Ullswater and Glenridding

I wandered lonely as a cloud,
That floats on high o'er vales and hills,
When all at once I saw a crowd,
A host of golden daffodils,
Beside the lake, beneath the trees,
Fluttering and dancing in the breeze.
William Wordsworth, *Daffodils*

It is said that Wordsworth was inspired to write these words after a trip to Ullswater. Certainly it's a beautiful lake and unlike neighbouring Grasmere and Haweswater there's plenty to do *on* the water too.

There is a **tourist information centre** (☎ 017684 82414, 🖳 ullswater tic@lake-district.gov.uk) in the main car park in Glenridding; it is open daily 9.30am-5.30pm March until the end of October and at weekends (roughly 9.30am-3.30pm, though phone first to check) only the rest of the year. On the board outside they put up a list of B&Bs with vacancies that evening, which could prove invaluable.

Boats (motorboats) can be hired from the café at the lake's southern corner. These boats are fine, though don't try to emulate Donald Campbell, who broke the 200mph water speed record on Ullswater in 1955.

For something more sedate, hire a rowing boat, or you can take a cruise on a **steamer** (☎ 017684 82229; 🖳 www.ullswater-steamers.co.uk). There have been steamers on the lake since 1859 and two of the four boats currently in service, *Lady of the Lake* and *Raven*, have been operating since the late 19th century. Services operate year-round 3-9/day) to Howton, Pooley Bridge and back.

For further details of accommodation, activities and events around Ullswater see 🖳 www.ullswater.co.uk.

just in case you thought you'd heard the last of him, it's said our old friend Wordsworth was a regular visitor to Side Farm.

On the other end of the village, *Patterdale Youth Hostel* (☎ 0845 371 9337, 🖳 patterdale@yha.org.uk; 82 beds; from £11.95) is on the main road. The 1970s building may not win any design awards, but inside has been refitted comfortably and, unusually, is open all day. Credit cards are accepted.

Just before the hostel, *Old Water View* (☎ 01768 482175, 🖳 www.oldwaterview .co.uk; 4D/1T/1F, all en suite some with bath) is a wonderful place and a favourite of Wainwright's. The current owner is a mine of information regarding the walk and is also the guy to speak to about short-cuts along High St to Shap. The accommodation itself has some nice touches including free internet access, but they insist on two nights on Fridays and Saturdays; rates are £35-42 per person for two sharing (single occupancy supplement £10 and only available in some rooms in the low season).

Very close to the path and the focus of the village is the 19th-century *White Lion* pub (☎ 01768 482214, 🖳 www.patterdale .org/Whitelion.htm; 1S/1S or D/2D/3T, all with private shower facilities). **B&B** starts at £36pp and they do **bar meals** (daily noon-9pm) too. The extensive menu includes steaks, curry and fish & chips; whatever dish you choose, it will be big! They also do **breakfasts** (Apr-Sep from 9am) for non-residents.

The smartest and most expensive lodgings in the village are at *Patterdale Hotel* (☎ 01768 482231, 🖳 www.patterdaleho tel.co.uk; 4S/10T/39D/4F, all en suite; most with bath). Part of a chain, it's an enormous establishment and their reluctance to accept bookings for anything less than two-night stays may deter trekkers; however, they are happy to take one-night bookings if there is a vacancy near the time. Unravelling the tariff takes a degree in metaphysics, but

expect to pay around £85 for DB&B for two sharing, from £70 for B&B with small discounts if booked early or if you're staying for more than two nights. **Food** is served daily noon-5pm & 6-8pm (6.30-8.30pm at weekends).

There are other B&Bs further south along the road beyond the youth hostel. Less than a mile south of the path, *Noran Bank Farm* (☎ 01768 482327, 🖳 www .patterdale.org/Noranbank.htm; 1F with private bathroom) is a whitewashed 16th-century farmhouse. Rates are £25-30pp; packed lunches available on request. Another old farmhouse, *Greenbank Farm* (☎ 017684 82292, 🖳 www.coast2coast.co .uk/greenbankfarm; 1S/1D/1D, T or F, shared shower facilities; Mar-Sep or Oct) is nearby, a working sheep farm charging £22.50-30pp and £12 for an evening meal (book in advance); packed lunches are about £4.50. Just after Greenbank Farm is *Deepdale Hall* (☎ 01768 482369, 🖳 www .deepdalehall.co.uk, 1D/1F, both with private facilities, bath available; closed Dec-Feb) with B&B from £40 per person and £65 for single occupancy.

Grisedale Lodge (☎ 01768 482155, 🖳 www.grisedalelodge.co.uk; 2D/2D or T, all with private facilities, one with bath) is set halfway between Patterdale and Glenridding villages, close to the shores of Ullswater. It's a lovely location and by all accounts a lovely B&B too, with swish rooms and large breakfasts. Rates are from £35pp, (£45 single occupancy Sun-Thurs only; full rate for two at weekends).

Transport (see also pp52-5)

Stagecoach's **Bus** No 517 (Kirkstone Rambler) is a seasonal and limited service between Windermere's Bowness Pier and Glenridding via Patterdale Hotel. Their No 108 (Patterdale Bus) travels to Penrith railway station and operates Mon-Sat year-round and on Sundays April to late August.

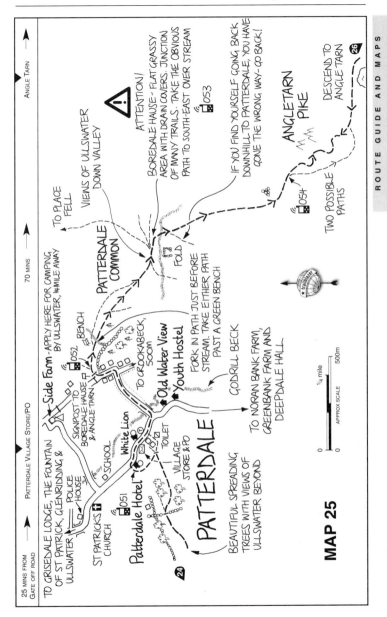

MAP 25

25 MINS FROM GATE OFF ROAD ➤ PATTERDALE VILLAGE STORE/PO ➤ 70 MINS ➤ ANGLE TARN ➤

TO GRISEDALE LODGE, THE FOUNTAIN OF ST PATRICK, GLENRIDDING & ULLSWATER

Side Farm - APPLY HERE FOR CAMPING, BY ULLSWATER, ¼ MILE AWAY

St PATRICK'S CHURCH

POLICE HOUSE

SIGNPOST TO BOREDALE HAUSE & ANGLE TARN

SCHOOL

White Lion

Patterdale Hotel

051

VILLAGE STORE & PO

TOILET

PATTERDALE

24

BEAUTIFUL SPREADING TREES WITH VIEWS OF ULLSWATER BEYOND

BENCH

052

TO CROOKABECK, 500M

Old Water View Youth Hostel

FORK IN PATH JUST BEFORE STREAM. TAKE EITHER PATH PAST A GREEN BENCH

GODRILL BECK

TO NORAN BANK FARM, GREENBANK FARM AND DEEPDALE HALL

PATTERDALE COMMON

VIEWS OF ULLSWATER DOWN VALLEY

TO PLACE FELL

ATTENTION!

BOREDALE HAUSE - FLAT GRASSY AREA WITH DRAIN COVERS. JUNCTION OF MANY TRAILS. TAKE THE OBVIOUS PATH TO SOUTH-EAST OVER STREAM

053

FOLD

IF YOU FIND YOURSELF GOING BACK DOWNHILL TO PATTERDALE, YOU HAVE GONE THE WRONG WAY - GO BACK!

ANGLETARN PIKE

054

TWO POSSIBLE PATHS

DESCEND TO ANGLE TARN

26

¼ mile

500m

APPROX SCALE

0

0

Trailblazer

STAGE 5: PATTERDALE TO SHAP **MAPS 25-34**

Introduction

Today is the day you leave the Lake District, but the crags, knotts, pikes and fells that have been your high-level chums for much of the past few days won't let you go without a struggle. Be prepared to feel very tired indeed at the end of this **16-mile (26km, 6¹⁄₂hr)** stage from Patterdale to Shap. The long climb up to Kidsty Pike, the gnarly descent from it to Haweswater (see box pp130-1) and the undulating trawl along the lake's edge adds up to well over **1300 metres** (4400ft) of total ascent. Together it all conspires to make the seemingly harmless spin down over field and farmland to Shap enough to curse the very name of 'Wainwright'.

With no accommodation directly on the route nor, indeed, any shops, tea-rooms or pubs, you have little choice but to grit your teeth and knuckle down to some serious long-haul trekking. To shorten the day, a few walkers now take a 1¹⁄₄ mile (2km) detour to Bampton (see p132). Otherwise, consider camping at Angle Tarn having come over from Grasmere and stocked up at Patterdale store. You won't find many more truly wild places like this in the days to come and at all other times the baggage van can carry the camping gear. *(cont'd on p132)*

ROUTE GUIDE AND MAPS

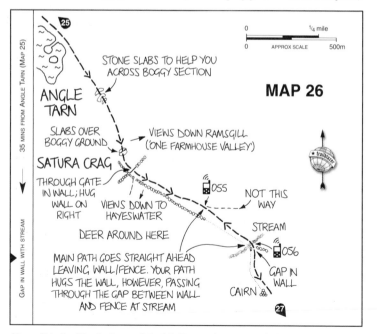

MAP 26

35 MINS FROM ANGLE TARN (MAP 25)

GAP IN WALL WITH STREAM

25

STONE SLABS TO HELP YOU ACROSS BOGGY SECTION

ANGLE TARN

SLABS OVER BOGGY GROUND

SATURA CRAG

THROUGH GATE IN WALL; HUG WALL ON RIGHT

VIEWS DOWN RAMSGILL ('ONE FARMHOUSE VALLEY')

VIEWS DOWN TO HAYESWATER

DEER AROUND HERE

MAIN PATH GOES STRAIGHT AHEAD LEAVING WALL/FENCE. YOUR PATH HUGS THE WALL, HOWEVER, PASSING THROUGH THE GAP BETWEEN WALL AND FENCE AT STREAM

055

NOT THIS WAY

STREAM

056

GAP IN WALL

CAIRN

27

0 — ¹⁄₄ mile
0 — APPROX SCALE — 500m

(**Opposite**) Looking back onto Grisedale Tarn on the ascent to St Sunday Crag on a hot summer's day and in mid-winter. (Top photo © CS, bottom photo © SG).

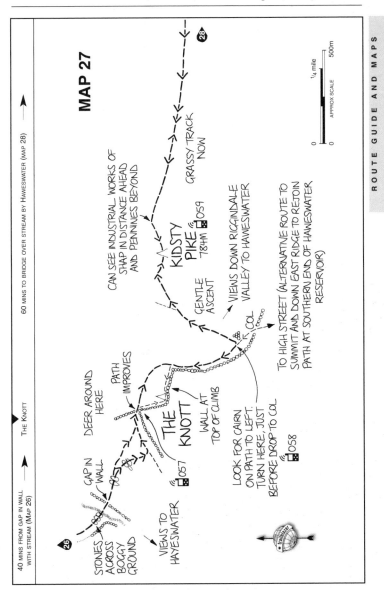

MAP 27

ROUTE GUIDE AND MAPS

CAN SEE INDUSTRIAL WORKS OF SHAP IN DISTANCE AHEAD AND PENNINES BEYOND

GRASSY TRACK NOW

KIDSTY PIKE 784M 059

VIEWS DOWN RIGGINDALE VALLEY TO HAWESWATER

GENTLE ASCENT

R. COL

TO HIGH STREET (ALTERNATIVE ROUTE TO SUMMIT AND DOWN EAST RIDGE TO REJOIN PATH AT SOUTHERN END OF HAWESWATER RESERVOIR)

PATH IMPROVES

DEER AROUND HERE

THE KNOTT

WALL AT TOP OF CLIMB

057

LOOK FOR CAIRN ON PATH TO LEFT. TURN HERE, JUST BEFORE DROP TO COL

058

GAP IN WALL

STONES ACROSS BOGGY GROUND

VIEWS TO HAWESWATER

0   ¼ mile
0   500m
APPROX SCALE

26

28

(Opposite) Top: Looking down Greenup, on the trail between Borrowdale and Grasmere; Skiddaw in the distance. Bottom: Wordsworth's Dove Cottage (see p117). (Photos © HS).

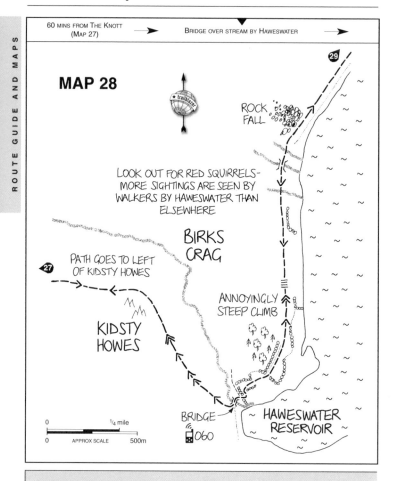

MAP 28

60 MINS FROM THE KNOTT (MAP 27) →

BRIDGE OVER STREAM BY HAWESWATER →

29

ROCK FALL

LOOK OUT FOR RED SQUIRRELS - MORE SIGHTINGS ARE SEEN BY WALKERS BY HAWESWATER THAN ELSEWHERE

BIRKS CRAG

27

PATH GOES TO LEFT OF KIDSTY HOWES

KIDSTY HOWES

ANNOYINGLY STEEP CLIMB

BRIDGE

060

HAWESWATER RESERVOIR

0   ¼ mile

0   APPROX SCALE   500m

ROUTE GUIDE AND MAPS

❑ Haweswater Reservoir
What is now one of Cumbria's largest bodies of water was once a small and fairly unassuming lake stuck on the eastern edge of the national park. In 1929, however, a bill was passed authorising the use of Haweswater as a reservoir to serve the needs of the population of Manchester. A concrete dam, 470m wide and 35m high, was constructed at the northern edge of the lake, raising the depth of the lake by over 30m and increasing the surface area to four miles long by half a mile wide (6km by 1km).

This project was not without its opponents. In particular, many protested at the loss of the settlements that had existed on Haweswater's shore for centuries. The largest of these was Mardale Green on Haweswater's eastern shore (near the pier).

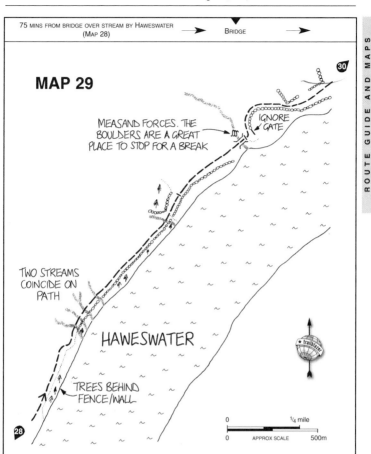

Before the village was flooded, coffins were removed from the graveyard and buried elsewhere and the 18th-century Holy Trinity Church was pulled down. Some of the windows from this church are now in the reservoir tower. Even today, during times of drought when the water level is low, the walls of Mardale emerge from the reservoir.

Despite man's interference the lake is still something of a wildlife haven. Swimming in the waters are wild brown trout, char, gwyniad and perch, while **Riggindale** is an RSPB haven, with wheatear, raven, ring ouzel and peregrine.

ROUTE GUIDE AND MAPS

The route

You'll have spotted the ramp rising up from the far side of Patterdale. After much huffing and puffing it drops you to the grassy platform known as **Boredale Hause** where the right way is actually the most obvious, continuing south-east, by one trail or another to the scalloped shoreline of Angle Tarn. The gradient levels off for a while until another haul leads up around The Knott and soon the hard-to-miss turn-off that brings you with rather less effort than you might expect to **Kidsty Pike**, at a modest 784m (2572ft) the high point on the original Coast to Coast route.

From the top, looking west, you can see the Pillar looking down onto Ennerdale Water from all those days ago, Scafell Pike, Helvellyn and St Sunday from the previous stage. To the south lie unknown lands including the deep cleft of Riggindale in whose crags is said to be the eyrie of England's last **golden eagle**. Re-occupying the area in the late 1960s, a female mate brought down from the healthier population in Scotland died prematurely in 2005 and so the future of 'Golden Boy' (as some call him) looks bleak.

The biggest descent on the walk now follows to the very shores of Haweswater reservoir, but a lakeside amble while spinning your dainty parasol is sadly not on the cards. Soon you're panting like a hippo on a treadmill high above the shore, measuring each streaming gill until the trapped waters terminate at the wooded glade along Haweswater Beck.

The 'model' village of **Burnbanks** (Map 30) at the head of the reservoir has a slightly sinister ambience along with an infrequent (Tue & Sat only) bus service (NBM Hire No 111) to Bampton, Penrith, and the outside world (see public transport map and services pp52-5).

BAMPTON   OFF MAP 30

Bampton offers two excellent accommodation possibilities including *Mardale Inn* (off Map 30; ☎ 01931 713244, 💻 www.mardale inn.co.uk; 4D or T, private facilities some with bath; £80 per room, single occupancy £50; **food** served daily noon-5pm & 6-9pm). Some may be thrilled to know that the cult 1987 film *Withnail & I* was filmed in the area and the telephone box from which Withnail calls his agent in London is actually a stone's throw from the Inn, in which one would be right to expect nothing less than the finest wines available

to humanity. (Incidentally, the famously decrepit cottage of 'Crow Crag' is actually a derelict farmhouse called Sleddale Hall, situated by a reservoir three miles south-west of Shap – off Map 34).

In **Bampton Grange**, about a mile away, the equally recommended *Crown and Mitre* (☎ 01931 713225; 💻 www .crown-and-mitre.co.uk; 2S/2D/1T/2F) charges £35pp for an en suite room with shower or £40pp for the double room with bath.

Back on the trail it now feels odd to suddenly be walking on the level for miles at a time and, free of the national park's edicts; helpful 'Coast to Coast' signposts reappear too. Wall follows stile follows field follows bog until, towards the end of the stage, you descend on **Shap Abbey** (see box p134 and Map 32),

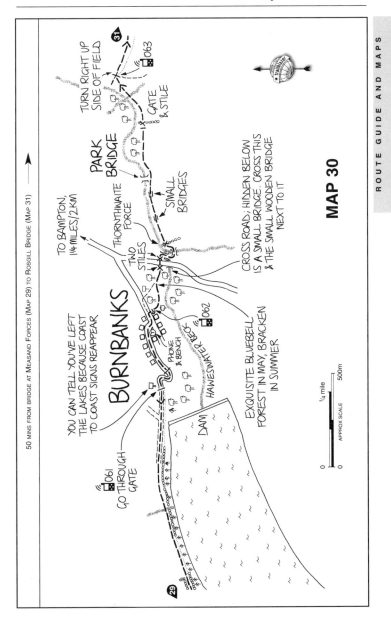

50 MINS FROM BRIDGE AT MEASAND FORCES (MAP 29) TO ROSGILL BRIDGE (MAP 31) ⟶

31

📷 063

TURN RIGHT UP SIDE OF FIELD

GATE & STILE

PARK BRIDGE

THORNTHWAITE FORCE

SMALL BRIDGES

CROSS ROAD; HIDDEN BELOW IS A SMALL BRIDGE. CROSS THIS & THE SMALL WOODEN BRIDGE NEXT TO IT

MAP 30

TO BAMPTON, 1¼ MILES/2KM

TWO STILES

YOU CAN TELL YOU'VE LEFT THE LAKES BECAUSE COAST TO COAST SIGNS REAPPEAR

BURNBANKS

PHONE & BENCH

📷 062

HAWESWATER BECK

EXQUISITE BLUEBELL FOREST IN MAY, BRACKEN IN SUMMER

📷 061 GO THROUGH GATE

DAM

29

¼ mile

APPROX SCALE   500m

0   0

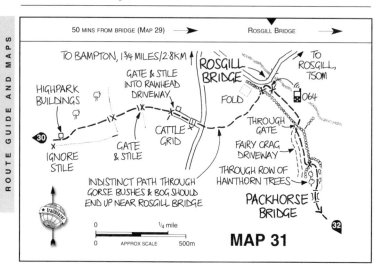

50 MINS FROM BRIDGE (MAP 29) ⟶   ROSGILL BRIDGE   ⟶

TO BAMPTON, 1¾ MILES/2·8KM
ROSGILL BRIDGE
TO ROSGILL, 750M

GATE & STILE INTO RAWHEAD DRIVEWAY

HIGHPARK BUILDINGS

FOLD

064

THROUGH GATE

CATTLE GRID

FAIRY CRAG DRIVEWAY

IGNORE STILE

GATE & STILE

THROUGH ROW OF HAWTHORN TREES

INDISTINCT PATH THROUGH GORSE BUSHES & BOG SHOULD END UP NEAR ROSGILL BRIDGE

PACKHORSE BRIDGE

0   ¼ mile
0   APPROX SCALE   500m

MAP 31

an atmospheric ruin set in a peaceful spot by the River Lowther. It's just regrettable that, by the time you get there, you'll probably be somewhat of a ruin yourself, your thoughts having long ago turned from holy orders to hors d'oeuvres following a hot bath. From the abbey, all that remains is to tick off the road or parallel paths for your triumphant entry into **Shap**.

❑ **Shap Abbey**
Shap Abbey (see Map 32) has the distinction of being the last abbey to be founded in England, in 1199. It was built by the French Premonstratensian order founded by St Norbert at Prémontré in Northern France, who were also known as the White Canons after the colour of their habits.

The abbey was also the last to be dissolved by Henry VIII, in 1540. Presumably Henry's henchmen would have had plenty of practice in plundering monasteries by this time, which is perhaps why the abbey is today in such a ruinous state. The best-preserved section is the **western belltower**, built around 1500.

Since its demise, the abbey has had to suffer the commonplace indignity of having some of its best carved stonework purloined by the locals for use in their own buildings. The cottage by the abbey clearly used a couple of remnants in its construction, albeit to good effect, while Shap's 17th-century market hall, just by the NatWest Bank, is built largely from abbey stone. Even some of the local stone walls contain abbey stones.

SHAP MAP 33 p136 & MAP 34 p137

Shap is a long, narrow village lining a wide street, the former A6, once the north-west's main route to Scotland and still the highest main road in the country as it passes over the Howgill Fells. The road used to supply Shap's traders with enough passing trade to

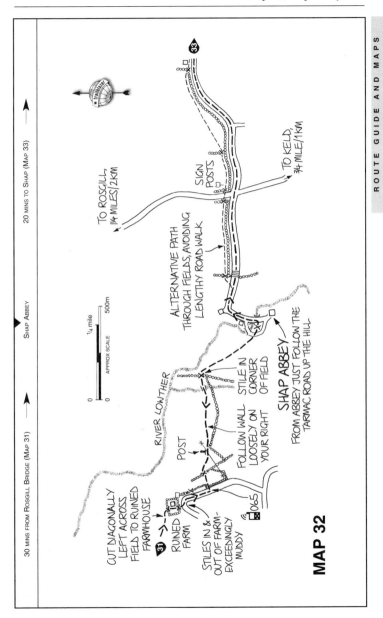

30 MINS FROM ROSGILL BRIDGE (MAP 31) → SHAP ABBEY → 20 MINS TO SHAP (MAP 33) →

ROUTE GUIDE AND MAPS

33

TO ROSGILL, 1¼ MILES/2KM

SIGN POSTS

TO KELD, ¾ MILE/1KM

ALTERNATIVE PATH THROUGH FIELDS, AVOIDING LENGTHY ROAD WALK

¼ mile
500m
0
0
APPROX SCALE

RIVER LOWTHER

POST

STILE IN CORNER OF FIELD

FOLLOW WALL LOOSELY ON YOUR RIGHT

SHAP ABBEY
FROM ABBEY JUST FOLLOW THE TARMAC ROAD UP THE HILL

CUT DIAGONALLY LEFT ACROSS FIELD TO RUINED FARMHOUSE

31
RUINED FARM

STILES IN & OUT OF FARM — EXCEEDINGLY MUDDY

065

MAP 32

make a living and the village prospered. But then they built the M6 and, like the motel in *Psycho*, things have been pretty quiet since, bar the presence of a couple of quarries and cement factories.

There are some attractive features in town, including a 17th-century **market hall** built with masonry from the **abbey** (see box p134), but overall the place is not exactly Las Vegas on New Year's Eve. However, now you're out of the Lakes you don't have to fight over the great accommodation, plus there's a chippy, a Co-op, a couple of pubs, internet access and even a bank.

Services
There are enough in the way of services in Shap to raise a sigh of relief. The village has its own website (www.shapcumbria .co.uk) and even has an outdoor heated (seasonal) **swimming pool**. By the **post office** (Mon-Thur 9am-12.30pm & 1.30-5.30pm; Fri 9am-12.30pm; Sat 9am-noon) is a decent-sized **Co-op** (Mon-Sat 8am-8pm) with an **ATM**. There's another cash machine in the Bull's Head (£1.50 charge).

The NatWest **bank** (Mon & Fri only 10.45am-12.45pm) is opposite the school and there's a **newsagent** (Mon-Sat 5am-5.30pm, Sun 7.30am-1pm) at the southern end of town.

The **library** (Mon 11am-2pm, Tue 2-5pm, Fri 2-7pm, Sat 10am-2pm) in the Old Courthouse has **internet access**.

Where to stay
Being out of the Lakes, many B&B owners need to make more of an effort to attract custom, and with most of their guests being Coast to Coasters, it's something that is appreciated by many of our readers. There's none of that 'two nights minimum stay at weekends' malarkey or overpricing you've put up with on previous days.

As you come into town *The Hermitage* (☎ 01931 716671; www .coast2coast.co.uk/thehermitage; 1D/3T, mostly en suite, bath available) is on your right and has been recommended by readers. The house itself is over 300 years old yet the rooms come with all mod cons. Rates are £30-35pp.

Over the road *New Ing Lodge* (☎ 01931 716719, www.newinglodge.co .uk, 1S/2D/2T/2F) offers a variety of accommodation. **B&B** costs £25-35 per person; apart from one family room which has en suite bath the rooms share shower facilities. Under the same roof there are also two notably spacious mixed **dorms** (sleeping 14 in all) for £16pp plus £2 for bedding. **Camping** in the small back garden under the washing lines costs £4-6pp. Evening **meals** (about £12) and breakfast (£4-6) are available but there is also a very basic 'kitchen'. The eggs from the free-roaming chickens taste like something out of a Roald Dahl fairy tale (that means delicious, by the way). There are plans to improve all these facilities and make use of the outbuildings.

Right at the southern end of town, few begrudge the walk to *Brookfield House*

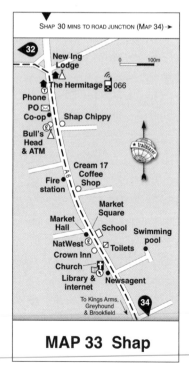

MAP 33 Shap

(Map 34; ☎ 01931 716397, 🖳 www.brook fieldshap.co.uk; 1S private bath/3D or T en suite with shower/1D with private bath; Mar-Nov) which has become a legend among Coast to Coasters and is frequently cited as the best stay on the entire walk. Nothing is too much trouble for Margaret, who charges £30-35pp. They have a bar and the breakfasts, and packed lunches (£5), are the talk of the walk.

When it comes to best pubs, *The Greyhound* (Map 34; ☎ 01931 716474, 🖳 www.greyhoundshap.co.uk; 2S/7D or T/ 2D/1F, all en suite some with bath) seems to be the favourite for accommodation. B&B starts at £35pp in standard rooms, £50pp in de luxe rooms and £45 for single occupancy. *The King's Arms* (Map 34; ☎ 01931 716277, 🖳 www.kingsarmsatshap .co.uk; 2D/3T, all en suite with shower, 2F

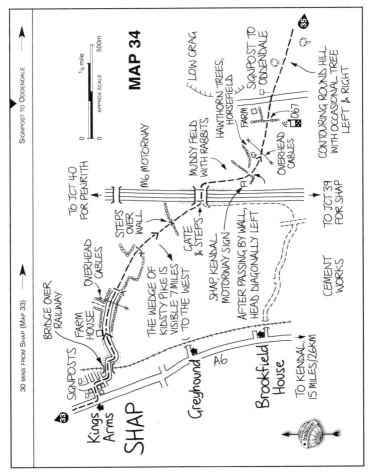

MAP 34

SIGNPOST TO ODDENDALE

30 MINS FROM SHAP (Map 33)

APPROX SCALE
¼ mile
500m

TO JCT 40 FOR PENRITH

M6 MOTORWAY

LOW CRAG

HAWTHORN TREES, HORSEFIELD

FARM

SIGNPOST TO ODDENDALE

CONTOURING ROUND HILL WITH OCCASIONAL TREE LEFT & RIGHT

067

OVERHEAD CABLES

MUDDY FIELD WITH RABBITS

STEPS OVER WALL

GATE & STEPS

SHAP KENDAL MOTORWAY SIGN

AFTER PASSING BY WALL, HEAD DIAGONALLY LEFT

TO JCT 39 FOR SHAP

CEMENT WORKS

BRIDGE OVER RAILWAY

FARM HOUSE

OVERHEAD CABLES

THE WEDGE OF KIDSTY PIKE IS VISIBLE 7 MILES (TO THE WEST

SIGNPOSTS

Kings Arms

SHAP

Greyhound

A6

Brookfield House

TO KENDAL 15 MILES/26KM

TO KENDAL 15 MILES/26KM

with shared bathroom) charges £75 for two sharing, £45 for single occupancy, £90-120 for the family rooms one of which sleeps four.

Campers alight at the more central *Bull's Head Inn* (☎ 01931 716678, 💻 www.bullsheadshap.co.uk), a busy locals' boozer with a small beer garden where you can pitch your tent for £5pp (with a 25% discount off one of their main courses if you've prebooked).

Where to eat and drink
The *Greyhound* (see Where to stay; daily noon-2pm & 6-9pm) is reputed to cook the best grub in town. The menu consists of mainly local dishes including a decent-sized plate of Cumberland sausage with mash or chips (£10.50), or the ever-succulent Lamb Henry (£13). Unfortunately, the Greyhound's location is over a mile from The Hermitage or New Ing Lodge at the top end of town. More convenient is the *Bull's Head* (see Where to stay; daily noon-2pm & 6.30-9pm) which does decent British food, either in their restaurant or in the bar. Breakfast is also available for campers (Mon-Sat 8.30-10am).

The *King's Arms* (see Where to stay; food served Easter to Oct Mon-Sat noon-3pm, Sun noon-2pm, daily 6-8.30pm; Nov to Easter Sat noon-3pm, Sun noon-2pm) sometimes has a 'happy hour' for food between 5 and 6pm Monday to Friday, when two meals cost £10. Opposite the Bull's Head is *Shap Chippy* (Mon-Sat 9am-1.30pm, daily 4.30-8pm) and a little further south is *Cream 17 Coffee Shop* (Mon-Sat 10am-3.30pm) which is good for cakes and sandwiches but usually closed by the time Coast to Coasters hobble into town.

Transport (see also pp52-5)
Bus No 106 operated by Stagecoach and Apollo 8 calls here en route between Kendal and Penrith. The buses leave from Shap's Market Square and take 30 minutes to reach Penrith, 12 minutes to Orton (see pp141-2) and 45 minutes to Kendal.

STAGE 6: SHAP TO KIRKBY STEPHEN   MAPS 34-43

Introduction
Those who struggled over the previous stage may be less than delighted to learn that today's hike is, at **20½ miles (33km, 7hrs)**, even longer. Indeed, it's one of the longest on the entire route but with no prolonged gradients, it can be regarded as something of a 'recovery day', a steady undulating transit over field and moorland as you flank the little-known Howgill Fells to the south and near the peat-sodden ridge they call the Pennine chain.

If you're not convinced, there's again a chance to break it in two by taking the short diversion into Orton, only eight miles from Shap. It's coming across 'lost' villages like Orton or later, Danby Wiske, that is part of the appeal of the Coast to Coast walk. Stranded far from well-established tourist trails or national parks, they're simply what they are; places where people live but in a manner and locale that for most of us is long past. It's then that it dawns on you that, away from the coach-tour honeypots, the forgotten corners of rural England are full of these charming places, scraping by with a shop, a pub, a church and maybe even a bus.

This stage is also replete with **prehistoric sites**, though it's fair to say that none of them will make your jaw drop in amazement and if you didn't know about them you'd probably pass by none the wiser but still cheered by another great day aboard the Coast to Coast path.

The route

With over 20 miles to cover, you leave Shap to cross first rail then two road arteries that funnel through north-west England. In a few minutes they're a forgotten memory as you skirt the isolated, walled village of **Oddendale** (Map 35) where, just a few minutes off the path to the west lie two **concentric stone circles**. If you watched Julia Bradbury stagger around on the Coast to Coast path TV show trying to locate them you may not be so curious, so continue south to cut past a strip of plantation and head over limestone pavements down into Lyvennet Beck. Now you turn north-east, passing **Robin Hood's Grave** (Map 37), a large cairn in a shallow fold in the moor and certainly not the grave of the man who gives his name to the bay that is the ultimate destination on this path.

Eventually the trail drops down past a quarry and traces a road, bending south to a junction with the B6260, leaving it to the left to drop down again past a well-preserved **limekiln** above Broadfell Farm. Those bound for Orton, whose white churchtower has been clearly visible since the brow of the hill, should continue down through the farm from here; the rest march resolutely on to join the farm's driveway and continue east round Orton Scar.

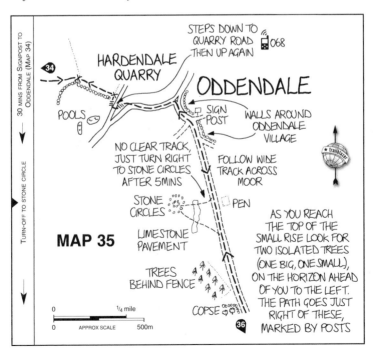

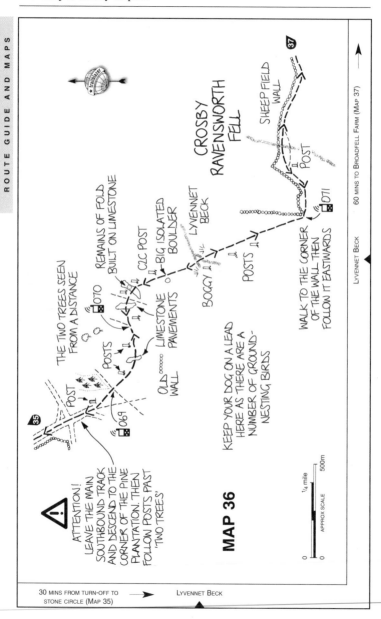

MAP 36

CROSBY RAVENSWORTH FELL

ATTENTION! LEAVE THE MAIN SOUTHBOUND TRACK AND DESCEND TO THE CORNER OF THE PINE PLANTATION. THEN FOLLOW POSTS PAST 'TWO TREES'

THE TWO TREES SEEN FROM A DISTANCE

REMAINS OF FOLD BUILT ON LIMESTONE

C2C POST

BIG ISOLATED BOULDER

LYVENNET BECK

POSTS

BOGGY

LIMESTONE PAVEMENTS

OLD WALL

POSTS

069

070

071

SHEEP FIELD WALL

POST

WALK TO THE CORNER OF THE WALL THEN FOLLOW IT EASTWARDS

KEEP YOUR DOG ON A LEAD HERE AS THERE ARE A NUMBER OF GROUND-NESTING BIRDS

¼ mile

500m

APPROX SCALE

0

0

60 MINS TO BROADFELL FARM (MAP 37)

LYVENNET BECK

30 MINS FROM TURN-OFF TO STONE CIRCLE (MAP 35)

LYVENNET BECK

35

37

ROUTE GUIDE AND MAPS

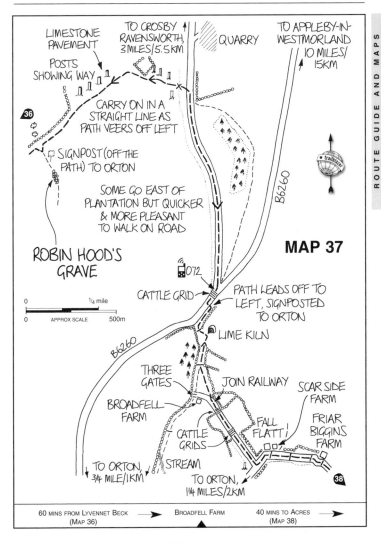

TO CROSBY
RAVENSWORTH,
3 MILES / 5.5 KM

QUARRY

TO APPLEBY-IN-
WESTMORLAND
10 MILES /
15KM

LIMESTONE
PAVEMENT

POSTS
SHOWING WAY

36

CARRY ON IN A
STRAIGHT LINE AS
PATH VEERS OFF LEFT

SIGNPOST (OFF THE
PATH) TO ORTON

SOME GO EAST OF
PLANTATION BUT QUICKER
& MORE PLEASANT
TO WALK ON ROAD

B6260

ROBIN HOOD'S
GRAVE

072

MAP 37

CATTLE GRID

PATH LEADS OFF TO
LEFT, SIGNPOSTED
TO ORTON

0   1/4 mile

0   APPROX SCALE   500m

B6260

LIME KILN

THREE
GATES

JOIN RAILWAY

SCAR SIDE
FARM

BROADFELL
FARM

FALL
FLATT

FRIAR
BIGGINS
FARM

CATTLE
GRIDS

TO ORTON,
3/4 MILE / 1KM

STREAM

TO ORTON,
1¼ MILES / 2KM

38

60 MINS FROM LYVENNET BECK ⟶
(MAP 36)

BROADFELL FARM

40 MINS TO ACRES ⟶
(MAP 38)

ORTON   see map p142

Orton is typical of the quaint 'unknown' villages in which the Coast to Coast specialises, but one with a couple of surprises in store for walkers. For one thing there's the **church** dating back to 1293 below

which are some **pillories** or stocks once used to punish wrongdoers. Perhaps they were spending too much time round the back of **Kennedy's chocolate factory**? Popping in here you may think you've been transported to a chocolaterie in some upmarket Parisian suburb but no, this is Orton, east Cumbria, and that is a fantasy of cocoa-based delicacies you see before you.

The well-stocked **village shop** (Mon-Sat 8am-6pm; **post office** hours Mon, Tues & Fri 9am-1pm, 2-5pm, Wed & Sat 9am-noon, closed Thurs) is nearby, in rude health we're pleased to report and with enough provisions to restock your travelling larder. Stagecoach's/Apollo 8's **Bus** No 106 (Kendal to Penrith and vice versa) stops in the village; see pp52-5 for details.

Where to stay and eat

Recommended time and again by Coast to Coasters, *Barn House* (☎ 015396 24259, 🖳 www.barnhouse-orton.freeserve.co.uk; 1D/2T, all en suite, bath available) on the southern side of the village on Raisbeck Rd has just three rooms but each is supremely comfortable, with Lillian or David serving tea and cakes on arrival. Rates start at £32 per person or £37 for single occupancy and they'll do you a packed lunch too.

The George Hotel (☎ 015396 24229, 🖳 www.thegeorgehotelorton.co.uk; 1S/2D/ 3T/1F, most en suite with shower, bath available) is in the centre of town. Rates start at £60-120 for two sharing (£40 for the single).

Mostyn House (☎ 015396 24258, 🖳 liv_bland@hotmail.com; 1D en suite shower/2T shared bathroom) charges £25-30pp with a single occupancy supplement of £5 (a packed lunch costs £4).

New House Farm (off Map 38; ☎ 015396 24324) offers **camping** (£6pp; £1 for a shower). Campers can order breakfast (£7.50) and an evening meal (£14 if booked

in advance). New House Farm is best reached from Knott Lane (see Map 38). Follow Knott Lane south to the T Junction. Turn left and continue for five minutes. The farm is on the right.

Having taken your penance in the stocks and said a few Hail Marys, you're free to sample *Kennedy's* (Mon-Sat 9am-5pm; Sun & bank hols 11am-5pm; café shuts 30 mins before closing) products in their attached coffee house and ice-cream parlour. For a chocoholic overdose, their chocolate cake washed down with a hot chocolate (made with pure chocolate) and topped with grated chocolate ought to hit the mark.

For pub grub it's got to be *The George Hotel* (Mon-Sat noon-2.30pm, Sun to 3pm, daily 6-9pm; all day Sat & Sun in the main season); the roast lamb jennings in Cumberland sauce was mighty fine.

Orton

There's a second and more impressive **stone circle** (Map 38) a mile to the east of Orton on the Coast to Coast path. It can be reached, for those who didn't take the Orton detour, via a driveable track running east from Broadfell Farm. (Those who *did* visit Orton can rejoin this track at the stone circle by taking the Raisbeck road east and heading up Knott Lane).

After this, the trail continues east across walled fields and on to **Tarn Moor** (Map 39). All being well you'll emerge from the moor on a backroad alongside **Sunbiggin Tarn**, an important bird sanctuary. Here, the Right to Roam laws (see p70) mean the arc of road walking along the original route has been super-seded by turning briefly south and then cutting directly east across the heather-

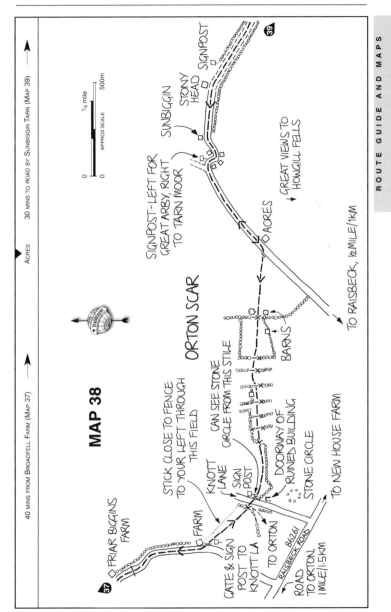

MAP 38

ORTON SCAR

¼ mile
APPROX SCALE
500m

trailblazer

37
◇ FRIAR BIGGINS FARM

GATE & SIGN POST TO KNOTT LA

STICK CLOSE TO FENCE TO YOUR LEFT THROUGH THIS FIELD

KNOTT LANE

SIGN POST

◇ FARM

CAN SEE STONE CIRCLE FROM THIS STILE

DOORWAY OF RUINED BUILDING

STONE CIRCLE

TO NEW HOUSE FARM

TO ORTON

RAISBECK ROAD
B6261

ROAD TO ORTON, 1 MILE/1.5KM

BARNS

SIGNPOST - LEFT FOR GREAT ARBY, RIGHT TO TARN MOOR

ACRES
◇

TO RAISBECK, ½ MILE/1KM

GREAT VIEWS TO HOWGILL FELLS

SUNBIGGIN

STONY HEAD

SIGNPOST

39

clad moor; you'll have seen the sign boards indicating the course. Reaching another lane on the far side of the moor, head for the hill-top water cistern and continue east. Tracing a thread of dry-stone walls (see box p178) below Great Ewe Fell will bring you past ***Bents Farm*** (Map 41; bookings ☎ 01946 758198, 🖥 www.bentscampingbarn.co.uk) with a **camping barn** which sleeps 12-14 (bed £8) and **camping** for £4 per person. Booking is recommended as occasionally groups take over the whole barn.

The next prehistoric site lies a short way past the farm where, having crossed a stile, a signpost urges you to stick to the recognised path so as not to disturb the archaeological site. This'll probably come as something of a surprise because, no matter how hard you look, there seems to be nothing remarkable. What you're actually looking at is the **Severals Village settlement**, which is said to be one of the most important prehistoric sites in Britain. The fact that it remains unexcavated does nothing to diminish this, or to quell the archaeologists' enthusiasm for the place. Without leaving the path, look for irregular or unnatural depressions and bumps in the land here; it's these undulations that have so excited the archaeologists. On the opposite side of Scandal Beck lies the final ancient site on this stage. The so-called **Giants' Graves** (called pillow mounds on OS maps) are a series of long narrow mounds which, some say, may have been prehistoric rabbit enclosures. *(cont'd on p149)*

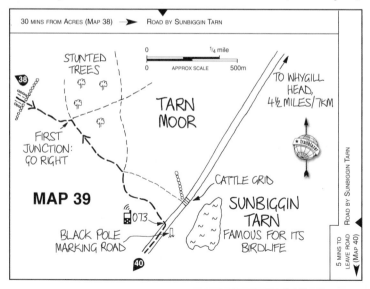

(**Opposite**) **Top**: Passing the Severals Village archaeological site on the way to Kirkby Stephen. (© CS). **Bottom**: Red deer at dawn near Angle Tarn. (© CS).

(**Overleaf**) **Top**: Made it at last and made to last. The mysterious Nine Standards (see p156) mark the boggy transit of the Pennines. (© HS). **Bottom**: Approaching Richmond. (© CS).

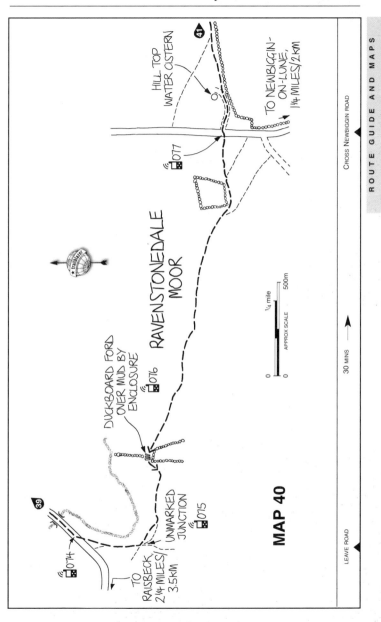

HILL TOP
WATER CISTERN

TO NEWBIGGIN-
ON-LUNE,
1¼ MILES/2KM

077

RAVENSTONEDALE
MOOR

DUCKBOARD FORD
OVER MUD BY
ENCLOSURE

016

UNMARKED
JUNCTION

015

014

TO
RAISBECK, 2¼ MILES/
3.5KM

MAP 40

¼ mile

500m

0

0

APPROX SCALE

LEAVE ROAD

30 MINS

CROSS NEWBIGGIN ROAD

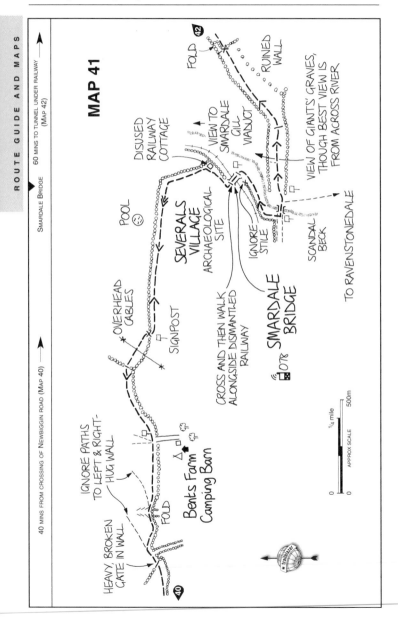

40 MINS FROM CROSSING OF NEWBIGGIN ROAD (Map 40) ▶

SMARDALE BRIDGE   60 MINS TO TUNNEL UNDER RAILWAY (Map 42) ▶

MAP 41

DISUSED
RAILWAY
COTTAGE

VIEW TO
SMARDALE
GILL VIADUCT

RUINED
WALL

VIEW OF GIANTS' GRAVES,
THOUGH BEST VIEW IS
FROM ACROSS RIVER

FOLD

POOL

SEVERALS
VILLAGE
ARCHAEOLOGICAL
SITE

IGNORE
STILE

SCANDAL
BECK

OVERHEAD
CABLES

SIGNPOST

CROSS AND THEN WALK
ALONGSIDE DISMANTLED
RAILWAY

SMARDALE
BRIDGE

TO RAVENSTONEDALE

IGNORE PATHS
TO LEFT & RIGHT-
HUG WALL

FOLD

Bents Farm
Camping Barn

HEAVY, BROKEN
GATE IN WALL

40

¼ mile

0   500m
APPROX SCALE
0

42

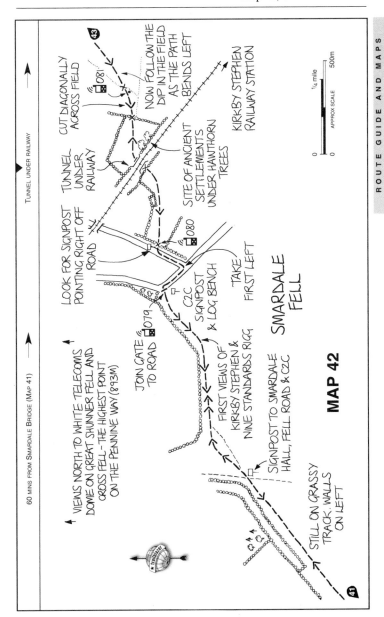

TUNNEL UNDER RAILWAY

CUT DIAGONALLY ACROSS FIELD

081

NOW FOLLOW THE DIP IN THE FIELD AS THE PATH BENDS LEFT

KIRKBY STEPHEN RAILWAY STATION

TUNNEL UNDER RAILWAY

SITE OF ANCIENT SETTLEMENTS UNDER HAWTHORN TREES

¼ mile
500m
0
0
APPROX SCALE

LOOK FOR SIGNPOST POINTING RIGHT OFF ROAD

080

C2C SIGNPOST & LOG BENCH

TAKE FIRST LEFT

SMARDALE FELL

60 MINS FROM SMARDALE BRIDGE (MAP 41)

VIEWS NORTH TO WHITE TELECOMS DOME ON GREAT SHUNNER FELL AND CROSS FELL – THE HIGHEST POINT ON THE PENNINE WAY (893M)

JOIN GATE TO ROAD   079

FIRST VIEWS OF KIRKBY STEPHEN & NINE STANDARDS RIGG

MAP 42

SIGNPOST TO SMARDALE HALL, FELL ROAD & C2C

STILL ON GRASSY TRACK. WALLS ON LEFT

trailblazer

43

41

35 MINS FROM TUNNEL UNDER RAILWAY (MAP 42) → KIRKBY STEPHEN → 35 MINS TO FELL HOUSE (MAP 44) →

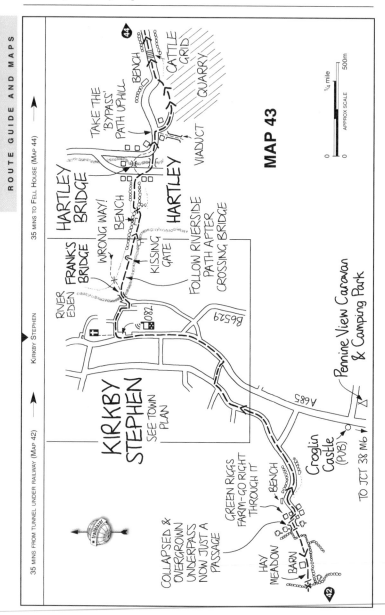

MAP 43

KIRKBY STEPHEN
SEE TOWN PLAN

HARTLEY BRIDGE

FRANK'S BRIDGE

RIVER EDEN

WRONG WAY!

BENCH

KISSING GATE

HARTLEY

TAKE THE 'BYPASS' PATH UPHILL

BENCH

CATTLE GRID

QUARRY

VIADUCT

FOLLOW RIVERSIDE PATH AFTER CROSSING BRIDGE

B6259

B6082

Pennine View Caravan & Camping Park

Croglin Castle (PUB)

A685

TO JCT 38 M6

GREEN RIGGS FARM - GO RIGHT THROUGH IT

BENCH

COLLAPSED & OVERGROWN UNDERPASS NOW JUST A PASSAGE

HAY MEADOW

BARN

0 ... 500m
0 ... 1/4 mile
APPROX SCALE

(cont'd from p144) Dropping down to the bridge across Scandal Beck, more recent archeological evidence can be spied in the form of the distant **Smardale Gill viaduct** along a former railway that once joined Kirkby Stephen to what is now the M6 corridor. Climbing to the crest of Smardale Fell, on a clear day the Pennines rise before like a standing wave with the cairns on Nine Standards Rigg just visible beyond the quarry west of Kirkby Stephen. Looking north across the Eden valley, with less difficulty you'll also spot the white dome of the radio station atop Great Shunner Fell and to the left, Cross Fell, at 893m (2930ft), the highest point on the Pennine Way, a great walk for another day.

By now, those nearing Kirkby Stephen will not be mindful of such distant prospects, as slowly the town's churches and then other buildings rise from the wooded vale below.

KIRKBY STEPHEN   See map p151

Kirkby Stephen (pronounced 'Kirby Stephen' without the second 'k') vies with Richmond as the biggest town on the route, though don't let that fool you into thinking that this place is a metropolis. In fact, Kirkby Stephen is a pleasant and prosperous market town built along the A685 with a population of around 1900, a figure that's swollen considerably during the summer months by walkers, runners, cyclists and other outdoor bon viveurs. If you're due a rest after the Lakeland stages, not least following the preceding 20-miler from Shap, a day off in town is the tonic to numerous woes.

There've been **markets** in Kirkby Stephen since at least 1361 when it was granted a market charter. Note the cobbled outline on the market square's floor; it marks the outer limits of a former bull-baiting area, a popular pastime in the town until 1820 when a bull broke free and ran amok, killing a number of bystanders.

The principle tourist attraction in Kirkby Stephen is the 13th-century **St Hedda church** (see box p150) although the town's front gardens are no eyesore either and in 2009 it again won a Village of the Year award. Other sites of note include the old and much-photographed **signpost** at the southern end of town, where the distances are given in miles and furlongs (see photo); and the curious but attractive **stone seats** in the form of sheep, that stand by the door of the tourist office. Carved by artist Keith Alexander, they're reputed to increase the

fertility of any who sit upon them, ovine or otherwise. **Frank's Bridge** is a pretty double-arched stone footbridge, a quiet place to sit by the grassy riverbank and feed the ducks. It's thought to be named after a local brewer, Frank Birkbeck, who lived here in the 19th century. One other item of note is the flock of **parrots** that fly around town during the day before returning home to their owner, a local resident, at dusk.

Services

Kirkby Stephen has become the spiritual (if not *quite* the geographical) heart of the Coast to Coast path. Packhorse (see p24) operate out of the town, and those who opt to take advantage of their 'taxi' service will spend the night in Kirkby Stephen before being shuttled to St Bees the next morning. If you've left your car here, the Packhorse van arrives back in town from Robin Hood's Bay at around 6.30pm.

Old roadsign with distances in furlongs and miles. In case you've forgotten eight furlongs equals one mile.

❏ St Hedda Church

The distinctive red sandstone church (part of the same formation found at St Bees) is separated from the market square by the peaceful lawn of the **cloisters**. On entering the main gate, on your right is the **Trupp Stone**, resembling a stone tomb or table, where until 1836 the locals' tithes were collected. Take half an hour or so to wander around inside the church, which is known locally as the Cathedral of the Dales. It is built on the site of a Saxon church, though the earliest feature (the nave) of the present structure dates only to 1220.

Features to look out for include the 17th-century **font**, a great stone lump at the rear of the church, and the nearby **bread shelves**, used for distributing bread to the poor. There's also a **Norman coffin** by the north wall, unearthed in 1980 during restoration work, and a glass display cabinet, also by the north wall, housing 16th- and 17th-century Bibles and, curiously, a **boar's tusk**, said to belong to the last wild boar shot in England. It was killed by the first Sir Richard Musgrave (died 1464), who was buried with the tusk in Hartley Chapel, to the south of the chancel. (The place where Sir Richard shot the boar, by the way, the appropriately named Wild Boar Fell, lies to the south of Kirkby Stephen.)

The church's most interesting feature, however, is the 8th-century **Loki Stone** facing the main door, a metre-high block carved by the Vikings with the horned figure of the Norse god Loki. A bit of a prankster, one of Loki's tricks backfired and resulted in the death of Odin's son, which led to Loki being bound in chains and thrown into a dungeon. When the church was built the locals interpreted the carving as a representation of a demon. The stone was thus placed in the church to remind parishioners of the terrifying creatures that awaited sinners in the afterlife.

Indeed, demons still play a big part in the folklore of Kirkby Stephen. At 8pm every day step outside to hear if they are still ringing the **Taggy Bell**, a warning to those who are still on the streets that Taggy, the local demon, now stalks the town looking for prey.

For details about St Hedda himself, see box p226.

The **tourist office** (☎ 017683 71199; 🖳 www.kirkby-stephen.com; Easter to Oct Mon-Sat 10am-4pm, Sun 11am-3pm, Nov to Easter Mon-Wed, Fri & Sat 10am-noon) is crammed with brochures and leaflets and the staff seem knowledgeable. They offer accommodation booking; the 10% charge will be deducted from the final bill.

Just down Market St a little way is the **library** (☎ 017683 71775; Mon & Wed 10.30am-12.30pm, 1.30-6pm, Fri 10.30am-12.30pm & 1.30-5pm, Sat 10am-1pm) with **internet** connection (£1 for 30 mins). There are two **banks** with **cash machines** while on the other side of the road the **post office** (Mon-Fri 9am-5.30pm, Sat 9am-12.30pm) is at the back of Emporium Deli. The best **supermarket** in the town centre is the Co-op (Mon-Sat 8am-10pm, Sun 9am-10pm).

There's also a Spar (daily 8am-10.30pm in high summer) at the southern end of town closer to the campsite and a bigger Co-op at the northern end of town past the chippy. These late opening hours are a treat if you've got in late from Shap and need a rest and a feed before stocking up. There's a **launderette** down the lane between the Emporium/post office and a chip shop.

Eden Outdoors (☎ 017683 72431; Mon-Fri 9am-5pm, Sat 9.30am-4.30pm) is a small **shop** with a little outdoor gear. Blister kits and other medications are on sale at Green Tree **pharmacy** (Mon-Fri 9am-5.30pm, Sat 9am-1pm).

Where to stay

The Pennine View Caravan and Camping Park (Map 43; ☎ 017683 71717; Mar-Oct) is a secure, no-nonsense spot just outside town near Croglin Castle pub, with a laundry room and a clean ablutions block. Camping costs £7-7.50 per person with a large, flat grassy area set aside for tents away from the motorhomes and caravans. Long-term parking (£3.25 per car per day) is available.

Kirkby Stephen Hostel (☎ 0845 371 9525, 🖳 www.kirkbystephenhostel.co.uk; 38 beds) is an independent hostel (and under new ownership) but beds can be booked via the YHA website. It is housed in a former Methodist chapel in the centre of town. Rates are £18pp and the hostel has self-catering facilities; breakfast is available for £5.

Of the B&Bs on the walk, we've received many recommendations for the *Old Croft House* (☎ 017683 71638, 🖳 www .oldcrofthouse.co.uk; 1S/2D/1T, all en suite bath available; closed January). It's a lovely old Georgian townhouse with a warm, oak-panelled interior full of books, made all the better by the warmth and generosity of the owners who know what Coasters want, welcoming guests with freshly baked scones and even providing foot spas in the rooms! They also offer food in the evenings (if booked in advance), with a choice of menus for £17-21. B&B costs £32-35pp.

Next to the hostel and a favourite with many readers, with spacious rooms *Fletcher House* (☎ 017683 71013, 🖳

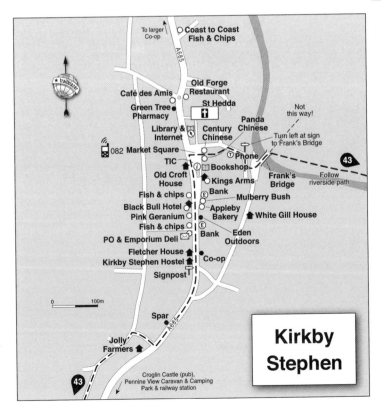

www.fletcherhousecumbria.co.uk; 2D/1T/ 1T or F, all en suite with shower plus separate bathroom) has free wi-fi and internet access (£1/hour) and TV in every room for £33pp (single occupancy £40).

Towards the southern end of town at 63 High St *The Jolly Farmers Guest House* (☎ 017683 71063; 🖳 www.thejollyfarmers .co.uk; 4D/4T, all en suite) is a converted pub with hydro-spa baths in a couple of the rooms which should help take those aches away, and of course tea and scones on arrival. Rates are from £35pp; single occupancy £40.

Not all the pubs in town are said to give a good service to walkers but back in the centre near the square, the *Kings Arms* (☎ 017683 71378, 🖳 www.kingsarmskirk bystephen.co.uk; 1S/7D or T/1F, some en suite, bath available) is a 17th-century former posting inn with many antiques in the rooms. Rates are £50 per room, or £60 for an en suite; single occupancy £30 or £45 if an en suite room.

Nearby the *Black Bull Hotel* (☎ 017683 71237, 🖳 www.blackbullkirkby stephen.co.uk; 2S/5D/2F, all en suite, bath available), 38 Market Sq, also gets good reports and charges £66 for two sharing, £35-40 for a single.

To the east of the main road on Melbecks *White Gill House* (☎ 017683 72238, 🖳 barbwgh@onetel.com; 1D/1T, both en suite with bath) has been highly recommended by many readers and walkers alike, where the rate is £32pp (£37 for single occupancy). As with most of the B&Bs they'll do packed lunches (£5) and also have drying facilities.

Where to eat and drink

On the main street there are no fewer than three **chippies** including the *Coast to Coast* (Mon & Thur-Sat 11.30am-1.30pm & 4.30-7pm, Sun 4.30-7pm) at the northern end of town that has them queueing out the door on a Friday evening.

As for tearooms, *Pink Geranium* (☎ 017683 71586; Wed-Sat 9am-4.30pm, Sun 9am-4pm) gives you a great big pot of tea and their food is some of the most imaginative and generous around.

The Mulberry Bush (☎ 017683 71572) is a popular Kirkby Stephen café (daily 9.15am-4pm) that turns itself into a restaurant (Fri-Sun 5-9pm; low season Fri-Sat only) in the evenings serving modern British and European cuisine.

For a picnic lunch to eat by the river, call in at *The Appleby Bakery* (Mon-Sat 8am-5pm, Sun 9.30am-3.30pm; 🖳 www .applebybakery.co.uk) for a mouthwatering range of speciality breads and sandwiches.

Another good place to pick up supplies is *The Emporium Deli* (Mon-Fri 9am-5.30pm, Sat 9am-2pm) over the road, in the front part of the post office building, with a great selection of the world's finer foodstuffs.

For evening meals, if you're up near the campsite (see pp150-1), *Croglin Castle* (Wed-Sun noon-2pm, daily 6-9pm) is a convenient stop though in 2009 this pub again had new owners and a walk down town may prove more rewarding. There, the *Kings Arms* (see Where to stay; food served daily 11.30am-9.30pm) is the pick of the pubs and has a fine reputation and a fair vegetarian selection. The moussaka here is tasty, while the grilled Lakeland lamb chops are good value.

Of the other pubs the *Black Bull* (see Where to stay; daily all day) does locally inspired meals including pork loin and black pudding in cider sauce.

The finest evening meals in town, and probably for a considerable radius beyond, are waiting for you at the intimate, some might say tiny, *Old Forge Restaurant* (☎ 017683 71832; Wed-Sun 6.30pm to late) at the northern end of town. If you're returning to your car having just completed the walk, or even if you're just passing through on the way east, we recommend you treat yourself to a feed at the Old Forge, a rare and welcome antidote to traditional pub fare and takeaways. A chicken salad starter followed by a fillet steak and a coffee will set you back about £25, an apparent extravagance easily offset by a couple of night's penance in a camping barn.

The *Café des Amis* and deli on the opposite side of the roundabout is another nice spot for a daytime snack.

Crashing back down to earth, both *Panda Chinese Takeaway* (☎ 017683 71283; Sun-Mon & Wed-Thur 5.30-11.30pm; Fri-Sat to midnight; closed Tue) and *Century Chinese Restaurant* (☎ 017683 72828; Tue-Sat noon-2pm & 5-11.30pm; Sun 5-11.30pm), next door, serve the usual array of Oriental fare.

Transport (see also pp52-5)

Kirkby Stephen is on the Carlisle to Leeds railway line. The **train** station – the only one, apart from St Bees, on the Coast to Coast path – lies over a mile to the south of the town centre.

As for **buses**, Grand Prix Coaches' No 563 runs to Penrith and back from the Market Square Mon-Sat (journey time around an hour), while Kirkby Lonsdale Coach Hire's No 564 runs from both the Market Square and the railway station to Kendal, a journey of 60-75 minutes.

Finally, for a **taxi** call ☎ 017683 72036, 72557 or 71682.

STAGE 7: KIRKBY STEPHEN TO KELD   MAPS 43-50

Introduction

This **14¹/₂-mile (24km, 5-6hrs via the high routes)** stage is something of a red-letter day. Not only do you cross the **Pennines** – the so-called backbone of the British Isles on whose flanks the Industrial Revolution gathered pace 200 years ago – but in doing so you cross the **watershed** on the Coast to Coast. From the summit at Nine Standards Rigg all rivers, including the infant headwaters of the Swale which you'll track for the next few days, flow eastwards to drain into the North Sea.

You also pass from the county of Cumbria into **Yorkshire**, your home for the rest of the trek and finally, by the end of this stage by our reckoning you're at the halfway point, having completed around 100 miles out of our estimated 200 (161km out of 322km).

Yet in spite of these significant landmarks, the one thing that most walkers remember about the transit of the Pennines is the **peat bogs** they have to negotiate along the way. The maps point out the boggiest sections and no matter what the weather or which of the **three routes** (see pp154-60) you take, it's a good stage to don gaiters, if you have them. If you do succumb to the mires, cheer yourself up with the thought that at the end of this stage you'll be spending the night in the gentle pastoral scenery of **Swaledale**, the most northerly of Yorkshire's Dales and some say its loveliest.

The route

From Kirkby Stephen you cross the Eden river at Frank's Bridge (Map 43) and continue up to **Hartley** village. The path climbs the hill and skirts around a working quarry on a steep metalled road which can be a strenuous start to the day.

At the end lies a wide dirt track up Hartley Fell where, five miles from town, the path divides (Map 45, WPT 083): the red and blue routes head east up the hill to the Nine Standards, while the green route parallels a stone wall for a while before striking off over a flat moorland path to the quiet, B6270 Kirkby Stephen–Keld road. The three routes are described in more detail overleaf.

The three routes over the moors Due to severe erosion of the peat by walkers, there are **three paths** (see pp156-7) across the Pennines to Keld, the exact route you take depending on the time of year or weather conditions. These three routes are marked on Maps 45a, 46 and 47 (they're missing on the current OS OL19 map), and are colour coded. They initially diverge at a signpost (Map 45, WPT 083) at which point boggy sections set in whichever route you take. Although there are colour-coded signposts at key points, as well as laminated maps showing the three routes nailed to the odd post, you'll see only few aged colour-coded waymarkers on the blue route.

Furthermore, it has to be said that the junction where the red and blue paths separate really has been ravaged by erosion from your predecessors' footwear and will get worse year by year; you can't even get near the signpost without making a mess of yourself.

If ever there was a part of the Coast to Coast path that urgently needed lining with stone slabs or duckboards, it's here at the southern end of Nine

35 MINS FROM KIRKBY STEPHEN (MAP 43)

FELL HOUSE   35 MINS TO SIGNPOST (MAP 45)

43

ROAD CONTOURS QUARRY

QUARRY

★ trailblazer

FELL HOUSE

CATTLE GRID

MAP 44

BIRKETT HILL

HAWTHORN & SCRUB

SIGNPOST AS METALLED ROAD ENDS. RIGHT TO LADTHWAITE. WE GO STRAIGHT ON TO 'ROLLINSON HAGGS'

ROUGH TRACK

0   ¼ mile

0   APPROX SCALE   500m

'REST-A-WHILE' CARVED SEAT

45

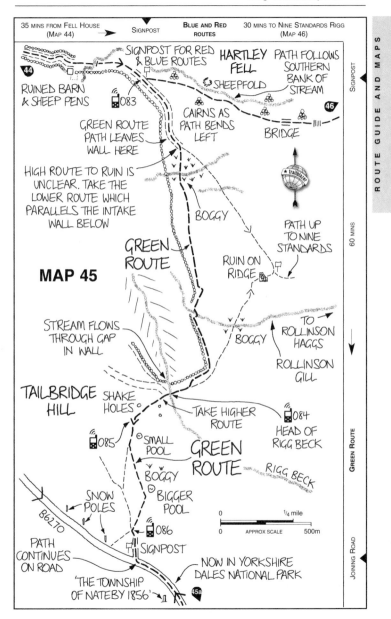

35 MINS FROM FELL HOUSE (MAP 44) → SIGNPOST

BLUE AND RED ROUTES

30 MINS TO NINE STANDARDS RIGG (MAP 46)

SIGNPOST FOR RED & BLUE ROUTES

HARTLEY FELL

PATH FOLLOWS SOUTHERN BANK OF STREAM

44

RUINED BARN & SHEEP PENS

083

SHEEPFOLD

46

GREEN ROUTE PATH LEAVES WALL HERE

CAIRNS AS PATH BENDS LEFT

BRIDGE

HIGH ROUTE TO RUIN IS UNCLEAR. TAKE THE LOWER ROUTE WHICH PARALLELS THE INTAKE WALL BELOW

BOGGY

trailblazer

GREEN ROUTE

MAP 45

PATH UP TO NINE STANDARDS

RUIN ON RIDGE

60 MINS

STREAM FLOWS THROUGH GAP IN WALL

BOGGY

TO ROLLINSON HAGGS

ROLLINSON GILL

TAILBRIDGE HILL

SHAKE HOLES

TAKE HIGHER ROUTE

084

085

SMALL POOL

GREEN ROUTE

HEAD OF RIGG BECK

GREEN ROUTE

BOGGY

RIGG BECK

SNOW POLES

BIGGER POOL

0   1/4 mile

B6270

086

0   500m

APPROX SCALE

PATH CONTINUES ON ROAD

SIGNPOST

NOW IN YORKSHIRE DALES NATIONAL PARK

'THE TOWNSHIP OF NATEBY 1856'

45a

SIGNPOST

60 MINS

GREEN ROUTE

JOINING ROAD

ROUTE GUIDE AND MAPS

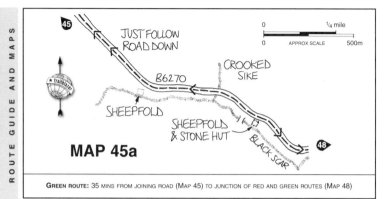

MAP 45a

JUST FOLLOW ROAD DOWN

CROOKED SIKE

B6270

SHEEPFOLD

SHEEPFOLD & STONE HUT

BLACK SCAR

0   ¼ mile
0   APPROX SCALE   500m

GREEN ROUTE: 35 MINS FROM JOINING ROAD (MAP 45) TO JUNCTION OF RED AND GREEN ROUTES (MAP 48)

Standards Rigg which looks like a scene from the Somme, circa 1916.

The **blue and red** high routes are about the same length (4 miles from Nine Standards to the point where all three paths converge just west of Ravenseat). The low-level **green route** is nearly a mile longer (adding up to 15½ miles for this stage), but with a couple of miles of road walking it takes about the same time.

The advice seems to be: if you can't see the Nine Standards by the Mile 5 junction (WPT 083) due to low cloud or mist, you'll see even less when you're up there and may even get lost, so take the green route.

It is possible to have your cake and eat it up here. Should you arrive at the Nine Standards and have the weather turn on you, follow a path south for three-quarters of a mile and then head west from the cairns, passing to the west of Rollinson Haggs to pick up Rollinson Gill and so the green route before it reaches the head of Rigg Beck (WPT 084). From there you can follow the road all the way to Keld if you wish.

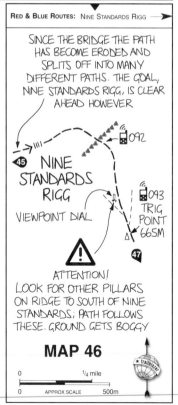

RED & BLUE ROUTES: NINE STANDARDS RIGG

SINCE THE BRIDGE THE PATH HAS BECOME ERODED AND SPLITS OFF INTO MANY DIFFERENT PATHS. THE GOAL, NINE STANDARDS RIGG, IS CLEAR AHEAD HOWEVER

092

NINE STANDARDS RIGG

VIEWPOINT DIAL

093 TRIG POINT 665M

ATTENTION! LOOK FOR OTHER PILLARS ON RIDGE TO SOUTH OF NINE STANDARDS; PATH FOLLOWS THESE. GROUND GETS BOGGY

MAP 46

0   ¼ mile
0   APPROX SCALE   500m

● **Blue route (Aug-Nov; Maps 45-49; 3hrs 20mins from where the green route separates)** Weather permitting, this is the route to choose to get the full Pennine experience. Up to Nine Standards (WPT 092), just 30 minutes from the junction with the green route it matches the red route. Heading south past the **trig point** (662m) and the low ruins to the end of the ridge, at the key junction marked by the mire-bound signpost (WPT 095) this route then takes an eastern course down to Whitsundale Beck.

Irregular and ageing posts daubed with forensic traces of light blue paint guide you east down to the Beck, but if you can't rely on seeing them, a compass bearing of 100° or so will do the same job. Once down in the Beck you follow its winding course south to a reunion with the other two paths, and just 15 minutes from a tea and scone at Ravenseat Farm (see p160).

● **Red route (May-July; Maps 45-49; 3hrs 35 mins from where the green route separates)** In clear conditions this route is straightforward enough. From the boot-ravaged divergence with the blue route (WPT 095; Map 47) things can get a little boggier still and there are no waymarkers as the route rolls south over the barely noticeable crest of **White Mossy Hill**.

From here you should be able to make out a large **pile of stones** (resembling a ruin) to the south; once there you hope to be able to see a tall stone **pillar** (WPT 106) to the south-south-east. At this point you drop south-east over a small bridge and then south down towards the green route where you turn east onto a track and, free of the worst mires, continue on to the farm at **Ravenseat**.

Note that on both these higher routes it's well worth taking your time to **avoid the worst bogs** by all means possible: backtracking, taking a running jump, using a pole, using your partner as a plank; whatever works for you. The one time I got a bit blasé here I sunk down over my knees. Perhaps those tales of calf-swallowing Pennine bogs were not so exaggerated after all.

● **Green route (Dec-Apr; Maps 45, 45a, 48-49; 3hrs 25mins from where the route separates from the red and blue routes)** This is the simplest route and in inclement weather the best one to take, regardless of the season. Note that we found the more used path from the junction post at WPT 083 no longer squelches pointlessly halfway up to Rollinson Haggs only to drop down again (as shown on OS maps).

The more practical route contours above the intake wall to the moderately impressive head of Rigg Beck which meanders away down its valley (a view, incidentally, evoking the more dramatic vista at High Cup Nick on the Pennine Way).

After Rigg Beck there follows a section of weathered limestone pavement before you join the B6270. Note too that later on, the point where the green route officially leaves the B6270 (Map 48, WPT 087) at a right-hand bend seems to be another pointless hiding to nothing, this time up a gully on all fours. Instead, continue along the road for another minute or so (Map 48) and turn north up the farm track. The 'official' path soon joins it. Shortly you'll pass the bootworn scar of the red route coming down from the pillar to join your track (WPT 109), and soon the track ends by a grouse hut.

From here you follow, and occasionally cross, Ney Gill as it wends its way towards the blue route junction at Whitsundale Beck just out of Ravenseat (WPT 102). All in all, keeping below 1700ft (530m) on a rainy day the green route need not be regarded as a 'consolation prize'. *(cont'd on p160)*

ROUTE GUIDE AND MAPS

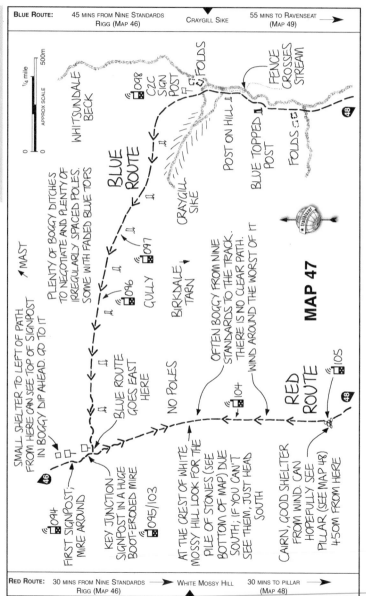

BLUE ROUTE: 45 MINS FROM NINE STANDARDS   CRAYGILL SIKE   55 MINS TO RAVENSEAT
RIGG (MAP 46)   (MAP 49)

APPROX SCALE   500m   ¼ mile

WHITSUNDALE BECK

FOLDS

FENCE CROSSES STREAM

098 C2C SIGN POST

POST ON HILL

BLUE TOPPED POST

FOLDS

48

BLUE ROUTE

MAST

PLENTY OF BOGGY DITCHES TO NEGOTIATE AND PLENTY OF IRREGULARLY SPACED POLES. SOME WITH FADED BLUE TOPS

CRAYGILL SIKE

097

096

GULLY

BIRKDALE TARN

OFTEN BOGGY FROM NINE STANDARDS TO THE TRACK. THERE IS NO CLEAR PATH. WIND AROUND THE WORST OF IT

MAP 47

SMALL SHELTER TO LEFT OF PATH FROM HERE CAN SEE TOP OF SIGNPOST IN BOGGY DIP AHEAD. GO TO IT

BLUE ROUTE GOES EAST HERE

NO POLES

104

105

RED ROUTE

48

46

FIRST SIGNPOST; MIRE AROUND

094

KEY JUNCTION SIGNPOST IN A HUGE BOOT-ERODED MIRE

095/103

AT THE CREST OF WHITE MOSSY HILL LOOK FOR THE PILE OF STONES (SEE BOTTOM OF MAP) DUE SOUTH; IF YOU CAN'T SEE THEM, JUST HEAD SOUTH

CAIRN, GOOD SHELTER FROM WIND. CAN HOPEFULLY SEE PILLAR (SEE MAP 48) 450M FROM HERE

RED ROUTE: 30 MINS FROM NINE STANDARDS   WHITE MOSSY HILL   30 MINS TO PILLAR
RIGG (MAP 46)   (MAP 48)

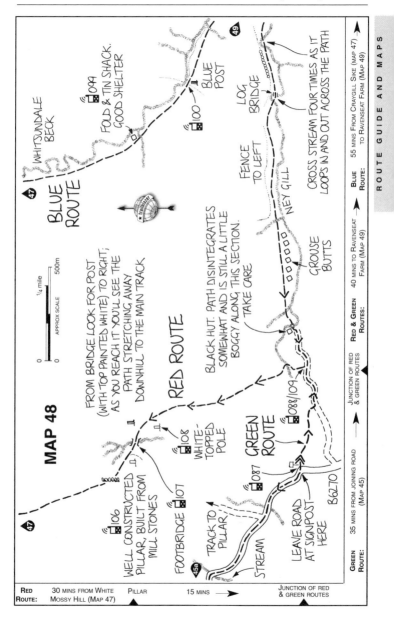

MAP 48

BLUE ROUTE

WHITSUNDALE BECK

FOLD & TIN SHACK. GOOD SHELTER

BLUE POST

¼ mile

APPROX SCALE

500m

FROM BRIDGE LOOK FOR POST (WITH TOP PAINTED WHITE) TO RIGHT; AS YOU REACH IT YOU'LL SEE THE PATH STRETCHING AWAY DOWNHILL TO THE MAIN TRACK

RED ROUTE

WELL CONSTRUCTED PILLAR, BUILT FROM MILL STONES

WHITE-TOPPED POLE

FOOTBRIDGE

BLACK HUT. PATH DISINTEGRATES SOMEWHAT AND IS STILL A LITTLE BOGGY ALONG THIS SECTION. TAKE CARE

FENCE TO LEFT

NEY GILL

CROSS STREAM FOUR TIMES AS IT LOOPS IN AND OUT ACROSS THE PATH

LOG BRIDGE

GROUSE BUTTS

GREEN ROUTE

TRACK TO PILLAR

STREAM

LEAVE ROAD AT SIGNPOST HERE

B6270

Green Route:	35 MINS FROM JOINING ROAD (MAP 45)	JUNCTION OF RED & GREEN ROUTES
Red & Green Routes:	40 MINS TO RAVENSEAT FARM (MAP 49)	
Blue Route:	55 MINS FROM CRAYGILL SIKE (MAP 47) TO RAVENSEAT FARM (MAP 49)	

RED ROUTE:	30 MINS FROM WHITE MOSSY HILL (MAP 47)	PILLAR
	15 MINS	JUNCTION OF RED & GREEN ROUTES

ROUTE GUIDE AND MAPS

RED AND GREEN 40 MINS FROM JUNCTION
ROUTES: OF ROUTES (MAP 48)   RAVENSEAT FARM

WHITSUNDALE BECK
BLUE ROUTE

RED & GREEN ROUTES

48 101

48 102/089

FOLD

OPTIONAL TWO
TRACK STREAMS

KEEP STREAM
TO YOUR RIGHT

MAP 49

0   ¼ mile
0   APPROX SCALE   500m

090

WATER FALL

WHITSUNDALE BECK

TO TAN HILL,
3 MILES/5KM

RAVENSEAT
FARM — CREAM
TEAS

SMALL GATE INTO
FIELD & SIGNPOST
TO KELD

BARN

TWO BARNS
RUINED WALL
GAP IN WALL

SIGNPOST
BOUNDARY
WALL

WOODED RAVINE

SIGNPOST
TO KELD

EDDY FOLD

TO B6270 ROAD
LEADING TO
PRYHOUSE FARM
AND BIRKDALE FARM
¾ MILE/1.3KM

RAVENSEAT FARM

70 MINS TO KELD (MAP 50)

50

BLUE   55 MINS FROM CRAYGILL   ➤   RAVENSEAT FARM
ROUTE: SIKE (MAP 47)

(cont'd from p157) Although it's a shame to miss out the mysterious cairns, it's a fine moorland walk in its own right, getting lost with no landmarks is not too great a risk and the road stage along Birkdale is a fine way to appreciate the peaty wastelands without necessarily sinking into them.

Whichever way you've come over the moors, many readers have confirmed that by the time they get to **Ravenseat Farm** they're unable to resist a sit down, **a tea and a scone** which Amanda offers here. However, be aware she may not always be around. From here the path tracks south alongside the engorged chasm of **Whitsundale Beck**, punctuated with some impressive waterfalls and the finely restored but otherwise unused stone barns or 'laithes' which are a feature of Swaledale. Passing the farmhouse of **Smithy Holme** (Map 50), you can join the B6270 immediately by crossing the bridge, or take the path above the riverside cliff of **Cotterby Scar**. (For once we recommend the road, as it allows you to visit Wainwath Force.) These two paths reunite by the bridge just by *Park*

House and Keld Bunkhouse (see below) from where it's a gentle half-mile stroll to what passes for Keld village centre. The tough first half of the Coast to Coast is now behind you; let's just hope your feet are keeping up with the pace.

KELD   MAP 50, p162

Keld sits at the head of Swaledale where the Coast to Coast dissects the longer, northbound, Pennine Way. Today it's a tiny hill village of little consequence, huddled against the often inclement weather. However, in common with the rest of Swaledale, in the mid-19th century Keld stood at the heart of the local lead-mining industry. Many of the buildings including the two **Methodist chapels** were constructed at this time, as a quick survey of the construction dates carved on the houses' lintels will confirm.

Keld is more about water than lead today. The name means 'spring' in Norse and the **Swale River**, dyed brown by the peat, rushes past the village. Do take the opportunity to visit some of the numerous nearby waterfalls – more accurately called cascades or, locally, **forces** (another Norse word) – including Catrake Force, just above the village, and East Gill Force below it.

Being a tiny village at the crossroads of two major long-distance paths, let alone situated in the ever-popular Swaledale, accommodation options in Keld can dry up fast if you leave it too late in the high season. Further down the valley the B&Bs in Thwaite and Muker (on the 'low level' route to Reeth) are no less popular. Indeed, such are the charms of Swaledale's gentle rolling scenery, dotted here and there with the distinctive 'laithes' – stone barns for housing hay and livestock – that many hikers forego Wainwright's high route (see pp164-70) via Swinner and Gunnerside gills in favour of the gentle stroll down the Swale valley to Reeth.

The only services in Keld are a **public toilet** and a **phone**. For more details on Keld and the rest of Swaledale visit 🖳 www .swaledale.net.

Where to stay and eat

The village has at least two **campsites**, although level pitches can be a bit of a premium once car-borne weekenders with their giant family tents have spread out. You'll have walked past *Park House Camping and Keld Bunkhouse* (☎ 01748 886549; 🖳 www.keldbunkhouse.com; camping £5pp; bunkhouse £17-20pp inc bedding) on the way into the village. Based around the farmhouse, the shower here has got some kick to it and they have a big shed for campers to take cover under and cook in during a downpour. The bunkhouse is just what Keld needed now the YHA hostel has gone, with a double (£40), a triple and a quad room, a kitchen plus a cosy lounge area with a TV and a kettle. Inexpensive evening meals (£5) and breakfast baguettes (£2.50) are also on offer.

Park Lodge (☎ 01748 886274, 🖳 www .rukins-keld.co.uk) is at the bottom of the village, though their actual **campsites** (Easter to Oct; from £5pp) are in several different places, including below Butt House and right by the river. They don't take bookings. They also have a lovely little **tearoom** (Easter to end Sep; daily 9am-6pm) in the farmhouse with tables and chairs in the front garden. There are bacon rolls and a limited selection of groceries including beer and wine and they also serve an extra pot of hot water when you order tea – always a sign of a good tearoom in our opinion.

The former youth hostel, *Keld Lodge* (☎ 01748 886259, 🖳 www.keldlodge.com; 1S/4T or F/4D, all en suite with shower; 2S 'pod rooms' share shower facilities) is now the village's de facto **pub** (daily noon-11pm) and the only place for a walk-in meal in the evening. All rooms have a TV, there is a drying room, most have wonderful views and dogs (£5 per dog) are welcome. Rates are £45pp (£40 for a single), although singletons have reported they were given a cushier double in Butt House (see p163) for the price of a single. The *restaurant* (open to non residents; daily noon-2pm & 6-9pm) has a good vegetarian selection (one of the owners is a veggie)

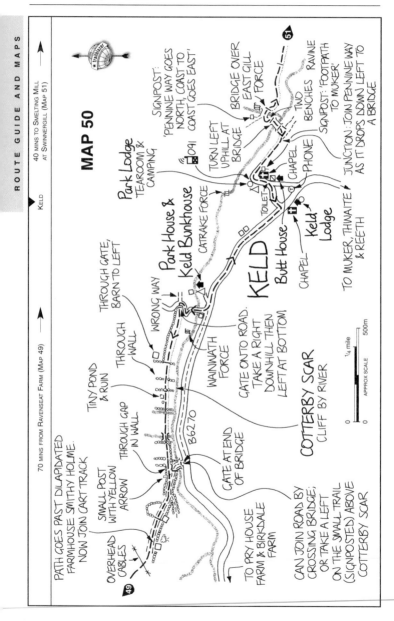

KELD ← 70 MINS FROM RAVENSEAT FARM (MAP 49) → 40 MINS TO SMELTING MILL AT SWINNERGILL (MAP 51) →

MAP 50

PATH GOES PAST DILAPIDATED FARMHOUSE SMITHY HOLME. NOW JOIN CART TRACK

OVERHEAD CABLES

SMALL POST WITH YELLOW ARROW

TINY POND & RUIN

THROUGH GAP IN WALL

THROUGH WALL

THROUGH GATE, BARN TO LEFT

WRONG WAY

GATE AT END OF BRIDGE

B6270

WAINWATH FORCE

GATE ONTO ROAD. TAKE A RIGHT DOWNHILL THEN LEFT AT BOTTOM

TO PRY HOUSE FARM & BIRKDALE FARM

CAN JOIN ROAD BY CROSSING BRIDGE; OR TAKE A LEFT ON THE SMALL TRAIL (SIGNPOSTED) ABOVE COTTERBY SCAR

COTTERBY SCAR CLIFF BY RIVER

¼ mile

APPROX SCALE

500m

Park House & Keld Bunkhouse

CATRAKE FORCE

Park Lodge TEAROOM & CAMPING

SIGNPOST: 'PENNINE WAY GOES NORTH, COAST TO COAST GOES EAST'

TURN LEFT UPHILL AT BRIDGE

BRIDGE OVER EAST GILL FORCE

TWO BENCHES RAVINE

SIGNPOST: 'FOOTPATH TO MUKER'

JUNCTION: JOIN PENNINE WAY AS IT DROPS DOWN LEFT TO A BRIDGE

TOILET

CHAPEL

PHONE

KELD

Butt House

Keld Lodge

CHAPEL

TO MUKER, THWAITE & REETH

51

49

and an extensive wine list; light meals are served at lunchtime.

Butt House (☎ 01748 886374, 🖥 www .butthousekeld.co.uk; 2D/1T/2F, all en suite, most with bath) is the B&B once run by Doreen Whitehead, who nowadays produces an accommodation guide to the Coast to Coast (see p48). It's now owned by Keld Lodge and rates start at £38pp with an evening meal available for £15 if booked in advance. Dogs (£5) are welcome.

Two miles back up the road to Kirkby (or just a mile back west from where the path joins the B6270 at the bridge) is **Pry House Farm** (☎ 01748 886845; 🖥 www.pryfarm house.co.uk; 1D en suite shower/1T private bath) where B&B costs £30-32pp or £37 for single occupancy. They can also lay on an evening meal for £13 (book in advance) and a packed lunch for £5.50. If you ask they'll collect you from Keld if you've chosen to end this stage right in the village.

On the same road, past the turn off north to Ravenseat (a useful short cut avoiding backtracking from Keld) and nearly three miles from the village is **Birkdale Farm** (☎ 01748 886044; 🖥 www.birkdalefarm.com;

1F sleeping up to five, en suite bath). Again, with advance notice they'll pick you up and drop you off the next day (although the OS map shows an interesting path from the farm down to the river, over Keld Side and around Kisdon Hill to Muker to pick up the valley route to Reeth).

Accommodation here is offered in a spacious cottage on a half-board basis at £40pp (no discount for single occupancy); the food for dinner and breakfast is provided and guests cook or heat it up in the cottage. Everyone will find it a real treat to spread out and enjoy this remote locale in Upper Swaledale. A packed lunch to see you on your way costs £5.

For further accommodation options in Muker and Gunnerside (on the recommended low-level path) see p170 and p174.

Transport (see also pp52-5)
Little Red **Bus** No 30 (Mon-Sat) travels to Reeth and Richmond via Thwaite, Muker and all the Swaledale villages. Kirkby Lonsdale Coach Hire's No 831 runs on Sunday between Hawes and Leyburn and also stops in Reeth.

THWAITE   OFF MAP 50
Two miles down the road from Keld, **Kearton Country Hotel** (☎ 01748 886277, 🖥 www.keartoncountryhotel.co.uk; 6D/ 5T/1F, all en suite, bath available; Feb-Dec) is a good-looking place. Rates are £39pp per night plus £10.50pp for dinner; room rates are reduced for longer stays.

Their smart *restaurant* is open to non-residents with local specialities on the menu; dinner is served daily 6.30-7.30pm.

Little Red **Bus** No 30 (Mon-Sat) stops here on its route between Keld and Richmond; see pp52-5 for details.

STAGE 8: KELD TO REETH   MAPS 50-56

Introduction
One might rightly assume the **original high-level route** (see pp164-70) is the way to go but many walkers who've done both find the **low-level (Swaledale Valley) route** (see pp170-4) most agreeable, and of course a tad less effortful.

The high-level walk as described in Wainwright's book begins at the foot of the village – a bit of a pain to those who've spent the night down in Thwaite or Muker (see p170) and where following the valley alternative to Reeth makes sense. But if you wish to take the high-level route you could catch the Little Red Bus (No 30) back up to Keld. There's one morning service a day Monday to Saturday from Muker (at the time of writing it left from near the Farmers Arms; check the website, see box p54, for the actual departure time) to Keld via Thwaite. Note that on this high-level route there's nowhere to buy any food or drink so come prepared.

The high-level route   Maps 51-56

The wildlife along this **12¹/₂-mile (20km, 4¹/₂hr)** walk can be abundant, so try to set off as early as possible to increase your chances of encountering rabbits, pheasants and even deer. However, as with Stage 6 from Shap to Kirkby Stephen, this route is mainly about archaeology and the evidence of man's industrial enterprise in the far north of England. Today's walk takes you through a part of Yorkshire that has been forever scarred by the activities of lead mining (see box below). The first sign of this crops up at **Crackpot Hall** (Map 51), 30 minutes from Keld along a gloriously pretty trail high above the Swale. Though there's been a house here since the 16th century, the ruin you see today actually dates from the 18th century and, while not directly connected to the mining industry, the farmhouse was once owned by one of the mine's managers. Quiet and ruined now, the location would be a nice spot for a wild camp were it

---

❑ Lead mining in Swaledale

According to the best estimates, lead has been mined in Swaledale since at least Roman times, and very possibly there was some small-scale mining back in the Bronze Age. A couple of pigs (ingots) of lead, including one discovered in Swaledale with the Roman name 'Hadrian' marked upon it, have been found. A versatile metal which oxidises slowly, lead is used in plumbing (indeed the word 'plumbing' comes from the Latin for lead), ship-building and roofing as well as in the manufacture of glass, pottery and paint. During medieval times lead was much in demand by the great churches and castles that were being built at that time.

The onset of the Industrial Revolution caused mining in Swaledale to become more organised and developed from the end of the 17th century. The innovation of gunpowder blasting, too, led to a sizeable increase in production, and the Yorkshire sites were at the centre of the British lead-mining industry. Indeed, during the mid-19th century Britain was producing over half the world's lead, and the mines in Yorkshire were producing 10 per cent of that.

But while some of the mine-owners grew fabulously wealthy on the proceeds, the workers themselves suffered appalling conditions, often staying for a week or more at the mine and spending every daylight hour inside it. Deaths were common as the mines were rarely built with safety in mind, and as advances in technology drove the mines ever deeper, so conditions became ever more hazardous. Illnesses from the cramped, damp and insanitary conditions were rife. As if to rub salt into the wounds, many of the workers did not even own their own tools, but instead hired them from an agent. The industry continued to prosper throughout much of the 19th century until the opening of mines in South America lead to an influx of cheaper imports and a fall in price, sending many British mines into bankruptcy. Many workers drifted away, usually to the coal mines around Durham, or to London and North America, in search of better prospects. By the early 20th century many of the villages were struggling to survive. Indeed, in the words of one resident of Reeth, when the mines closed the village became a 'City of the Dead'. Thankfully, tourism today has gone some way to securing the future of these attractive mining villages, and with the establishment of the Yorkshire Dales National Park, the future looks a lot brighter for the villages of Swaledale.

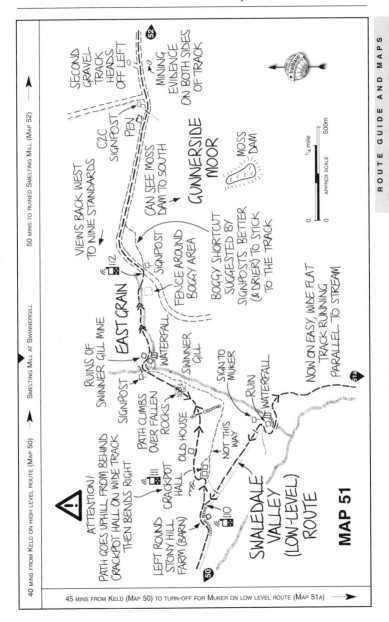

40 MINS FROM KELD ON HIGH LEVEL ROUTE (MAP 50) → SMELTING MILL AT SWINNERGILL. → 50 MINS TO RUINED SMELTING MILL (MAP 52) →

MAP 51

SECOND GRAVEL TRACK HEADS OFF LEFT

MINING EVIDENCE ON BOTH SIDES OF TRACK

C2C SIGNPOST PEN

GUNNERSIDE MOOR

MOSS DAM

VIEWS BACK WEST TO NINE STANDARDS

CAN SEE MOSS DAM TO SOUTH

SIGNPOST

FENCE AROUND BOGGY AREA

BOGGY SHORTCUT SUGGESTED BY SIGNPOSTS, BETTER (& DRIER) TO STICK TO THE TRACK

EAST GRAIN

RUINS OF SWINNER GILL MINE

SIGNPOST

WATERFALL

SWINNER GILL

SIGN TO MUKER

RUIN

WATERFALL

NOW ON EASY, WIDE FLAT TRACK RUNNING PARALLEL TO STREAM

PATH CLIMBS OVER FALLEN ROCKS

OLD HOUSE

NOT THIS WAY

ATTENTION!
PATH GOES UPHILL FROM BEHIND CRACKPOT HALL ON WIDE TRACK THEN BENDS RIGHT

CRACKPOT HALL

LEFT ROUND STONY HILL FARM (BARN)

SWALEDALE VALLEY (LOW-LEVEL) ROUTE

APPROX SCALE

0 ¼ mile

0 500m

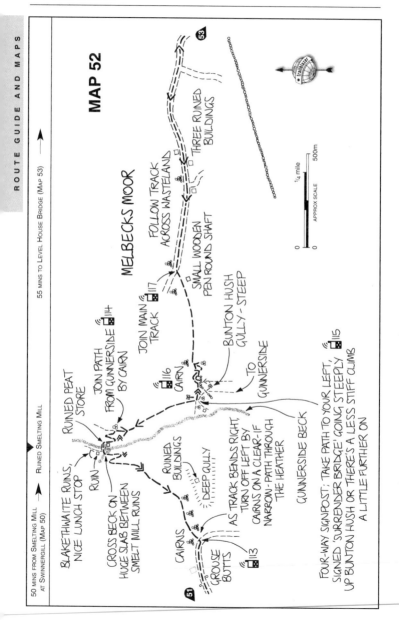

50 MINS FROM SMELTING MILL
AT SWINNERGILL (MAP 50) → RUINED SMELTING MILL

55 MINS TO LEVEL HOUSE BRIDGE (MAP 53) →

MAP 52

MELBECKS MOOR

THREE RUINED BUILDINGS

FOLLOW TRACK ACROSS WASTELAND

SMALL WOODEN PEN ROUND SHAFT

BUNTON HUSH GULLY - STEEP

JOIN MAIN TRACK

🏕117

JOIN PATH FROM GUNNERSIDE 🏕114 BY CAIRN

RUINED PEAT STORE

BLAKETHWAITE RUINS, NICE LUNCH STOP

RUIN

CROSS BECK ON HUGE SLAB BETWEEN SMELT MILL RUINS

🏕116 CAIRN

TO GUNNERSIDE

🏕115

RUINED BUILDINGS

DEEP GULLY

CAIRNS

GROUSE BUTTS

🏕113

GUNNERSIDE BECK

AS TRACK BENDS RIGHT, TURN OFF LEFT BY CAIRNS ON A CLEAR - IF NARROW - PATH THROUGH THE HEATHER

FOUR-WAY SIGNPOST: TAKE PATH TO YOUR LEFT, SIGNED 'SURRENDER BRIDGE' GOING STEEPLY UP BUNTON HUSH OR THERE'S A LESS STIFF CLIMB A LITTLE FURTHER ON

APPROX SCALE
0   ¼ mile
0   500m

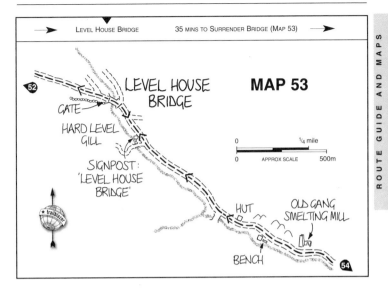

allowed, as would be many of the mining ruins on this stage. 'Crackpot', by the way, means 'Deep hole or chasm that is the haunt of crows', and is not a comment on the value of the endeavours of the former residents.

The path bends north now from behind the Hall to climb above the narrow gorge of Swinner Gill. Make sure you head uphill to follow the correct trail or you'll eventually find yourself on a lower, parallel but precipitous sheep track barely two boots wide and clinging to the side of the gorge below the correct route – see Map 51. Whichever route you stumble on, before long you arrive at the eerie remains of **Swinner Gill smelting mill** with waterfalls alongside. Again, from here it's possible to stray onto a tricky path alongside the north bank of **East Grain Beck** instead of the easier way a little higher up the valley side, but both deliver you with a sweaty brow onto the breezy expanse of **Gunnerside Moor**.

On the level now and passing **Moss Dam** to the south, you leave the track to curve north-east and descend steeply to another picturesque set of ruins at **Blakethwaite** (Map 52) in the valley of Gunnerside Beck. This is an ideal, if slightly premature, location to enjoy a picnic lunch out of the wind. While sitting on the grassy bank behind the large ruined peat store with its impressive arched windows (peat was used with coal to heat the smelting furnace), look for the flue coming down from the hill, finishing near the kiln on the western banks.

From here the path continues east, steeply back up onto **Melbecks Moor**. It's not uncommon to lose your way on the final climb onto the moor; we recommend that at the signpost for 'Surrender Bridge' (Map 52, WPT 115), you get stuck into **Bunton Hush gully** as indicated until you're on the top where cairns

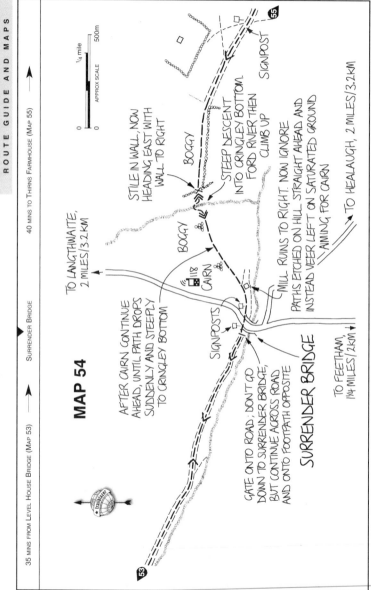

MAP 54

AFTER CAIRN CONTINUE AHEAD, UNTIL PATH DROPS SUDDENLY AND STEEPLY TO CRINGLEY BOTTOM

TO LANGTHWAITE, 2 MILES/3.2KM

BOGGY

118 CAIRN

STILE IN WALL, NOW HEADING EAST WITH WALL TO RIGHT

BOGGY

STEEP DESCENT INTO CRINGLEY BOTTOM. FORD RIVER THEN CLIMB UP

SIGNPOST

SIGNPOSTS

MILL RUINS TO RIGHT. NOW IGNORE PATHS ETCHED ON HILL STRAIGHT AHEAD AND INSTEAD VEER LEFT ON SATURATED GROUND AIMING FOR CAIRN

TO HEALAUGH, 2 MILES/3.2KM

SURRENDER BRIDGE

TO FEETHAM, 1¼ MILES/2KM

GATE ONTO ROAD; DON'T GO DOWN TO SURRENDER BRIDGE, BUT CONTINUE ACROSS ROAD AND ONTO FOOTPATH OPPOSITE

APPROX SCALE

0   ¼ mile

0   500m

★ Trailblazer

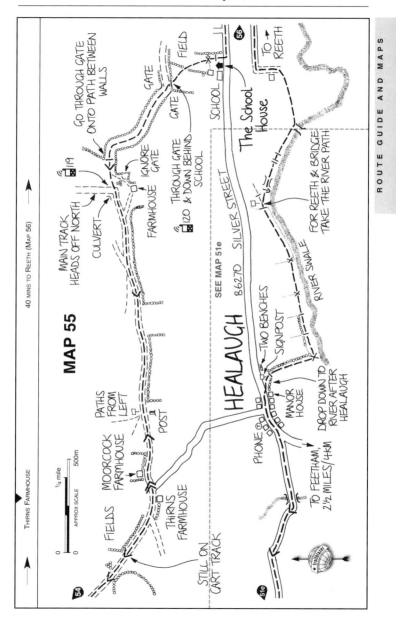

lead to the big track (WPT 117), which everybody eventually passes. The landscape at the top is a bit of a shock. Whereas the mining relics encountered thus far have been rather quaint, what confronts you now is a gravel desolation, stripped of any topsoil by artificially channelled water released by the miners to expose the minerals underneath. Such gullies, like the one you just clambered up, are known as a *hush*.

At the end of your 'moon walk' lies **Level House Bridge** (Map 53), where you cross **Hard Level Gill** before following it down to the remains of **Old Gang Smelting Mill**, the most extensive ruins yet where warning notices beseech you not to 'ruin the ruins'. Soon you arrive at **Surrender Bridge** (Map 54) where you cross a minor road leading up to obscure Arkengarthdale and continue past another smelt-mill ruin, dropping in and out of the excellently named **Cringley Bottom** to continue with fine views of Swaledale's iridescent verdure and drystone walls (Map 55, p169; see box p178) as the track rolls down to Reeth.

The low-level Swaledale Valley alternative route
Map 51 p165, Map 51a, Maps 51b-e pp172-4, Map 56, p179

This option adds up to about 4½ hours of level walking (11½ miles, 18.5km) and you may well end up in Reeth soon after lunch. Some Coasters are tempted to roll it in with the previous stage, making a hefty 23-mile day, but doing so you can expect to hobble into Reeth in a bit of a state. Others in a rush knock out Keld to Richmond in one day; about the same distance and probably with the same consequences. Our advice? Kick back and enjoy the first leisurely stage for a while, stop frequently to admire the valley and commune with nature, take the diversion to Muker. Suppress the urge to press on with a pint or two of Old Peculier while overlooking Reeth's village green. It's a beautiful stroll, particularly in the early morning before the crowds gather. The path is so easy that for once you can fully appreciate your surroundings, looking for riparian wildlife such as herons, ducks and, so it is said, otters. It's not all so rosy down in the valley. One thing you'll remember about Swaledale all the way to Marrick, is the number of awkwardly **narrow stone stiles** barely a leg wide and often embellished with a tiny, sprung gate. If you're lame, stiff or just lugging a heavy backpack, getting jammed on one of these trekkers' traps really can upset your composure.

The villages passed on the way are a joy. **Muker** (off Map 51a and actually slightly off the route) is a very pleasant little place and one of James Herriot's (see p175) favourites. Pronounced 'Miu-ker', you'll find a church and the *Farmers Arms* (☎ 01748 886297; food served daily noon-2.30pm & 6-8.45pm). It has also been the home for 30 years of **Swaledale Woollens** (🖳 www.swaledalewoollens.co.uk), their raw material shorn from the hardy Swaledale sheep whose tough wool is considered ideal for carpets. The shop boasts that it actually saved the village following the depression caused by the collapse of the mining industry. Following a meeting in the local pub, a decision was made to set up a local cottage industry producing knitwear, and today over 30 home workers are employed knitting the jumpers, hats and many other items available in the store.

Muker Village Store and Teashop (☎ 01748 886409, 🖥 www.mukervil lage.co.uk) comprises the **village shop** (Mar/Apr to end Oct Mon-Sat 9am-5pm, Sun 9.30am-5pm, Nov to Mar/Apr Mon-Fri 9am-1pm, Sat 9am-4pm, Sun 9.30am-4pm, a **tearoom** (Mar/Apr to end Oct, Wed-Mon 11am-ish to 'when it goes quiet'; weekends only in winter) and **B&B** (1D or T; £32.50pp en suite shower). Accommodation is also available at *Chapel House* (☎ 01748 886822, 🖥 www.mukerchapel.co.uk; 1D en suite shower; Easter to Nov), just up from Swaledale Woollens, where the room costs from £35pp with a £5 single occupancy supplement; the 18th-century *Swale Farm* (☎ 01748 886479, 🖥 www.dalesandvaleswalks.co.uk/swalefarm.html; 1D/1T, en suite shower; Mar-Nov), near the shop, charges £28.50pp, single occupancy £30. From Monday to Saturday Little Red **Bus** 30 calls here, and

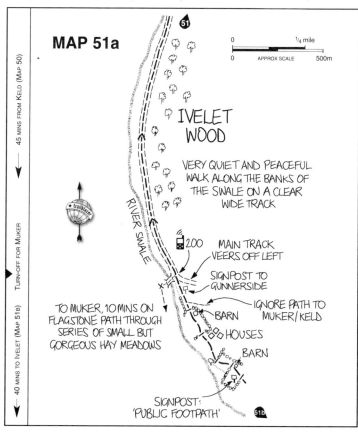

MAP 51a

0   ¼ mile

0   APPROX SCALE   500m

IVELET WOOD

VERY QUIET AND PEACEFUL WALK ALONG THE BANKS OF THE SWALE ON A CLEAR WIDE TRACK

RIVER SWALE

★ trailblazer

📱200   MAIN TRACK VEERS OFF LEFT

SIGNPOST TO GUNNERSIDE

IGNORE PATH TO MUKER/KELD

BARN

HOUSES

BARN

TO MUKER, 10 MINS ON FLAGSTONE PATH THROUGH SERIES OF SMALL BUT GORGEOUS HAY MEADOWS

SIGNPOST: 'PUBLIC FOOTPATH'

51b

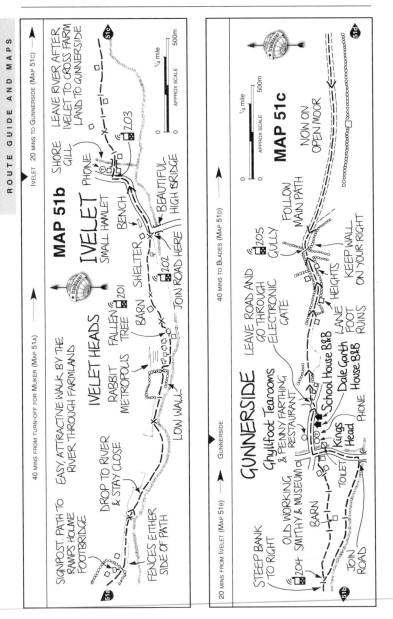

40 MINS FROM TURN-OFF FOR MUKER (MAP 51A) →

IVELET 20 MINS TO GUNNERSIDE (MAP 51c)

MAP 51b

IVELET
SMALL HAMLET

EASY, ATTRACTIVE WALK BY THE
RIVER THROUGH FARMLAND

LEAVE RIVER AFTER
IVELET TO CROSS FARM
LAND TO GUNNERSIDE

IVELET HEADS

RABBIT
METROPOLIS

SHORE
GILL

103

SIGNPOST. PATH TO
RAMPS HOLME
FOOTBRIDGE

DROP TO RIVER
& STAY CLOSE

FENCES EITHER
SIDE OF PATH

LOW WALL

FALLEN
TREE

201

BARN

SHELTER

202

PHONE

BENCH

BEAUTIFUL
HIGH BRIDGE

JOIN ROAD HERE

¼ mile
0   500m
0   APPROX SCALE

51c

20 MINS FROM IVELET (MAP 51B) →   GUNNERSIDE

40 MINS TO BLADES (MAP 51D) →

MAP 51c

NOW ON
OPEN MOOR

GUNNERSIDE

Ghyllfoot Tearooms
& Penny Farthing
Restaurant

LEAVE ROAD AND
GO THROUGH
ELECTRONIC
GATE

205

GULLY

FOLLOW
MAIN PATH

STEEP BANK
TO RIGHT

204

OLD WORKING,
SMITHY & MUSEUM

BARN

Kings
Head

School House B&B

Dale Garth B&B

Penny House B&B

TOILET

PHONE

JOIN
ROAD

LANE
HEIGHTS

LANE
FOOT
RUINS

KEEP WALL
ON YOUR RIGHT

¼ mile
0   500m
0   APPROX SCALE

51d

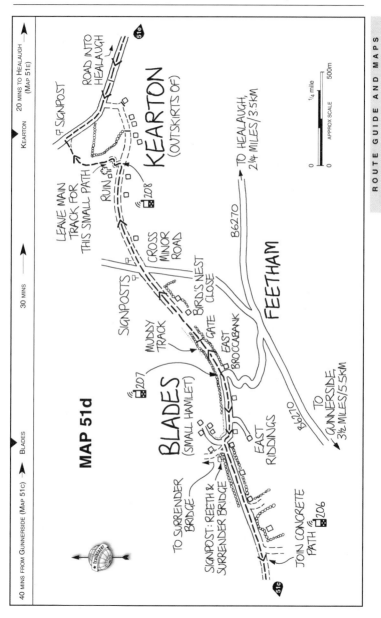

MAP 51d

40 MINS FROM GUNNERSIDE (MAP 51c) → BLADES → 30 MINS → KEARTON → 20 MINS TO HEALAUGH (MAP 51e)

BLADES (SMALL HAMLET)

TO SURRENDER BRIDGE

SIGNPOST: REETH & SURRENDER BRIDGE

JOIN CONCRETE PATH 206

EAST RIDDINGS

SIGNPOSTS

MUDDY TRACK

GATE

EAST BROCCABANK

BIRD'S NEST CLOSE

CROSS MINOR ROAD

FEETHAM

TO GUNNERSIDE 3½ MILES/5.5KM

B6270

TO HEALAUGH, 2¼ MILES/3.5KM

B6270

LEAVE MAIN TRACK FOR THIS SMALL PATH

RUIN 208

KEARTON (OUTSKIRTS OF)

SIGNPOST

ROAD INTO HEALAUGH

207

1/4 mile   500m
0   APPROX SCALE   0

in Gunnerside, and on Sunday Kirkby Lonsdale Coach Hire's No 831 bus stops in both villages; see pp52-5 for details.

Gunnerside (💻 www.gunnerside.info; Map 51c, p172) which lost out to Kirkby Stephen in a recent Village of the Year award, has a post office, public toilet and public phone, and even an old **smithy** with an attached museum (Easter to Oct 11am-5pm, closed Mon; £2.50).

The genteel *Ghyllfoot Tearooms* (☎ 01748 886239; 10.30am-5pm, closed Tue) transforms into the *Penny Farthing Restaurant* (7.15-9pm) serving meals on Wednesday and Saturday evenings and a roast at lunchtime (12.30-2pm) on Sunday; they also do a curry takeaway on Monday evenings (Apr-Oct only).

The *Kings Head* (💻 www.kingsheadgunnerside.co.uk) was under new ownership at the time of writing but it wasn't possible to check opening days/hours.

There's accommodation at *Dalegarth House* (☎ 01748 886275, 💻 www.dalegarthhousebandb.co.uk; 1T, en suite shower) on the way out of the village towards Reeth. B&B costs £25pp, or £27 for single occupancy. The *School House* (☎ 01748 886874, 💻 SchoolHouseBandB@aol.com; 1D en suite shower/2T private bathroom) is another B&B with simple rooms costing from £30pp (£40 single occupancy).

From Gunnerside the path crosses moor and farmland, eventually dropping down to **Healaugh** (Map 51e), from where it returns to the river to continue past the suspension bridge to Reeth, which it enters via Quaker Rd.

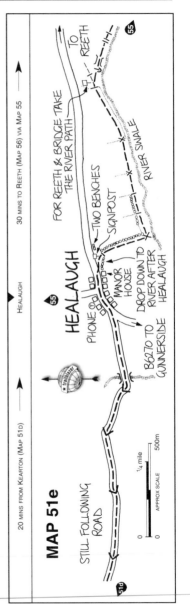

REETH   see map p177

Reeth, the 'capital' of Swaledale, is the archetypal Yorkshire dale village: flanked to north and south by mine-scarred valleys and ringed by dry-stone walls. At its heart lies a village green surrounded on all sides by several examples of those twin institutions of Yorkshire hospitality: the **tearoom** and the **pub**. As if to underline its Yorkshire credentials still further, it also has a renowned brass band. Hardly surprising, therefore, that the village was used as a location for many episodes of the quintessential 1980s Yorkshire TV saga *All Creatures Great and Small* based on the books of rural vet, James Herriot.

Mentioned in the Domesday survey nine centuries earlier, the village grew on the profits of the 19th-century mining boom, though unlike other nearby villages it could always claim a second string to its bow as the main market town for Swaledale (the market is still held on The Green on Fridays). Thankfully, after the mines closed tourism gave Reeth a new lease of life and today the town hosts a number of B&Bs and hotels, as well as some **gift shops** (Garden House and Dales Centre) and a small **museum** (see p177).

Services

The **tourist office** and **National Park centre** (☎ 01748 884059, 🖳 www.yorkshire dales.org; Apr-Oct daily 10am-5pm, Nov-Mar Sat & Sun 10am-4pm) is to the west of The Green in Hudson House.

On the other side of The Green the **general store** (Mon-Sat 9am-5.30pm, Sun 10am-4pm) has a **post office** (Mon-Fri 9am-5.30pm, Sat 9am-4pm). Otherwise there are **cash machines** or cashback in both the Black Bull or the **newsagents** (Mon-Fri 7am-7.30pm, Sat 7.30am-7pm, Sun 8am-4pm; £1.85) at the bottom of the hill on the way out of town. **Internet access** is available at the tourist office or the Buck Hotel (see p176).

Transport

From Monday to Saturday the Little Red Bus (No 30) stops here en route between Keld and Richmond and on Sundays

Kirkby Lonsdale Coach Hire's No 831 calls here; see pp52-5 for details.

Where to stay

There is no shortage of accommodation in Reeth so some selection is necessary. The nearest **youth hostel** is *Grinton Lodge* (off Map 56; ☎ 0845 371 9636, 🖳 grinton @yha.org.uk; 71 beds; from £15.95), a lovely old shooting lodge, but at just over a mile on past Reeth and up a very steep hill, it can be too much to bear. However it is only half a mile from the path and offers superior lodgings with meals, is licensed and has a TV and a games room as well as internet access.

Just half a mile from Reeth and even closer to the path are the converted stone barns which make up the *Dales Bike Centre* (Map 56; ☎ 01748 884908, 🖳 www.dales bikecentre.co.uk; 14 beds) in **Fremington** village. You don't need to be cycling to stay here and the dorms have no more than four beds each so reducing the chance of getting lumbered with a dreaded snorer. Bunk and breakfast at the Centre costs £24, or £35 for a two-bed room to yourself, if available. There's also a *café*/lounge with wi-fi and the *Bridge Inn* (Map 56) is just down the road for a steak and a Martini, shaken, not stirred.

Campers pitch up at *The Orchard Caravan Park* (☎ 01748 884475; check-in at the house signed 'Warden Enquiries' at the cottage; April-Oct; book in advance in peak season). The enthusiastic owners have transformed the place and though dominated by caravans, it's still popular with Coasters. You can camp here for £5pp and, wonderfully, if it's raining they'll allow you to shelter in one of their old caravans for the same price.

If you've taken the high route over the moors and can't walk another inch, just as you rejoin the road you'll pass alongside *The School House* (Map 55, p169; ☎ 01748 884284; 🖳 www.theschoolhouse-reeth .com; 1D/1T, both en suite one with bath), not to be confused with the one in Gunnerside. Less than five minutes' walk from the village, it offers free wi-fi, a drying

ROUTE GUIDE AND MAPS

room, packed lunches by prior arrangement, a guest lounge and rooms for £39pp (single occupancy rates on request).

Hackney House (☎ 01748 884302; 🖳 www.coast2coast.co.uk/hackneyhouse; 1S/1D/1T/3D, T or F, most with en suite shower, bath available), Bridge Terrace, at the bottom of the village has received commendations from readers; the breakfasts are big and the welcome friendly. Rates are £28-33pp. Another place to try is **Walpardo** (☎ 01748 884626, 🖳 walpardoreeth@aol .com; 1S/1T shared bathroom), just off The Green on Anvil Square, where B&B is just £25pp. **Hillary House** (☎ 01748 884171; 1D/1T, shared bathroom), 4 Hillary Terrace, offers B&B for £25pp (£35 single occupancy) and comes recommended. **The Olde Temperance** (☎ 01748 884401; 1S/1D/1F, shared bathroom) is situated above a Christian bookshop and charges £22pp.

Across The Green, **Ivy Cottage** (☎ 01748 884418, 🖳 www.ivycottagereeth.co .uk; 2D en suite with shower/1T private bathroom) charges £25-40pp (minimum two-night stay at weekends) and £5 for packed lunches.

The three pubs add up to: **Buck Hotel** (☎ 01748 884210, 🖳 www.buckhotel.co .uk; 1S/6D/2T/1F, all en suite some with bath), which charges £80-85 per room, £60 single occupancy; **The Black Bull** (☎ 01748 884213; 🖳 www.theblackbullreeth .co.uk; 5D/3T/2F, all private facilities with bath) dates back to 1680 and has rooms overlooking The Green and down Swaledale. Rates are £35-40pp and, hallelujah, there is no single room supplement, dogs are welcome and kids under 10 stay for free; packed lunches cost £4.50. **The Kings Arms** (☎ 01748 884259, 🖳 www .thekingsarms.com; 2T/7D/1F, en suite some with bath), next door, is over 50 years younger, and they charge £35pp for their rear bedrooms which we found to be bright and clean and with a spacious bathroom, or £40pp for those overlooking The Green, but single occupancy is £45-50.

Cambridge House (☎ 01748 884633, 🖳 www.cambridge-house-reeth.co.uk; 1S/3D/1T, all en suite, some with bath) lies about a quarter of a mile (400m) north from Buck Hotel on the road to Arkengarthdale; you'll find it on the left and stuffed full of antiques and curios. The rooms all face south with views over Reeth; for a night's B&B they charge £40pp and they will make a packed lunch for £5.

Arkleside Country Guest House (☎ 01748 884200, 🖳 arkleside@supanet.com; 4D/3D or T, all with private facilities, one with bath; annexe 1F with bath) charges £85 for B&B, £50 single occupancy.

Where to eat and drink

On the way into Reeth it's a real shame **Reeth Bakery** (☎ 01748 884735; Apr-Oct Mon-Sat 10am-4pm, Sun 11am-5pm; Nov-Mar days/hours variable so check in advance), on Silver St, opens late and closes early most days. Along with a variety of breads and heavenly cakes, the still-warm filled rolls sure make a change from the plastic-cocooned sandwiches found at most village shops. If you can't squeeze into the tiny **tearoom**, take your purchases out onto one of the The Green's many benches.

The **Copper Kettle** (☎ 01748 884748; Apr-Sep Sat-Thur 10am-7.30pm, Fri 10am-3pm; Mar & Oct 10.30am-5pm; closed Nov-Feb) is a traditional establishment serving such delights as a proper cream tea (£3) and Swaledale afternoon tea (£6.50). They also offer more substantial fare throughout the day, with most dishes, including beef lasagne and lamb moussaka, around the £8 mark.

The **White House Tea Shop** (☎ 01748 884763; Mar-Jan Fri-Tue 10.30am-4.30pm), on the corner of Anvil Square, sells ice cream and filling lunches. However, they have built up such a loyal clientele that you would be incredibly lucky to get a table on a Sunday (they are only open for lunch on Sundays).

Cuckoo Hill View (☎ 01748 884929; daily in summer 11.30am-5pm, occasionally up to 8pm, weekends only in winter) is an ice-cream parlour at the foot of The Green serving such flavours as 'rhubarb crumble' and 'chocoholic'.

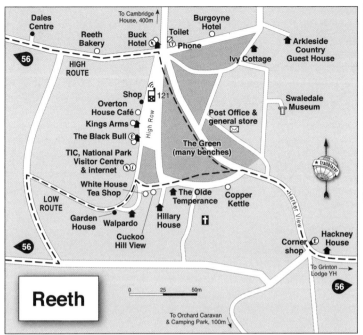

Reeth

Next to the Kings Arms the licensed *Overton House Café* (☎ 01748 884332; Wed 11am-3pm, Fri 10am-2.30pm & 6-10pm, Thurs & Sat 11am-2.30pm & 6-10pm) offers all sorts of coffees and cakes by day and specials (£12-17), such as grilled swordfish in garlic butter with Caesar salad and king prawns, in the evening. Otherwise the pubs like the *Buck Hotel*, *Kings Arms*, *Black Bull* put on the usual spreads with the latter known for its homemade pies. Turn up at the Black Bull early and you should be able to get a seat in the quieter Old Draper's Shop at the centre of the pub.

If you've something to celebrate the exclusive and pricey *Burgoyne Country House Hotel* (☎ 01748 884292, 🖳 www.theburgoyne.co.uk; daily 8pm book in advance; closed Jan to mid Feb) at the top of The Green could be the place for you.

What to see

Swaledale Museum (☎ 01748 884118, 🖳 www.swaledalemuseum.org; Easter to Oct, Mon-Sat 10.30am-5.30pm; £3) is housed in the old 19th-century Methodist school room. It holds some surprisingly intriguing exhibits and is well-worth an hour of your time, particularly if you want to learn more about the local mining and farming industries. The dry-stone wallers' craft (see box p178) is examined, and the museum also looks at the social history of the area in some detail, attempting to show how the locals used to live a hundred or more years ago.

ROUTE GUIDE AND MAPS

STAGE 9: REETH TO RICHMOND   MAPS 56-61

Introduction

There are a couple of lovely tracts of woodland on this **12¹/₂-mile (20km, 4¹/₂hr)** stage, a simple walk that should allow you time to explore the sights of Richmond at the end of the day if you set off early enough and don't lose your way.

A couple of charming villages are passed on the way too, as well as the remains of an old priory. Overall, it's not a spectacular day as you leave the Pennines behind but, if the weather's fine, an exceedingly pleasant one.

The route

The walk starts out along the B6270 which you've been tracking since Kirkby Stephen, but soon after leaving Reeth and crossing the bridge over Arkle Beck, you leave the road and follow the beck along riverside pastures to meet the road again at Grinton Bridge over the meandering Swale. On the far side of the road you continue along the Swale and then, like a startled badger, dart uphill to

---

❏ Dry-stone walls

I am a Dry Stone Waller
All day I Dry Stone Wall
Of all appalling callings
Dry Stone Walling's worst of all
Pam Ayres (British poet), 1978

Along the Coast to Coast path you'll pass hundreds of dry-stone walls out of Britain's estimated 125,000 miles-worth. Beautiful and photogenic, particularly when covered in a layer of velvety green moss, they're probably the most ubiquitous feature of northern England's landscape. That said, few walkers give much thought to who built them, nor have any idea just how much skill and effort goes into making these walls.

Dry-stone walls, so called because they are built without mortar, have been around since Elizabethan times when, as now, they were used to demarcate the boundaries between one farmer's land and another. Many others were built during the Enclosure Acts between 1720 and 1840, when previously large fields shared between a number of farmers were divided into strips of land. A very few of these 18th-century walls are still standing: those nearest to a village tend to be the oldest, as it was this land that was divided and enclosed first. The fact that the walls have lasted so long is largely due to the care that goes into construction.

The first step is to dig some deep, secure foundations. That done, the next step is to build the wall itself, or rather walls, for a typical dry-stone wall is actually made up of two thinner walls built back to back; a design that helps make the wall as sturdy as possible. Every metre or so a through or tie stone is built into the wall to bind the two halves together. It's estimated that one tonne of stone is required for one square yard of wall. Each stone is chosen carefully to fit exactly: a bad choice can upset the pressure loading, leading to an early collapse. Smaller chippings or pebbles are used to fill the gaps and a dry-stone waller we once met in the North Pennines reckoned he could erect just two metres of wall on a good day.

Dry-stone walling has had its heyday; it now faces competition from the wire fence which is a cheaper, simpler and just as effective a way of dividing land, and while the existing dry-stone walls have to be repaired occasionally, more often than not the farmer would rather do it himself than call in a professional. However, the art is certainly not dead; for further information visit the Dry Stone Walling Association's website (🖳 www.dswa.org.uk).

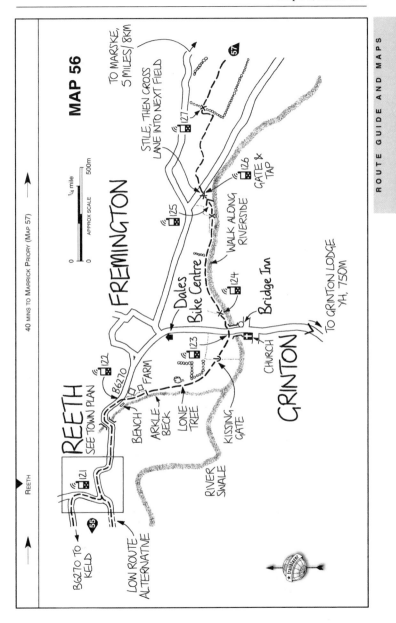

cross a minor road and follow pastures new to **Marrick Priory** (Map 57), just 40 minutes outside Reeth. Though it's visible from a distance, casual visitors are not now allowed to visit the adjacent ruins which have been incorporated into an Outdoor Education Centre. Nevertheless, it seems that staff are pretty used to seeing people walking down the drive to inspect the remains and are quite relaxed about it. The abbey was founded by local noble, Roger de Aske, for Benedictine nuns who numbered 17 at the priory's dissolution in 1540. There are a couple of tomb slabs in the grounds, including one by the entrance belonging to a Thomas Peacock who died in 1762 at the grand old age of 102.

Those disappointed at not being able to explore the ruins thoroughly will find some consolation in the walk up to Marrick village, a pretty uphill amble through the first of this stage's woods, known as Steps Wood and notable as the first dense shade you may have experienced on the trail for several days. The path you're ascending is known as the **Nuns' Steps**, so-called because the nuns are said to have constructed the 375 steps as a walkway to the abbey. At the top, through a couple of fields, lies the village that gave Marrick Priory its name.

MARRICK   MAP 57

Mentioned in *The Domesday Book* as Mange and Marig, the derivation of the name Marrick is something of a mystery. According to one school of thought it has something to do with marshes; according to another, it means something like 'The Habitation of Mary'. Still others believe it to mean Horse or Boundary Ridge from old Norse.

There are no pubs or shops here, in fact very little save for some 25 houses, a public phone and a village institute, but there is a delightful B&B, *Marrick Lodge* (☎ 01748 884474, 🖳 www.marricklodge.co.uk; 1D/ 1T, shared bath, Easter to Oct), tucked down a driveway. They also have a small orchard for **camping** (£5pp) nearby and dogs are welcome. B&B costs from £27.50pp and there's no single occupancy supplement; a three-course dinner is around £15 (book in advance).

From Marrick the trail begins a long north-easterly march up to Marske through farmland punctuated by any number of tiny stiles and gates. If you manage to miss the signs (see photo p20) for *Elaine's Country Kitchen* at *Nun Cote Nook Farm* (Map 57; ☎ 01748 884266; daily 9am to late; **camping** £5pp; bed in a static caravan sleeping up to six, £18pp) you need to get on to Specsavers fast. She serves snacks and drinks overlooking a quiet open field that gives farm **camping** a good name. They also offer a two-course evening meal (with the meat coming from their farm) for campers for just £12. Even if you're not camping here, many Coasters agree *Elaine's* is well worth a detour for a brew, a snack and a chat about the price of wool.

Nun Cote Nook is just about the last hill farm and so you bid farewell to The Pennines and tramp diagonally across pastures until you join the road to **Marske** and impressive Marske Hall (Map 58) on the right. Continuing up the hill, you pass the crenellated profile of **St Edmund the Martyr**, built on the site of an earlier church dating back to 1090, of which the north and south doors and hexagonal supporting pillars survive. St Edmund, incidentally, was a Saxon king put to death by the Danes in AD870. *(cont'd on p185)*

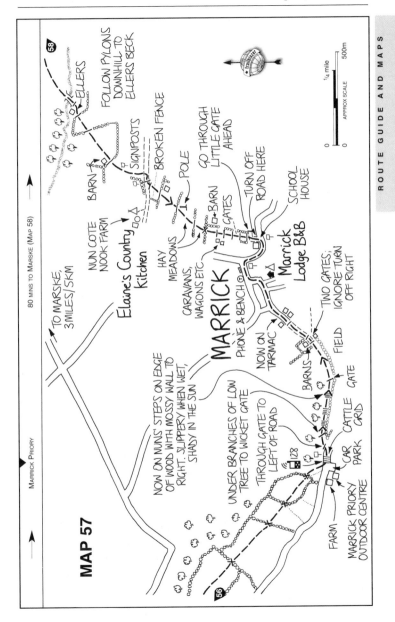

MAP 57

MARRICK PRIORY

TO MARSKE, 3 MILES/5KM

80 MINS TO MARSKE (MAP 58)

58

ELLERS

FOLLOW PYLONS DOWNHILL TO ELLERS BECK

SIGNPOSTS

BROKEN FENCE

POLE

GO THROUGH LITTLE GATE AHEAD

BARN

NUN COTE NOOK FARM

Elaine's Country Kitchen

HAY MEADOWS

BARN GATES

TURN OFF ROAD HERE

SCHOOL HOUSE

CARAVANS, WAGONS ETC

MARRICK

PHONE & BENCH

Marrick Lodge B&B

TWO GATES; IGNORE TURN OFF RIGHT

FIELD

GATE

NOW ON TARMAC

BARNS

CATTLE GRID

CAR PARK

NOW ON NUNS' STEPS ON EDGE OF WOOD WITH MOSSY WALL TO RIGHT. SLIPPERY WHEN WET, SHADY IN THE SUN

UNDER BRANCHES OF LOW TREE TO WICKET GATE

THROUGH GATE TO LEFT OF ROAD

128

MARRICK PRIORY OUTDOOR CENTRE

FARM

56

APPROX SCALE

¼ mile

0   500m

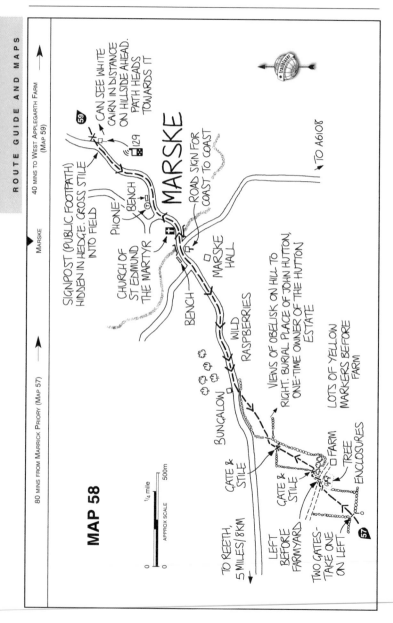

80 MINS FROM MARRICK PRIORY (MAP 57)

MARSKE

40 MINS TO WEST APPLEGARTH FARM (MAP 59)

MAP 58

¼ mile

APPROX SCALE

500m

TO REETH,
5 MILES/8KM

LEFT
BEFORE
FARMYARD

TWO GATES-
TAKE ONE
ON LEFT

57

GATE &
STILE

GATE &
STILE

FARM

TREE
ENCLOSURES

BUNGALOW

LOTS OF YELLOW
MARKERS BEFORE
FARM

VIEWS OF OBELISK ON HILL TO
RIGHT. BURIAL PLACE OF JOHN HUTTON,
ONE-TIME OWNER OF THE HUTTON
ESTATE

WILD
RASPBERRIES

BENCH

MARSKE
HALL

MARSKE

CHURCH OF
ST EDMUND
THE MARTYR

ROAD SIGN FOR
COAST TO COAST

SIGNPOST (PUBLIC FOOTPATH)
HIDDEN IN HEDGE. CROSS STILE
INTO FIELD

PHONE

BENCH

59

129

CAN SEE WHITE
CAIRN IN DISTANCE
ON HILLSIDE AHEAD.
PATH HEADS
TOWARDS IT

TO A6108

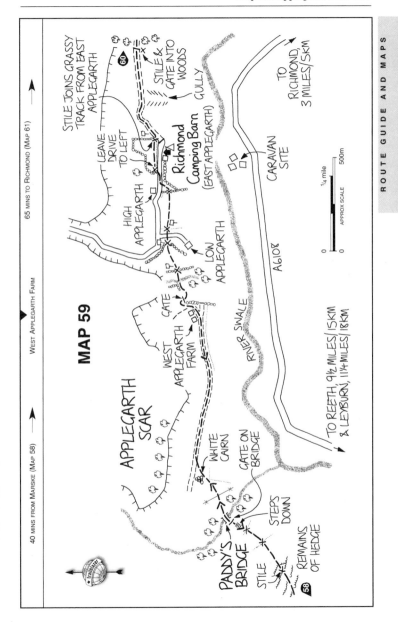

40 MINS FROM MARSKE (MAP 58) ⟶

WEST APPLEGARTH FARM

65 MINS TO RICHMOND (MAP 61) ⟶

MAP 59

STILE JOINS GRASSY TRACK FROM EAST APPLEGARTH

STILE & GATE INTO WOODS

GULLY

60

LEAVE DRIVE TO LEFT

HIGH APPLEGARTH

Richmond Camping Barn (EAST APPLEGARTH)

TO RICHMOND, 3 MILES/5KM

CARAVAN SITE

A6108

LOW APPLEGARTH

WEST APPLEGARTH FARM

GATE

RIVER SWALE

APPLEGARTH SCAR

¼ mile
500m
APPROX SCALE

WHITE CAIRN

GATE ON BRIDGE

TO REETH, 9½ MILES/15KM & LEYBURN, 11¼ MILES/18KM

PADDY'S BRIDGE

STEPS DOWN

STILE

REMAINS OF HEDGE

58

Trailblazer

ROUTE GUIDE AND MAPS

65 MINS FROM WEST APPLEGARTH FARM (MAP 59) TO RICHMONDSHIRE CRICKET CLUB (MAP 61)

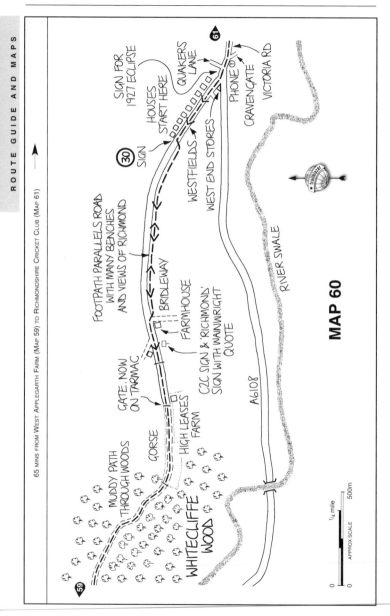

MAP 60

SIGN FOR 1927 ECLIPSE

QUAKERS LANE

HOUSES START HERE

PHONE

CRAVENGATE

VICTORIA RD

30 SIGN

WESTFIELDS

WEST END STORES

FOOTPATH PARALLELS ROAD WITH MANY BENCHES AND VIEWS OF RICHMOND

BRIDLEWAY

FARMHOUSE

C2C SIGN & 'RICHMOND' SIGN WITH WAINWRIGHT QUOTE

GATE NOW ON TARMAC

GORSE

HIGH LEASES FARM

A6108

RIVER SWALE

MUDDY PATH THROUGH WOODS

WHITECLIFFE WOOD

trailblazer

¼ mile

500m

APPROX SCALE

0

0

(cont'd from p180) Half a mile out of the village the road is once again forsaken in favour of grassy pasture as the trail unfolds, bending east at the white cairn below **Applegarth Scar** to pick up the farm track to West Applegarth (Map 59).

The farms of Low and High Applegarth are passed before the trail reaches a third farm at **East Applegarth** where, high above the wooded valley, the rustic ***Richmond Camping Barn*** (☎ 01748 822940; Mar-Nov) is the nearest cheap accommodation option this side of Richmond, three miles on. However, booking in advance is essential either direct (as above) or through the YHA (see p17) because the barn may be booked for sole occupancy. There's an 8- and a 4-bed **dorm** (£7pp with bedding). Electricity (including the shower but not lighting) is on a meter (£1). There's also a grassy patch for **camping** (£4).

The trail continues into sometimes muddy **Whitecliffe Wood**, emerging 15 minutes later at High Leases Farm where the ensuing road walk can actually be paralleled on a footpath behind the fence on the right. Fine views of Richmond soon emerge; terracotta and slate roofs backed by the distant Cleveland Hills until you enter the town's suburbs. As you reacquaint yourself with urban etiquette you'll spot the welcoming sign on the back wall of the West End Stores with a Coast to Coast map showing just how far you've come and what yet remains.

ROUTE GUIDE AND MAPS

RICHMOND   MAP 61, p187

Up above a castle! Down below a stream!
Up above a ruin! Down below a dream!
Man made the castle, rude, forbidding, bare.
God made the river, swift, eternal, fair.
From the recollections of **Mr M Wise** as recorded in ***Richmond Yorkshire in 1830s*** (Wenham Publishers 1977).

This is the largest settlement on the Coast to Coast and feels it. Richmond is a busy market town that evolved around the **castle**, built by one Alan the Red in the 11th century.

As the castle fell into disrepair over time its stones were scavenged to build the surrounding houses, giving the entire town the same sombre hue. During the Georgian era, as the town's fortunes waned still further, Richmond discovered a new source of prosperity as a centre for fine cabinet-making. Many of the buildings leading off the main market-place date back to this era (indeed, the town museum is housed in a former cabinet-maker's workshop) and, following its restoration in 2003, the **Georgian theatre** is now said to be the finest in the land.

At the centre of the town is the large, cobbled **market-place** off which run numerous winding alleys, known as *wynds*. Most of the town's attractions can be found on or near this market-place, though a couple of the ruins nearby may also warrant further investigation.

Although it beat off Chichester and Stirling to win a 'greatest town' accolade in 2009, the size and scale of Richmond – to say nothing of the noise, the bustle and the traffic – can come as something of a shock to fell-weathered Coasters used to more rural locales. As with so many provincial English towns, Richmond can get rowdy at weekends, but it does have its advantages in terms of the facilities it provides, as well as enough sights to keep amused those who decide to rest here for a day.

Services
The **tourist office** (☎ 01748 828742, 🖥 www.richmond.org; Easter to end Oct daily 9.30am-5.30pm, Nov to Easter Mon-Sat 9.30am-4.30pm), on the junction of Victoria

Rd and Queens Rd, stocks all manner of souvenirs, books and brochures about nearby attractions and has an accommodation-booking service (see Where to stay).

The **library** (Mon, Tue, Fri 9.30am-7pm, Thur 9.30am-5pm, Sat 9.30am-4pm; closed Wed and Sun) offers **internet** access (it has ten terminals) and charges £1.50 for 30 minutes to temporary members.

The **post office** (Mon, Tues & Fri 9am-7pm, Thur 9.30am-5pm, Sat 9.30am-4pm) does foreign exchange and all the major banks are represented on the main square and have longed-for **cashpoints**. Having got your money you'll then want something to spend it on. The **outdoors shop**, Yeoman's (Mon-Sat 9am-5.30pm, Sun 10am-5pm), on Finkle St, is worth checking out for replacement equipment; Stepping Out is another outdoor clothes and shoe shop nearby. There's a Boots on the main square and a second **pharmacy**, Richmond Pharmacy, by the roundabout on King St.

Castle Hill **Bookshop**, below the castle, has a good range of books and an interesting selection on local history. For **food shopping** there's a Somerfield (Mon-Sat 7am-10pm, Sun 9am-6pm) on the main square, and a Co-op superstore (Mon-Fri 8am-10pm, Sat 8am-8pm, Sun 11am-5pm) to the north of Grey Friars Tower.

Where to stay

Currently there are no hostels in Richmond and the nearest **cheap accommodation** (camping/camping barn) is either three miles back at East Applegarth (see p185), the *Hildyard Arms* (see p192) in Colburn three miles further along the Coast to Coast path, or the better-appointed *Brompton Camping Barn* (see p192) two miles after Colburn.

So if you want to stay in town it's going to have to be a B&B or a hotel. If you haven't pre-booked, your best bet is the tourist office which runs a free accommodation-booking service and posts lists of available accommodation in the window. What follows is our selection of the options based on readers' feedback and our own experiences. Fellow Coasters recommend *Willance House* (☎

01748 824467, 🖳 www.willancehouse.com; 1D/2D or T, all en suite with shower), at 24 Frenchgate, an oak-beamed house (or rather, three houses) dating back to the 17th century. It's named after the first alderman of Richmond and stands just a few yards off the main square. You'll find free wi-fi and a guest lounge; rates are from £35pp or £50 for single occupancy.

Further up this road, away from the square is *Frenchgate Guesthouse* (☎ 01748 823421, 🖳 www.66frenchgate.co.uk; 2D/2T/2F, all en suite; some with bath), 66 Frenchgate, which, like the others, has fine views down across the Swale. Other features include TVs and free wi-fi. Rates are from £39pp; single occupancy is from £60.

Almost opposite Willance House is the smart *Frenchgate Restaurant & Hotel* (☎ 01748 822087, 🖳 www.thefrenchgate .co.uk; 2S/6T or D/1 suite, all en suite, some with bath), 59-61 Frenchgate. With marble floors, stone walls, oak-framed beds and showcasing local artists, it's a classy venue for a relaxing stay with rates from £59pp for two sharing a standard room with plusher options at £79pp. Sadly, the weary solo traveller must hand over at least £88.

On the square itself is *The Kings Head* (☎ 01748 850220, 🖳 www.kingsheadrich mond.co.uk; 5S/28D/7D or T), probably the smartest hotel in town though it doesn't look much on the outside. All rooms are en suite (most with bath) with wi-fi and variable rates which start from £58pp (£82 for a single) for B&B.

Another good choice is *Nuns Cottage* (☎ 01748 822809, 🖳 www.nunscottage.co .uk; 1D/1T, private bath; closed late Dec to Jan), 5 Hurgill Rd, which is actually three cottages converted into one Grade II listed house. The house is filled with antiques and guests are welcomed with a sherry and will find fresh fruit in the room as well as a TV with DVD player; nevertheless, the favourite part for most trekkers is the enclosed garden surrounded by high stone walls, a tranquil sanctuary from the hubbub beyond. B&B here costs £75-80, £60 for single occupancy. No dogs.

The Buck Inn (☎ 01748 822259, 🖳 www.thebuck-richmond.co.uk; 1S or D/3D

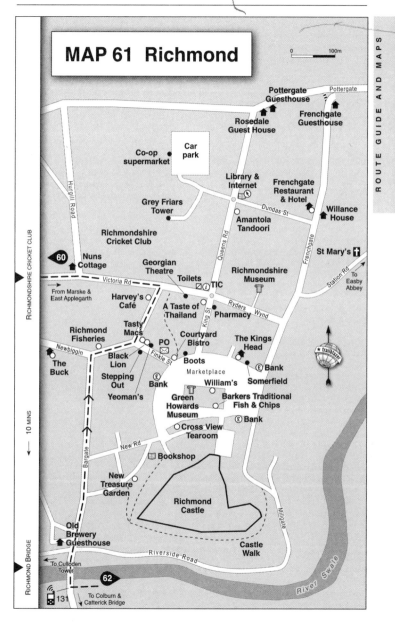

or T/2D/T or F) on Newbiggin is an unpretentious, friendly place with six en suite shower rooms. Parts of the inn date back to the 14th century and rates start at £65 for a room and £50 for single occupancy.

On Pottergate to the north are the friendly *Pottergate Guesthouse* (☎ 01748 823826; 1S/2D/2T/1F, most with shared/en suite shower, bath available), 4 Pottergate, charging £30-33pp, and *Rosedale Guest House* (☎ 01748 823926 ☐ www.rich mondbedandbreakfast.co.uk; 2T/4D, all en suite with shower; £65 for a twin, £74-84 for a double, from £55 for single occupancy), where the silver-starred, high-ceilinged Georgian rooms all come with sherry and chocolates on your bedside table and a pleasingly varied breakfast menu.

On the small green in the south of the town is *The Old Brewery Guesthouse* (☎ 01748 822460, ☐ www.oldbreweryguest house.com; 2S/3D/2D or T/2T, all with private facilities, bath available), another Grade II Georgian building and the nerve centre for Sherpa Van (see p25). Rates are £45-55 for a single and from £36 per person for two sharing.

Where to eat and drink
Disregarding fast-food outlets which you'll have not necessarily walked across the country to visit, *Harvey's Café* (☎ 01748 829505; Mon, Tue, Thur-Sat 9am-3pm, Sun 11.30am-3pm), on Rosemary Lane, has a specials board (two courses for £6); the menu has vegetarian options and may include roasts.

A more modern, swish tearoom, *Williams* (☎ 01748 824052; Tue-Sat 9am-5.30pm in summer, to 4.30pm in winter) stands in the centre of the market-place and their scones are £1.60. More traditional and unfussier, *Cross View Tearooms* (☎ 01748 825897; Mon-Sat 9am-5pm, Sun 10am-5pm) is friendly and cheap.

The opening hours are rather limited but for the biggest selection of sandwiches in the shire, *Tasty Macs* (☎ 01748 822597; Mon-Sat 10am-3pm), on Finkle St, has a menu the size of a wall. Richmond is well-served by fish and chipperies, the most popular of which is *Richmond Fisheries*

(☎ 01748 822937; Mon-Sat daily 11am-10pm, summer Sun 11.30am-8pm) at 4 Newbiggin. If the thought of more fish and chips or another pub meal gives you a migraine, a delicious curry is the only cure. Point yourself confidently towards *Amantola Tandoori* (☎ 01748 826070; ☐ www.amontola-restaurant.co.uk; Sun-Thur 5-11.30pm, Fri-Sat to midnight) up on Queen's Rd; we think it's the best curry house on the Coast to Coast. There's plenty of space, the service is great and you can eat all you want for £10 or enjoy a slightly better selection of dishes as part of a three-course deal for £9. The spicy aromas of *Amantola* will stay with you all the way to Robin Hood's Bay.

The *Black Lion* (☎ 01748 826217; food Mon-Fri 11.30am-2.30pm, Sat to 3.30pm, Sun noon-3.30pm, Mon-Fri & Sun 5.30-8.30pm, Sat to 9pm), Finkle St off Market Place, serves tasty and unusual dishes such as rabbit casserole while *New Treasure Garden* (☎ 01748 825827; Wed-Mon 6-11pm), 7 Castle Hill, is a Cantonese restaurant with an interesting Szechuan selection; if you're unfamiliar with this spicy Chinese fare, you may care to try the Szechuan House Special (around £8.30 to eat in) which has a sample of every dish including chicken, squid, bean curd, duck and pork, much of it covered with a special sauce made with chillies, garlic, 'five spicy powder' and yellow bean sauce.

At 5 Chantry Wynd *Courtyard Bistro* (Mon-Sat 9.30am-5pm, Sun 10am-4pm, Fri & Sat 7-10pm) is a fair-value place doing a reasonable 'workers' lunch' of sandwiches, crisps and tea or coffee from £5.95 during the day, and smarter dishes in the evening from around £11, including a tasty poached salmon in Hollandaise sauce.

A Taste of Thailand (☎ 01748 829696, daily 5-11pm), on King St, has been recommended and does a green curry for £6-8 plus you can bring your own drinks with £1 corkage.

The smartest place to eat on Market Place is the **restaurant** at the *Kings Head* (see Where to stay; daily 6-9pm) where you can dine on such fancy dishes as roast fillet of lamb with pancetta and spinach, thyme and orange jus, dauphinoise potato and wilted greens (£18.95). They also do meals at the **bar** (daily noon-2pm & 6-9.15pm) which are less expensive.

Frenchgate Restaurant and Hotel (see Where to stay; daily noon-2pm & 7-9pm) is another good, if expensive, choice for a relaxed evening's dining with guinea fowl, turbot and your old friend, Swaledale lamb, on the menu. Their three-course set meal costs £34.

For drinking, there are some pubs lining Market Place, but they can be extremely noisy with a couple catering largely to groups of local youths looking for a fight. A safe option is *The Buck Inn* (see Where to stay; food Mon & Wed-Fri noon-2.30pm & 6-8pm, Sat noon-7pm, Sun noon-4pm), on Newbiggin, which, though it still has live music some nights, is a lot more friendly and relaxed and has great views across the river.

What to see and do

Richmond is a great town to walk around, with plenty of twisting 'wynds' to explore and plaques installed here and there pointing out places of historical interest. The following sights are all on 🖳 www.richmond.org.

● **Richmond Castle** (☎ 01748 822493; Apr-Sep daily 10am-6pm, Oct Thur-Mon 10am-5pm, Nov-Mar Thur-Mon 10am-4pm, closed Tue & Wed in winter; £4.50/3.80 adult/concs, English Heritage members free; for website see box p57) Without Richmond Castle it's arguable there would be no Richmond and while it ceased performing its castellian duties centuries ago, in the middle of the 1800s it found a new purpose as a tourist attraction and has been welcoming visitors ever since.

Visitors are advised not to rush headlong at the ruins like a troupe of marauding barbarians, but instead first acquaint themselves with the **exhibition** in the reception building; it gives a thought-provoking account of the history of the castle and the town as well as a display on how the castle was originally built. There's also an interesting section on First World War conscientious objectors (absolutists) who were held captive here. Their poignant graffiti still exists on the cell walls, though for protection these cells are today kept locked; copies of the graffiti can be seen in the exhibition.

Now advancing to the ruins in an orderly and newly informed manner, you may be a little disappointed at first by the lack of surviving structures within the castle walls, though by reading the information boards dotted around, you should get a reasonable idea of how the castle once looked.

Scholars may be similarly entranced by the ruins of **Scolland Hall**, the finest ruins surviving from Alan the Red's time; most visitors, however, will find the views from the **keep** overlooking the town far more engrossing.

● **Richmondshire Museum** (☎ 01748 825611, 🖳 www.richmondshiremuseum .org.uk; Apr to end Oct daily 10.30am-4.30pm; £2.50) Another surprisingly absorbing local museum, similar in content to Reeth's Swaledale Museum (see p177), though bigger and with even more impressive exhibits. Highlights include **Cruck House**, a 15th-century building moved wholesale from Ravensworth in 1985, an exhibition tracing the history of transport (including an original penny farthing bicycle), and tellingly, most popular of all, the set of the vet's surgery from the TV series of *All Creatures Great and Small* (see p175).

● **Green Howards Museum** (☎ 01748 826561; 🖳 www.greenhowards.org.uk) Richmond has a long military association and is the garrison town of Catterick, now many times larger than Richmond itself. The town's regiment, the Green Howards, have their own museum and headquarters (Feb-Nov Mon-Sat 10am-4.30pm; £3.50) in the market-place at the former Holy Trinity Church. With a history spanning the Crimean and Boer wars, as well as military engagements on the North-West Frontier of India and current operations in neighbouring Afghanistan, the story of the regiment is a fascinating one. Highlights include the staggering 3750-strong medal collection awarded to members of the regiment.

● **Easby Abbey** Formerly and more properly known as **St Agatha's Monastery**, Easby Abbey lies about a mile to the east of Richmond Castle. You may get a distant view of it from across the Swale during the next stage's walk, but if you've got the time we strongly advise you make a detour and pay a proper visit. Like those at Shap, the ruins at Easby were once part of a Premonstratensian Abbey, this one built in 1152, just 31 years after the founding of the order by St Norbert in Prémontré in Picardy, northern France. The monastery served the community for almost 400 years because, unlike many other orders who chose to cut themselves off from the outside world, the Premonstratensians saw it as their duty to administer and serve the laity until Henry VIII brought about the dissolution. Unwilling to bow to Henry's demands, they joined the Pilgrimage of Grace in 1536, the most popular rebellion against Henry. Many monasteries were briefly rescued by the rebels – St Agatha's at Easby among them. They were subsequently defeated and Henry set about exacting a chilling revenge on those who had dared to defy his orders, instructing his forces in the north to

'*cause such dreadful execution upon a good number of inhabitants, hanging them on trees, quartering them and setting their heads and quarters in every town, as shall be a fearful warning*'.

While visiting, be sure to check out the **parish church** here at Easby, which has survived in remarkable condition and plays host to some wonderful 13th-century **wall paintings**. Look out, too, for the 12th-century **panel of glass** depicting St John.

Other sights There are a couple of magnificent ruined towers in town. The first you'll come across is **Grey Friars Tower**, in the gardens behind the tourist office. This was once part of a Franciscan monastery, founded in 1258, though the tower itself wasn't built until sometime around 1500. The second, clearly visible to the west of town from Richmond Castle, is **Culloden Tower**, a folly dating back to 1746. Amazingly, it's now a novelty holiday cottage let out by the Landmark Trust (🖥 www .landmarktrust.org.uk).

Built in 1788, the beautifully restored **Georgian Theatre** (☎ 01748 825252, 🖥 www.georgiantheatreroyal.co.uk) now hosts regular plays and events and is also well worth visiting.

Transport (see also pp52-5)
The nearest **railway station** is in Darlington, but there are plenty of **buses** from Market Place. Arriva's buses (X26, 27, X27, 29 & 34) run to Darlington and take around 45 mins. The Little Red Bus (No 30) runs up Swaledale (Mon-Sat), calling at Reeth, Gunnerside and Keld, and Dales & District's No 54 and No 55 go to Northallerton.

Those who wish to skip some of the next section can catch one of the many buses to Catterick Bridge or the No 55 to Bolton-on-Swale – your conscience may torment you but the truth is you won't have missed much.

For a **taxi** call Amalgamated (☎ 01748 825112 or ☎ 07552 160547).

STAGE 10: RICHMOND TO INGLEBY CROSS   MAPS 61-72

Introduction

This is the longest stage in this book, so long that you may want to break it up with a night at Danby Wiske. True, there's something to be said for Wainwright's preference in traversing the **Vale of Mowbray** to the Cleveland Hills in one fell swoop. It is a fairly uneventful trudge by the lofty standards of the Coast to Coast, much of it conducted on back roads and with barely a hill to pant over, and though the **23 miles (37km, 8¾hrs)** to Ingleby Cross sounds a long way, it's actually achievable. What you may want to factor in is the following stage; a gruelling 21-miler to Blakey Ridge. There's more on p206 to help make up your mind how you stage the next couple of days.

The Lakeland fell-loving Wainwright lost little love on this tepid agricultural tract, not least the innocent hamlet of Danby Wiske, claiming it to be a low point in his project in more than just elevation. Things have obviously changed for the better (and were probably never that bad), and now there are not only two B&Bs, but by the time you read this the pub will be operating again. So, in our opinion, there's a lot to be said for spending a morning ticking off a couple of sights in Richmond before heading on to Danby Wiske in the afternoon.

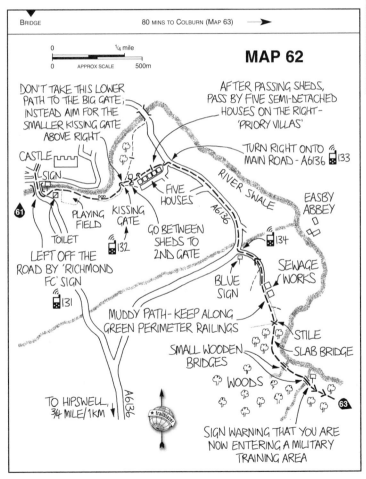

BRIDGE   80 MINS TO COLBURN (MAP 63) ➡

0   ¼ mile

0   APPROX SCALE   500m

MAP 62

DON'T TAKE THIS LOWER PATH TO THE BIG GATE, INSTEAD AIM FOR THE SMALLER KISSING GATE ABOVE RIGHT

AFTER PASSING SHEDS, PASS BY FIVE SEMI-DETACHED HOUSES ON THE RIGHT - 'PRIORY VILLAS'

CASTLE

SIGN

TURN RIGHT ONTO MAIN ROAD - A6136 🔋133

RIVER SWALE

A6136

FIVE HOUSES

EASBY ABBEY

61

PLAYING FIELD

KISSING GATE

🔋132

GO BETWEEN SHEDS TO 2ND GATE

🔋134

TOILET

LEFT OFF THE ROAD BY 'RICHMOND FC' SIGN

🔋131

BLUE SIGN

SEWAGE WORKS

MUDDY PATH - KEEP ALONG GREEN PERIMETER RAILINGS

STILE

SLAB BRIDGE

SMALL WOODEN BRIDGES

WOODS

63

TO HIPSWELL, ¾ MILE/1KM

A6136

★ trailblazer

SIGN WARNING THAT YOU ARE NOW ENTERING A MILITARY TRAINING AREA

The route

Starting off from **Richmond Bridge** with a quick stroll along the Swale's southern bank, you pass alongside a terrace of houses and join the A6136, leaving it shortly by following a lane to the left that leads to the **sewage works** and subsequently a dark, muddy stretch of riverside woodland. Slithering about over this clammy, saturnine mush, you may find yourself recalling the Pennine peat bogs with rather greater fondness as you pop out of the trees, quite possibly to the sound of gunfire from the nearby garrison at Catterick.

A little further on is the village of **Colburn** (Map 63), with little to distract the eastbound hiker apart from the unprepossessing exterior of *The Hildyard Arms* (after 7pm ☎ 01748 832353, 🖳 http://thehildyardarms.wordpress.com; Mon-Sat 7-11pm, Sun to 10.30pm; 1T, private facilities with shower). Evening meals (served daily 7-9pm) won't break the bank. **B&B** costs £60 for two sharing (£50 without breakfast). **Camping** (shower available) costs £5pp; dogs are welcome with campers. Book in advance for an evening meal or to camp. *The Hildyard* comes recommended.

From Colburn at one point the path skirts past the former site of St Giles Hospital that flourished alongside the river some 800 years ago, although if any trace of it remains today, they're best observed following a prolonged session at the *Hildyard*. More conspicuous is *St Giles Farm* (☎ 01748 811372; 1T/1D/1F, all en suite, bath available; booking essential) providing B&B for £32.50pp or £35 for single occupancy, as well as **camping** for £6pp including shower/toilet facilities.

From here the path continues above the river past *Thornborough Farm* (Map 64; ☎ 01748 811421) where very basic **camping** is offered (£3pp), and under the throbbing A1 trunk road to **Catterick Bridge**. Famed for its racecourse and army camp, the name Catterick reaches back 2000 years when a strategic Roman garrison and town developed where Dere Street (today's A1 or Great North Road) bridged the Swale. By today's busy bridge you'll see *The Bridge House Hotel* (☎ 01748 818331; 🖳 www.thebridgehousehotelcatterick.co.uk; 3S/6D/3T/3F, all en suite, some with bath), with origins dating back to the 15th-century coaching era. Rates are £50-70 for a single room or £42.50-50pp for two sharing a room.

There are other pubs offering accommodation in **Brompton-on-Swale**, as well as *Brompton Camping Barn* (☎ 01748 818326; 🖳 bromptonbarn@fsmail .net). The barn has three rooms (each sleeping four) with bunk beds including bedding (sleeping sacks cost £1); the rate is £8pp. There's a fully equipped kitchen, dining/lounge area and shower facilities (10p). There's also **camping** (£4pp inc shower) for half a dozen tents. Book through the YHA (see p17) or direct. Dales & District's No 55 **bus** stops in Brompton; see pp52-5. To get to the barn continue north once over the bridge and turn left down Bridge Rd; it's less than half a mile on your right on West Richmond Rd. Or take a daring short cut by scrambling down to the small bridge over the Swale river by Colburn Beck Woods (see Map 63).

Continuing along the north bank of the river, you leave the Swale for good as you march into the hamlet of **Bolton-on-Swale** (Map 65). *(cont'd on p198)*

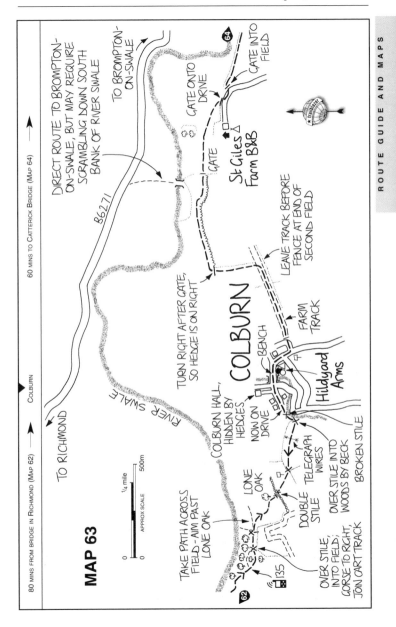

ROUTE GUIDE AND MAPS

MAP 63

80 MINS FROM BRIDGE IN RICHMOND (MAP 62) ◄— COLBURN ► 60 MINS TO CATTERICK BRIDGE (MAP 64)

0 _____ 1/4 mile

0 _____ 500m

APPROX SCALE

TO RICHMOND

TO BROMPTON-ON-SWALE

TO BROMPTON-ON-SWALE

DIRECT ROUTE TO BROMPTON-ON-SWALE, BUT MAY REQUIRE SCRAMBLING DOWN SOUTH BANK OF RIVER SWALE

B6271

RIVER SWALE

GATE

GATE ONTO DRIVE

GATE INTO FIELD

St Giles Farm B&B

64

LEAVE TRACK BEFORE FENCE AT END OF SECOND FIELD

TURN RIGHT AFTER GATE, SO HEDGE IS ON RIGHT

COLBURN HALL, HIDDEN BY HEDGES

NOW ON DRIVE

COLBURN

BENCH

Hildyard Arms

FARM TRACK

LONE OAK

TELEGRAPH WIRES

DOUBLE STILE

OVER STILE INTO WOODS BY BECK

BROKEN STILE

TAKE PATH ACROSS FIELD - AIM PAST LONE OAK

135

OVER STILE, INTO FIELD; GORSE TO RIGHT, JOIN CART TRACK

62

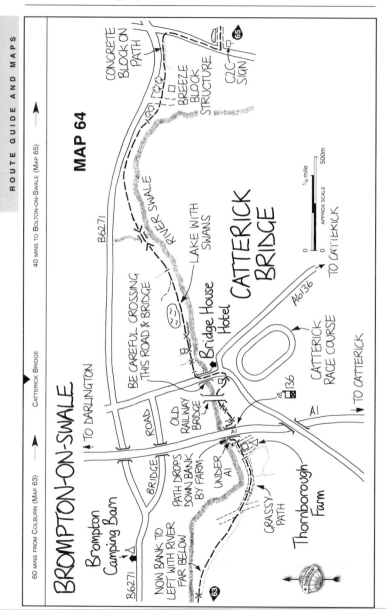

MAP 64

BROMPTON-ON-SWALE

CONCRETE BLOCK ON PATH

BREEZE BLOCK STRUCTURE

C2C SIGN

65

B6271

RIVER SWALE

BE CAREFUL CROSSING THIS ROAD & BRIDGE

TO DARLINGTON

LAKE WITH SWANS

Bridge House Hotel

CATTERICK BRIDGE

ROAD

OLD RAILWAY BRIDGE

A6136

CATTERICK RACE COURSE

TO CATTERICK

BRIDGE

PATH DROPS DOWN BANK BY FARM

136

A1

TO CATTERICK

UNDER A1

A1

Brompton Camping Barn

B6271

NOW BANK TO LEFT WITH RIVER FAR BELOW

GRASSY PATH

Thornborough Farm

63

¼ mile

500m

0   0

APPROX SCALE

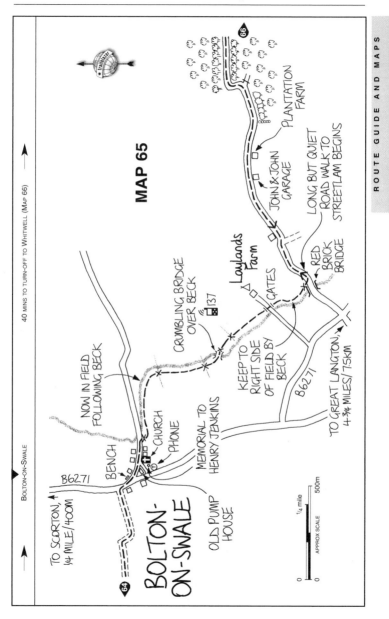

BOLTON-ON-SWALE

40 MINS TO TURN-OFF TO WHITWELL (MAP 66)

MAP 65

TO SCORTON, ¼ MILE/400M

B6271

66

NOW IN FIELD FOLLOWING BECK

BENCH

CHURCH PHONE

BOLTON-ON-SWALE

MEMORIAL TO HENRY JENKINS

OLD PUMP HOUSE

64

CRUMBLING BRIDGE OVER BECK

137

Laylands Farm

GATES

KEEP TO RIGHT SIDE OF FIELD BY BECK

B6271

TO GREAT LANGTON, 4¾ MILES/7.5KM

RED BRICK BRIDGE

JOHN & JOHN GARAGE

LONG BUT QUIET ROAD WALK TO STREETLAM BEGINS

PLANTATION FARM

66

¼ mile
500m
APPROX SCALE
0
0

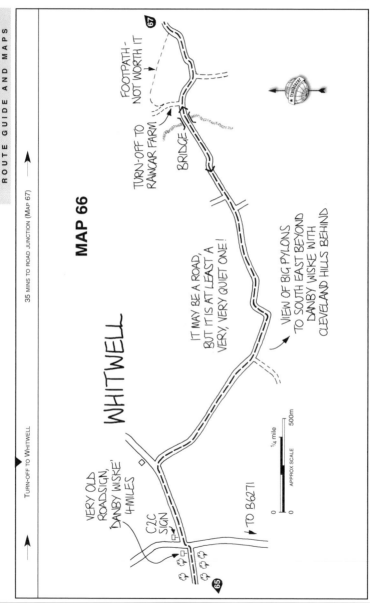

ROUTE GUIDE AND MAPS

TURN-OFF TO WHITWELL

35 MINS TO ROAD JUNCTION (MAP 67)

MAP 66

WHITWELL

VERY OLD
ROADSIGN,
'DANBY WISKE'
4 MILES

C2C SIGN

TO B6271

IT MAY BE A ROAD,
BUT IT IS AT LEAST A
VERY, VERY QUIET ONE!

VIEW OF BIG PYLONS
TO SOUTH EAST BEYOND
DANBY WISKE WITH
CLEVELAND HILLS BEHIND

APPROX SCALE

¼ mile

500m

TURN-OFF TO
RAINCAR FARM

BRIDGE

FOOTPATH -
NOT WORTH IT

67

65

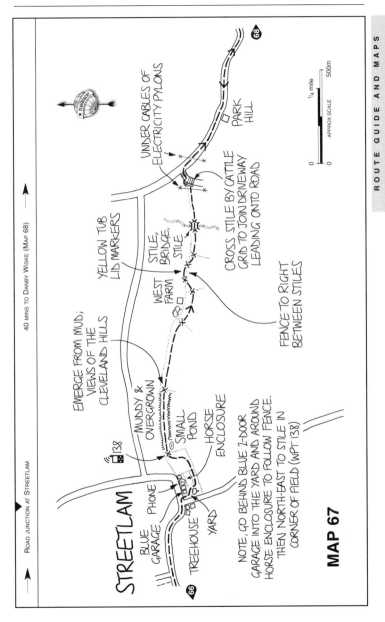

ROAD JUNCTION AT STREETLAM

40 MINS TO DANBY WISKE (MAP 68)

STREETLAM

BLUE
GARAGE   PHONE

138

TREEHOUSE
YARD

66

EMERGE FROM MUD;
VIEWS OF THE
CLEVELAND HILLS

MUDDY &
OVERGROWN

SMALL
POND

HORSE
ENCLOSURE

YELLOW TUB
LID MARKERS

WEST
FARM

STILE,
BRIDGE,
STILE

UNDER CABLES OF
ELECTRICITY PYLONS

CROSS STILE BY CATTLE
GRID TO JOIN DRIVEWAY
LEADING ONTO ROAD

FENCE TO RIGHT
BETWEEN STILES

PARK
HILL

68

NOTE: GO BEHIND BLUE 2-DOOR
GARAGE INTO THE YARD AND AROUND
HORSE ENCLOSURE TO FOLLOW FENCE.
THEN NORTH-EAST TO STILE IN
CORNER OF FIELD (WPT 138)

MAP 67

APPROX SCALE

0   ¼ mile

0   500m

(cont'd from p192) Don't search for refreshments here – your hopes will be dashed – but do visit the churchyard, famous for its **monument to Henry Jenkins**, a local man who lived an unremarkable life except for its length: he claimed he was 169 when he died, a fact which may explain the popularity of the village with retirees (incidentally, the current verifiable record is a more credible 122). The church itself is of course older, dating back to the 14th century, with Norman and Saxon ancestors; you can see various bits of masonry from these earlier churches inside, including part of an Anglo-Danish cross shaft in the vestry and part of a pointed arch in the vestry roof. Also if you need a break Dales & District's No 55 **bus** calls here en route from Richmond to Northallerton; see pp52-5.

More unexceptional field-tramping ensues, with **camping** at *Laylands Farm* (Map 65; ☎ 01748 811491; £4.50pp), followed by a 3½-mile stretch of road-walking, the longest on the entire trail (Maps 65-68). With an OS map you might string together a network of footpaths but here in the Vale, is it worth it? The roads are nearly as quiet as they'd have been in Wainwright's day, while the intrusive odours and racket of industrial farming will be present whichever route you take.

At **Streetlam** (Map 67) there's an opportunity to hack along an overgrown footpath towards more fields of pasture and livestock so if you're on the long haul to Ingleton, stick to the roads where indicated, a pleasant chance to switch to autopilot. You'll shortly rejoin the road and march on to see what awaits in Danby Wiske.

DANBY WISKE   MAP 68

Chances are you'd never heard of Danby Wiske before you set your sights on the Coast to Coast, but this tiny village with an 11th-century Norman church and a tidy village green is a renowned staging post on your trek. Having long outgrown the hurtful comments in Wainwright's guide, the proud villagers seem to go out of their way to greet trail-weary Coasters, and with a bit of luck your transit will coincide with a lavish array of cakes laid on in the village hall.

A new licensee took over the *White Swan* (☎ 01609 775131; snacks available daily at lunchtime, meals 6-8pm) in September 2009 and they expect to be up and running by Easter 2010. **B&B** (2T/1F sleeping four; shared bathroom) costs £30pp (£10 single occupancy supplement) and **camping** (£5pp; breakfast £6) is also available in a field; shower/toilet facilities and a cold water tap are available. They have drying facilities and can make packed lunches (£5).

The previous owners of the pub now run *The Old School* (☎ 01609 774227; 🖳 www.coasttocoastguides.co.uk/accommo dation/old school; 1D/2T; Easter to end Sep). A 19th-century schoolhouse as its name implies, all the rooms are bright, neat and smart. The double is en suite (with shower) and the twin rooms share a bathroom. Rates are £60-65 for two sharing, £35 for single occupancy. Evening meals from £15 by prior arrangement. The other choice is *Ashfield* (☎ 01609 771628; 3T all with private facilities, bath available, Apr-Sep) where B&B costs £32pp (£37 single occupancy). Packed lunch from £2; evening meals (main course about £10) available if booked in advance. The owner, Jean Norris, has also taken the enterprising step of offering self-service **hot drinks and snacks** in her front garden with tables, chairs and a gazebo. No need to ring the bell, just put the kettle on and leave a couple of pounds in the honesty

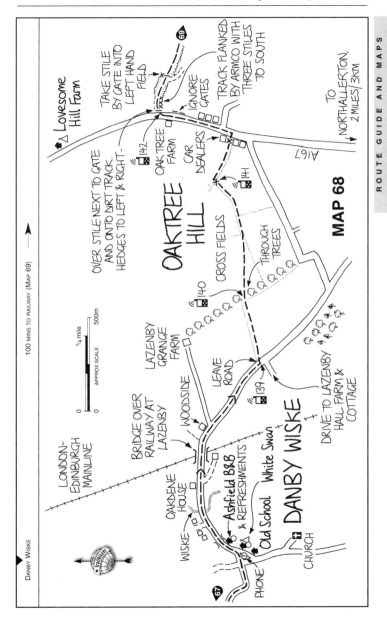

DANBY WISKE

100 MINS TO RAILWAY (MAP 69)

Lovesome Hill Farm

TAKE STILE BY GATE INTO LEFT HAND FIELD

TRACK FLANKED BY ARMCO WITH THREE STILES TO SOUTH

IGNORE GATES

142

OVER STILE NEXT TO GATE AND ONTO DIRT TRACK - HEDGES TO LEFT & RIGHT

OAK TREE FARM

CAR DEALERS

141

TO NORTHALLERTON, 2 MILES/3KM

A167

OAKTREE HILL

MAP 68

CROSS FIELDS

THROUGH TREES

140

LAZENBY GRANGE FARM

LONDON-EDINBURGH MAINLINE

¼ mile

500m

APPROX SCALE

0

0

LEAVE ROAD

BRIDGE OVER RAILWAY AT LAZENBY

WOODSIDE

139

DRIVE TO LAZENBY HALL FARM & COTTAGE

DANBY WISKE

OAKDENE HOUSE

Ashfield B&B & REFRESHMENTS

WISKE

Old School

White Swan

CHURCH

PHONE

67

box. In a lesser form, it's a refreshment system that seems to have become popular along this stage.

As for the **church** – one of the very few in England that has no known dedication – only the solid oak door and the font are 11th-century originals, though much of the north aisle is only slightly younger. Look above the main door at the tympanum and you should be able to make out the outlines of three weathered figures who've been interpreted as the Angel of Judgement weighing the soul of the figure on the right using the scales that he holds in his other hand. Though the evil deeds in one of the scale's pans outweigh the other, the third figure, the Angel of Mercy (Jesus Christ), has slipped his fingers under the pan containing the bad deeds, thus causing the good deeds to seem heavier.

From the bridge crossing the River Wiske outside the village, you can see the outline of the Cleveland Hills in the distance. Unfortunately half the Vale of Mowbray still lies before you, much of it, as before, on roads, but with a nifty back route sneaking up on **Oaktree Hill**, a garage and a string of houses lining the A167.

Despite the noise of the road, *Lovesome Hill Farm* (Map 68; ☎ 01609 772311, 🖳 www.lovesomehillfarm.co.uk; 1S/3D/1T/1F, all en suite, one with bath; closed Christmas/New Year) has been praised by walkers for the quality of its accommodation as well as the opportunity to take a tour of the 165-acre farm. **B&B** rates are £35-40pp (£36 for the single room) and evening meals (£15-22) can be arranged with advance notice. They also have a luxury cottage (1D) with a spa bath (£40-45pp) and a **bunkhouse** with two rooms each sleeping four (£10pp inc shower; bedding £3-4). The farm lies less than a quarter of a mile north of the point where the route turns off to the east.

Here more tracks and quiet backroads link a series of busy farms, many leaving drinks and snacks out for you, as you cross a railway line and a beck or two to finally meet the busy A19 (Map 71) at **Exelby Services**. Campers should note that, unless you pop into Osmotherley, from here on there are no village shops along the path until Glaisdale, two days away. However, if you traipsed all the way from Richmond, a more pressing concern will be finding the energy to dash across four lanes of the A19 without causing a pile-up.

INGLEBY CROSS   MAP 72, p205
& INGLEBY ARNCLIFFE
Sandwiched between two busy 'A' roads, Ingleby Cross and its twin Ingleby Arncliffe are actually surprisingly peaceful places if you're not camping. Ingleby Cross is said to be named after its war memorial and has nothing more than the **post office** (Mon-Wed 9.30am-noon), situated in the Blue Bell Inn (see p204). Abbots No 80 and No 89 **bus** services stop here en route between Northallerton and Stokesley; see pp52-5 for details.

If you've walked from Danby Wiske and have the time, spend it visiting **Mount Grace Priory** (see the box on p204), the best of the ruined abbeys on the Coast to Coast. When a heritage site advertises itself by saying that it has one of the most remarkable medieval drainage systems in the country, you'd be forgiven for thinking that there's not much point in visiting. But you'd be wrong.

Where to stay and eat
In **Ingleby Arncliffe**, *Elstavale* (☎ 01609 882302, 🖳 www.elstavale.co.uk; 2D or T, shared shower facilities) is situated right on the path and offers B&B at £55 for two sharing. The rooms are in a separate annex and come with foot spas.   *(cont'd on p204)*

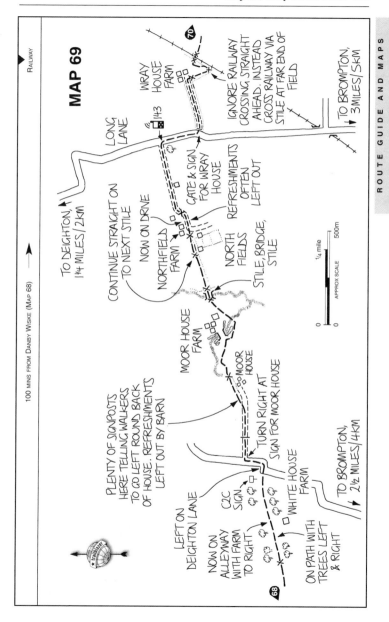

RAILWAY

MAP 69

100 MINS FROM DANBY WISKE (MAP 68)

TO DEIGHTON, 1¼ MILES / 2KM

LONG LANE

WRAY HOUSE FARM

70

IGNORE RAILWAY CROSSING, STRAIGHT AHEAD. INSTEAD CROSS RAILWAY VIA STILE AT FAR END OF FIELD

TO BROMPTON, 3 MILES / 5KM

143

CONTINUE STRAIGHT ON TO NEXT STILE

NOW ON DRIVE

NORTHFIELD FARM

GATE & SIGN FOR WRAY HOUSE

REFRESHMENTS OFTEN LEFT OUT

NORTH FIELDS

STILE, BRIDGE, STILE

MOOR HOUSE FARM

MOOR HOUSE

TURN RIGHT AT SIGN FOR MOOR HOUSE

PLENTY OF SIGNPOSTS HERE TELLING WALKERS TO GO LEFT ROUND BACK OF HOUSE. REFRESHMENTS LEFT OUT BY BARN

WHITE HOUSE FARM

TO BROMPTON, 2½ MILES / 4KM

LEFT ON DEIGHTON LANE

NOW ON ALLEYWAY WITH FARM TO RIGHT

C2C SIGN

ON PATH WITH TREES LEFT & RIGHT

68

¼ mile

APPROX SCALE

500m

ROUTE GUIDE AND MAPS

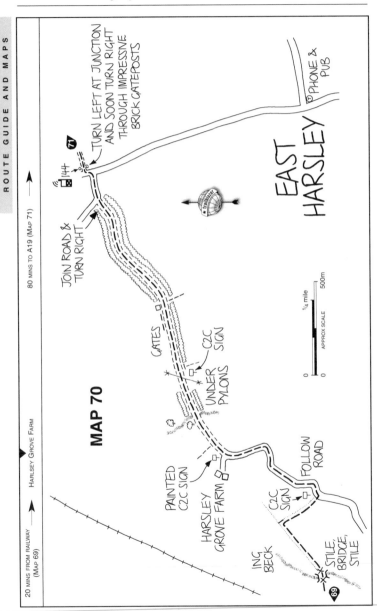

MAP 70

20 MINS FROM RAILWAY (MAP 69)

HARLSEY GROVE FARM

80 MINS TO A19 (MAP 71)

TURN LEFT AT JUNCTION AND SOON TURN RIGHT THROUGH IMPRESSIVE BRICK GATEPOSTS

71

JOIN ROAD & TURN RIGHT

PHONE & PUB

EAST HARSLEY

GATES

UNDER PYLONS

C2C SIGN

PAINTED C2C SIGN

HARLSEY GROVE FARM

ING BECK

C2C SIGN

FOLLOW ROAD

STILE, BRIDGE, STILE

69

¼ mile

500m

0

0

APPROX SCALE

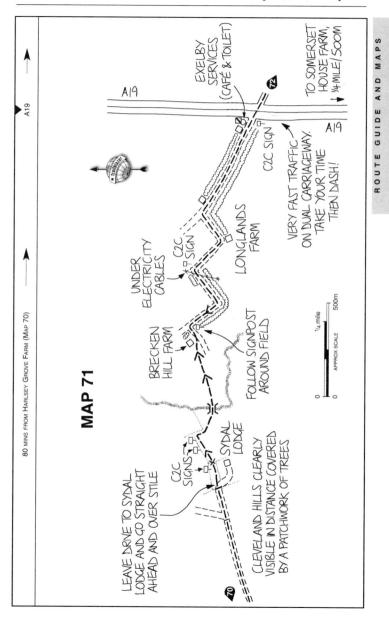

(cont'd from p200) Dogs are welcome. There are great breakfasts, packed lunches cost around £5 and a most welcome cream tea on arrival. *Monk's House* (☎ 01609 882294; 1S/1D, shared bath; Easter to Oct), also right on the path, is a 500-year-old building with mullioned windows. The single is tiny but B&B costs £26pp and they'll pack you a lunch for a fiver.

Somerset House Farm (☎ 01609 882555, 💻 www.somersethousefarm.co .uk; 4T/2D, all en suite, bath available) charges £35pp (£50 for single occupancy). They also do packed lunches and laundry (both £5). To get there, at the water tower in the village walk south, or walk down the A19 (see Map 71) for five minutes though this is not recommended; the farm's on the left. *The Blue Bell Inn* (☎ 01609 882272, 💻 www.the-blue-bell-inn.co.uk; 2S/2T/1D, en suite with showers) in the centre of **Ingleby Cross** serves real ales and standard **bar meals** (daily noon-2pm & 6-9pm)

including the Middlesborough staple: chicken parmesan which is less Italian than it sounds. You can also **camp** in the field out back for just £3 including shower, and breakfast is available in the mornings. B&B is £54-56 for a room with two sharing, £30 for a single.

Although it's just over a mile further along the path, and agonisingly uphill too, from what readers tell us *Park House* (☎ 01609 882899, 💻 www.parkhousebb.co.uk; 2D/2T/2F, all en suite) is well worth the effort. With a lovely lounge and grounds that hopefully you'll have the energy to appreciate, there's also a laundry service (about £5) and wi-fi access. They provide **lifts** to the pub but as they have a licence, you may well prefer an evening meal here (book 24 hrs in advance, main courses £8-11). Rates are £32.50pp, £50 for single occupancy.

Should you find all the above booked up, hobble on to Osmotherley (see p207) for more options, including a youth hostel.

❏ **Mount Grace Priory**   **Map 72**

Mount Grace Priory was built in 1398, by the ascetic **Carthusian** order, founded in 1084 by St Bruno, a canon of the Cathedral Church of Rheims. He established a religious community that settled at La Grande Chartreuse near Grenoble, from which the name Carthusian (and also the word for all Carthusian monasteries, which are known as charterhouses) comes. St Bruno and his followers saw the world as inherently wicked so lived as hermits undistracted by temptation. The monastic order that evolved from this community followed much the same principles. The prior was the only person in the monastery allowed access to the outside world, while each monk lived an essentially solitary existence, eating his meals alone and spending much of his life in his cell. The monk's day was fairly hard, rising at 5.45am and returning to bed only at 2.30am the next morning, following a day spent mainly in prayer or contemplation.

There are two people to thank for the preservation of Mount Grace. Following the priory's dissolution on December 18, 1539, James Strangways bought the land from the government but did not destroy the church as required by law at that time. Instead he let it stand as it was, intact save for the roof, possibly because his parents and grandparents had all been buried on the site. In 1899, more than two and a half centuries later, Sir Lowthian Bell bought the adjoining 17th-century house and during the course of his 30-year residency did some restoration to the priory, including the first attempt to rebuild cell number 8, one of 25 cells in total.

The priory today, though definitely a ruin, is an absorbing one, and one that clearly shows in its foundations the basic layout of the place. The restoration of **cell number 8** also makes clear that, for their time, these cells were remarkably comfortable, built on two floors with cabinets, a loom, a small bed, water closet and a small garden.

And the **drainage system**? Well with latrines fitted and clean water piped into every cell, the plumbing was indeed ahead of its time. Little of the system remains today save for the channels in which the water flowed around the priory.

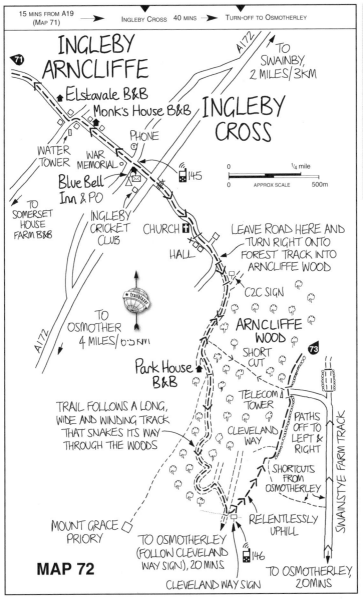

15 MINS FROM A19 (MAP 71) → INGLEBY CROSS 40 MINS → TURN-OFF TO OSMOTHERLEY

INGLEBY ARNCLIFFE

71

Elstavale B&B
Monk's House B&B

INGLEBY CROSS

PHONE

WATER TOWER

WAR MEMORIAL

A172

TO SWAINBY, 2 MILES/3KM

📱 145

Blue Bell Inn & PO

TO SOMERSET HOUSE FARM B&B

INGLEBY CRICKET CLUB

CHURCH ✝

HALL

0   ¼ mile
0   APPROX SCALE   500m

LEAVE ROAD HERE AND TURN RIGHT ONTO FOREST TRACK INTO ARNCLIFFE WOOD

C2C SIGN

ARNCLIFFE WOOD

★ trailblazer

TO OSMOTHER 4 MILES/6.5KM

A172

SHORT CUT

73

Park House B&B

TRAIL FOLLOWS A LONG, WIDE AND WINDING TRACK THAT SNAKES ITS WAY THROUGH THE WOODS

TELECOM TOWER

CLEVELAND WAY

PATHS OFF TO LEFT & RIGHT

SHORTCUTS FROM OSMOTHERLEY

SWAINSTYE FARM TRACK

MOUNT GRACE PRIORY

RELENTLESSLY UPHILL

TO OSMOTHERLEY (FOLLOW CLEVELAND WAY SIGN), 20 MINS

📱 146

MAP 72

CLEVELAND WAY SIGN

TO OSMOTHERLEY, 20 MINS

Introduction

At **21 miles (34km, 8hrs)**, this is another stage that many walkers consider splitting in two. Unfortunately, unless wild camping, it's less easily done than Stage 10 which is one reason you might want to spare yourself if coming from Richmond; you'll need to be in good shape to reach Blakey Ridge without looking like an extra from a George Romero movie on arrival.

If you do divide the walk at **Clay Bank Top** and spend the night in one of the nearby villages, such as Great Broughton to the north or Urra to the south, the next day (having returned to Clay Bank Top) is an effortless 9 miles (14.5km) to Blakey Ridge so you can easily walk on to Glaisdale or beyond and needn't lose much time. Providing you book in advance, the B&Bs at Great Broughton, Urra and the other nearby villages are more than happy to collect you at Clay Bank Top and return you there next morning.

The second option has its plus points, however. For one thing, though the first half is a rollercoaster of inclines, once you've climbed one last time onto Urra Moor, 12 miles (19.5km) from Ingleby Cross and following well over 1000 metres (nearly 3800ft) of accumulated ascent, the second half is blessedly level as you follow the course of a dismantled railway. Secondly, many consider the *Lion Inn* at Blakey to be one of the more memorable pubs on the route, an isolated but busy tavern stranded on a windswept moor.

Thus our advice is as follows: if your feet are in good shape and there's room at the Inn (or elsewhere, see p215), grab it and attempt the 21 miles in a day. If that doesn't suit your schedule, organise a B&B near Clay Bank Top.

One final thing: campers should note that there's free **camping** at Lord Stones Café (see p211) and the *Lion Inn* has camping for Coast to Coasters only.

As for the walk itself, this stage takes us into the **North York Moors National Park**, the third national park on the route with, it is said, the world's largest expanse of heather. Depending on the weather, this could be a pleasant stage as you tramp merrily up and down the moors, stopping only to admire the iridescent plumage of the pheasant, gaze at the heather that swathes the moor in a variegated sea of colour, or savour the views south to the valleys of Farndale or north to the industrial glories of Teeside and your first view of the North Sea. Or it could be a miserable, muddy, rain-soaked trudge with all views obscured by a bone-chilling mist while paramotors buzz overhead. Let's hope it's the former but either way, on the bright side the waymarking is good so you're unlikely to get lost.

The route

From Ingleby Cross the walk begins with a climb up past the **church** (note the triple-decker pulpit and purple box pews) and on up into **Arncliffe Wood**, where the path takes a turn to the south.

Having passed the turn-off for Park House (see Map 72, p205) you come to the junction for **Mount Grace Priory** (see p200 and box p204); take the right-hand fork for the priory (April-Sep Mon, Thur, Fri-Sun 10am-6pm, Oct-Mar

Thur-Sun 10am-4pm) which is free for English Heritage and NT members but everyone else must pay an **entrance fee** of £4.50/3.80 adult/concessions; don't be tempted to duck out of paying, even though the path from the Coast to Coast trail brings you out at the gate at the back of the priory, while the ticket office is by the front.

Stay on the Path if not visiting the priory and at the southernmost point of the wood a hairpin bend sees Wainwright's climbing trail meet the Cleveland Way, established a couple of years before Wainwright's original book was published and which you'll follow for almost the entire way to Blakey Moor. Those wishing to visit Osmotherley should turn off south through the gate.

OSMOTHERLEY
OFF MAP 72 p205/MAP 73, p208

Though a 20-minute walk off the Coast to Coast trail, Osmotherley is a delight and energetic walkers may want to visit, even if they're not staying there. In the centre stands a **market cross** and a **barter table**, believed to be the same one from which John Wesley preached. Indeed, in Chapel Yard you can find what's believed to be Britain's oldest practising **Methodist chapel**, constructed in 1754.

Another sight is **Thompson's**, a dusty, empty shop that's been in the same family since 1786 – and looks it. And finally there's the church, **St Peter's**, which is said to have been built on Saxon foundations. The most distinctive things about Osmotherley, however, are its beautiful, **stone terraced cottages**, built for the workers who laboured at the flax mill that now houses the youth hostel (see Where to stay).

In the village there's a **post office** (Mon, Tue, Thur & Fri 9am-5.30pm, Wed & Sat 9am-12.30pm) inside the small **village store** (Mon-Sat 8.30am-5.30pm, Sun 9am-1pm) where they sell basic provisions as well as sandwiches (from £1.50). If your boots are on their uppers, a door or two from Thompson's is **Osmotherley Walking Shop** (☎ 01609 883818; daily 9am-5pm), selling discounted outdoor equipment.

To rejoin the trail, you needn't return to the junction with the Cleveland Way, but can take a short-cut up along Swainstye Farm track (found on the left as you walk from the village towards Cote Ghyll caravan park), meeting up with the Cleveland and Coast to Coast paths at the Telecom Tower (see Map 72 and Map 73).

Where to stay
Osmotherley Youth Hostel (☎ 0845 371 9035, ✉ osmotherley@yha.org.uk; 72 beds; from £15.95) serves meals, accepts cards, is licensed and also has a TV and games room. Coming from Arncliffe Wood, at the top end of the village turn left when you hit the road, rather than right down the hill into town. Just before the hostel, *Cote Ghyll Caravan Park* (☎ 01609 883425, ✉ www.coteghyll .com; Mar-Oct) has **camping** for £7.50pp, or £8pp during school holidays. As its name suggests, its main business is caravans and during the school holidays it can be crammed with sugar-high kids, though they do have a few places to pitch a tent on the far side of the site.

Across the road from Osmotherley Walking Shop, *Queen Catherine Hotel* (☎ 01609 883209, ✉ www.queencatherineho tel.co.uk; 1S/1D/2T, all en suite with shower), 4 West End, charges £32.50pp and the rooms have free wi-fi. The pub is named after Henry VIII's wife, Catherine of Aragon, who is believed to have sheltered with monks at Mount Grace Priory (see box p204). It is, surprisingly, the only pub in England named after her. Back up the hill a little way is charming *Vane House* (☎ 01609 883448, ✉ www.vanehouse.co.uk; 4T/2D/1F, all en suite with shower), 11A North End, with rooms from £37.50pp (£50 single occupancy) in high season.

The Three Tuns (☎ 01609 883301, ✉ www.threetunsrestaurant.co.uk; 5D/1T/1F, all en suite, bath available) is a restaurant that offers pleasant rooms in the neighbouring Moon House. Rates start at £85, £55 for single occupancy.

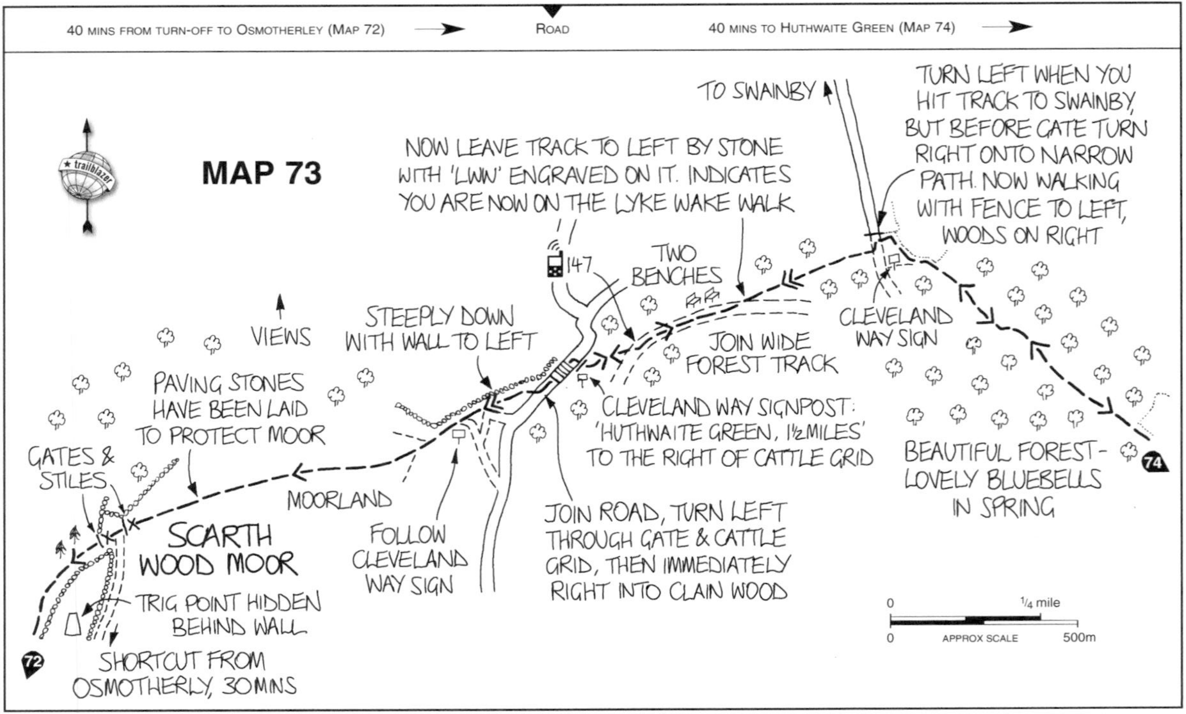
40 MINS FROM TURN-OFF TO OSMOTHERLEY (MAP 72)
ROAD
40 MINS TO HUTHWAITE GREEN (MAP 74)
MAP 73
trailblazer
VIEWS
NOW LEAVE TRACK TO LEFT BY STONE WITH 'LWW' ENGRAVED ON IT. INDICATES YOU ARE NOW ON THE LYKE WAKE WALK
147
TWO BENCHES
TO SWAINBY
TURN LEFT WHEN YOU HIT TRACK TO SWAINBY, BUT BEFORE GATE TURN RIGHT ONTO NARROW PATH. NOW WALKING WITH FENCE TO LEFT, WOODS ON RIGHT
CLEVELAND WAY SIGN
STEEPLY DOWN WITH WALL TO LEFT
JOIN WIDE FOREST TRACK
PAVING STONES HAVE BEEN LAID TO PROTECT MOOR
CLEVELAND WAY SIGNPOST: 'HUTHWAITE GREEN, 1½MILES' TO THE RIGHT OF CATTLE GRID
BEAUTIFUL FOREST - LOVELY BLUEBELLS IN SPRING
GATES & STILES
MOORLAND
SCARTH WOOD MOOR
FOLLOW CLEVELAND WAY SIGN
JOIN ROAD, TURN LEFT THROUGH GATE & CATTLE GRID, THEN IMMEDIATELY RIGHT INTO CLAIN WOOD
TRIG POINT HIDDEN BEHIND WALL
SHORTCUT FROM OSMOTHERLY, 30MINS
72
74
0
¼ mile
0
APPROX SCALE
500m

Where to eat and drink

Queen Catherine Hotel (see p207) has the most popular bar in town, with live blues or jazz music every Sunday. It also has some great homemade meals (daily noon-2pm & 6-9pm) including cod from £7.60, or in the evening stilton and bacon chicken for £10 and, regional favourite, chicken parmesan.

Down the road at *The Three Tuns* (see p207; food served Mon-Sat noon-2.30pm & 5.30-9.30pm, Sun noon-6pm), also opposite The Green, is another surprisingly smart establishment that's more a restaurant than a pub and with starters from around £6 and mains from £9 for veggie pasta up to £17 for something like lamb roasted with garlic, shallots and gratin potato.

For something lighter try *The Coffee Pot* (☎ 01609 883536; Mar-Oct Mon-Thur 10.30am-2.30pm, school hols and Fri-Sun 10.30am-5pm, Nov-Feb Fri lunchtime only), a pleasant little café just round the corner from the walking shop with scones and sandwiches to take away.

Cheapest of all is *Osmotherley Fish and Chip Shop* (☎ 01609 883557; summer Thurs-Sat noon-2.30pm, Wed & Thurs 5.30-9pm, Fri & Sat 5-9.30pm, winter Fri & Sat noon-2.30pm, Thur & Sat 5.30-8.30pm, Fri to 9pm), where it's £5 for a large haddock and chips or £1 for a chip bun.

Transport

Abbott's No 80/89 **bus** services stop here en route to Stokesley and Northallerton. Moorsbus's M9 service to Helmsley calls here; see pp52-5 for details.

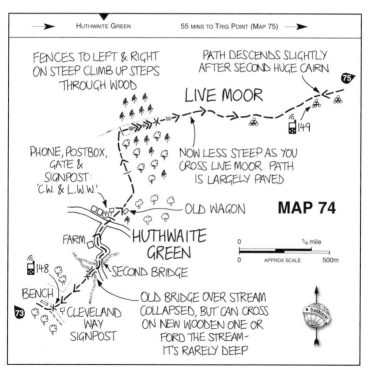

The route continues steeply up through Arncliffe Wood (get used to it, there's plenty more of it on this stage), with cleared forestry providing views back to the Vale of Mowbray as you pass a humming telecoms station to emerge onto the heather-clad **Scarth Wood Moor**. You soon join the Lyke Wake Walk (see box below) in **Clain Wood** before joining the road briefly to pretty **Huthwaite Green**. Here, haul yourself up a steep, wooded climb onto **Live Moor** (Map 74), dutifully noting the first appearance of a number of stone boundary markers along the wayside.

The path now drops slightly and then ascends to **Carlton Moor** (Map 75), with its gliding club, runway and paragliders. At the far end of the moor is a trig point and another boundary marker, from where you may see the **North Sea** beyond the industrial installations of Teeside, and where the path drops steeply around a quarry to a road.

❏ The Lyke Wake Walk

The Lyke Wake Walk, which the Coast to Coast trail joins for part of the stretch across the moors, was the invention of one man. Local farmer and journalist Bill Cowley came up with the idea in 1955 when he claimed that, with the exception of one or two roads that run across the moors, one could walk the entire 40 miles over the North York Moors from east to west (or vice-versa) on **heather**. Several walkers enthusiastically agreed to see if Mr Cowley was right, and it was agreed that the trail should start on Scarth Wood Moor, near Osmotherley, and finish in Ravenscar. To make the challenge tougher, it was decided that the whole 40 miles should be completed in 24 hours.

The curious name comes from the Lyke Wake Dirge, possibly the oldest verse in the Yorkshire dialect and starts:

> *This yah neet, this yah neet,*
> *Ivvery neet an' all,*
> *Fire an' fleet an' cannle leet,*
> *An' Christ tak up thy saul.*

> *When thoo frae hence away art passed*
> *Ivvery neet an' all,*
> *Ti Whinny Moor thoo cums at last*
> *An' Christ tak up thy saul.*

'Lyke' was the local term for corpse and the song recounts the passage of the soul through the afterlife. Bill himself became the chief dirger and handed out black-edged cards to those who successfully completed the trial. There was also a Wake Club which he founded for those who completed the walk.

Unfortunately, the trail has suffered from hard times recently. Firstly, the popularity of the walk, which saw thousands of people accepting the challenge through the '60s and '70s, led to a fair amount of environmental damage to the moors. These days there are a number of different paths to choose from and the National Park Authority now seeks to limit the damage caused by the walkers. The death of Bill Cowley in 1994 dealt another blow to the trail and the demise of the original Lyke Wake Club in 2005 was a further setback. However, the New Lyke Wake Club (🖳 www.lyke wake.org) has been set up to continue along much the same lines as the original organisation. See the website for details of the club and the walk which it promotes.

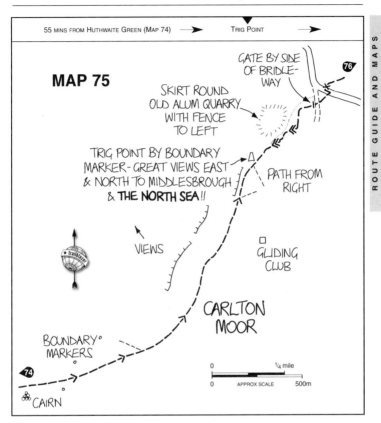

55 MINS FROM HUTHWAITE GREEN (MAP 74) ⟶ TRIG POINT ⟶

MAP 75

GATE BY SIDE OF BRIDLE-WAY

76

SKIRT ROUND OLD ALUM QUARRY WITH FENCE TO LEFT

TRIG POINT BY BOUNDARY MARKER - GREAT VIEWS EAST & NORTH TO MIDDLESBROUGH & **THE NORTH SEA**!!

PATH FROM RIGHT

VIEWS

GLIDING CLUB

CARLTON MOOR

BOUNDARY MARKERS

74

CAIRN

0 ¼ mile

0 APPROX SCALE 500m

Crossing this and its adjacent stile, by a car park *Lord Stones Café* (Map 76; ☎ 01642 778227; Apr-Oct daily 9am-9pm, Nov-Mar daily 10am-4pm) is well staged for a break, a busy hub serving both day and dog walkers who you'll meet and greet between here and Clay Bank Top. They also allow **campers** to stay for free. All they ask is that you patronise their café – which, with its cheap beer and good food, is no great burden. It's also the only place on this stretch where **tap water** is available.

Another steep climb follows – this time up to **Cringle Moor** (Map 76), with the superbly situated **Alec Falconer Memorial Seat** from where you can take in more views over the smokestacks of Teeside, the outlying cone of Roseberry Topping, and just ahead of it, an obelisk on Easby Moor commemorating locally born Captain James Cook.

Follow the bends south then east (towards and then away from the summit of Cringle Moor), skirt the cliffs of **Kirby Bank** and then tackle a steep descent.

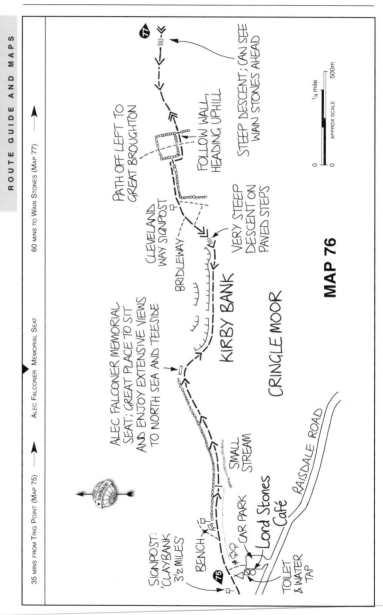

35 MINS FROM TRIG POINT (MAP 75) ➞   ALEC FALCONER MEMORIAL SEAT   60 MINS TO WAIN STONES (MAP 77) ➞

SIGNPOST: 'CLAYBANK 3½ MILES'

BENCH

CAR PARK

Lord Stones Café

TOILET & WATER TAP

RAISDALE ROAD

SMALL STREAM

ALEC FALCONER MEMORIAL SEAT; GREAT PLACE TO SIT AND ENJOY EXTENSIVE VIEWS TO NORTH SEA AND TEESIDE

KIRBY BANK

CRINGLE MOOR

BRIDLEWAY

CLEVELAND WAY SIGNPOST

VERY STEEP DESCENT ON PAVED STEPS

PATH OFF LEFT TO GREAT BROUGHTON

FOLLOW WALL HEADING UPHILL

STEEP DESCENT; CAN SEE WAIN STONES AHEAD

MAP 76

0   ¼ mile
0   500m
APPROX SCALE

75

77

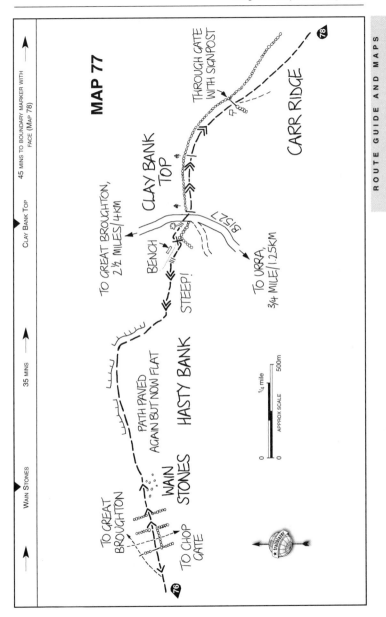

MAP 77

45 MINS TO BOUNDARY MARKER WITH FACE (Map 78)

CLAY BANK TOP

35 MINS

WAIN STONES

TO GREAT BROUGHTON, 2½ MILES/4KM

BENCH

STEEP!

CLAY BANK TOP

B1257

TO URRA, ¾ MILE/1.25KM

CARR RIDGE

THROUGH GATE WITH SIGNPOST

78

PATH PAVED AGAIN BUT NOW FLAT

HASTY BANK

TO GREAT BROUGHTON

WAIN STONES

TO CHOP GATE

76

¼ mile   500m
0   0
APPROX SCALE

The **Wain Stones** are clearly visible on top of your next moor, the outcrops (a favourite of Wainwright's), resembling cake decorations atop **Hasty Bank** (Map 77). If staying at Great Broughton (see below), you may wish to divert from the path on the signposted low-level trail before the climb up to the stones as the road walk is said to be no fun. Otherwise, from the Wain Stones the path continues east to **Clay Bank Top** steeply dropping one more time to the B1257 and, for those staying in the nearby villages, a possible rendezvous with your hosts. Moorsbus's M2 service calls here; see pp52-5 for details.

URRA   OFF MAP 77, p213

Accommodation-wise the nearest place to Clay Bank Top, where the B1527 bisects the Coast to Coast path, is at Urra a mile to the south along the road. Gerry and Wendy have been running *Maltkiln House* (☎ 01642 778216, 🖥 www.maltkiln.co.uk; 2T/ 1D) for many years and charge £24-35pp for B&B, from £13.50 for an evening meal and £4.50 for a packed lunch. One of the twins is en suite with a shower and the other rooms share a shower room. They'll also show you the short cut from the back of the house directly onto Urra Moor the next morning.

GREAT BROUGHTON
OFF MAP 77, p213

Great Broughton lies nearly three miles to the north of the trail at Clay Bank Top. It boasts several pubs; the walker-friendly *Bay Horse* (☎ 01642 712319; food served Mon-Sat 11.30am-2pm & 6-9.30pm, Sun noon-9pm), on the High St, is a good choice for both bar meals and more formal meals (à la carte menu) in their restaurant.

As far as accommodation goes, almost all B&Bs offer lifts from and back to Clay Bank Top, some for a small fee; the ride back up is something you may appreciate in the morning. Of these, *Ingle Hill* (☎ 01642 712449; 2T share bathroom/1F en suite shower) has beautiful gardens with B&B from £25pp (£30 for single occupancy) and at *Newlands House* (☎ 01642 712619;

🖥 www.newlandshouse.co.uk; 1D/1T/1F, all en suite with bath; Apr-Oct), at 7 Ingleby Rd; the tariff starts at £35pp (£45 for single occupancy).

The Wainstone's Hotel (☎ 01642 712268, 🖥 www.wainstoneshotel.co.uk; 3S/14D/7T, all en suite, most with bath), on Great Broughton High St, is a rather extravagant choice. Rooms cost from £125 for two sharing, £89.50 for a single. **Eating** (Mon-Sat noon-2pm & 5-10pm, Sun noon-9pm) here is a better bet, with several main courses under £10.

Abbotts No 89 **bus** stops here en route between Stokesley and Northallerton; see pp52-5 for details.

From Clay Bank Top the penultimate steep climb on the Coast to Coast follows and after 20 minutes of effort the top of **Urra Moor** is reached where the gradient relents to near nothing. A wide track unrolls over the moor past a **trig point** (Map 78) and after the **boundary marker with a face** carved onto it, you arrive at a junction of tracks. It's here that the Cleveland Way breaks away to the north, to return as you reach the sea cliffs north of Robin Hood's Bay, while you continue on the wide track of the former Rosedale Ironstone Railway (Map 79) that used to serve the nearby iron mines a century and a half ago.

Passing above the head of pretty **Farndale**, renowned for its daffodils in spring, the track curves round High Blakey Moor towards your probable destination, the isolated Lion Inn.

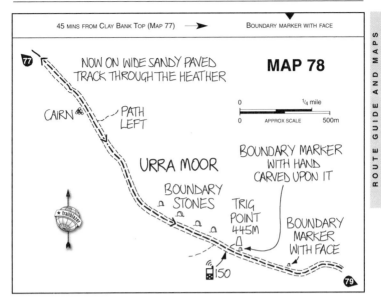

BLAKEY RIDGE MAP 81, p219

For everybody, be they a walker or driver, Blakey Ridge *is* the *Lion Inn* (☎ 01751 417320, 🖳 www.lionblakey.co.uk; 1T/8D/4F, all with private bath), the fourth highest inn in Britain (the highest, the Tan Inn, lies near Keld) and one of the most charming on the route. The inn is nothing much to look at on the outside. Indeed, its orange-tiled roofs are rather disappointing for those expecting the rustic image suggested by the website. But inside, with its dark time-worn beams and open fires, it looks like the inn dating back to at least 1553 that it claims to be. The (small) twin is £20pp, but most other rooms cost £35-42pp. During the week the single occupancy supplement is £7.50; the full rate must be paid at weekends.

The **food**, served at the bar or in the restaurant (daily noon-10pm), is tailor made for walkers, being hearty and tasty. Most dishes, which include a sumptuous steak and ale pie, cost about £10.

Camping is allowed in the adjacent field for £2.50pp, with a bit of shelter offered by the walls; toilet and showers are accessible when the pub's open. They prefer you book your pitch in advance to help filter out beery louts intent on mischief, but as long as you rock up in a Gore-Tex cagoule and not a Middlesbrough FC outfit, they'll probably let you stay.

Across the road from the inn is *High Blakey House* (☎ 01751 417186, 🖳 www .highblakeyhouse.co.uk; 1S/1T share bathroom, 1D or F en suite) which caters almost exclusively for walkers with rates starting at £32 per person. Note that the front door gets locked at 10pm.

Readers have recommended an alternative to these two options which are often booked up. *Feversham Arms Inn* (☎ 01751 433206, 🖳 www.fevershamarmsinn.co.uk; 3D or T/cottage sleeping two; all en suite with showers) in **Church Houses**, down the hill in **Farndale**, can be reached by following a path south from where the Lion Inn comes into view (Map 81, WPT 151) for about a mile and a half (an OS map, or an OS print out of this section may help). B&B costs £65-75 (single occupancy is £40); the

ROUTE GUIDE AND MAPS

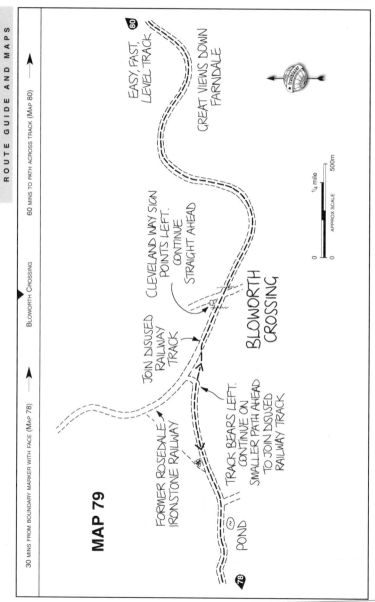

30 MINS FROM BOUNDARY MARKER WITH FACE (MAP 78) → BLOWORTH CROSSING → 60 MINS TO PATH ACROSS TRACK (MAP 80) →

MAP 79

POND

FORMER ROSEDALE IRONSTONE RAILWAY

TRACK BEARS LEFT. CONTINUE ON SMALLER PATH AHEAD TO JOIN DISUSED RAILWAY TRACK

JOIN DISUSED RAILWAY TRACK

BLOWORTH CROSSING

CLEVELAND WAY SIGN POINTS LEFT. CONTINUE STRAIGHT AHEAD

EASY, FAST, LEVEL TRACK

GREAT VIEWS DOWN FARNDALE

APPROX SCALE

0   ¼ mile

0   500m

78

80

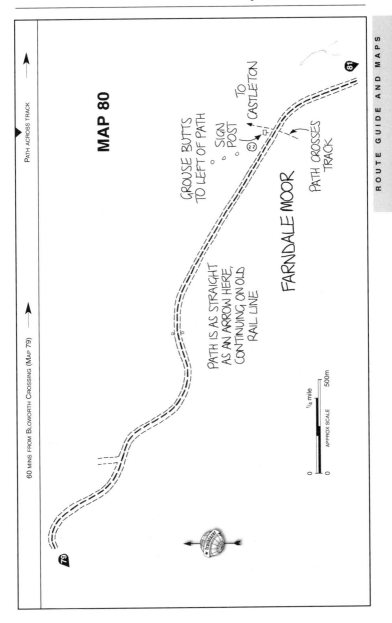

MAP 80

60 MINS FROM BLOWORTH CROSSING (MAP 79)

PATH ACROSS TRACK

GROUSE BUTTS
TO LEFT OF PATH

SIGN
POST

TO
CASTLETON

PATH CROSSES
TRACK

FARNDALE MOOR

PATH IS AS STRAIGHT
AS AN ARROW HERE,
CONTINUING ON OLD
RAIL LINE

¼ mile

500m

APPROX SCALE

79

81

cottage costs £95. The food (Mon-Sat noon-2pm, to 3pm on Sun, daily 6-9pm; daffodil season daily all day) is reportedly excellent, the welcome friendly and the owner is happy to drive walkers back up the hill in the morning. A packed lunch is £5.50 and dogs are welcome.

STAGE 12: BLAKEY RIDGE TO GROSMONT   MAPS 81-87

Introduction

For those who enjoy cosy English villages hidden amongst the gentlest, most bucolic scenery this fine country has to offer, the **14-mile (22.5km, 5hr)** stroll down the **Esk Valley** from Glaisdale to Grosmont may be the best section of this walk. For charm, only the lakeland villages of Borrowdale and Grasmere come close to matching the beauty of Egton Bridge and Grosmont, and it comes as no surprise that the nostalgic '60s village bobby TV show, *Heartbeat*, is filmed nearby.

As a final destination on this stage, either Egton Bridge or Grosmont will do nicely. Glaisdale, too, for that matter, though that will be a very short stage, leaving you with a lot to cover on the final stage to Robin Hood's Bay. But first you have to get to the valley, and that means getting down off the moors.

The route

The walk begins by following the tarmac north towards **Young Ralph Cross** (off Map 82), which just pokes its head over the horizon as you turn off right onto another road, this one signposted to Rosedale Abbey.

Soon you pass the stumpy white landmark known as **Fat Betty** off the path to the left, where tradition requires you both take and leave a snack or a sweet; here's your chance to finally offload those galling muesli bars! Suitably revived, you then turn north-east into the wonderfully named **Great Fryup Lane** (Map 83 and where one suspects Betty spent too much time) and leave the road to pass **Trough House**. The path can clearly be made out continuing eastwards round the southern side of Great Fryup Dale until the end of **Glaisdale Moor** where, on rejoining the road, the **North Sea** ought to be obvious at the far end of the valley.

After a mile of road-walking, Coast-to-Coasters take the rough track along **Glaisdale Rigg** (Map 85) past various standing stones (and a particularly well-hewn **boundary marker** to the right of the path) and on down to a junction with a number of paths by a small tarn. Passing through farmland, the path descends to the houses of Glaisdale.

GLAISDALE   MAP 86, p225

Ten miles (16km) from Blakey, the village of Glaisdale sprawls across its lofty perch above the Esk Valley.

The terraced houses that are a feature of the town were originally built to house the workers in the ironstone mines of the late 19th century and today the **Robinson**

Institute is a village hall that also acts as a small theatre.

The late 18th-century **Church of St Thomas the Apostle**, near the upper end of Glaisdale, is notable for its 16th-century wooden font cover and communion table.

(cont'd on p224)

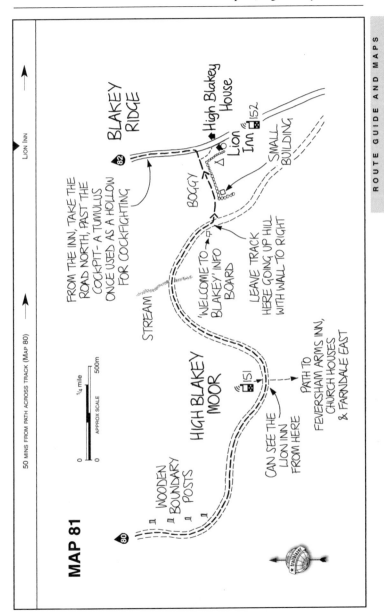

MAP 81

50 MINS FROM PATH ACROSS TRACK (MAP 80)

LION INN

¼ mile
APPROX SCALE
0   500m

BLAKEY RIDGE

High Blakey House

Lion Inn 152

SMALL BUILDING

BOGGY

FROM THE INN, TAKE THE ROAD NORTH, PAST THE COCKPIT - A TUMULUS ONCE USED AS A HOLLOW FOR COCKFIGHTING

STREAM

'WELCOME TO BLAKEY' INFO BOARD

LEAVE TRACK HERE GOING UP HILL WITH WALL TO RIGHT

HIGH BLAKEY MOOR

151

CAN SEE THE LION INN FROM HERE

PATH TO FEVERSHAM ARMS INN, CHURCH HOUSES & FARNDALE EAST

WOODEN BOUNDARY POSTS

80

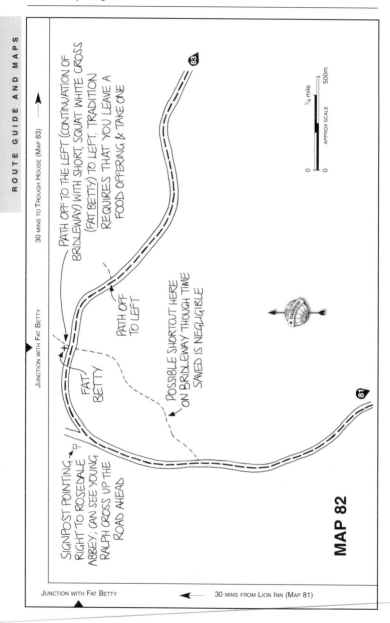

30 MINS TO TROUGH HOUSE (MAP 83) →

PATH OFF TO THE LEFT (CONTINUATION OF BRIDLEWAY) WITH SHORT, SQUAT WHITE CROSS (FAT BETTY) TO LEFT. TRADITION REQUIRES THAT YOU LEAVE A FOOD OFFERING & TAKE ONE

PATH OFF TO LEFT

JUNCTION WITH FAT BETTY

FAT BETTY

POSSIBLE SHORTCUT HERE ON BRIDLEWAY THOUGH TIME SAVED IS NEGLIGIBLE

SIGNPOST POINTING RIGHT TO ROSEDALE ABBEY; CAN SEE YOUNG RALPH CROSS UP THE ROAD AHEAD

MAP 82

¼ mile

APPROX SCALE

500m

JUNCTION WITH FAT BETTY

← 30 MINS FROM LION INN (MAP 81)

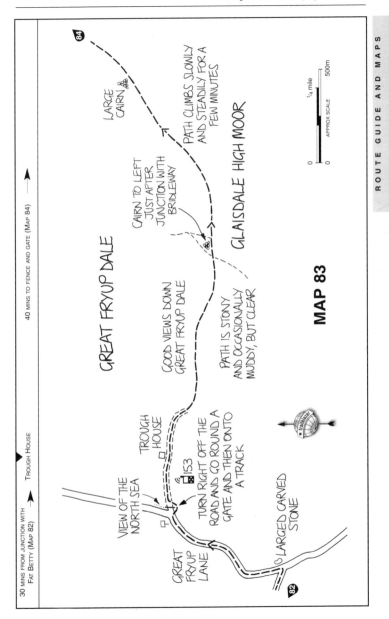

30 MINS FROM JUNCTION WITH FAT BETTY (MAP 82) →→ TROUGH HOUSE →→ 40 MINS TO FENCE AND GATE (MAP 84) →→

84

LARGE CAIRN

PATH CLIMBS SLOWLY AND STEADILY FOR A FEW MINUTES

GLAISDALE HIGH MOOR

CAIRN TO LEFT JUST AFTER JUNCTION WITH BRIDLEWAY

GREAT FRYUP DALE

GOOD VIEWS DOWN GREAT FRYUP DALE

PATH IS STONY AND OCCASIONALLY MUDDY, BUT CLEAR

MAP 83

1/4 mile
500m
0
0
APPROX SCALE

TROUGH HOUSE

153

TURN RIGHT OFF THE ROAD AND GO ROUND A GATE AND THEN ONTO A TRACK

VIEW OF THE NORTH SEA

GREAT FRYUP LANE

LARGED CARVED STONE

82

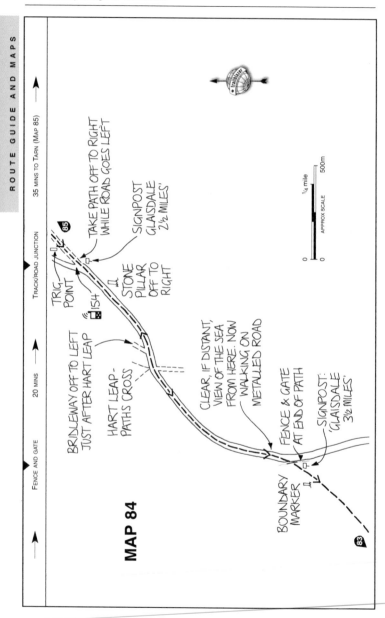

MAP 84

FENCE AND GATE

20 MINS

TRACK/ROAD JUNCTION

35 MINS TO TARN (MAP 85)

85

BRIDLEWAY OFF TO LEFT
JUST AFTER HART LEAP

HART LEAP -
PATHS CROSS

TRIG-
POINT

154

STONE
PILLAR
OFF TO
RIGHT

TAKE PATH OFF TO RIGHT
WHILE ROAD GOES LEFT

SIGNPOST
GLAISDALE
2½ MILES'

CLEAR, IF DISTANT,
VIEW OF THE SEA
FROM HERE. NOW
WALKING ON
METALLED ROAD

FENCE & GATE
AT END OF PATH

SIGNPOST:
'GLAISDALE
3½ MILES'

BOUNDARY
MARKER

83

¼ mile   500m

0   0

APPROX SCALE

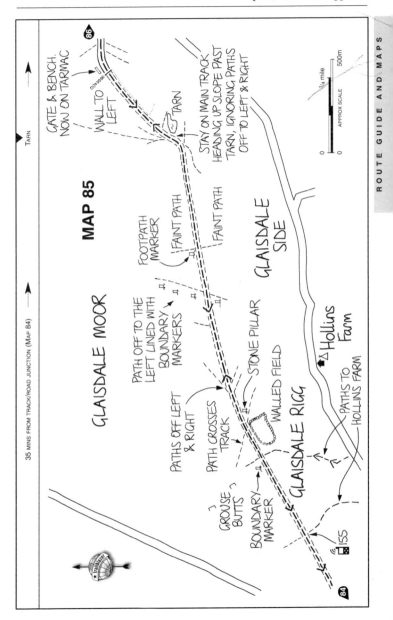

TARN →

35 MINS FROM TRACK/ROAD JUNCTION (MAP 84) ←

GLAISDALE MOOR

MAP 85

GATE & BENCH. NOW ON TARMAC

WALL TO LEFT

TARN

STAY ON MAIN TRACK HEADING UP SLOPE PAST TARN, IGNORING PATHS OFF TO LEFT & RIGHT

PATH OFF TO THE LEFT LINED WITH BOUNDARY MARKERS

FOOTPATH MARKER

FAINT PATH

FAINT PATH

GLAISDALE SIDE

PATHS OFF LEFT & RIGHT

PATH CROSSES TRACK

STONE PILLAR

WALLED FIELD

Hollins Farm

GROUSE BUTTS

BOUNDARY MARKER

GLAISDALE RIGG

PATHS TO HOLLINS FARM

155

0   ¼ mile
0   500m
APPROX SCALE

ROUTE GUIDE AND MAPS

(cont'd from p218) (Don't be fooled by the '1585' date stone in the side of the steps leading to the tower, it's from an earlier chapel).

The church also contains a picture of Thomas Ferris, the beggar made famous in Glaisdale's other main sight, the **Beggar's Bridge** at the other end of the village. In the 17th century, Ferris, a humble pauper, was courting the daughter of the wealthy local squire. In order to win her hand Ferris thought he needed to improve his standing in the community so with this in mind he struck upon a plan to set sail from Whitby and seek his fortune on the high seas. The night before he put this plan into action, however, Ferris went to visit his beloved who lived across the river. Unfortunately, the river was swollen by heavy rains and Ferris's dreams of a romantic farewell were dashed. The story, however, does have a happy ending: Thomas returned from his adventures on the sea a wealthy man and married his sweetheart, and with part of his fortune built the Beggar's Bridge so that other young lovers from the neighbourhood would not suffer the same torment as he had that stormy night.

As for facilities, the **shop** (Mon-Sat 7am-6pm, Sun 9am-2pm) is also home to the **post office** (Mon, Tue, Thur and Fri 8.30am-12.30pm & 1.30-5.30pm, Wed and Sat morning only). There is also a **public phone**, and a **public toilet** near the station.

Where to stay and eat
Down near the train station *The Arncliffe Arms* (☎ 01947 897555; 🖳 www.arncliffearms.co.uk; 1D/2T/1D or F, all en suite with showers) charges £58 or £45 for single

occupancy. It also lays on **food** (Mon-Sat noon-2pm & 6-8.45pm; Sun 6-8pm only; Nov-Mar hours variable).

Half a mile from the village centre is the award-winning 17th-century **Red House Farm** (☎ 01947 897242, 🖳 www.redhousefarm.com; 1S/2D/1F, en suite with bath and shower). Once a working farm and still the home of a number of farm animals, it's been tastefully converted to retain many of the original features to the point where it would be a shame to spend only one night here. Dogs are welcome but in the stable not in the house; B&B costs from £32.50 per person.

At the very end of the village just across the tracks from the railway station is **Beggar's Bridge** (☎ 01947 897409, 🖳 www.beggarsbridge.co.uk; 2D with en suite shower/1T with bath), close to the lovelorn bridge. Rates here are £28pp or £38 for single occupancy.

Campers can head for the well-equipped **Hollins Farm** (☎ 01947 897516, 🖳 www.coast2coast.co.uk/hollinsfarm; 1D or T en suite shower/1D or F private bath), just over a mile south-west of Glaisdale and most easily reached by taking the path as indicated on Map 85. **Camping** is £3.50pp (showers are 30p) and if you lose your nerve **B&B** costs £22-26pp. They offer lifts to the pub, and packed lunches (if ordered in advance).

Transport (see also pp52-5)
M&D's **Bus** No 99 travels up and down the Esk Valley from Lealholm to Whitby 4-5/ day, Mon-Sat.

Trains stop here en route between Middlesbrough and Whitby.

From Glaisdale you enter East Arncliffe Wood, walking along the river until the path winds up at a road where a left leads down the hill and into Egton Bridge.

❏ **Important note – walking times**
Unless otherwise specified, **all times in this book refer only to the time spent walking**. You will need to add 20-30% to allow for rests, photography, checking the map, drinking water etc. When planning the day's hike count on 5-7 hours' actual walking.

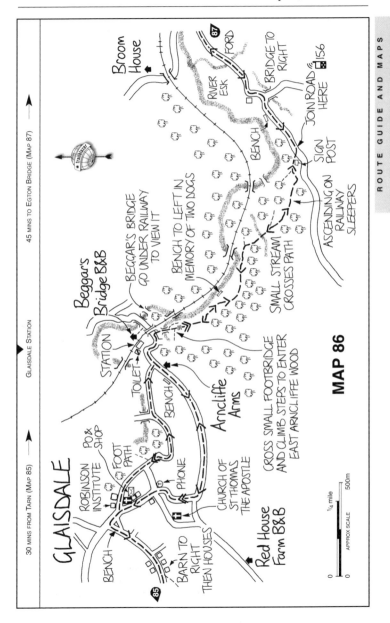

30 MINS FROM TARN (MAP 85) →

GLAISDALE STATION

45 MINS TO EGTON BRIDGE (MAP 87) →

Broom House

RIVER ESK

87 FORD

BRIDGE TO RIGHT

JOIN ROAD HERE 156

SIGN POST

BENCH

ASCENDING ON RAILWAY SLEEPERS

SMALL STREAM CROSSES PATH

BENCH TO LEFT IN MEMORY OF TWO DOGS

BEGGAR'S BRIDGE GO UNDER RAILWAY TO VIEW IT

Beggar's Bridge B&B

STATION

TOILET

BENCH

Arncliffe Arms

CROSS SMALL FOOTBRIDGE AND CLIMB STEPS TO ENTER EAST ARNCLIFFE WOOD

MAP 86

GLAISDALE

ROBINSON INSTITUTE

PO & SHOP

FOOT PATH

PHONE

CHURCH OF ST THOMAS THE APOSTLE

BENCH

BARN TO RIGHT THEN HOUSES

85

Red House Farm B&B

¼ mile

500m

APPROX SCALE

0

0

EGTON BRIDGE   MAP 87

A strong competitor for the accolade of prettiest village on the Coast to Coast, Egton Bridge is a delight, a hamlet of grand houses surrounding an uninhabited island on the Esk. Everything about the place is charming, from the bridge itself – a 1990s' copy of the original 18th-century structure washed away in a flood in 1930 – to the stepping stones that lead across to the island and the mature trees that fringe the settlement.

The Catholic **St Hedda's Church**, too, is incredibly grand given the tiny size of the village. On the exterior are a series of friezes while inside, behind glass to the right of the altar, are the relics of Nicholas Postgate, a local Catholic priest and martyr hung, drawn and quartered for continuing to practise his faith in 1679. See box below for details about St Hedda himself.

Where to stay and eat

It would be a surprise indeed if somewhere like Egton Bridge didn't have decent accommodation, and the village doesn't disappoint. *The Horseshoe Hotel* (☎ 01947 895245; ⌨ www.thehorseshoehotel.co.uk; 4D/2T), right on the walk at the start of the village, fulfils every expectation of a country inn, with an expansive beer garden, a lavish array of local ales and a snug interior. Main courses are typically under £10 (sandwiches or hot baguettes cost £4-6) and are served daily noon-2pm & 7-9pm.

B&B costs £55 in a room with shared bathroom or £70 for an en suite room with shower. No discount for single occupancy.

A little way to the west of the village, the four-star *Broom House* (Map 86, p225; ☎ 01947 895279, ⌨ www.egton-bridge.co .uk; 1S/1T/5D/1D or F, all en suite some with bath; closed Jan) is a 19th-century farmhouse described by one reader as more of a country house hotel with a touch of class. They charge £33-65pp (single occupancy £60) and recently opened an in-house *bistro* (Mar-Oct Wed-Sun 6-9pm, Sun lunch noon-2pm; hours variable in winter), which is open to non residents; book in advance.

The Postgate Inn (☎ 01947 895241, ⌨ www.postgateinn.com; 1D/1D or T/1F, all en suite, bath available) is another top choice with food served daily (light lunches noon-2.30pm, snacks 2.30-6.30pm, meals 6.30-9pm), and B&B for £75 for two sharing, £25-30pp in the family room. To get there, head up the hill from the church past the point where the Coast to Coast path turns down the track.

Transport (see also pp52-5)

Egton Bridge is on the **railway** line between Whitby and Middlesbrough. In addition, M&D's **bus** No 99 travels from Whitby up the Esk Valley to Glaisdale and Lealholm.

❑ Saint Hedda

The seventh-century British saint, Hedda, crops up a few times on the Coast to Coast walk, even though he is these days more closely associated with Winchester, Hampshire. He began his Episcopal career at Whitby Abbey (whose striking remains you'll have spied from Glaisdale Moor), where he was educated and rose to become abbot.

His big break came in 676AD when he was consecrated as the Bishop of Wessex by Saint Theodore of Tarsus, at that time the Archbishop of Canterbury. He ruled over the diocese for thirty years, during which time he moved the see from Dorchester to Winchester and became chief advisor to King Ina. Described by the Venerable Bede as 'a good and just man, who in carrying out his duties was guided rather by an inborn love of virtue than by what he had read in books', he died in 705AD and is buried at Winchester Cathedral.

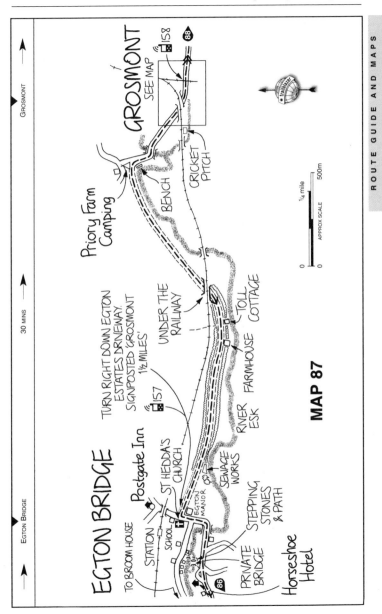

EGTON BRIDGE

30 MINS

GROSMONT

EGTON BRIDGE

TO BROOM HOUSE

STATION

SCHOOL

Postgate Inn

ST HEDDA'S CHURCH

157

EGTON MANOR

SEWAGE WORKS

PRIVATE BRIDGE

STEPPING STONES & PATH

Horseshoe Hotel

86

RIVER ESK

FARMHOUSE

TOLL COTTAGE

UNDER THE RAILWAY

TURN RIGHT DOWN EGTON ESTATES DRIVEWAY. SIGNPOSTED 'GROSMONT ½ MILES'

Priory Farm Camping

BENCH

CRICKET PITCH

GROSMONT
SEE MAP

158

88

MAP 87

trailblazer

¼ mile

APPROX SCALE

0   500m

ROUTE GUIDE AND MAPS

The next mile or so from Egton Bridge to Grosmont takes you past the elegant **Egton Manor** along an old toll road (the original toll charges are still written on a board hanging from **Toll Cottage**, halfway along). It's an easy walk now, taking you under the railway and along the Esk, past Priory Farm (see below), and into Grosmont.

GROSMONT see map opposite

After the quaint, picture-perfect settlements of the preceding few miles, Grosmont emerges as a grittier and more distinctive sibling. Indeed literally so as from the rail crossing in the village centre, a row of soot-stained terraces claw their way up the hill, caked by the acrid fumes that once belched from three ironstone smelting furnaces 150 years ago.

These days this less glamorous heritage is all but forgotten as tourists and steam rail enthusiasts alike flock to ride the locomotives of the **North York Moors Railway**. Featured as the 'Hogwarts Express' in the original *Harry Potter* movie, it's definitely worth hanging about to see at least one loco in motion before leaving Grosmont, if not timing your arrival to take a return ride to Pickering or Whitby. By now you deserve to take the weight off your feet; for full details see 'Transport' opposite.

While you're waiting, follow the alleyway leading through a long train tunnel to the **sidings and loco sheds** to gain an insight into what it takes to keep these engines on track. The tunnel is thought to be the oldest passenger train tunnel in the world, hewn out around 1829 to serve a horse-drawn railway designed by no less than George Stephenson. Regarded as the 'Father of Railways', it was Stephenson who foresaw a future in a network of inter-linked rail lines along which engines powered by steam would go on to span and help consolidate the riches of the British Empire. It was during the tunnel excavations that viable quantities of iron ore were uncovered, leading to the ironstone mining boom along the Esk Valley.

There's a **church**, too, with a boulder of Shap granite outside the west door, deposited here by a glacier which lost its way back in the Ice Age.

The settlement, originally known as 'Tunnel', went on to gain the name Grosmont and is today a one-street village where both modern and heritage rail lines intersect, and that has all of the essentials a weary trekker needs: a **store**, **pub** (the Station Tavern, of course!), two **tearooms** and a few B&Bs.

The **Co-op** (Mon-Fri 7.30am-5.30pm, Sat 8am-5.30pm, Sun 9am-5.30pm) is one of the oldest community-run village shops in the country and is also home to the **post office** (Mon-Fri 9am-noon). As well as the post office, the Station Tavern does **cash-back**.

Where to stay and eat

A little before the village, **campers** stop at *Priory Farm* (Map 87, p227; ☎ 01947 895324; closed Dec-Feb) offering basic facilities for just £3 per person including a small room alongside the farmhouse with a toilet, sink and a kettle.

As you come into town *Hazelwood* (☎ 01947 895292, 💻 www.hazelwoodhouse .net; 1S/1D/1T or F; Easter to Oct; no dogs) is on the right before the rail crossing, a family-run place with an adjacent **tearoom** (daily Easter to Oct 10am-5pm). B&B is £33pp; the single and double share a bathroom and the other room has an en suite shower. There's another **tearoom** and **café** on the station platform.

Just over the rails *Linten House* (☎ 01947 895386, 💻 valerie@vsmith648 .orangehome.co.uk; 1D or F with private bath) offers plain accommodation in an old terrace house for £60 for two sharing.

Over the road is the *Station Tavern* (☎ 01947 895060, 💻 www.stationtavern-gros mont.co.uk; 1S/1D/1T or F, all with private facilities) which serves **pub grub** (daily Easter to late Oct noon-3pm & 7-9pm, Nov to Easter weekends noon-3pm,

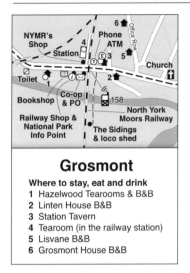

Grosmont

Where to stay, eat and drink
1 Hazelwood Tearooms & B&B
2 Linten House B&B
3 Station Tavern
4 Tearoom (in the railway station)
5 Lisvane B&B
6 Grosmont House B&B

daily 7-9pm) and has become something of a venue for spontaneous Coast to Coast banquets before people go their separate ways at Robin Hood's Bay. B&B costs £65-75 (£35 for single occupancy).

Just up the hill and left down Office Row, *Lisvane* (☎ 01947 895969, 🖳 www

.lisvane.me.uk; 1S/1T shared shower facilities; 1D or T en suite shower; Mar-Oct) is a grand Victorian villa with wi-fi and B&B from £32.50pp (£35 for the single). Further on, *Grosmont House* (☎ 01947 895539, 🖳 www.grosmonthouse.co.uk; 3D with en suite shower/1T/1F share bathroom) is a delightful place whose gardens also have wonderful views down over the railway. Rates are from £35pp. **Evening meals** (daily around 6.30pm) are available only if you pre-book (even if you're not staying there) and are worth it: the fresh lobster salad is said to be divine.

Transport (see also pp52-5)
North York Moors Railway's **steam train** (☎ 01751 472508, 🖳 www.nymr.co.uk) to Pickering (70 mins), or Whitby (25 mins) leaves Grosmont between four and eight times a day depending on the season. Some of the trains are drawn by a diesel engine rather than a steam engine, so if you want that authentic chuff-chuff sound check the timetable or give them a call. Northern Rail's **trains** go to Whitby (20 mins) and to Middlesbrough (70 mins).

M&D's **Bus** No 99 also travels to Whitby (15 mins) from the railway station.

STAGE 13: GROSMONT TO ROBIN HOOD'S BAY   MAPS 87-95

Introduction

The last stage, but don't be fooled into thinking this is a mere formality as the climb out of Grosmont will soon demonstrate. It's a long stretch totalling **15½ miles (25km, 6hrs)** with enough ups and downs to ensure that you arrive in Robin Hood's Bay suitably dishevelled. The scenery is largely similar to what's gone before: desolate moorland punctuated with short road stages and, in an echo of the first leg, a finale along the sea cliffs prior to the final descent to the Bay. The most pleasant surprise, especially on a hot day, is the transit of Little Beck Wood, a narrow belt of the most heavenly woodland in north Yorkshire.

The route

First, there's a 700ft (230m) climb up to **Sleights Moor**, part of the intriguingly named Eskdaleside Cum Ugglebarnby, which is how you may feel if you missed breakfast. With views north-east to the well-ventilated ruins of **Whitby Abbey** or back down into misty Eskdale, you pass the **High Bride Stones** – five ancient standing monoliths – to the right of the road.   *(cont'd on p232)*

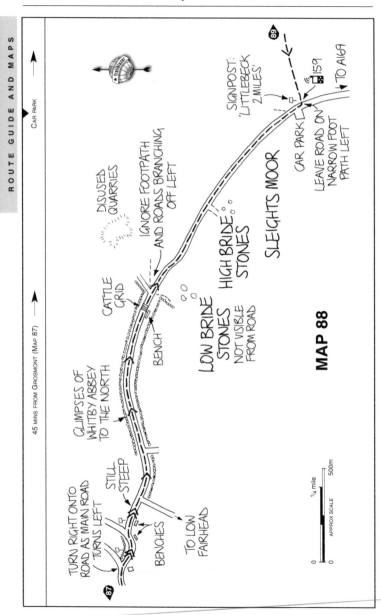

MAP 88

ROUTE GUIDE AND MAPS

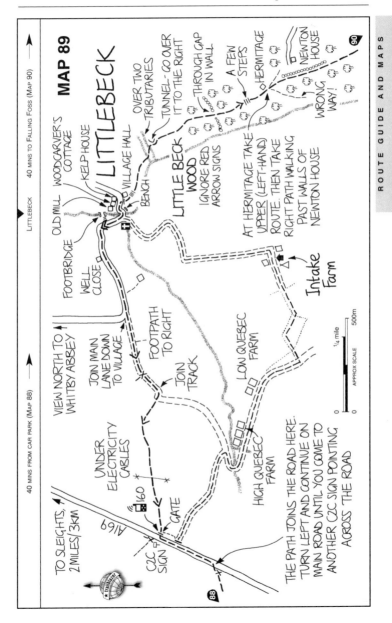

40 MINS FROM CAR PARK (MAP 88)

LITTLEBECK

40 MINS TO FALLING FOSS (MAP 90)

MAP 89

LITTLEBECK

VIEW NORTH TO WHITBY ABBEY

OLD MILL

WOODCARVER'S COTTAGE

KELP HOUSE

FOOTBRIDGE

VILLAGE HALL

BENCH

OVER TWO TRIBUTARIES

TUNNEL – GO OVER IT TO THE RIGHT

THROUGH GAP IN WALL

A FEW STEPS

HERMITAGE

WELL CLOSE

LITTLE BECK WOOD

IGNORE RED ARROW SIGNS

NEWTON HOUSE

90

JOIN MAIN LANE DOWN TO VILLAGE

FOOTPATH TO RIGHT

JOIN TRACK

AT HERMITAGE TAKE UPPER (LEFT-HAND) ROUTE. THEN TAKE RIGHT PATH WALKING PAST WALLS OF NEWTON HOUSE

WRONG WAY!

Intake Farm

UNDER ELECTRICITY CABLES

160

GATE

LOW QUEBEC FARM

¼ mile

APPROX SCALE

0   500m

0

TO SLEIGHTS, 2 MILES/3KM

A169

C2C SIGN

HIGH QUEBEC FARM

THE PATH JOINS THE ROAD HERE. TURN LEFT AND CONTINUE ON MAIN ROAD UNTIL YOU COME TO ANOTHER C2C SIGN POINTING ACROSS THE ROAD

88

trailblazer

(cont'd from p229) (Incidentally, the confusing jumble of the Low Bride Stones stands just below them on a terrace, to your right as you passed over the cattle grid.)

Opposite a car park turn left onto a path (Map 88, WPT 159) and follow it down to the A169 at which point you turn left again for a few hundred metres until a Coast to Coast sign heralds the path dropping down through more heather to Littlebeck.

LITTLEBECK   MAP 89, p231

Littlebeck is another tiny hamlet with a lengthy past, it's hard to imagine today's picturesque rural idyll was actually once a centre of alum-mining in the 17th to 19th centuries. Alum, by the way, is used in dyeing as well as tanning leather. A hundred tons of shale would be produced in order to extract just one ton of alum, so it seems remarkable the surrounding land appears so unscarred.

The village has one other minor claim to fame as the home of master woodcarver Thomas Whittaker who died in 1991 (his house, now called **Woodcarver's Cottage**, is on the bend above the **Old Mill**). Whittaker exclusively used English oak and would 'sign' every piece of his furniture with a gnome; in German folklore the oak tree's guardian. Above the cottage is **Kelp House**, where kelp, used in the processing of alum, was stored.

Fifteen minutes south of the village and half a mile from the path, staying at *Intake Farm* (☎ 01947 810273, 🖳 intake farm@farming.co.uk; 2D/1T/1F, one en suite with shower, bath available) is regularly and warmly recommended by readers who want to spin out the last day into an easy 12-miler. B&B costs £25-30pp for two sharing, £22.50pp for three and £30 for single occupancy – and £4 to **camp** out the back. It's a way to the nearest pub but they'll happily lay on an evening meal (£15 for three courses if booked in advance) as well as a packed lunch (£4) in the morning.

Whilst you can reach the farm from the centre of the village, it's quicker to join the track to the right (south) of the Coast to Coast path heading off the A169 via both High Quebec Farm and Low Quebec Farm.

Pretty as Littlebeck is, it's nothing when compared to the beauty that awaits in **Little Beck Wood**. This really is a stunning 65 acres of woodland, filled with oak trees, deer, badgers, foxes and birdlife galore. There are also a couple of man-made features to see on the way including the mysterious **Hermitage** (Map 89), a boulder hollowed out to form a small cave. Above the entrance is etched the year '1790'.

More delights await as the path from the Hermitage leads you down to **Falling Foss** (Map 90), a 20m-high waterfall alongside the former ruins of **Midge Hall**, now rebuilt and enterprisingly converted into the *Falling Foss Tea Garden* (☎ 07723 477929, 🖳 www.fallingfossteagarden.co.uk; Mar-Oct Tue-Sun 10.30am-5pm, Aug daily, closed Nov-Feb), a great place for a coffee and cake, an ice cream or a light lunch before you leave the woods for the final hike to the sea.

Suitably refreshed, cross the road and head along **May Beck** to the car park at the southern extremity of the wood. Here you turn back north and walk along the road, looking back over the valley you've just walked through and the moors beyond. *(cont'd on p236)*

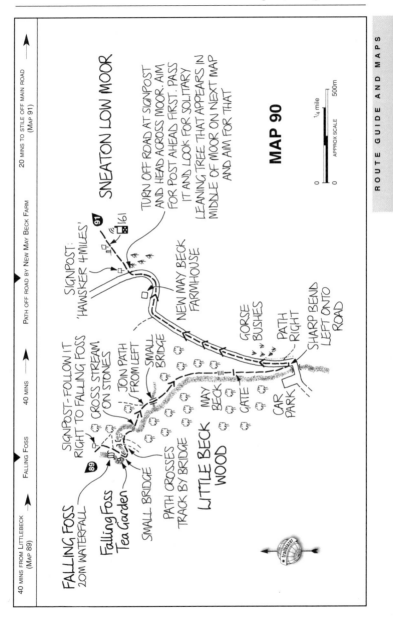

40 MINS FROM LITTLEBECK (MAP 89) → FALLING FOSS → 40 MINS → PATH OFF ROAD BY NEW MAY BECK FARM → 20 MINS TO STILE OFF MAIN ROAD (Map 91) →

FALLING FOSS
20M WATERFALL

Falling Foss Tea Garden

SMALL BRIDGE

PATH CROSSES TRACK BY BRIDGE

LITTLE BECK WOOD

SIGNPOST – FOLLOW IT RIGHT TO FALLING FOSS

CROSS STREAM ON STONES

JOIN PATH FROM LEFT

SMALL BRIDGE

MAY BECK

GATE

CAR PARK

SIGNPOST: 'HAWSKER 4 MILES'

NEW MAY BECK FARMHOUSE

GORSE BUSHES

PATH RIGHT

SHARP BEND LEFT ONTO ROAD

SNEATON LOW MOOR

TURN OFF ROAD AT SIGNPOST AND HEAD ACROSS MOOR. AIM FOR POST AHEAD FIRST. PASS IT AND LOOK FOR SOLITARY LEANING TREE THAT APPEARS IN MIDDLE OF MOOR ON NEXT MAP AND AIM FOR THAT

MAP 90

¼ mile
500m
0
0
APPROX SCALE

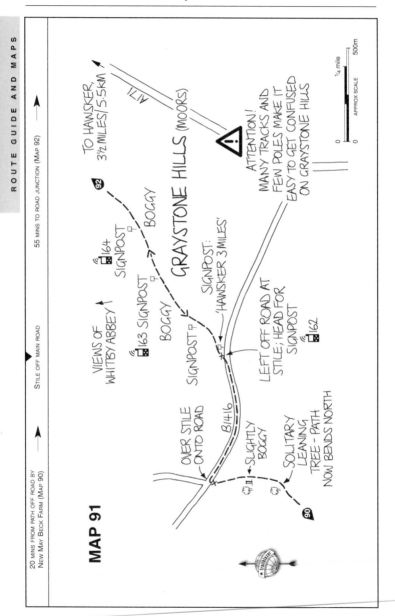

20 MINS FROM PATH OFF ROAD BY
NEW MAY BECK FARM (MAP 90)

STILE OFF MAIN ROAD

55 MINS TO ROAD JUNCTION (MAP 92)

MAP 91

TO HAWSKER,
3½ MILES/5.5KM

A171

92

GRAYSTONE HILLS (MOORS)

164
SIGNPOST

BOGGY

163 SIGNPOST

BOGGY

VIEWS OF
WHITBY ABBEY

SIGNPOST

SIGNPOST:
'HAWSKER 3 MILES'

OVER STILE
ONTO ROAD

B1416

SLIGHTLY
BOGGY

SOLITARY
LEANING
TREE - PATH
NOW BENDS NORTH

LEFT OFF ROAD AT
STILE; HEAD FOR
SIGNPOST

162

ATTENTION!
MANY TRACKS AND
FEW POLES MAKE IT
EASY TO GET CONFUSED
ON GRAYSTONE HILLS

90

¼ mile
0

APPROX SCALE
0   500m

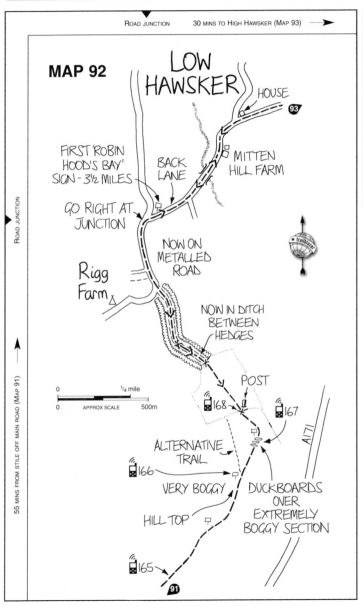

ROUTE GUIDE AND MAPS

MAP 92

LOW HAWSKER

HOUSE

93

FIRST 'ROBIN HOOD'S BAY' SIGN - 3½ MILES

BACK LANE

MITTEN HILL FARM

GO RIGHT AT JUNCTION

NOW ON METALLED ROAD

Rigg Farm

NOW IN DITCH BETWEEN HEDGES

POST

ROAD JUNCTION

55 MINS FROM STILE OFF MAIN ROAD (MAP 91)

0   ¼ mile
0   APPROX SCALE   500m

168

167

A171

ALTERNATIVE TRAIL

166

VERY BOGGY

HILL TOP

DUCKBOARDS OVER EXTREMELY BOGGY SECTION

165

91

ROUTE GUIDE AND MAPS

(cont'd from p232) A traverse of two other moors, Sneaton Low Moor and the innocuously named Graystone Hills, follows; the rather lean waymarks and confusing paths across Graystone Hills to Normanby Hill Top (north of the B1416) can require a good sense of direction or some luck, even in bright sunshine; see box p82.

You soon emerge on a road and should turn left here if planning to camp at Rigg Farm (see below). If not, continue down the road where before long you will no doubt be thrilled to spot the first road sign to Robin Hood's Bay indicating it's only '3½ miles' away. Turn right to follow Back Lane past *York House Hotel* and into the village of **High Hawsker** (Map 93) on the A171 Whitby road.

HIGH HAWSKER   MAP 93
In the village the *Hare & Hounds* (☎ 01947 880453; daily noon-2pm & 6.30-9pm) serves hot meals as well as ploughman's lunches and sandwiches. You'll have passed *York House Hotel* & *Caravan Park* on the way there, a large complex with expensive camping and more regulations than the Highway Code. If you're set on **camping**, the smaller *Rigg Farm Caravan Park* (☎ 01947 880430; 🖥 www.riggfarm caravanpark.co.uk), a couple of minutes' walk west from where you rejoined the road (Map 92), charges only £4pp to camp, though it's said they have plans for expansion in 2010.

Arriva's **bus** No 93 calls here; see pp52-5 for details.

From Hawsker, what's left of your eastward progression continues down past sprawling caravan parks and *Woodland Tearoom and Shop* (Map 93; Mon-Thur 9am-2pm, Fri 9am-2pm & 4.30-10pm, Sat 9am-10pm, Sun 9am-4pm), where you can get a last-minute snack for the final stretch.

And so you arrive at the **North Sea** to rejoin the Cleveland Way and stride along the blustery clifftops leading towards Robin Hood's Bay. Though the tiny beach at Robin Hood's Bay appears half an hour before you actually set foot on it, the village itself, tucked away by the headland, is concealed until the very last moment.

But soon enough, having passed a coastguard station and **Rocket Post Field** (Map 94) from which coastguards used to practise aiming their rescue rockets, you join Mount Pleasant North Rd at the top end of Robin Hood's Bay. Take a left at the end of the road and at the roundabout follow either the cliff path or the steep road down, down, down to the bay.

You arrive at the slipway, or Dock as it's known and, all that remains is to dip your toes in the sea, liberate the pebble you've carried from St Bees beach, and toast your achievement in Wainwright's Bar at Bay Hotel (see p242 for opening hours), not forgetting to sign their book.

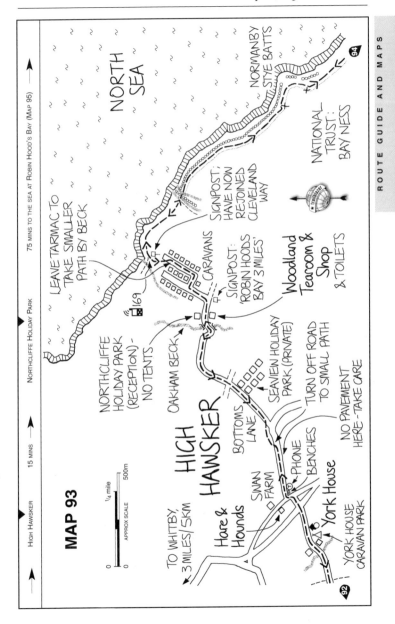

MAP 93

¼ mile
500m
APPROX SCALE

HIGH HAWSKER · 15 MINS · NORTHCLIFFE HOLIDAY PARK · 75 MINS TO THE SEA AT ROBIN HOOD'S BAY (MAP 95)

NORTH SEA

94

NORMANBY STYE BATTS

NATIONAL TRUST: BAY NESS

SIGNPOST: HAVE NOW REJOINED CLEVELAND WAY

LEAVE TARMAC TO TAKE SMALLER PATH BY BECK

CARAVANS

169

SIGNPOST: 'ROBIN HOODS BAY 3 MILES'

Woodland Tearoom & Shop & TOILETS

NORTHCLIFFE HOLIDAY PARK (RECEPTION) - NO TENTS

OAKHAM BECK

SEAVIEW HOLIDAY PARK (PRIVATE)

TURN OFF ROAD TO SMALL PATH

HIGH HAWSKER

BOTTOMS LANE

PHONE

BENCHES

NO PAVEMENT HERE - TAKE CARE

TO WHITBY, 3 MILES/5KM

SWAN FARM

Hare & Hounds

York House

YORK HOUSE CARAVAN PARK

92

And that's it. The walk is over. Congratulations: you've walked the width of England, a total of at least 200 miles, which is certainly something to tell the grandchildren. But that leaves one question unanswered: What are you going to do for an encore?

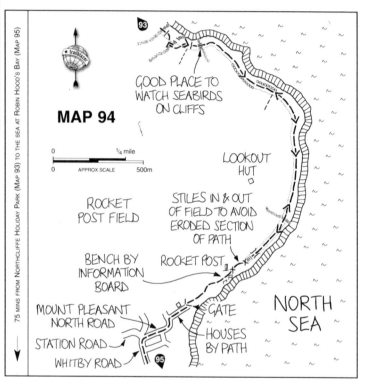

MAP 94

GOOD PLACE TO WATCH SEABIRDS ON CLIFFS

LOOKOUT HUT

ROCKET POST FIELD

STILES IN & OUT OF FIELD TO AVOID ERODED SECTION OF PATH

BENCH BY INFORMATION BOARD

ROCKET POST

MOUNT PLEASANT NORTH ROAD

GATE

HOUSES BY PATH

NORTH SEA

STATION ROAD

WHITBY ROAD

0   ¼ mile

0   APPROX SCALE   500m

❑ **The rescue of *The Visitor***

A small memorial just above the old village celebrates the heroic rescue of the brig, *The Visitor,* which ran aground off Robin Hood's Bay during a storm in 1881. With the village's small lifeboat unable to help in such rough seas, the villagers summoned help from Whitby. That night, the lifeboat from Whitby was dragged over the snow to Robin Hood's Bay, a distance of some 8 miles (13km). Sometimes the snowdrifts were up to 2m deep and it took 200 men to clear a path for the lifeboat. Yet having arrived at the bay it managed to launch safely and by some miracle all the crew of *The Visitor* were saved.

ROBIN HOOD'S BAY   MAP 95, p241

Robin Hood's Bay is the perfect place to finish, a quaint, cosy little fishing village that in high summer becomes a busy seaside resort that is entirely in keeping with the picturesque theme of the walk.

Though fishing has declined since its heyday in the 19th century, there's been a revival thanks to its crab grounds, said to be amongst the best in the north.

The old town huddles around the Dock, row after row of terraced, stone cottages arranged haphazardly uphill with numerous twisting interconnecting alleyways and paths to explore. Within them are a number of pubs and tearooms where you can celebrate. There are also gift, souvenir and antique shops aplenty, as well as plaques or certificates (see Bay Hotel, p240 & p242) for newly ennobled Coast to Coasters and a **museum** (July-Aug Sun-Fri noon-4pm).

And what is the connection with Robin Hood? Who knows, but after the effort and energy you may have expended over the past fortnight or so to get here – who honestly cares?

Services

The **Old Coastguard Station Visitor Centre** (☎ 01947 885900; June-Sep Tue-Sun 10am-5pm, Mar-May & Oct weekends only 10am-5pm, Nov-Feb weekends only 11am-4pm) sits right by the end of the trail but seems to be struggling to meet its posted opening hours, though the official tourist information **website** (🖥 www.robin-hoods-bay.co.uk) has plenty of useful information, including a comprehensive list of **accommodation**.

The **post office and general store** (Mon-Fri 9am-5.30pm, Sat 9am-12.30pm) do **cashback** if you spend a minimum of £5.

Where to stay

Robin Hood's Bay is divided into Upper Bay, the development dating from the Victorian era at the top of the hill, and the quainter and more congested 17th-century Lower Bay or 'Old Town' down by the sea, where there are fewer accommodation options and rooms are less spacious. Not

since Grasmere have you paused to stay in such a busy tourist 'honeypot', and as most Coasters end their walk on a Thursday or Friday, it's worth knowing that rooms on a summer's weekend may be hard to come by and some places may even insist on a minimum of two nights stay.

There are two **campsites** and both can be pretty crowded in summer with families, dogs and caravans. The first, *Middlewood Farm Holiday Park* (☎ 01947 880414, 🖥 www.middlewoodfarm.com; Apr-Oct) is a smart and efficient operation with a laundry room and according to some, the finest ablutions block north of the 52nd parallel. It costs from £7pp; showers and toilets are free but for £1 you can even take a bath. To get there, from the end of the walk by the Bay Hotel head up Albion Rd past the chippy for ten minutes along the path.

High on a hill above the town, you may want to check into the no less popular *Hooks House Farm* (☎ 01947 880283, 🖥 www.hookshousefarm.co.uk) before walking the last mile or two down to the sea as the walk back can be quite an effort. **Camping** here costs from £5pp.

Boggle Hole Youth Hostel (☎ 0845 371 9504, 🖥 bogglehole@yha.org.uk; 80 beds; £13.95-19.95) is a former corn mill located in a ravine about a mile south of the village and reachable either along the shore or the inland road which passes Middlewood Farm Holiday Park. The hostel is open round the clock (as long as you've checked in), serves meals and has a bar.

Back in town there are nearly three dozen hotels, guesthouses and B&Bs to choose from; the official town website mentioned above has a fuller list. Accommodation is most prolific in Upper Bay, the top of the village, where *Thackwood* (☎ 01947 880858, 🖥 www.thackwood.com; 2D en suite with shower/1T en suite with bath) is the first B&B you spot as the trail comes into town. Rates are £70 for two sharing or £50 for single occupancy.

This is followed by *Northcliff* (☎ 01947 880481, 🖥 www.north-cliff.co.uk; 2D/1T, all en suite with shower) also on Mount Pleasant North Rd, a Victorian villa where every room comes with TV and you get a varied breakfast menu. Rates are £60, £35 single occupancy. On the same street is *Manning Tree* (☎ 01947 881042, 🖳 www .manningtreebnb.co.uk; 1T/2D, all en suite with shower) offering a similar standard of accommodation; rates are £65, £40 for single occupancy.

On Mount Pleasant South Rd there's more of the same with the pick of the bunch including *Lee-Side* (☎ 01947 881143; 🖳 lee-side.rhbay.co.uk; 1T/2D, all en suite, bath available) with rooms starting at £68 (£50 for single occupancy), and *Streonshalh* (☎ 01947 881065, 🖳 www .streonshalh.co.uk; 3S/1D/3D or T, all en suite with shower), with free wi-fi and costing £70 for two sharing and £40 in a single. Most credit cards are accepted.

On Station Rd, at the junction with Whitby Rd, is *The Grosvenor Hotel* (☎ 01947 880320, 🖳 www.thegrosvenor.info; 6D/T/3F, all en suite, some with bath) with B&B from £65 (single occupancy £50), while still on Station Rd, *The Villa* (☎ 01947 881043, 🖳 www.thevillarhb.co.uk; 4D or T) is another Victorian property. They have retained the period features such as the cast-iron fireplaces and the servant bells, though from 2010 rooms will be en suite (some with bath); internet access is available and rooms have a TV. Rates are from £65 (£45 for single occupancy).

Below, a further string of B&Bs on Station Rd lead down towards the old town. They're all pretty similar. Readers have recommended the rooms at *The Wayfarer* (☎ 01947 880240, 🖳 www.wayfarerbistro .co.uk; 4D/1D or T, all en suite with shower), B&B costs £32.50pp.

The elegant *West Royd* (☎ 01947 880678, 🖳 www.westroyd.co.uk; 2D/1F, all en suite) comes next, built in 1897 and maintaining its Victorian charm. The family room has a bath. Rates start at £35 per person, £45 for single occupancy.

This is followed by: *Devon House* (☎ 01947 880197, 🖳 www.devonhouserhb.co .uk; 4D, all en suite, one with bath) charging £70 (£50 for single occupancy); *Clarence Dene* (☎ 01947 880478, 🖳 www .clarencedene.co.uk; 2D/1F, all en suite with shower) where B&B is £70 (£90 in the family room), or from £50 single occupancy midweek, dogs are accepted; and *Birtley House* (☎ 01947 880566, 🖳 www.birtley housebedandbreakfast.co.uk; 4D/1T, all en suite one with bath) charging around £32.50-37.50pp.

Alongside these *Victoria Hotel* (☎ 01947 880205, 🖳 www.victoriarhb.com; 10D/2T or D, all en suite with shower) charges from £80 (£60 for single occupancy). Take the alleyway next to the Victoria and it leads onto a road with great views down to the old town. This is where you'll find *Raven House* (☎ 01947 880444, 🖳 http://ravenhouse.rhbay.co.uk; 1S/2D/1D or F, all en suite with shower), which more than one reader has recommended. Edwardian rather than Victorian, most of the rooms enjoy great panoramas and gorging on the generous hospitality tray can save you a trip downtown. Rates start at £65 or £35 for the single.

In the **old town**, most of the accommodation has been given over to holiday apartments for those intending to stay for a week or more. Of the B&Bs, many request a minimum stay of two nights, including *Marnardale Cottage* (☎ 01947 880677, 🖳 www.marnardalecottage.co.uk; 2D, private facilities one with bath) which charges £70 for a room. To get there walk up Tyson's Steps and head for 8 Sunnyside. Right in the centre of the action, *The Boathouse* (☎ 01947 880099, 🖳 www. boathouserhb.co.uk; 2D/2T/1F, all en suite) charges from £70 (£65 single occupancy).

Close to the Dock, *Bramblewick* (☎ 01947 880187; evenings ☎ 01723 871476 🖳 www.bramblewick.org; 4D, all en suite

---

(Opposite) Top: The Hermitage (see p232), a hollowed out boulder in Little Beck Woods. (© JM). **Bottom**: The North York Moors Railway at Grosmont (see p229). (© HS).

(Overleaf) Top: A most welcome sight for weary walkers: Robin Hood's Bay. (© CS). **Bottom**: The last few steps to the Slipway below the Bay Hotel. (© CS).

ROUTE GUIDE AND MAPS

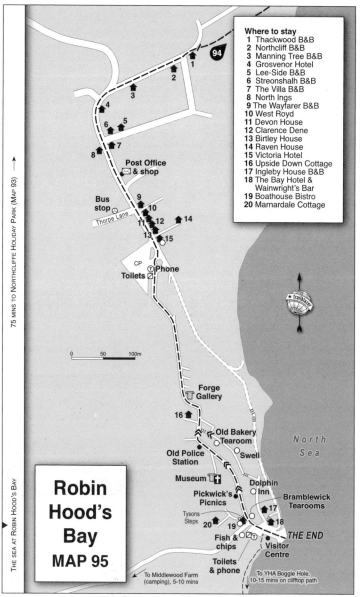

Where to stay
1 Thackwood B&B
2 Northcliff B&B
3 Manning Tree B&B
4 Grosvenor Hotel
5 Lee-Side B&B
6 Streonshalh B&B
7 The Villa B&B
8 North Ings
9 The Wayfarer B&B
10 West Royd
11 Devon House
12 Clarence Dene
13 Birtley House
14 Raven House
15 Victoria Hotel
16 Upside Down Cottage
17 Ingleby House B&B
18 The Bay Hotel &
   Wainwright's Bar
19 Boathouse Bistro
20 Marnardale Cottage

94

Post Office
✉ & shop

Bus
stop
Thorpe Lane

CP
Ⓣ Phone
Toilets ✉

0   50   100m

75 MINS TO NORTHCLIFFE HOLIDAY PARK (MAP 93) →

THE SEA AT ROBIN HOOD'S BAY ▶

Forge
Gallery

Old Bakery
Tearoom

Old Police
Station

Swell

North
Sea

Museum

Pickwick's
Picnics

Dolphin
Inn

Bramblewick
Tearooms

Tysons
Steps

**Robin
Hood's
Bay
MAP 95**

20   19

Fish &
chips

THE END

Visitor
Centre

Toilets
& phone

To Middlewood Farm
(camping), 5-10 mins

To YHA Boggle Hole,
10-15 mins on clifftop path

with shower), 2 King St, retains the feel of its 17th-century origins with B&B from £80, and finally, as close to the walk's end as the tides will allow, *Bay Hotel* (☎ 01947 880278; 3D en suite with shower) where rates are £65-80 per room.

Where to eat and drink
It has to be said that Robin Hood's Bay is not the easiest place to celebrate your monumental achievement with fine dining. The cuisine here seems strictly sea side-traditional: pubs, takeaways and bucket 'n' spade snackeries, but there are a few notable exceptions.

There are plenty of good tea rooms to relax in should you arrive early and need to spin down. *Swell* (10am-3.30pm, to 4 or 5pm in summer), in the heart of the old-town alleyways, is the smartest place and even includes a small cinema and a gift shop.

For evening dining, *Bay Hotel* (see Where to stay; food served daily noon-2pm & 6.30-9pm) is said to have a great restaurant and of course, Wainwright's Bar (Easter to July & Sep to end Oct weekends only, daily in school summer holidays). The pub sells various mementos of the walk including keyrings, certificates, T-shirts as well as magnetised fridge ornaments; don't forget to sign their book to record your success (if the bar is closed, the log book will be in the upstairs bar. Victoria Hotel's (see Where to stay) *Bay & Sea View restaurant* (daily noon-2pm & 6-9pm, no bar meals Sunday evening) is also a safe bet.

Close to Bay Hotel and under new ownership *Bramblewick* (see Where to stay; Thur-Sat 6-9pm; Fri & Sat only out of season) serves home-made crab cakes (£6.95) and a variety of main courses for around £11-17. Further up King St *Ye Dolphin* (food served noon-2pm & 6.30-8.30pm) serves local fish dishes, as well as

boasting a good range of real ales and live music sessions on Fridays and Mondays.

Fish and chips under a mashed pea sludge never did Alfred Wainwright any harm, so the like-minded will queue expectantly at the takeaway **chippy** (Mon & Wed noon-4pm; Tue & Thur noon-7.30pm; Fri & Sat noon-8.30pm; Sun noon-7pm) up an alleyway by the Boathouse. Up near the top of the hill, by the Esplanade, *Maryondale Fisheries* (similar hours) also has a cosy café and right up at the top of town, *The Wayfarer's* bistro (see Where to stay; Feb-Oct Tue-Sun from 6pm; Nov-Dec Tue-Sat from 6pm, closed Jan) features grills and seafood with a new menu every month.

Transport (see also pp52-5)
Arriva's **bus** No 93 runs north to Whitby (20 mins) and on to Middlesbrough (90 mins) for train connections to Darlington – or heads south to Scarborough (40 mins), the nearest place from where you can get a train to York. A single fare to Whitby is £2.80; the last buses to Whitby leave at 9.20pm and 11.55pm, and to Scarborough at 10.34pm. However, times can change so check in advance. The bus stop is on Thorpe Lane, just north of the main car park.

For a **taxi**, call Bay Private Hire on ☎ 01947 880603.

APPENDIX A: MAP KEY

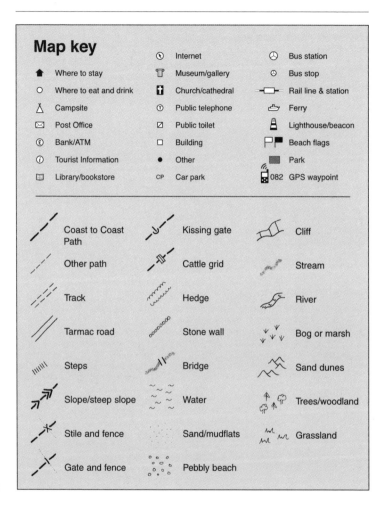

Map key

- ♠ Where to stay
- O Where to eat and drink
- Λ Campsite
- ⊠ Post Office
- £ Bank/ATM
- ⓘ Tourist Information
- 📖 Library/bookstore

- ⓢ Internet
- ⊤ Museum/gallery
- ⊞ Church/cathedral
- ⓣ Public telephone
- ⊠ Public toilet
- ☐ Building
- ● Other
- CP Car park

- ☺ Bus station
- ☉ Bus stop
- ▬□▬ Rail line & station
- ⛴ Ferry
- 🗼 Lighthouse/beacon
- ⚑⚑ Beach flags
- ▬ Park
- 📱082 GPS waypoint

- Coast to Coast Path
- Other path
- Track
- Tarmac road
- Steps
- Slope/steep slope
- Stile and fence
- Gate and fence

- Kissing gate
- Cattle grid
- Hedge
- Stone wall
- Bridge
- Water
- Sand/mudflats
- Pebbly beach

- Cliff
- Stream
- River
- Bog or marsh
- Sand dunes
- Trees/woodland
- Grassland

APPENDIX B: GPS WAYPOINTS

MAP NO	WAY-POINT	OS GRID REF	DESCRIPTION
Stage 1		**St Bees to Ennerdale Bridge (14½ miles)**	
1	001	NX 96042 11791	Mile Zero; Coast to Coast sign on St Bees beach
3	002	NX 97898 14269	Gate on right, then downhill to railway tunnel
4	003	NX 98932 14175	By woods continue N then E to disused railway/cycle route
4	004	NX 99608 14346	Cross A595 and pass Coast to Coast statue; east into Moor Row
4	005	NY 00768 13923	Turn E into field
4/5	006	NY 01558 13494	Cleator Stores, Main St; cross road into Kiln Brow
5	007	NY 02295 13356	Black How Farm. Backroad N to Ennerdale or track E to Dent Hill
5	008	NY 03055 13338	End of trees; follow wall ESE towards Dent Hill summit.
5	009	NY 03743 13052	Cairn along walls; not the summit
5	010	NY 04148 12893	Dent Hill summit (353m), small cairn
5	011	NY 04352 12765	Stile in fence, continue SE
6	012	NY 04535 12668	Junction, follow track going ENE to tall stile
6	013	NY 05532 12979	Having crossed over Kirk Beck continue NE along stream
6	014	NY 05744 13873	Opposite gorse hillside head NE
7	015	NY 06942 15811	Ennerdale Bridge over river
Stage 2		**Ennerdale Bridge to Borrowdale low route (16½ miles)**	
8	016	NY 08831 15257	Weir at western end of Ennerdale Water
9	017	NY 12493 13874	Bridge at eastern end of Ennerdale Water
9	018	NY 13091 14222	Cross River Liza and turn east on forestry track
10	019	NY 14564 14122	Turn off north for high-level route via Red Pike
11	020	NY 19118 12508	Path comes down from Scarth Gap
11/12	021	NY 19464 12385	Black Sail YH. Take minor path E for Loft Beck
12	022	NY 20278 12033	Cross Loft Beck by two cairns and ascend
12	023	NY 20548 12383	Top of Loft Beck at boggy saddle; turn E for stile in fence
12	024	NY 20802 12417	Stile in fence
12	025	NY 21135 12465	Cairns; now head NE
13	026	NY 21366 12632	Join bigger track coming from Brandreth
13	027	NY 21593 13455	Drum House
14	028	NY 24661 13975	Short cut avoiding Seatoller; down steep grassy bank
14	029	NY 24731 13892	End of short cut; follow path through woods
14	030	NY 25825 14939	At bridge turn off by bus stops in Rosthwaite
Stage 3		**Borrowdale to Grasmere (8½ miles)**	
16	031	NY 28180 11635	Downhill briefly into drumlin basin
16	032	NY 28313 11202	Top of Lining Crag; now bogs and cairns to Greenup Edge
16	033	NY 28543 10774	Cairn
16	034	NY 28602 10526	Greenup Edge; twin cairns just after fence post
17	035	NY 29297 10460	Cross a beck, carry on SE

MAP NO	WAY-POINT	OS GRID REF	DESCRIPTION

Stage 3 *(cont'd)*

17	036	NY 29558 10287	Top of Easedale; two routes separate
17	037	NY 30160 10411	Top of Calf Crag (538m)
18	038	NY 32744 09202	Near Helm Crag summit
18	039	NY 32802 09117	Big cairn; steep descent to Grasmere
18	040	NY 32735 08607	At the wall turn right then left onto slate track
18	041	NY 32712 08536	Gate on left for Poet's Walk route
18	042	NY 33260 08458	At road just east of Thorney How YH

Stage 4 Grasmere to St Sunday to Patterdale (7½ miles)

18	043	NY 33593 09169	Cross A591 and head up Tongue Gill
19	044	NY 33952 09817	Two Tongue paths separate
19	045	NY 34908 11680	Grisedale Hause
20	046	NY 35365 12187	Point where paths meet
21	047	NY 36932 13393	Summit of The Cape (841m); head N briefly to cairn
21	048	NY 36975 13678	Cairn; descent NE from St Sunday Crag begins
24	049	NY 37927 14728	Wall joins from east
24	050	NY 38680 15699	Turn right (SE) at oak tree
25	051	NY 39561 15898	Patterdale Hotel

Stage 5 Patterdale to Camp to Shap (16 miles)

25	052	NY 40053 16146	Behind Rooking, path heads off SE uphill to Boredale Hause
25	053	NY 40793 15619	Boredale Hause; grassy flat by two drain covers
25	054	NY 41104 14953	Paths diverge but soon join up near Angle Tarn
26	055	NY 42432 13650	Soon after Satura Crag take right path heading E and later SE
26	056	NY 43106 13121	Cross stream before gap in wall
27	057	NY 43629 12849	Just after corner of a wall; path improves and curves to the S
27	058	NY 43924 12259	Turn left (NE) at cairn for track to Kidsty Pike
27	059	NY 44735 12583	Kidsty Pike summit (784m)
28	060	NY 46839 11894	End of descent at Haweswater reservoir
30	061	NY 50559 16134	East of the dam, a gate leads through the trees to Burnbanks
30	062	NY 50798 16108	Cross road and head through kissing gate into woods
30	063	NY 52026 16221	Turn right up side of field
31	064	NY 53372 16466	After bog, turn right, SE, just before Rosgill Bridge
32	065	NY 53868 15625	Head east here across fields to Shap Abbey
33	066	NY 56210 15555	Shap (northern end by The Hermitage)

Stage 6 Shap to Kirkby Stephen (20½ miles)

34	067	NY 57916 13829	Cross wall by farm and head east across farm access drive
35	068	NY 58568 13573	Steps across quarry access road
36	069	NY 59961 11826	Southern corner of plantation. Head ESE towards twin tree landmark
36	070	NY 60406 11733	Limestone pavement near twin trees; track soon curves to S
36	071	NY 60836 10784	E at wall corner then NE past gully near Robin Hood's Grave

MAP NO	WAY-POINT	OS GRID REF	DESCRIPTION
Stage 6 *(cont'd)*			
37	072	NY 62856 09942	Join road heading S to Orton; soon leave it to SE, passing limekiln
39	073	NY 67383 07661	Join road near Sunbiggin Tarn
40	074	NY 67138 07336	Leave road to SE
40	075	NY 67101 06984	Faint, unmarked junction; turn east across Ravenstonedale Moor
40	076	NY 67621 06930	Duckboard ford over mud by enclosure
40	077	NY 69342 06501	Drain by the road with a hilltop reservoir to the E
41	078	NY 72068 05957	Smardale Bridge over Scandal Beck
42	079	NY 74695 07269	Join road
42	080	NY 74871 07302	Signpost in verge; head across fields for tunnel
42	081	NY 75630 07479	Head for corner of the field then take dip to Green Riggs Farm
43	082	NY 77423 08375	Kirkby Stephen Market Square
45	083	NY 81047 06732	Signpost; Red and Blue routes go E, Green route goes S

Stage 7 Kirkby to Keld Green/Blue/Red routes (15^1/$_2$/14^1/$_2$/14^1/$_2$ miles)

● **Green route**

45	084	NY 81278 05146	Head of Rigg Beck
45	085	NY 81090 05046	Path through limestone pavements
45	086	NY 80810 04467	Four paths meet, head S then SSE to B6270
48	087	NY 83106 02787	Leave road; or carry on a bit and take easier track left uphill.
48	088/109	NY 83542 02774	Red route comes down from pillar cairn to N (WPT 106)

● **Green and Red routes**

49	089/102	NY 85583 03012	Signpost; Blue route joins from the north
49	090	NY 86035 02972	Point where path joins track near Ravenseat Farm
50	091	NY 89200 01050	Keld village centre by shop

● **Blue and Red routes**

46	092	NY 82495 06561	Nine Standards
46	093	NY 82544 06111	Trig point 665m
47	094	NY 82689 05836	Signpost by ruins
47	095/103	NY 82736 05728	Blue and Red routes diverge

● **Blue route**

47	096	NY 83608 05632	Waypoint on Blue route
47	097	NY 84157 05563	Waypoint on Blue route
47	098	NY 84635 05204	Signpost at descent to Whitsundale Beck
48	099	NY 84873 03745	Tin hut shelter
48	100	NY 85250 03380	Vicinity of stile and blue post by fence
49	101	NY 85536 03263	Turn south
49	102/089	NY 85583 03012	Signpost; Blue route joins other two by beck and wall

● **Red route**

47	103/95	NY 82736 05728	Blue and Red routes diverge
47	104	NY 82830 04950	White stick nearby

MAP NO	WAY-POINT	OS GRID REF	DESCRIPTION

Stage 7 Red route *(cont'd)*

47	105	NY 82823 04381	Cairn. Can see pillar cairn S of here
48	106	NY 83098 03785	Pillar cairn; head SE here
48	107	NY 83280 03636	Footbridge; ignore 'no access' sign to east and head for next waypoint
48	108	NY 83352 03582	White-topped pole; descent continues to Green route track
48	109/088	NY 83542 02774	Point where Red route joins Green route; turn east on track
51	110	NY 90464 00863	Fork; high route goes left, low route goes downhill

Stage 8 High route to Reeth (12½ miles)

51	111	NY 90594 00864	Crackpot Hall; turn N towards spoil heaps then E onto stony track
51	112	NY 91865 01300	Climb out of East Gill ends and path joins track
52	113	NY 93189 01309	Leave track to NE; descent to Gunnerside Beck
52	114	NY 93782 01747	Point above Blakethwaite ruins on zigzag path
52	115	NY 93988 01332	Signpost for Surrender Bridge; turn east up Bunton Hush (gully)
52	116	NY 94388 01333	Cairn. Continue directly E to next WPT on main track
52	117	NY 94709 01420	Join track near wooden pen around mine shaft
54	118	NY 99363 00007	Cairn after Surrender Bridge
55	119	SE 02712 99739	Cairn; head ENE for wall corner
55	120	SE 03321 99494	Cross field SE to the east side of the school buildings
56	121	SE 03813 99295	Reeth village green

Swaledale low route to Reeth (11½ miles)

51a	200	SD 91014 98674	Main track goes left, take path to right
51b	201	SD 92579 97809	Fallen tree
51b	202	SD 93295 97817	Join road
51b	203	SD 93600 97989	Leave road in Ivelet, cross Shore Gill, head E
51c	204	SD 94488 98054	Direct route to Gunnerside unclear; take river path
51c	205	SD 96355 98286	Gully
51d	206	SD 97385 98160	Join concrete path
51d	207	SD 98420 98436	Leave road, follow muddy track
51d	208	SD 99535 98999	Leave main track for small path

Stage 9 Reeth to Richmond (14 miles)

56	122	SE 04272 99087	Leave main road to right, take path along river behind farm
56	123	SE 04647 98581	Cross road by bridge and continue along northern side of Swale
56	124	SE 04771 98602	Waypoint by river
56	125	SE 05286 98591	Leave river NNE for tap by gate
56	126	SE 05412 98630	Tap by gate; cross road and enter field to north
56	127	SE 05708 98625	Head for this stile
57	128	SE 06622 97883	Field path rejoins road at Marrick Abbey farm
58	129	NZ 10897 00916	Leave road to right for path NE up to white cairn
61	130	NZ 17033 01012	Opposite Rosemary Lane where C2C goes down to bridge

MAP NO	WAY-POINT	OS GRID REF	DESCRIPTION

Stage 10 Richmond to Ingleby Cross (23 miles)

MAP NO	WAY-POINT	OS GRID REF	DESCRIPTION
61/62	131	NZ 16990 00546	After bridge turn left into playing field
62	132	NZ 17494 00656	Gate on right leads to sheds and path to houses
62	133	NZ 17694 00725	Turn right onto A6136 road
62	134	NZ 18057 00218	Leave A6136 to the left for sewage plant
63	135	SE 18611 99429	Continue SE past site of Hagg Farm; at the track head E then SE
64	136	SE 22732 99420	North of bridge turn right (E) along river bank
65	137	SE 26050 98454	Crumbling bridge over beck
67	138	SE 31230 98932	Join muddy, overgrown path
68	139	SE 34873 98550	Leave the road and head ENE along edge of field
68	140	SE 35186 98680	Pass through band of trees then diagonally east across next field
68	141	SE 35842 98822	At this stile turn SE towards Oakhill Garage by the A167
68	142	SE 36146 99166	Turn E off the A167
69	143	SE 38890 99773	No obvious sign but turn south here
70	144	NZ 41763 01057	Brick gateposts
72	145	NZ 44962 00629	Crossroads opposite Blue Bell Inn

Stage 11 Ingleby Cross to Blakey Ridge (20½ miles)

MAP NO	WAY-POINT	OS GRID REF	DESCRIPTION
72	146	SE 45403 98603	Footpath for Osmotherley
73	147	NZ 47460 00404	Join track, leave woods, head ENE
74	148	NZ 48952 00288	Leave track and turn NE down across field
74	149	NZ 50499 01301	Cairn (324m)
78	150	NZ 59411 01512	Near trig point (445m)
81	151	SE 66677 99442	A path leads south to Church Houses pub
81	152	SE 67914 99725	Lion Inn pub

Stage 12 Blakey to Grosmont (14 miles)

MAP NO	WAY-POINT	OS GRID REF	DESCRIPTION
83	153	NZ 69990 01919	Turn east off road for Glaisdale Moor
84	154	NZ 73998 04022	Junction near trig point
85	155	NZ 74458 04328	First path down to Hollins Farm
86	156	NZ 79303 04644	Path emerges from Arncliffe Wood by road
87	157	NZ 80452 05265	Turn right here down the track
87	158	NZ 82819 05246	Grosmont level crossing

Stage 13 Grosmont to Robin Hood's Bay (15½ miles)

MAP NO	WAY-POINT	OS GRID REF	DESCRIPTION
88	159	NZ 85514 04255	Leave moorland road here and take path E to A169
89	160	NZ 86174 04720	Turn E off A169 for descent to Littlebeck
90	161	NZ 89912 03519	Coast to Coast signpost; solitary tree visible to NNE
91	162	NZ 90712 03993	Turn NE off B1416
91	163	NZ 91309 04415	Signpost
91	164	NZ 91491 04509	Signpost
92	165	NZ 91778 04649	Low pole
92	166	NZ 91992 04894	Two-metre high Coast to Coast pole; soon tracks fork, go right
92	167	NZ 92094 05072	Duckboards
92	168	NZ 92088 05505	Post by stile and gate
93	169	NZ 94062 08147	NE end of caravan park, just before sea cliffs
95	170	NZ 95325 04849	Slipway by Bay Hotel in Robin Hood's Bay

INDEX

Page references in bold type refer to maps

Kilimanjaro: the trekking guide to Africa's highest mountain
Henry Stedman, 3rd edition, 368pp, 40 maps, 30 photos
ISBN 978-1-905864-24-9, £12.99

At 19,340ft the world's tallest freestanding mountain, Kilimanjaro is one of the most popular destinations for hikers visiting Africa. It's possible to walk up to the summit: no technical skills are necessary. Includes town guides to Nairobi and Dar-Es-Salaam, excursions in the region and a colour guide to flora and fauna. **Includes Mount Meru**.

Inca Trail, Cusco & Machu Picchu
Alexander Stewart, 4th edition, 352pp, 74 maps, 40 photos
ISBN 978-1-905864-15-7, £12.99

The **Inca Trail** from Cusco to Machu Picchu, is South America's most popular trek. Practical guide including detailed trail maps, plans of Inca sites, plus guides to Cusco and Machu Picchu. Route guides to other trails in the area: the **Santa Teresa Trek** and the **Choquequirao Trek** as well as the **Vilcabamba Trail** plus the routes linking them. This entirely rewalked and rewritten fourth edition includes a new history of the Incas by Hugh Thomson.

Nepal Trekking & The Great Himalaya Trail *Robin Boustead*
1st edition, 320pp, 8pp colour maps, 40 colour photos
ISBN 978-1-905864-31-7, £14.99   **Due late 2010**

This guide includes the most popular routes in Nepal – the Everest, Annapurna and Langtang regions – as well as the newest trekking areas for true trailblazers. This is the first guide to chart **The Great Himalaya Trail**, the route which crosses Nepal from east to west. Extensive planning sections to help visitors choose a trek.

Trekking in the Everest Region *Jamie McGuinness*
5th edition, 320pp, 30 maps, 30 colour photos
ISBN 978-1-873756-99-7, £12.99

Fifth edition of this popular guide to the Everest region, the world's most famous trekking region. Includes planning, preparation and getting to Nepal; detailed route guides – with 30 route maps and 50 village plans; Kathmandu city guide – where to stay, where to eat, what to see. Written by a professional trekking and mountaineering leader.

Tour du Mont Blanc *Jim Manthorpe*
1st edition, 208pp, 60 maps, 30 colour photos
ISBN 978-1-905864-12-6, £11.99

At 4810m (15,781ft), Mont Blanc is the highest mountain in western Europe. The snow-dome summit is the top of a spectacular massif stretching 60 miles by 20 miles, arguably the most magnificent mountain scenery in Europe. The trail (105 miles, 168km) circumnavigates the massif, passing through France, Italy and Switzerland. Includes Chamonix and Courmayeur guides.

The Walker's Haute Route – Mt Blanc to the Matterhorn
Alexander Stewart,1st edn, 256pp, 60 maps, 30 colour photos
ISBN 978-1-905864-08-9, £12.99

From Mont Blanc to the Matterhorn, Chamonix to Zermatt, the 180km (113-mile) Walkers' Haute Route traverses one of the finest stretches of the Pennine Alps – the range between Valais in Switzerland and Piedmont and Aosta Valley in Italy. Includes Chamonix and Zermatt guides.

TRAILBLAZER'S LONG-DISTANCE PATH (LDP) WALKING GUIDES

We've applied to destinations which are closer to home Trailblazer's proven formula for publishing definitive practical route guides for adventurous travellers. Britain's network of long-distance trails enables the walker to explore some of the finest landscapes in the country's best walking areas. These are guides that are user-friendly, practical, informative and environmentally sensitive.

● **Unique mapping features** In many walking guidebooks the reader has to read a route description then try to relate it to the map. Our guides are much easier to use because walking directions, tricky junctions, places to stay and eat, points of interest and walking times are all written onto the maps themselves in the places to which they apply. With their uncluttered clarity, these are not general-purpose maps but fully edited maps drawn by walkers for walkers.

● **Largest-scale walking maps** At a scale of just under 1:20,000 (8cm or 3¹/₈ inches to one mile) the maps in these guides are bigger than even the most detailed British walking maps currently available in the shops.

● **Not just a trail guide – includes where to stay, where to eat and public transport** Our guidebooks cover the complete walking experience, not just the route. Accommodation options for all budgets are provided (pubs, hotels, B&Bs, campsites, bunkhouses, hostels) as well as places to eat. Detailed public transport information for all access points to each trail means that there are itineraries for all walkers, for hiking the entire route as well as for day or weekend walks.

Coast to Coast *Henry Stedman* ISBN 978-1-905864-30-0, £11.99
4th edition, 256pp, 109 maps & town plans, 40 colour photos

Cornwall Coast Path *Edith Schofield* ISBN 978-1-905864-19-5, £9.99
3rd edition, 256pp, 112 maps & town plans, 40 colour photos

Cotswold Way *Tricia & Bob Hayne* ISBN 978-1-905864-16-4, £9.99
1st edition, 192pp, 60 maps & town plans, 40 colour photos

Hadrian's Wall Path *Henry Stedman* ISBN 978-1-905864-14-0, £9.99
2nd edition, 208pp, 60 maps & town plans, 40 colour photos

Offa's Dyke Path *Keith Carter* ISBN 978-1-905864-06-5, £9.99
2nd edition, 208pp, 88 maps & town plans, 40 colour photos

North Downs Way *John Curtin* ISBN 978-1-873756-96-6, £9.99
1st edition, 192pp, 60 maps & town plans, 40 colour photos

Peddars Way & Norfolk Coast Path *Alexander Stewart* £9.99
1st edition, 192pp, 60 maps & town plans, 40 colour photos   **Due late 2010**

Pembrokeshire Coast Path *Jim Manthorpe* ISBN 978-1-905864-27-0, £9.99
3rd edition, 224pp, 96 maps & town plans, 40 colour photos

Pennine Way *Keith Carter & Chris Scott* ISBN 978-1-905864-02-7, £11.99
2nd edition, 272pp, 135 maps & town plans, 40 colour photos

The Ridgeway *Nick Hill* ISBN 978-1-905864-17-1, £9.99
2nd edition, 192pp, 53 maps & town plans, 40 colour photos

South Downs Way *Jim Manthorpe* ISBN 978-1-905864-18-8, £9.99
3rd edition, 192pp, 60 maps & town plans, 40 colour photos

West Highland Way *Charlie Loram* ISBN 978-1-905864-13-3, £9.99
3rd edition, 192pp, 53 maps, 10 town plans, 40 colour photos

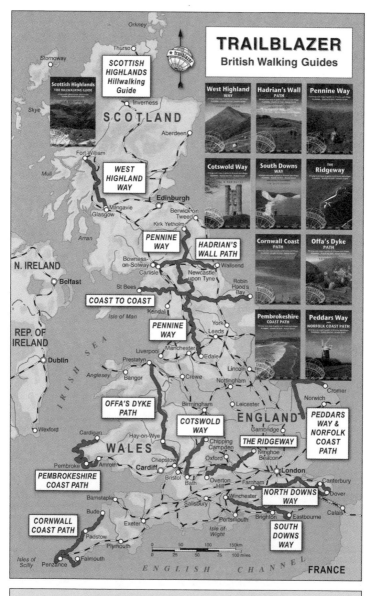

TRAILBLAZER
British Walking Guides

SCOTTISH HIGHLANDS Hillwalking Guide

WEST HIGHLAND WAY

PENNINE WAY

HADRIAN'S WALL PATH

COAST TO COAST

PENNINE WAY

OFFA'S DYKE PATH

COTSWOLD WAY

THE RIDGEWAY

PEMBROKESHIRE COAST PATH

PEDDARS WAY & NORFOLK COAST PATH

NORTH DOWNS WAY

CORNWALL COAST PATH

SOUTH DOWNS WAY

'The same attention to detail that distinguishes its other guides
has been brought to bear here'. **The Sunday Times**

TRAILBLAZER GUIDES – TITLE LIST

www.trailblazer-guides.com

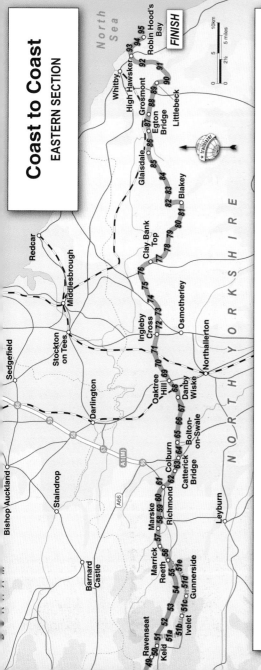

Coast to Coast
EASTERN SECTION

FINISH

North Sea

Robin Hood's Bay
Whitby
High Hawsker
Grosmont
Glaisdale
Egton Bridge
Littlebeck
Blakey
Clay Bank Top
Ingleby Cross
Osmotherley
Oaktree Hill
Danby Wiske
Bolton-on-Swale
Catterick Bridge
Colburn
Richmond
Marske
Reeth
Gunnerside
Ivelet
Keld
Ravenseat

Redcar
Middlesbrough
Stockton on Tees
Darlington
Northallerton
Sedgefield
Staindrop
Bishop Auckland
Barnard Castle
Leyburn

NORTH YORKSHIRE

trailblazer

0 10km
0 5 5 miles

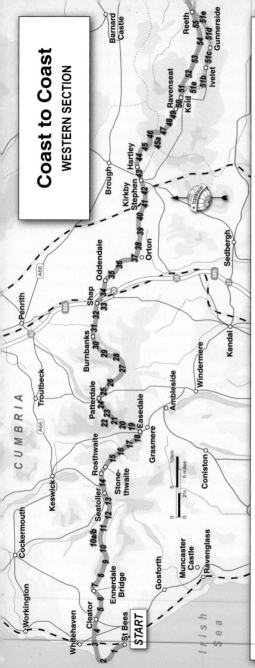

Coast to Coast
WESTERN SECTION

MAP KEY
Map 1 – p84 South Head
Map 2 – p85 Fleswick Bay
Map 3 – p87 Sandwith
Map 4 – p88 Moor Row
Map 5 – p89 Cleator
Map 6 – p91 Raven Crag
Map 7 – p93 Ennerdale Bridge
Map 8 – p95 Ennerdale Water
Map 9 – p95 Ennerdale Water
Map 10 – p97 Ennerdale YH
Map 10a – p99 Red Pike route
Map 10b – p100 High Crag
Map 11 – p101 Black Sail YH
Map 12 – p103 Blackbeck Tarn
Map 13 – p105 Seatoller Fell

Map 14 – p107 Borrowdale
Map 15 – p109 Eagle Crag
Map 16 – p110 Greenup Edge
Map 17 – p111 Far Easedale
Map 18 – p112 Easedale
Map 19 – p119 Great Tongue
Map 20 – p121 Grisedale Tarn
Map 21 – p122 St Sunday Crag
Map 22 – p123 Striding Edge
Map 23 – p123 Elmhow Plantation
Map 24 – p124 Harrison Crag
Map 25 – p127 Patterdale
Map 26 – p128 Satura Crag
Map 27 – p129 Kidsty Pike
Map 28 – p130 Haweswater Reservoir
Map 29 – p131 Haweswater Reservoir

Map 30 – p133 Burnbanks
Map 31 – p134 Rosgill Bridge
Map 32 – p135 Shap Abbey
Map 33 – p136 Shap
Map 34 – p137 Shap
Map 35 – p139 Oddendale
Map 36 – p140 Crosby Ravensworth Fell
Map 37 – p141 Robin Hood's Grave
Map 38 – p143 Orton Scar
Map 39 – p144 Tarn Moor
Map 40 – p145 Ravenstonedale Moor
Map 41 – p146 Smardale Bridge
Map 42 – p147 Smardale Fell
Map 43 – p148 Kirkby Stephen
Map 44 – p154 Birkett Hill
Map 45 – p155 Hartley Fell

Map 45a – p156 B6270, Green Route
Map 46 – p156 Nine Standards Rigg
Map 47 – p158 Whitsundale Beck
Map 48 – p159 Ney Gill
Map 49 – p160 Ravenseat Farm
Map 50 – p162 Keld
Map 51 – p165 Gunnerside Moor
Map 52 – p166 Melbecks Moor
Map 53 – p167 Level House Bridge
Map 54 – p168 Surrender Bridge
Map 55 – p169 Healaugh
Map 51a – p171 Ivelet Wood
Map 51b – p172 Ivelet
Map 51c – p172 Gunnerside
Map 51d – p173 Blades
Map 51e – p174 Healaugh